Palm™ Database Programming: The Complete Developer's Guide

Eric Giguère

Wiley Computer Publishing

John Wiley & Sons, Inc.
NEW YORK • CHICHESTER • WEINHEIM • BRISBANE • SINGAPORE • TORONTO

To my wife, Lisa, who has shown me other ways to synchronize

Publisher: Robert Ipsen
Editor: Carol Long
Managing Editor: Angela Murphy
Electronic Products, Associate Editor: Mike Sosa
Text Design & Composition: North Market Street Graphics

Designations used by companies to distinguish their products are often claimed as trademarks. In all instances where John Wiley & Sons, Inc., is aware of a claim, the product names appear in initial capital or ALL CAPITAL LETTERS. Readers, however, should contact the appropriate companies for more complete information regarding trademarks and registration.

This book is printed on acid-free paper. ∞

Copyright © 1999 by Eric Giguere. All rights reserved.

Published by John Wiley & Sons, Inc.

Published simultaneously in Canada.

No part of this publication may be reproduced, stored in a retrieval system or transmitted in any form or by any means, electronic, mechanical, photocopying, recording, scanning or otherwise, except as permitted under Sections 107 or 108 of the 1976 United States Copyright Act, without either the prior written permission of the Publisher, or authorization through payment of the appropriate per-copy fee to the Copyright Clearance Center, 222 Rosewood Drive, Danvers, MA 01923, (978) 750-8400, fax (978) 750-4744. Requests to the Publisher for permission should be addressed to the Permissions Department, John Wiley & Sons, Inc., 605 Third Avenue, New York, NY 10158-0012, (212) 850-6011, fax (212) 850-6008, E-Mail: PERMREQ @ WILEY.COM.

This publication is designed to provide accurate and authoritative information in regard to the subject matter covered. It is sold with the understanding that the publisher is not engaged in professional services. If professional advice or other expert assistance is required, the services of a competent professional person should be sought.

Library of Congress Cataloging-in-Publication Data:
Giguere, Eric.
    Palm database programming : the complete developer's guide /
   Eric Giguere.
       p.   cm.
    ISBN 0-471-35401-5 (pbk.)
    1. Database design.   2. Palm OS.   I. Title.
QA76.9.D26G52   1999
005.74—dc21   99-36711
                                                                         CIP

Printed in the United States of America.

10 9 8 7 6 5 4 3 2 1

CONTENTS

Chapter 1	**Introduction**	1
	Why Develop for the Palm Platform?	1
	Why Read This Book?	3
	Expected Background	4
	Examples and Sample Programs	5
	The Phone Book Sample	5
	The Time Book Sample	7
	Chapter Summaries	7
	Part One: Platform Basics	7
	Part Two: Databases	8
	Part Three: Database Applications	8
	Reference Material	9
	Web Site and CD-ROM	10
Part One	**Platform Basics**	**11**
Chapter 2	**What You Need to Know about Palm Devices**	13
	Hardware	13
	The Main Processor	13
	The Screen	14
	Running Modes	14
	Operating System	15
	The Kernel	15
	The Managers	16
	Palm OS Versions	16
	Memory	18
	ROM and RAM	20
	Cards and Heaps	20
	Handles and Local IDs	22
	Allocating from the Dynamic Heap	23
	Databases and the Storage Heap	23

	Resetting the Device	25
	Soft Resets	25
	Modified Soft Resets	25
	Hard Resets	26
Chapter 3	**Development Tools and Software Development Kits**	**27**
	Palm Operating System Software Development Kit	27
	CodeWarrior	30
	The Origins of CodeWarrior	30
	CodeWarrior versus CodeWarrior Lite	31
	Starting a Project	32
	Modifying Resources with Constructor	35
	Building the Project	38
	Debugging with CodeWarrior	38
	GCC and the GNU Tools	41
	What Are the GNU Tools?	42
	Starting and Building a Project	43
	Debugging with GDB	45
	C/C++ Programming Issues	46
	The C Runtime Library	46
	Assertions and Error Messages	47
	Exception Handling	50
	Callbacks and GCC	51
	C++ Programming Issues	52
	Multisegment Applications	70
	Floating-Point Support	70
	The Palm Operating System Emulator	71
	History	71
	Using the Emulator	72
	The Console	74
	The Conduit Development Kit	74
Chapter 4	**Writing Palm Applications**	**77**
	Applications	77
	What's an Application?	77
	How Applications Are Launched	80
	How Applications Use Memory	91
	Structuring an Application	92
	Checking the Palm Operating System Version	93
	Event Processing	94
	The Event Loop	94
	The EventType Structure	95
	Event Handling	97

Keyboard and Pen Events	100
Performing Long Operations	102
An Application Skeleton	105
Building the User Interface	110
Designing a User Interface	111
User Interface Resources	112
Alerts	114
Strings	116
String Lists	117
Forms and Dialogs	122
Dialogs	130
Menus	131
Controls and Other Components	134
Bitmaps and Icons	156
Miscellaneous Tasks	157
Handling Find Requests	157
Saving and Restoring State	163
The Phone Book User Interface	164
Application Design	164
The User Interface	165
The Data Interface	166

Part Two   Databases   169

Chapter 5   Palm Databases   171

What's a Palm Database?	171
Records versus Resources	172
The Database Header	172
Basic Database Management	173
Creating a Database	173
Opening a Database	175
Closing a Database	176
Deleting a Database	177
Database Information	177
Custom Information Blocks	181
Enumerating Databases	184
Resource Databases	185
Reading Resources	185
Creating Resources	186
Managing Resources	186
Record Databases	187
What's a Record?	187
Creating Records	189

	Accessing and Modifying Records	190
	Removing Records	190
	Finding Records	192
	Sorting Records	192
	Categories	197
	Secret Records	200
	Phone Book and Palm Databases	201
Chapter 6	**Relational Databases**	**203**
	What's a Database?	204
	Record-Oriented Databases	204
	Database Management Systems	206
	Database Management System Interfaces	207
	Database Classifications	208
	Relational Databases	209
	Object-Oriented Databases	211
	Other Classifications	212
	Database Design	212
	Mapping Data into Tables	212
	Table Normalization and Optimization	219
	Database Design Is Hard Work	223
	Structured Query Language	224
	SQL Basics	224
	Data Description Language	225
	Data Manipulation Language	226
	Mapping Phone Book Data to the Relational Model	236
	The Data	237
	The Abstract Model	237
	The Physical Model	238
	The Database	240
	Sample Queries	241
Part Three	**Database Applications**	**243**
Chapter 7	**Data Synchronization**	**245**
	What Is Synchronization?	245
	Why Synchronization Is Difficult	247
	The Learning Curve	247
	A Database Synchronization Example	248
	Synchronization Challenges	251
	Strategies for Synchronization	254
	Extracting and Subsetting Data	255
	Resolving Conflicts	258
	Primary Key Pooling	259

Chapter 8 Sybase UltraLite — 261

- What Is UltraLite? — 261
  - A Relational Database in Your Application — 262
  - MobiLink Synchronization — 262
  - Supported Platforms — 263
  - Limitations — 263
  - Licensing — 265
- How UltraLite Works — 265
  - Development Phase — 266
  - Deployment Phase — 268
- Building and Deploying UltraLite Applications — 272
  - UltraLite Development — 272
  - UltraLite Deployment — 283
  - Using UltraLite without Synchronization — 288
- Embedded SQL — 290
  - The SQL Preprocessor — 290
  - The SQL Communications Area — 291
  - Error Handling — 292
  - Initialization and Deinitialization — 293
  - Executing Simple SQL Statements — 295
  - Host Variables — 297
  - Fetching Data — 302
  - Transactions — 304
- Synchronization Channels — 304
  - User Identification — 305
  - HotSync Synchronization — 306
  - TCP/IP Synchronization — 307
  - Serial Synchronization — 308
  - Which Channel to Use? — 309
- Synchronization — 310
  - Understanding UltraLite Synchronization — 310
  - Scripts and Events — 310
  - Event Types and Script Parameters — 311
  - The Synchronization Process — 312
  - Synchronization Examples — 315
  - Conflict Resolution — 320
  - Primary Key Pooling — 321
  - Error Handling — 321
- Debugging UltraLite Applications — 322
- Phone Book and UltraLite — 323

Chapter 9 Oracle Lite Consolidator

- What Is the Consolidator? — 325
  - Oracle Lite — 326

Contents

The Consolidator		326
Requirements		326
Consolidator Samples		327
How the Consolidator Works		327
Development Phase		327
Deployment Phase		328
Building and Deploying Consolidator Applications		328
Consolidator Development		328
Consolidator Deployment		336
Conflict Resolution		337
Primary Key Pooling		337
Phone Book and the Consolidator		338
Chapter 10	**Conclusion**	**339**
Appendix A	**CD-Rom Contents**	**341**
Appendix B	**Sybase Adaptive Server Anywhere**	**343**
Index		**348**

ACKNOWLEDGMENTS

Many fine people spent time reading and commenting on the chapters in this book, primarily at Sybase's Waterloo site. The author especially thanks Chris Irie, Graeme Kemkes, and Rob Close for their extensive feedback The author also appreciates the efforts and attention of the Wiley staff involved in the creation of this book, including Carol Long, Christina Berry, Emilie Herman, and Angela Murphy. Last, but certainly not least, the author would like to acknowledge the love, support, and patience of his wife and family.

CHAPTER 1

Introduction

Do you remember the thrill you felt when you first used a Palm organizer? If your next thought was *how do I program this thing?* then this book is for you, because in it and its accompanying CD-ROM you'll find the tools and information you need to write applications for Palm devices, specifically applications that connect to external databases using technology from Sybase and Oracle. You'll learn the basics of the Palm operating system and how to use the development tools to build, run, and debug applications. You'll explore the code behind the Palm user interface. You'll learn about Palm databases, relational databases, and data synchronization. When you're done reading this book you'll be able to write interactive database programs for the Palm platform. All you need is a basic knowledge of C/C++ and the desire to learn about Palm and database programming.

Why Develop for the Palm Platform?

This book is focused exclusively on handheld devices running the Palm Computing platform. This includes Palm Computing's own connected organizers, such as the PalmPilot Professional and the Palm III, as well as other devices such as IBM's WorkPad and the QUALCOMM pdQ Smartphone digital phone. At this writing, the Palm platform has anywhere from a 45 to a 70 percent market share, among personal digital assistants (PDAs), depending on who is doing the surveying and how PDAs are defined. This places the platform ahead of its nearest competitor, Microsoft's Windows CE platform. These numbers are sure to change by the time you read this, but whether you're writing software to sell to others or for use in your own organization, the Palm platform is one of the platforms you should seriously consider targeting.

Why is the Palm platform the dominant player in the PDA market? It's successful because Palm Computing focused on the *users* of the device as opposed to the *technology* in the device. A Palm device isn't pretentious. It doesn't claim to understand your handwriting—in fact, it forces you to learn its own special character recognition system. Nor does it pretend it's a desktop computer—if you want serious number crunching, do it on a desktop computer and download the results to the handheld device. There are no lengthy boot cycles to worry about—press the power button and it's ready to work. Your valuable data is always safe— it gets backed up every time you synchronize with a desktop computer. Palm Computing made the devices useful right out of the box, and it's sold a lot of them because of that.

Not that the technology in the Palm devices is unimportant. The small form factor of a Palm device makes it possible to hold it with one hand and write on it with another. The low-power circuitry and a well-written operating system make it possible to use a Palm device for weeks without having to change batteries. But the technology is just a way to implement the vision behind the platform.

In fact, there's really nothing new in the operating system that manages the Palm platform. If you've had experience with any operating system that uses an event-driven graphical user interface (GUI)—such as Microsoft Windows, the Macintosh, or X Windows—the Palm platform will seem very familiar. It may also seem quite different. Most of you are probably Microsoft Windows programmers, and there's no denying that making the transition from Win32 programming (Windows 95/98/NT) to Windows CE programming is easier than to make the transition from Win32 programming to Palm programming. Win32 and Windows CE share most of the same concepts, terminology, and development tools. The transition from Win32 to Palm is more work—you must learn a new operating system and a new set of development tools. To some of you, Palm programming will be like returning to the days of Windows 3.1 programming, writing single-threaded, memory-limited, event-driven programs.

If anything can be considered revolutionary on the Palm platform, it is its synchronization capabilities. Synchronizing is more than just backing up data. It's about *exchanging* data between two applications, one on the device and one on the desktop. The desktop application, called a *conduit*, can process the data in ways that are not practical on the Palm device. This is why Palm Computing recommends offloading as much processing as possible onto the desktop computer—it keeps the applications on the Palm devices small and responsive. Complex synchronization is not required, however—a default conduit is always available to back up your data if that's all you need.

When it comes right down to it, you choose to develop applications for the Palm platform because Palm Computing's devices are popular. And because they're so cool.

A note about terminology: This book uses the term *Palm Computing platform* (or sometimes just *platform*) wherever possible when not dealing with a specific device. In some cases, however, the term *Palm* or *Palm device* is used when *Palm Computing platform* is just too awkward.

Why Read This Book?

If you haven't realized it yet, there's a wealth of programming information available for you to download from the Palm Computing Web site. You can download a complete reference guide to the Palm operating system in Adobe PDF format, suitable for online browsing or printing. You can also download tutorials and whitepapers, as well as tools and software development kits.

So why read this book? There are two reasons.

First, it's a concise introduction to Palm programming. While there's nothing stopping you from downloading the Palm reference guide (it's also included on the CD-ROM) and reading it from front to back, that's not the easiest way to learn about the platform. The reference guide presents too much information to be an overview, and the answers to many of the questions you ask yourself as a novice are either scattered throughout the document or else not addressed at all. This book covers the basics to get you started and then shows you where to go to get the information you need later on.

Second, this book introduces you to database programming for the Palm platform. Databases are a vital part of any organization, whether they are large relational databases or small desktop databases. Your applications need to interact with these external databases, to allow users to download and browse data on their Palm devices. If a user changes any of the information, those changes have to be uploaded back to the database. Writing programs that do all of this is quite a challenge because you need to know how to select and update data from an external database, how to write programs for the Palm platform, and how to synchronize the data between the device and the external database. The required combination of database programming experience, platform knowledge, and user interface design skills is rare. This book fills in the gaps you might have in any of those areas.

This book is *not* a guide to *using* your Palm device. There are several good books available that explain how to use a Palm device, and if you've never actually used one before, you should take some time to explore the device before you start programming it—it will make you a better programmer.

It's also important to note that this book is not a guide to conduit programming, either, although the topic is briefly discussed in Chapter 3. Conduits run on non-Palm platforms and are developed with a different set of tools—you can even develop conduits in Java instead of C++. But both Sybase and Oracle provide solutions for synchronizing data with an external database, and any conduit you write would really be duplicating their efforts. Data synchronization is a complicated problem, as you'll see in Chapter 7. You're probably already using third-party conduits such as EasySync or IntelliSync to synchronize the built-in applications with your desktop software, and this book assumes you'd rather use pre-canned database connectivity solutions, whether they be from Sybase, Oracle, or some other vendor.

Expected Background

This book makes the following assumptions about you:

- You own or have access to a Palm device of some kind and are familiar with its use and terminology. Terms such as HotSync and Graffiti don't confuse you.

- You have C or C++ programming experience, preferably C++. Although there are alternatives available, C/C++ is still the language of choice for programming the Palm Computing platform. Examples in this book are written in C++.

- You have experience with an event-driven graphical user interface, whether it's Windows, OS/2, the Macintosh, X Windows, or any other similar system.

Prior experience with databases is *not* required, although it certainly doesn't hurt.

Most of the non-Palm software that is discussed in this book runs under Microsoft Windows, so it's assumed that you also have access to a PC running Windows. In fact, this book is written from the viewpoint of a Windows programmer making the transition to Palm programming. This isn't meant to exclude anyone, rather it's meant to reflect market realities and what the typical reader has experienced.

Examples and Sample Programs

There's nothing like staring at some working code to understand how to use a new system. This is true whether you're learning about the Palm operating system or relational databases. You'll find code snippets sprinkled liberally throughout the text to clarify or demonstrate concepts. The book also presents two complete, working sample programs: Phone Book and Time Book.

The Phone Book Sample

Phone Book is a simple application that allows you to view and edit an organization's phone list. It lets you quickly find a coworker's extension number, external number, and fax number. Figure 1.1 shows what the Phone Book looks like given the sample data shown in Table 1.1. Apart from the phone numbers, the information to display includes the names of the employees, their departments, and their email addresses.

You're probably thinking: "Why do I need this application when an Address Book comes preinstalled on my Palm device?" There's no denying that it looks and feels much like the built-in Address Book—the similarities are intentional. The point of the sample is to demonstrate various concepts:

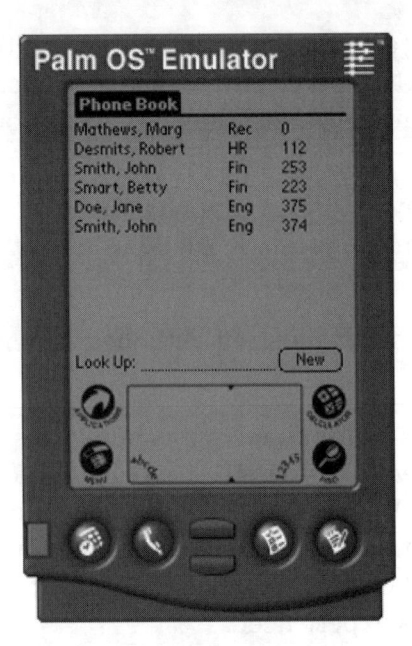

Figure 1.1 The Phone Book application in action.

- How applications are built and how they run.
- How to design a graphical user interface.
- How to store the data in a Palm database.
- How to synchronize the data with an external (relational) database, using Sybase UltraLite and Oracle Lite Consolidator technologies. (An evaluation version of Sybase UltraLite is included on the CD-ROM, while the Oracle Lite Consolidator is free to download from the Oracle Web site.)

Table 1.1 Sample Phone Book Data

NAME	SURNAME	DEPT.	EMAIL	EXTENSION	EXTERNAL	FAX
John	Smith	Engineering	jsmith	374	none	none
Jane	Doe	Engineering	jdoe	375	none	none
Betty	Smart	Finance	bsmart	223	555-888-9223	555-767-2345
John	Smith	Finance	smithj	253	555-888-9253	555-767-2345
Robert	Desmits	Human Resources	desmits	112	555-888-9112	555-767-2344
Marg	Mathews	Reception	mmathews	0	555-888-9000	555-767-2340

The application is used as an example throughout the book. To simplify matters, the following assumptions are made about the phone data:

- Each phone number is assigned to at most one employee.
- Each employee has at least one (but possibly more than one) phone number, but at most one of any given type.
- Phone numbers are either office extensions, external numbers, or fax numbers.

A more complete application would also allow for phone numbers to be shared between groups of people (i.e., technical support), allow numbers to be assigned to a position (i.e., receptionist) instead of a specific employee, and allow for more types of numbers (i.e., toll-free numbers). For our purposes, however, the preceding assumptions are enough to build a reasonable and useful application.

The Time Book Sample

A second, more complicated sample is the Time Book sample. Time Book tracks the time that you spend at various activities throughout your working day. It's designed to be multiuser and lets managers see information about their subordinates. The Time Book sample works with the Ultra-Lite synchronization technology and is discussed briefly in Chapter 7.

Chapter Summaries

The chapters in this book are meant to be read in sequence, since the later chapters will be hard to understand without the information presented in the earlier chapters.

Part One: Platform Basics

The first part introduces you to the Palm Computing platform. You'll learn about the hardware and the software in your Palm device and how to build applications for it.

Chapter 2, What You Need to Know About Palm Devices, provides basic information on how the device works. This includes the hardware, the operating system, and the memory. Even if you're not very interested in the hardware, it's important to know something about the device because it affects what your programs can and cannot do. This chapter also shows you how to reset your device, which is a skill you should master *before* you start programming!

Chapter 3, Development Tools and SDKs, introduces you to the set of development tools you'll need to master to do any programming. The Palm OS Software Development Kit, the CodeWarrior compiler, and the GCC compiler are covered, as well as the Palm OS Emulator, a key part of your programming arsenal. The chapter shows you how to use the tools to write new applications and how to debug those applications. It also presents the C and C++ programming issues that are specific to the platform.

Chapter 4, Writing Palm Applications, explores how applications work and how to write them. Program launches, event processing, and user interface programming are all explained in depth. This includes the contexts in which your application gets started, how to perform long operations while keeping the device responsive, and how to build and use forms and dialogs to create a user interface. A skeletal application is developed, and on the CD-ROM you'll find an application called UI Test that demonstrates the various user interface options that are available. The user interface for the Phone Book sample is also developed in this chapter.

Part Two: Databases

The second part introduces you to Palm and relational databases. You'll learn the basics of what a database is, how to get data in and out, and how to interface to a database from C/C++.

Chapter 5, Palm Databases, introduces the built-in database interfaces that are available on the Palm Computing platform. Palm database support is added to the Phone Book sample.

Chapter 6, Relational Databases, introduces relational databases and the SQL query language. Tables and database design are covered, and you're shown how to get the data you want out of the database and how to update it. An evaluation version of Sybase's Adaptive Server Anywhere is included on the CD-ROM (installation instructions are in Appendix B) and is used to demonstrate the concepts.

Part Three: Database Applications

The third part shows you how to build database-centric applications. You'll learn how to combine what you learned in the first two parts with some exciting database technology to build Palm applications that know how to talk to external databases.

Chapter 7, Data Synchronization, discusses what data synchronization is, why it's challenging, and strategies for synchronizing with external databases. The Time Book sample is used to demonstrate the challenges of data synchronization.

Chapter 8, Sybase UltraLite, shows you how applications are built with UltraLite. A database model is designed to store the phone book information and the Phone Book sample is modified to use UltraLite.

Chapter 9, Oracle Lite Consolidator, shows you how applications are built with the Consolidator. The Phone Book sample is modified to use the Consolidator.

Chapter 10, Conclusion, wraps everything up.

Reference Material

Palm Computing publishes comprehensive documentation on the Palm Computing platform in the Development Zone section of its Web site, at www.palm.com/devzone. The documentation is in Adobe Acrobat (PDF) format and is free to download. At the time of writing, this documentation included the following:

Palm OS Programmer's Companion. Conceptual and how-to information about the Palm Computing platform, for Palm OS 3.1 or earlier.

Palm OS SDK Reference. A complete reference guide to the Palm OS APIs, for Palm OS 3.1 or earlier.

Palm OS Tutorial. A complete tutorial on Palm OS programming. Requires the CodeWarrior compiler and the examples from the Palm OS Software Development Kit.

These documents complement the material in this book and are included on the CD-ROM for your convenience, although you should check the Palm Web site regularly for updates. The following documents are also available on the CD-ROM:

Palm OS Cookbook. An older version of the Programmer's Companion.

Developing Palm OS Applications. An older reference guide, distributed as three separate .PDF files.

References to the "Palm OS reference guide" throughout this book refer to either *Palm OS SDK Reference* or *Developing Palm OS Applications*.

Web Site and CD-ROM

No programming book today would be complete without both a Web site and a CD-ROM. The CD-ROM that accompanies this book includes all the examples discussed in the text along with some useful software to aid you with the development process. A complete listing of what's on the CD-ROM can be found in Appendix A.

The book also has a Web site, www.ericgiguere.com/palm. You'll find updates, corrections, and additional information not available in the book. You'll also find links to all the important places a Palm Computing platform developer should know about, so be sure to check it out.

You can contact the author at eric@ericgiguere.com.

PART ONE

Platform Basics

CHAPTER 2

What You Need to Know about Palm Devices

There are more constraints on what you can do on a Palm device than on a regular desktop computer. Even if you're not a hardware person, it's important to understand the limitations of the device, so that your applications remain responsive and don't drain the batteries unnecessarily. This chapter presents a short overview of the hardware, the operating system, and the memory in a Palm device. You'll also learn how to reset your device in order to recover from a crash.

Hardware

Palm devices are marvels of low-power, small form–factor technology. The two AAA batteries in most models (for a thinner profile, the Palm V uses built-in rechargeable batteries instead) can last for several weeks of continuous use because of low-power components and clever power management.

The Main Processor

The main processor in the current Palm devices is the Motorola MC68328 DragonBall processor. The DragonBall is a low-power version of the MC68000 processor, a popular chip used in computers such as the original Macintosh and the Amiga. The 68328 and 68000 share the same instruction sets, but the DragonBall processor is designed specifically for the portable consumer market. Detailed information on the chip can be found on Motorola's Web site at www.mot.com/SPS/WIRELESS/products/MC68328.html.

> **NOTE**
> If you're interested in writing assembly language programs for the Palm, the Pila cross-assembler is available for download from numerous sites, including www.massena.com/darrin/pilot/asdk/asdknews.htm. Please note that this book doesn't discuss assembly language programming on the Palm.

Compared to the processor in a desktop computer, the DragonBall is slow. A faster processor requires more power, and low power consumption was a primary design goal of the Palm platform. In fact, Palm Computing recommends that you offload computationally expensive processing to a desktop computer in order to save power and to keep the device responsive to the user.

The Screen

The screen on the Palm device is currently 160 pixels wide by 160 pixels high. Your application's user interface has to fit within these constraints. These dimensions may change at some point—they may get bigger. The ScrDisplayMode() function (available in later versions of the operating system) returns the screen dimensions of the current device.

A digitizer makes the screen touch-sensitive. The operating system transforms raw pen movements and taps into higher-level events (such as keystrokes) that an application can process. Your application has access to the raw events, though, and Chapter 4 shows you how to intercept them before the system processes them. Most applications just deal with the higher-level events.

Running Modes

Apart from the lower-power circuitry, the key to the Palm device's miserly ways is its power management via its *running modes*. A Palm device has three modes of operation:

- **Sleep mode** occurs when there has been no user activity on the device for a certain number of minutes. The default is two minutes, but you can change the wait period to one or three minutes using the Preferences application. Sleep mode is also entered when you turn off the device using the power button. In sleep mode, the processor, screen, and most of the other hardware do not receive any power, but the memory chips, the real-time clock, and some low-level circuitry do stay powered. Pressing a button restores power to the processor and the other hardware. The real-time clock can also wake the device at a predetermined time.

- **Doze mode** (sometimes referred to as *idle mode*) occurs when an application is waiting for user input. The processor is halted until a hardware interrupt signals user activity, such as the press of a button or a stroke of the pen. Most of an application's time when the device is on is spent in doze mode.

- **Running mode** occurs when the processor is executing instructions. This mode consumes the most power, so the device returns to doze mode as soon as possible in order to conserve battery power.

As you can see, the power is never really turned off unless you pull out the batteries and let the internal capacitors (which keep the device charged while you change batteries) discharge completely. The active application is simply in a halted state when in sleep mode, ready to resume where it left off as soon as power is reapplied to the processor.

Operating System

The Palm operating system (Palm OS) provides the environment for your applications to run in and consists of two parts, the kernel and the managers.

The Kernel

The *kernel* is the core of Palm operating system (Palm OS). It provides the interface between the hardware (such as trapping interrupts when the user strokes the screen with the pen) and the rest of the operating system and also manages multiple threads of execution. The kernel in current use is licensed from Kadak Products Ltd. (www.kadak.com).

Although Palm OS uses several threads internally, applications cannot create or use any threads other than the one they're running on. *You can only write single-threaded applications*, which means that you'll have to perform long operations in small chunks to avoid the appearance of hanging the device. We discuss this further in Chapter 4 when we deal with event processing.

Although applications are single-threaded and only one application ever appears active to the user, a second copy of the active application sometimes runs on another thread but in a more limited environment. This is also covered in Chapter 4 when we discuss application launching.

The Managers

Apart from the kernel, Palm OS consists of a series of *managers*, which are collections of APIs grouped by function. Your applications use the managers to obtain system resources and interact with the user. The managers can be grouped as follows:

- The UI managers handle all interaction with the user. This includes general functions for drawing on the screen as well as functions related to specific user interface elements such as fields and lists.
- The system managers handle non-UI interaction with the device, including access to the timers and the system event queue.
- The memory managers handle memory allocation and management of Palm OS *databases* and *resources*, discussed later in this chapter.
- The communication managers handle communications between the Palm device and the external world, using the serial port or the infrared port.

We discuss most of the managers as we explore Palm programming.

Palm OS Versions

As the Palm devices have evolved, Palm Computing has released new versions of the operating system. Palm OS 3.2 is the most recent version of the operating system at the time this book was written and is available on the Palm VII. The Palm IIIx and Palm V run Palm OS 3.1, while the Palm III runs Palm OS 3.0. The original Pilot 1000 and Pilot 5000 machines run Palm OS 1.0. The PalmPilot Personal and PalmPilot Professional models run Palm OS 2.0. All Palm models prior to the Palm III can be upgraded to run the latest operating system by ordering a new memory card from Palm Computing. The upgrade also provides more RAM (random-access memory) and adds some new capabilities such as infrared beaming that are missing in those models. More recent models such as the Palm III can be upgraded simply by downloading the new operating system into the device's flash memory.

To detect which version of Palm OS is installed, an application calls the FtrGet function, part of the Feature Manager:

```
// Get ROM version
DWord romVersion;
FtrGet( sysFtrCreator, sysFtrNumROMVersion, &romVersion );
```

The OS version number is returned as a four-byte value, whose format is documented in the Palm OS header file <System/SystemMgr.h> (see the next chapter for information about the Palm OS header files) as follows: 0xMMmfsbbb, where *MM* is the major version, *m* is the minor version, *f* is a bug fix number, *s* is the code stage (0 for internal development, 1 for an alpha release, 2 for a beta release, 3 for a final release), and *bbb* is the build number for the releases that are not final. In general, all you check are the major and minor build numbers:

```
if( romVersion < 0x02000000 ){
    // Palm OS 1.x
}

if( romVersion >= 0x03100000 ){
    // Palm OS 3.1 or higher
}
```

The version number is often checked when the application starts to ensure that the correct version of Palm OS is being used, as you'll see in Chapter 4.

Palm Computing has done its best to make each version of Palm OS upwardly compatible. Applications written for Palm OS 1.0 devices will work equally well on Palm OS 2.0 or 3.0 devices. Palm OS 2.0 applications will work on Palm OS 3.0 devices but may not work on Palm OS 1.0 devices. In some cases, an application written for an older operating system will not work correctly on a newer OS because it relied on an OS bug that the newer OS fixed. Apart from these bugs, if your application is developed using a newer OS but doesn't actually use any features specific to that version of the OS, then it will also run on older operating systems.

How can you tell if you're using a feature specific to Palm OS 2.0 or 3.0? The surest way to tell is to try running your application on a Palm OS 1.0 or 2.0 device (or using the Palm OS Emulator, which we'll discuss in the next chapter, with an older ROM image). Or you can try compiling your application using an older version of the Palm OS software development kit (SDK). The problem with both these approaches is that it is increasingly harder to get older versions of the device or the SDKs. Your best bet is to know what features were added to the OS. Since this book does not discuss Palm OS 1.0, here is a summary of what's new in Palm OS 3.0 in comparison to Palm OS 2.0:

- More dynamic memory (96K instead of 64K). See the discussion about the dynamic heap in the next section.
- New functions for supporting the infrared beaming capability new to the Palm III device.
- Support for MIDI sound files.
- The ability to dynamically create user interface objects at run time as opposed to only loading them from static definitions.
- A simple file-streaming API for dealing with large blocks of data.
- A Progress Manager for displaying progress dialogs during lengthy operations.

Full details of these and other changes can be found in Appendix B of *Palm OS SDK Reference*. Note that besides adding new routines, some Palm OS 2.0 routines were modified in Palm OS 3.0 to take extra parameters. The original routines are still available but with a V20 appended to their name. For example, Palm OS 3.0 supports both the CategoryEdit and the CategoryEditV20 routines. If you want your program to work on a Palm OS 2.0 device, you must call the V20 version of the routine, otherwise your program will crash when it tries to call the new version. There are a few Palm OS 1.0 routines that were similarly changed when 2.0 was released. The V10 suffix is used for the original version of the routine.

All applications in this book will work with Palm OS 2.0 and up unless otherwise mentioned.

Memory

Unlike desktop computers, which can use *virtual memory* (memory that is swapped to and from a hard disk as needed) to increase the

How V10 and V20 Functions Work

For a library developer, the promise of upward compatibility can be a hard one to keep. It's often only after you make a piece of code public that you discover one of your routines could have used an extra parameter or two, or that changing the order of the parameters would make the routine easier to understand. How can you make these changes without requiring the recompilation of existing applications?

When you call a Palm OS routine, your compiler doesn't generate a call directly to the routine in ROM, but rather to an entry in a dispatch table instead. A *dispatch table* is an array of pointers or offsets. In C++, for example, the virtual functions of a class are stored in a dispatch table called the *vtable* and all calls to the virtual functions are done through the vtable entries. This allows derived classes to easily override a function by simply writing a new address for the function in the vtable.

On the Palm, the dispatch table entries—called *system traps*—are initialized by the operating system. Whenever a routine is added to Palm OS, the developers add a new system trap to the end of the table. Once added, a system trap's index in the dispatch table is forever fixed.

How does the compiler know which system trap to use for a particular routine? In the header files that come with the Palm OS SDK you'll see that there is a mapping for each Palm OS routine to a particular system trap. These mappings provide the link from the symbolic name—the name you use in your code—to the actual routine in ROM. When you call a Palm OS routine, the compiler uses the mapping in the header file to generate a call into the dispatch table. Change the mapping and you change which ROM routine gets called. As long as the old system trap is still valid then code compiled using the original mapping will continue to work unchanged. Only when the code is compiled using a newer SDK will changes be required, at which point the generated code will use the new mapping and hence the new system trap.

Take, for example, the CategoryEdit routine. In Palm OS 3.0 there are actually three versions of this routine: CategoryEdit, CategoryEditV20, and CategoryEditV10. In Palm OS 1.0 there was only a single CategoryEdit routine, and it took two parameters. The SDK defined a mapping from the CategoryEdit name to a system trap. Palm OS 2.0 added a three-parameter version of the routine and hence a new system trap. The new SDK remapped CategoryEdit to the new (second) system trap and mapped the "new" routine CategoryEditV10 to the old (first) system trap. Palm OS 3.0 added a four-parameter version of the routine and another new system trap. The 3.0 SDK remapped CategoryEdit to the third trap and mapped the new routine CategoryEditV20 to the second trap. Thus, calling CategoryEdit using the 1.0 SDK is equivalent to calling CategoryEditV10 when using the 2.0 or 3.0 SDKs.

amount of memory available to an application, the memory chips that come with the Palm device are all you have to work with. Memory is a precious commodity on the Palm platform.

ROM and RAM

Palm devices come with varying amounts of memory, both read-only (ROM) and read-write (RAM). ROM memory is used to store the operating system, the built-in applications (such as the Address Book), and some default data for those applications. Newer models such as the Palm III use flash memory instead of ROM so that the operating system can be upgraded without replacing the memory chips.

RAM memory is where everything else is stored—the applications you've installed on the device, the data for those applications, user settings, and various system data areas. The original Palm devices came with very little memory, as low as 512K of ROM and 128K of RAM, but the Palm III comes with 2MB of RAM, a significant increase. Table 2.1 lists the RAM sizes in the various Palm devices.

Remember that unlike a desktop computer, the Palm device is never actually turned off—when you press the power button the device merely goes into sleep mode. Anything placed in RAM stays there until explicitly erased.

Cards and Heaps

ROM and RAM are packaged together on what is known as a memory *card*. Palm devices can support multiple cards, but so far only one card

Table 2.1 Palm Device RAM Sizes

DEVICE	RAM
Pilot 1000	128K
Pilot 5000	512K
PalmPilot Personal	512K
PalmPilot Professional and IBM WorkPad	1MB
Palm III	2MB
Palm IIIx	4MB
Palm V	2MB
Palm VII	2MB

is installed in each device. The memory card number (starting at 0) is a required parameter in some system calls, but until more memory cards are added to the device you can safely pass 0 in all cases.

The memory on a card is divided into *heaps*. ROM is considered a single heap. RAM consists of at least two heaps, the first of which is referred to as the *dynamic heap*, while the rest are called *storage heaps*.

The dynamic heap is used both by the operating system and by applications. Among other things, the dynamic heap stores the following:

- Operating system data, including the system trap dispatch table, user interface structures, and various buffers
- The application stack, where local variables and function return addresses are stored
- The application global and static variables, referred to as the global data block
- Dynamically allocated memory used by an application

The size of the dynamic heap can be quite small. On Palm OS 1.0 devices it's only 32K. On Palm OS 2.0 devices it's either 32K (PalmPilot Personal) or 64K (PalmPilot Professional), but if TCP/IP is available (only on the Professional) it uses 32K of the memory. So, effectively there is only 32K of memory available in the dynamic heap for Palm OS 1.0 and 2.0. In Palm OS 3.0, the dynamic heap size is 96K, but again TCP/IP requires 32K of this, leaving 64K for general use.

There are two important differences between the dynamic heap and the storage heaps. First, the contents of the dynamic heap are always cleared when the device is reset. The dynamic heap is not meant for use as long-term storage. The contents of the storage heaps are preserved, except in the most extreme cases, such as when the batteries are removed from the device for more than a minute or when a hard reset (explained subsequently) is performed. Second, the storage heaps are write-protected (in fact, all writing has to be done via system functions) to prevent an application from writing over another application's permanent storage, while the contents of the dynamic heap are not write-protected, making it possible for badly behaved applications to crash the device.

In Palm OS 1.0 and 2.0 there are multiple storage heaps, each no more than 64K in size. Thus, the maximum size of memory that can be allocated as a single chunk from any heap in the system is just under 64K. Palm OS 3.0 consolidates all the storage heaps into a single storage heap but keeps the allocation limit. The limit may be removed in a future version of the operating system.

Handles and Local IDs

Because physical memory is limited, heap fragmentation is to be avoided whenever possible. Fragmentation occurs when there are chunks of allocated memory spread throughout the heap, interspersed between the blocks of free memory. If two blocks of free memory are adjacent, for example, the Memory Manager can merge them into a single *contiguous* chunk. The larger a block of free memory is, the greater the likelihood that a request for memory will succeed.

In an ideal world all the allocated memory would sit at one end of the heap and the free memory at the other end, but real applications rarely behave this way. One way to avoid heap fragmentation is to relocate the allocated chunks so that more of the free chunks can be combined into larger blocks. The Memory Manager needs to know which blocks can be moved and which must stay fixed in place, otherwise the application will crash if one of the blocks it was using is suddenly shifted to another location. This is done by using memory *handles*.

A handle uniquely identifies a moveable block of memory. Conceptually, you can think of it as a pointer to a fixed memory block which itself holds a pointer to the moveable block. When the Memory Manager needs to move a block, it adjusts the pointer inside the handle—all references to the handle itself remain valid because the handle is fixed. At any point an application can use the handle to *lock* the moveable block. Locking a handle in Palm OS fixes the moveable block in memory to prevent the Memory Manager from moving it. The application then obtains a pointer to the newly fixed block. When the application is finished with the block, it *unlocks* the handle, making the block moveable again.

Applications can also allocate nonmoveable memory blocks, but their use is discouraged. They're best used for temporary memory allocations and should be freed as soon as possible.

Whether fixed or moveable, a block of memory can also be accessed by its *local ID*. The local ID is an offset relative to the start of the memory card. Palm OS provides APIs to convert handles and pointers to local IDs and vice versa. Local IDs are used mostly with certain system functions, in particular the Data Manager functions. Future Palm devices may allow the user to add and remove memory cards—using local IDs allows the base address of a card to change without affecting the data it holds.

Allocating from the Dynamic Heap

Palm OS provides functions analogous to the C runtime library's malloc, realloc, and free functions for allocating fixed memory blocks from the dynamic heap:

```
VoidPtr MemPtrNew( ULong size );
Err     MemPtrResize( VoidPtr ptr, ULong newSize );
Err     MemPtrFree( VoidPtr ptr );
```

All fixed-block memory allocation occurs with these functions: the C++ new and delete operators call MemPtrNew and MemPtrFree, for example.

Moveable blocks in the dynamic heap are allocated using MemHandleNew and deallocated using MemHandleFree:

```
VoidHand MemHandleNew( ULong size );
Err      MemHandleFree( VoidHand handle );
```

Before using a handle, you must lock it to obtain a pointer to a block of memory and unlock it when you're done:

```
VoidHand CopyStringIntoHandle( Char *string )
{
    VoidHand handle = MemHandleNew( StrLen( string ) );
    Char *dst = (Char *) MemHandleLock( handle );
    StrCopy( dst, string );
    MemHandleUnlock( handle );
    return handle;
}
```

You can also unlock a moveable block using the locked pointer because Palm OS can determine the handle that corresponds to a given pointer. The Palm OS Memory Manager also provides a number of functions for mapping handles to local IDs and back, resizing handles, and other miscellaneous operations.

Databases and the Storage Heap

Memory in the storage heap (or heaps) is accessed using the Data Manager API (application programming interface), which provides higher-level abstractions built on top of the Memory Manager that are useful when dealing with permanent storage. From the Data Manager's point of view, the storage heap is divided into databases. In Palm terminology, a *database* is just a collection of memory blocks allocated from the storage heap. We discuss Palm databases in detail in Chapter 5, so in this section we limit the discussion to a few basic facts. Note that most of the Memory Manager APIs can be used with blocks of memory from the storage heap as well as the dynamic heap.

There are two kinds of Palm OS databases: record and resource. A *record database* stores *records*, which are blocks of memory of arbitrary size (they don't have to be of equal size) that hold user-defined data. Records can be accessed by linear index, by a unique identifier, or by an application-defined key. The records in a database can also be sorted. A *resource database* has less overhead than a record database because it just stores a set of *resources*, which are memory blocks grouped by type and unique identifier only. No sorting is possible, and searching for a particular resource requires a linear search. The maximum size of any record or resource in a database is just under 64K.

All databases have a name, a type, and a creator ID. The name of the database must be unique and must be less than 32 characters long. The type is a four-byte value that identifies the kind of data in the database. By convention, the type value is represented using a four-character ASCII string, with each character in the string mapping to one of the bytes. (For readability, only printable ASCII characters, those in the range 32 to 127, are used.) The *creator ID* is a four-byte value, also represented as a four-character string, registered with Palm Computing that identifies the person or company who created the database. It's used to link databases of different types together with the application that created them. We'll talk more about creator IDs when we discuss applications in Chapter 4. Because registered creator IDs are unique, a common strategy to ensure that the database name is also unique is to append the creator ID to the name. For example, if you had a database that you wanted to call "Memos" and a creator ID of "ERIC," using the name "Memos-ERIC" or even "ERIC-Memos" should ensure uniqueness.

Resource databases are typically used by the system. For example, your application is really just a resource database, with different resources for the code, the initialization data for global and static variables, and for the static user interface elements. When programming, you'll be mostly dealing with record databases, not resource databases.

Resetting the Device

At some point, an application you're developing is going to corrupt memory and crash or else freeze the device. Pressing the power button is unlikely to help, since all it does is switch from one running mode to another. At times like these you'll need to manually reset your device.

There are three kinds of reset, and you should learn how to do each one. But before you experiment, be sure to do a HotSync to backup your device's current configuration. In fact, if you don't have a dedicated testing device, regular HotSyncs will ensure that you don't lose any data if you're forced to perform a hard reset as described in the following section.

Soft Resets

The gentlest and most basic form of reset is known as the *soft reset*. A soft reset clears the contents of the dynamic heap and resets the operating system. The storage heaps, and hence all applications and their data, are left untouched. All applications are notified that the system has been reset, the details of which are discussed in Chapter 4.

You perform a soft reset by using the tip of a straightened paper clip to press gently into the Reset hole on the back of your device. On the newer Palm III models, the unscrewed top of the stylus can serve in place of a paper clip.

Modified Soft Resets

A step up from the soft reset is the *modified soft reset*. A modified soft reset also clears the contents of the dynamic heap and resets the operating system, but applications are not notified that a reset has occurred. This allows you to get the device up and running again if an application crashes while processing the notification sent by a soft reset. System patches, which are primarily bug fixes to the operating system, are also not loaded, in case they are the cause of a crash.

You perform a modified soft reset by first pressing and holding down the scroll up button and then performing a soft reset with a paper clip.

If the system crashes immediately after a soft reset, try the modified soft reset to avoid the crash.

Hard Resets

The final form of reset is the *hard reset*. A hard reset erases the contents of the dynamic heap and all the storage heaps and then resets the operating system. Any applications you've installed and all their data are lost—the device is in the state it was when you first took it out of its box. Regular backups will allow you to recover your data after performing a hard reset.

You perform a hard reset by pressing and holding down the power button, pushing the paper clip into the Reset hole, removing the paper clip, and then releasing the power button. You will be asked to confirm the hard reset by pressing the scroll up button. The device then wipes itself clean.

A hard reset is hardly ever necessary. You're more likely to use it to purposely wipe a device clean than to recover from a crash. One time in which you'll need to do it is to change the user name of the device. Assuming you've defined two or more user names using the Palm Desktop software, the first HotSync after a hard reset lets you choose which user name the device will use. If you only have a single device, this is useful for impersonating different users in order to fully test an application. Be sure to do a complete backup before doing the hard reset and resetting the user name. When you're done testing, do another hard reset, use the HotSync Manager to make the desktop files overwrite the handheld files, and then perform a HotSync, choosing the original user name for the device. Your device will be restored to its previous state.

CHAPTER 3

Development Tools and Software Development Kits

Although you can write programs for the Palm Computing platform in several languages, the language of choice for most development is still C or C++. C/C++ allows you to write very small programs that interface directly to the operating system APIs. In this chapter we'll discuss the Palm OS Software Development Kit, the two C/C++ compilers (Code-Warrior and GCC) that you can use for Palm development, and some C/C++ programming issues specific to the Palm Computing platform. We'll also look at the Palm OS Emulator, which emulates a Palm device in software so that you can run your applications without downloading them to an actual device, and the Palm console. At the end of this chapter you'll be able to create, compile, and debug a new, but very basic, Palm application with the tool of your choice. In the next chapter we'll discuss how applications work and how to write them.

Palm Operating System Software Development Kit

The Palm OS Software Development Kit (SDK) is available for download from the Palm Computing Web site. The SDK contains a complete reference guide (either *Palm OS SDK Reference* or *Developing Palm OS Applications*) to Palm OS, the complete set of Palm OS header files and runtime libraries, the source to the built-in applications (such as the Address Book), the examples for the Palm OS Tutorial (available separately from the Web site), and a version of the Palm OS Emulator (discussed later in this chapter).

Although the compilers include a version of the SDK (CodeWarrior Release 5 includes the Palm OS 3.0 SDK, GCC includes the Palm OS 2.0 SDK), you should check the Palm Computing Web site regularly for new and updated versions of the SDK, especially if you're targeting the newer Palm devices like the Palm V. The most recent version of the SDK at the time this book was written is included on the accompanying CD-ROM.

The reference guide and the header files are the most important pieces of the SDK. You'll want to have links to the reference guide on your desktop for quick access. You might even want to print a copy of the complete reference guide, but given that it's about 1,000 pages in length you might find it simpler to purchase a printed copy instead. See the Web site for instructions on obtaining printed copies.

The header file directory structure isn't very complicated. A few header files are in the base directory, but most are found in the System and UI subdirectories and are referenced relative to the base directory:

```
#include <Common.h>
#include <System/SystemMgr.h>
#include <UI/UIAll.h>
```

Here is a short description of the most important header files:

- <Common.h> defines the types common to all Palm OS header files; see the summary in Table 3.1. You should familiarize yourself with these types.

- <System/SysAll.h> includes all the system header files.

- <UI/UIAll.h> includes all the user interface header files.

- <Pilot.h> includes <Common.h>, <System/SysAll.h> and <UI/UIAll.h>. Most application source files include <Pilot.h> as the first header file. Compile times for CodeWarrior users are shortened because a precompiled version of this header file is used.

- <System/Globals.h> and <UI/UIGlobals.h> define the global variables used by Palm OS itself. These global variables are stored in dynamic memory. Don't use these variables directly, always use the equivalent Palm OS APIs.

A number of header files are private to Palm OS. These have names like <System/AlarmPrv.h> or <System/SystemPrv.h>. These header files should not be used by your programs, as the functions, types, and macros they define are reserved for use by the operating system.

The Palm Computing platform uses 16-bit integers, so in both compilers

Table 3.1 Common Palm OS Types

TYPE	DESCRIPTION
Boolean	Unsigned 8-bit Boolean (true or false)
Byte	Unsigned 8-bit integer
Char	Signed character (8-bit)
CharPtr	Character pointer (Char *)
DWord	Unsigned 32-bit integer
Err	Signed 16-bit error code
Int	Signed 16-bit integer
IntPtr	Pointer to Int (Int *)
LocalID	Unsigned 32-bit card-relative memory offset
Long	Signed 32-bit integer
LongPtr	Pointer to Long (Long *)
SByte	Signed 8-bit integer
SDWord	Signed 32-bit integer
Short	Signed 16-bit integer
ShortPtr	Pointer to Short (Short *)
SWord	Signed 16-bit integer
UChar	Unsigned character (8-bit)
UCharPtr	Unsigned character pointer (UChar *)
UInt	Unsigned 16-bit integer
UIntPtr	Pointer to UInt (UInt *)
ULong	Unsigned 32-bit integer
ULongPtr	Pointer to ULong (ULong *)
UShort	Unsigned 16-bit integer
UShortPtr	Pointer to UShort (UShort *)
VoidHandle	Memory handle (void **)
VoidPtr	Generic pointer (void *)
Word	Unsigned 16-bit integer

the int type is a 16-bit type unless specified otherwise with a compiler option.

CodeWarrior

The official C/C++ development tool for the Palm Computing platform is CodeWarrior for Palm Computing platform, a commercial product. Although developed by Metrowerks, CodeWarrior for Palm Computing platform is now sold and supported exclusively by Palm Computing. As the official platform, you can expect more support for it than any other development tool. The current version of CodeWarrior at the time of writing is Release 5 and includes support for writing Palm OS 3.0 applications. Release 5 is required to run the CodeWarrior samples on the CD-ROM.

In this section we'll explore the basics of how to build and debug applications with CodeWarrior. For more details on CodeWarrior, consult the documentation that comes with the product. You can also download a Palm programming tutorial from the Palm Computing Web site that also doubles as an introduction to CodeWarrior.

The Origins of CodeWarrior

CodeWarrior is actually a family of development tools from Metrowerks. Originally a C/C++ compiler for Macintosh development, CodeWarrior can now also run on Microsoft Windows and generate code for a number of platforms and processors, including the Motorola 68000 series, the Intel 80x86 series, and embedded systems such as the Sony PlayStation. On some platforms, the CodeWarrior family supports programming in Java and Pascal as well as C/C++.

CodeWarrior for Palm Computing platform includes a C/C++ compiler, the CodeWarrior integrated development environment (IDE), a Motorola 68000 code generator, and other related tools. Also included are the Palm OS header files and a version of the Palm OS Emulator. In short, everything you need to write C or C++ for the Palm Computing platform.

Although it runs on Windows, CodeWarrior was first developed for and on the Macintosh, so it doesn't always follow Windows user interface guidelines. For example, a CodeWarrior message box looks like Figure

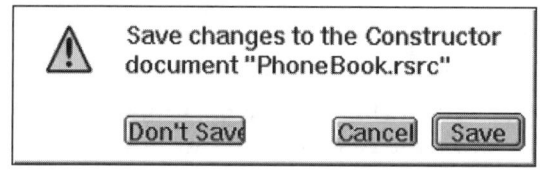

Figure 3.1 A Macintosh-like CodeWarrior dialog.

3.1. These differences are mostly annoyances, although references in the documentation to Macintosh-only tools such as ResEdit can sometimes be confusing. Macintosh programmers will feel right at home on either platform.

A Note for Windows Users

The Macintosh user interface model uses an approach similar to the multiple document interface (MDI) in Windows. In MDI, the child windows are contained in a parent window and share the parent's menubar. On the Macintosh windows do not have their own menubars, instead they all share the menubar at the top of the screen. Just as in MDI, the active window on the Macintosh determines the contents of the menubar. Although CodeWarrior on the Windows platform is not, strictly speaking, an MDI application (the windows are not contained within a parent window), it has a single menubar on its main window that all the windows share. As on the Macintosh, the contents of the menubar change depending on which window is active when you activate the main window. To use menu items with a particular window in mind, remember to activate the window before selecting an item from the menubar. If you find this too confusing, you can configure CodeWarrior to run as a true MDI application using a setting in the Preferences dialog.

CodeWarrior versus CodeWarrior Lite

Metrowerks makes an evaluation version of CodeWarrior available for downloading from its Web site. The evaluation version is known as CodeWarrior Lite and is also available on the CD-ROM that accompanies this book. It has all the features of the regular CodeWarrior except that it can only modify existing projects—it can't create new projects or add new files to existing projects. It's an option to consider if you want to try the software before buying it.

Starting a Project

You launch CodeWarrior just like any other Windows or Macintosh program. To start a new project, select the New Project menu item from the main window, which we'll refer to as the IDE window. You'll be presented with a dialog asking you what kind of project you want to create, as shown in Figure 3.2. Although you can create a new, completely empty project, CodeWarrior comes with some predefined project templates called *project stationery*. Selecting a project stationery creates a new project with some boilerplate C/C++ code and predefined project settings. Project stationery is included for building Palm applications in C or C++, as is stationery for building multisegment targets (discussed later in this chapter). You'll find it easy to get started with a new application if you always base your new projects on the Palm OS project stationery.

Once you've created a new project, CodeWarrior opens a project window with views listing the files, segments, and targets in the project, as shown in Figure 3.3. You switch between views by clicking on the tabs at the top of the window. The files view lists all the source files, runtime libraries, and resources used to build the application. The files view can also include other files, such as text files with documentation about the project. The segments view organizes the files in the project into segments, which are the individual code and data resources that comprise the final application. Segments are discussed in more detail later in this chapter. The final view is the targets view, which lets you control the tool settings for building your application. Applications have a single target, a .prc target.

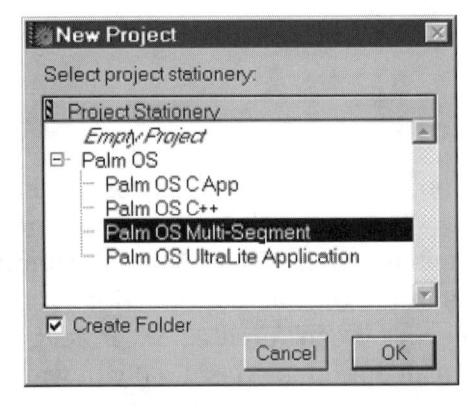

Figure 3.2 Selecting project stationery in CodeWarrior.

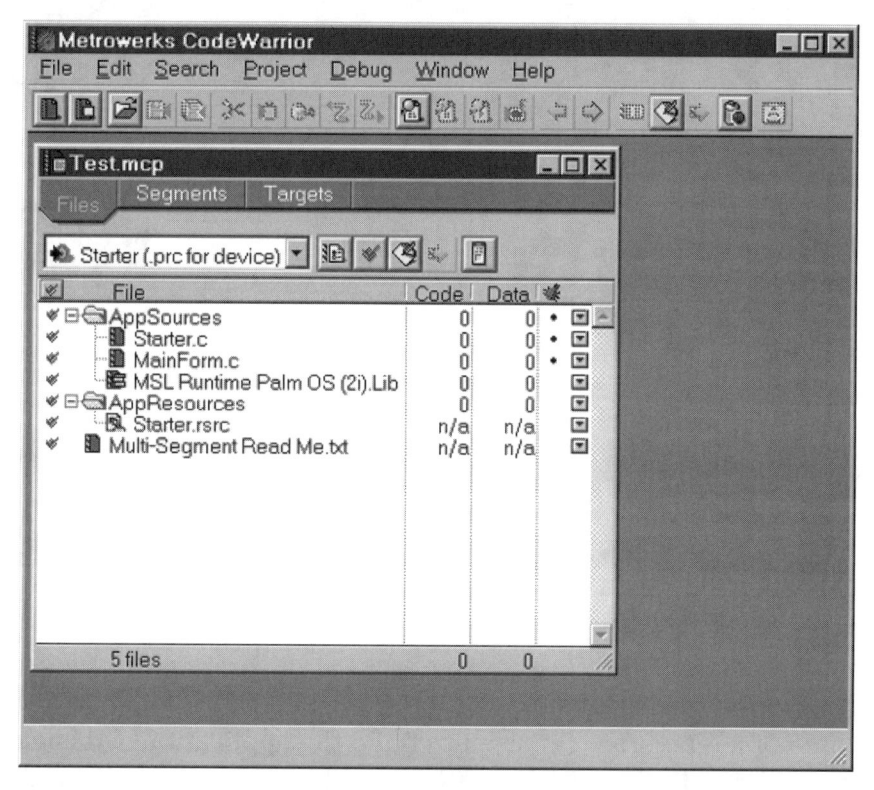

Figure 3.3 The CodeWarrior project window.

The first thing to do with any new project is to change the target settings to reflect the name of the application and its creator ID. Get into this habit now and you won't run into problems with applications overwriting each other on installation. Obtaining a creator ID is simple and is discussed in the next chapter.

To change the application name, several steps are required. Select the targets view and bring up the settings for the lone target (either by pressing the Target Settings button on the project window toolbar or by selecting the equivalent item from the Edit menu on the IDE window). The settings window shown in Figure 3.4 consists of two panes, with a tree view on the left and a details view on the right. In the tree view, select the "Target Settings" item. Change the Target Name shown in the right-hand pane to a descriptive name for your application. Then, back in the tree view, select the "68K Target" item and change the File Name in the right-hand pane to the name of your application suffixed with ".tmp." This is not the final name of your application, it's only the

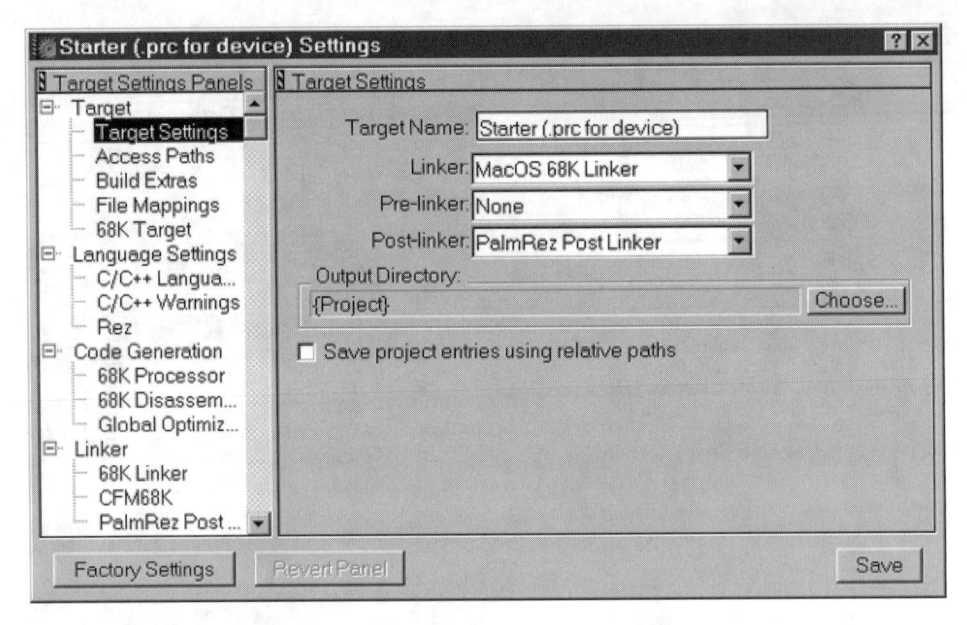

Figure 3.4 The CodeWarrior settings window.

name of a temporary file used to build the application. Go back to the tree view and select the "PalmRez Post Linker" item. In the right-hand pane, enter the name of the temporary file (the one you just set in the "68K Target" item) in the Mac Resource Files field. Enter the application name suffixed with ".prc" in the Output File field—this is the name of the file you'll install on your Palm device. Finally, enter your creator ID in the Creator field.

You'll probably want to change the name of the C/C++ source file as well. To do this, return to the files view, select the file and double-click to edit it. Activate the editor window, select the "Save As..." item from the File menu (Windows users remember that the menubar is on the IDE window, not the editor window; just make sure the editor window is open and active before you access the menubar) and type in the new name. The file will be renamed on disk and in the project.

If at this point you were to build the application and install the newly built .prc file onto your device, you would notice that the old name was still being used. The name of the .prc file does not determine the name of the application shown to the user by the Palm device. That application's name and icon are in fact stored as resources in the .prc file. In CodeWarrior, resources are edited with the Constructor tool.

Modifying Resources with Constructor

Although resources on the Palm platform can hold any kind of data, including the compiled code for your application, on a platform like Windows, resources usually hold a program's *static user interface elements*—such things as windows, menus, and strings. Constructor is a resource editor for creating these user interface elements for the Palm platform. It's a separate tool that you can launch from your desktop or from within the CodeWarrior environment. Constructor reads and writes resource files, which end in a .rsrc extension, and which it refers to as project files. (Don't confuse Constructor project files with CodeWarrior project files.)

To edit the resources for your new project, double-click on the .rsrc file shown in the project window's file view. The resource editor is shown in Figure 3.5. Like CodeWarrior itself, on the Windows platform the menubar for Constructor is in a separate window, so if you're editing several resource files simultaneously, be sure to activate the correct editor before selecting a menu item.

The resource editor window has two parts to it. The upper part of the window lists all the resource types that are available for editing. The bottom part is for Constructor project settings, which is where you set the name, icon, and version number of the application. The project settings also control the name of the header (.h) file that Constructor generates to map resource identifiers (which are integers) into more meaningful names.

For now all we'll do is change the name and icon for the application. To change the name, click on the existing name (to the left of the "Applica-

Another Note for Windows Users

On the Macintosh, files have two parts, called *forks*: a data fork and a resource fork. When you move a Macintosh file to another platform, each fork is a separate file. CodeWarrior on Windows uses the two-file approach for .rsrc files. The file you see on disk is the data fork and is empty. In the same directory as the data fork is a (possibly hidden) directory called Resource.frk which holds the resource fork. The resource fork has the same name as the data fork. CodeWarrior manages these files for you automatically, but if you ever need to copy files from a project to another directory or another machine, be sure to copy both forks.

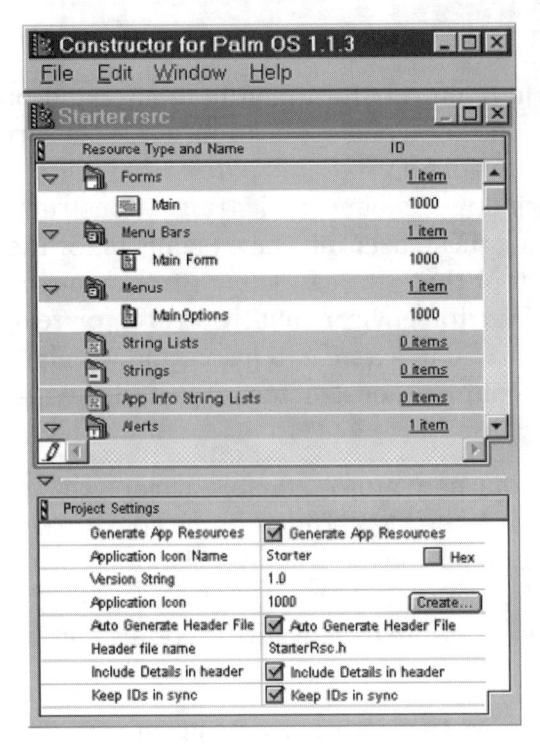

Figure 3.5 The Constructor resource editor.

tion Icon Name" field) and type the new name. Keep the name short but descriptive. To change the icon, click on the small button (labeled "Create" or "Edit") to the right of the "Application Icon" field. This brings up a small bitmap editor, shown in Figure 3.6, for creating monochrome icons. Create a simple icon and quit the bitmap editor.

> **TIP** Since Constructor and CodeWarrior are actually separate tools, changes you make to a resource file with Constructor are not automatically reflected in the CodeWarrior project. Always save your resource file before building your project.
>
> To rename a resource file, load it in Constructor and save it under a different name. Then return to CodeWarrior, select the files view for your project, and add the resource file to the project using the "Add Files" menu item in the Project menu. Finally, select the old resource file in the files view and select "Remove Selected Items" from the Project menu to remove the old file from the project.

The final step is to change the name that the application displays in its titlebar. Return to the resource editor window and find the "Forms"

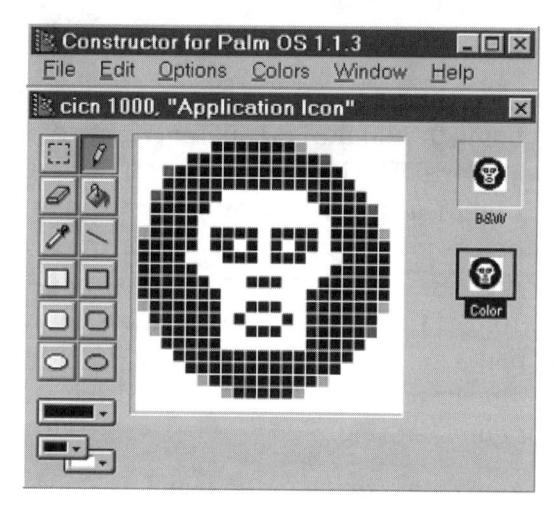

Figure 3.6 Constructor's bitmap editor.

resource type. There should be a single form listed there. Double-click on it to open the form editor shown in Figure 3.7. In the form editor, click on the field to the right of "Form Title" and change the title to the name of the application. Quit the form editor. Go to the menubar and save the resources you've just modified. Now you're ready to compile your project.

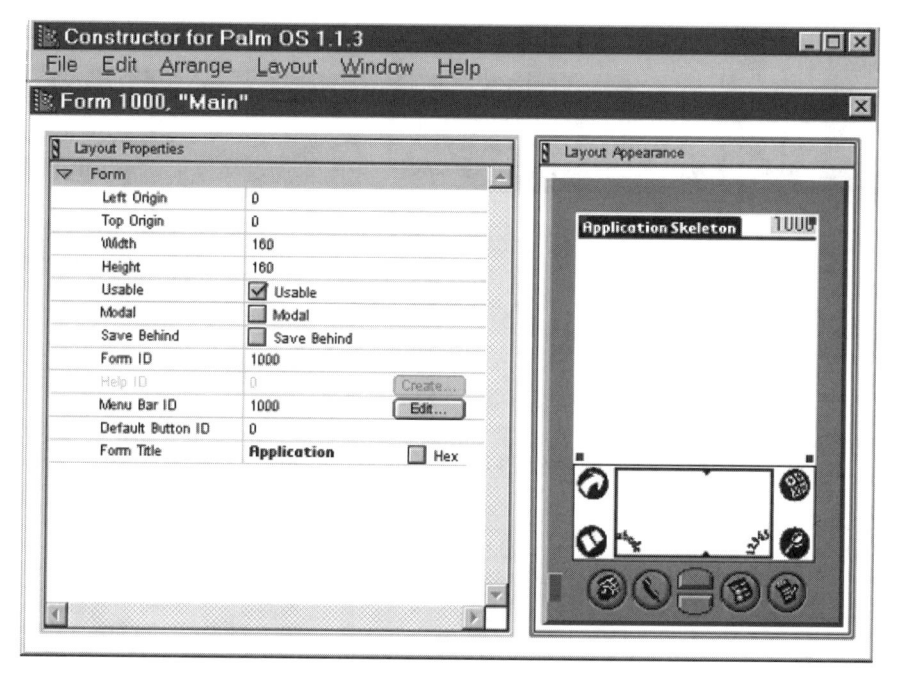

Figure 3.7 Constructor's form editor.

Building the Project

After changing the target settings and the resources, the next step is to build and run your project using the "Make" menu item or the equivalent button on the project window or IDE window toolbars. The application is compiled and linked to build a .prc file. Any errors and warnings appear in a separate window, as shown in Figure 3.8. Errors are easily fixed by selecting an error message and making the appropriate changes in the text editor at the bottom of the window. You can also double-click on the error message to open a separate editor window. In either case, the text editor jumps to the line in the source file where the error occurred, which makes for quick editing.

Download the .prc file to your Palm device in the usual manner and run it. You've just built your first application with CodeWarrior!

Debugging with CodeWarrior

At some point your application is going to crash and you're going to wonder why. CodeWarrior includes a full source-level debugger that is integrated into the development environment. With it you can debug your programs from your desktop computer as they run on the Palm-

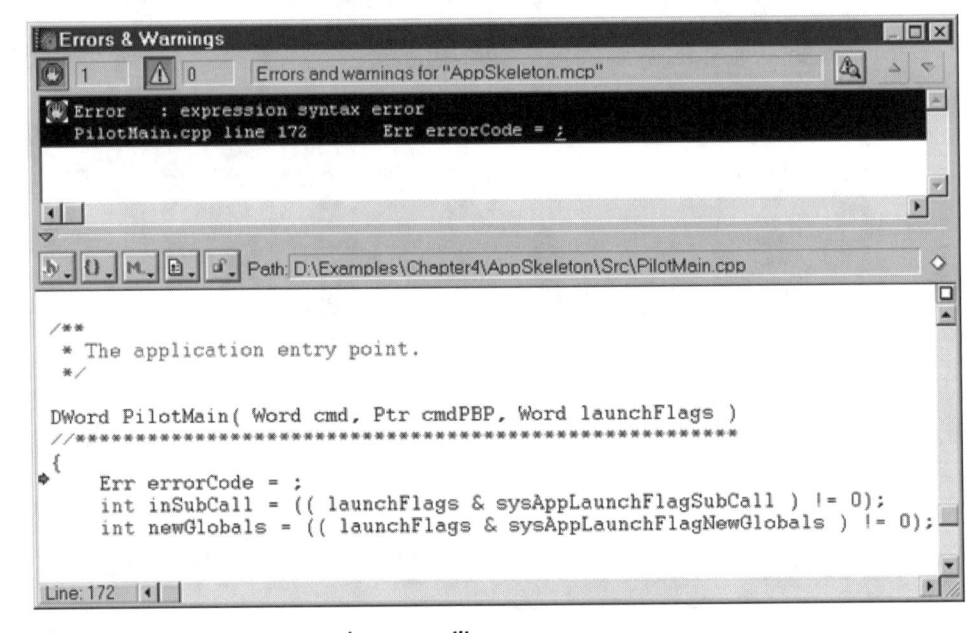

Figure 3.8 Error messages when compiling.

Pilot. The debugger can also debug programs running in the Palm OS Emulator. Even if you're planning on using the Emulator for most of your testing and debugging (most developers do), you should try a live debugging session with an actual device.

The debugger has to be configured before you can use it. On Windows, for example, it needs to know which serial port to use to communicate with the device. Or if you're using the Emulator, it needs to know where to find it. To configure the dialog, select the "Preferences" item from the Edit menu in the IDE window. In the resulting window, select the "Palm Connection Settings" in the tree view on the left side of the window, as shown in Figure 3.9. On the right side you can choose whether you want to debug with a device or the Emulator and configure either option.

To debug an application, load its project file into CodeWarrior and build it to make sure it's up to date. Select the "Debug" menu item from the Project menu to start the debugging process. What happens next depends on whether you're using a real device or the Palm OS Emulator.

If you're debugging with a real device, CodeWarrior will prompt you to place the device in *console mode*. Console mode is a low-level debugging mode that is available in each device, and which we discuss later in this chapter. When console mode is active, CodeWarrior can communicate

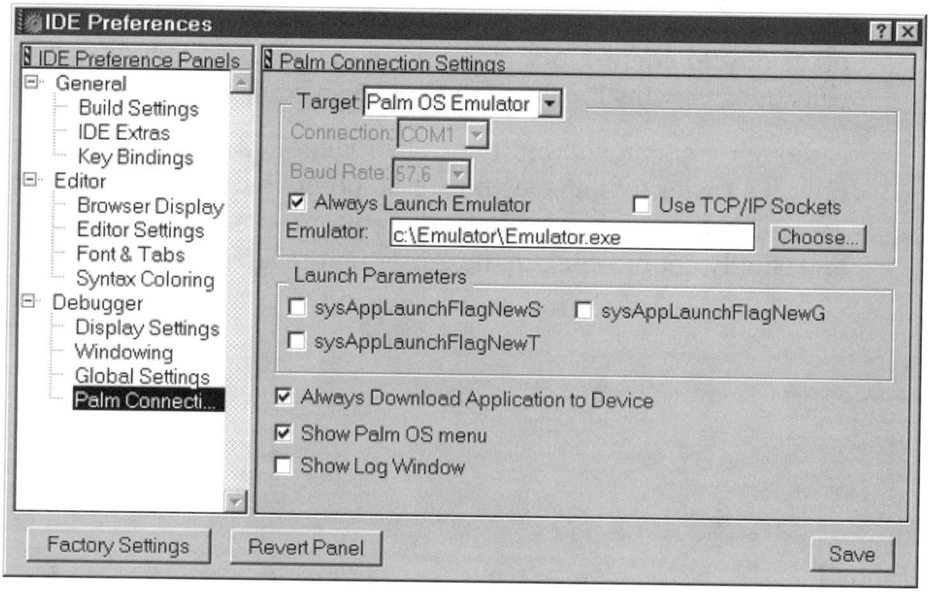

Figure 3.9 Configuring CodeWarrior to use the Emulator.

with the device through its HotSync cradle to install and debug your application. Place the device in its cradle and then write a sequence of Graffiti characters: the *shortcut* sequence (shown in Figure 3.10) followed by a period (two taps) and the number 2. Once you've done this, the device listens on its serial port for the debugger. Return to your desktop computer and dismiss the dialog. CodeWarrior will transfer the application to the device and start it running. If it doesn't, there could be a problem with your connection settings; consult the CodeWarrior documentation for steps on how to fix the problem.

If you're debugging with the emulator, there's no need to place the emulator in console mode. CodeWarrior transfers the application and starts it running without your help.

> **TIP**
> If you're having trouble with the Graffiti shortcut sequence, press the Find button before writing the shortcut. The shortcut character will appear in the Find dialog's text field if you're doing it right, otherwise another character will appear. This makes it much easier to correct writing problems.

Once the application is running, CodeWarrior brings up the debugger window, shown in Figure 3.11. The debugger stops at the entry point to the application, the PilotMain function, which we'll be discussing in some detail in the next chapter. The debugger window allows you to perform all the normal source-level debugging functions you're used to in other development tools: stepping in and out of functions, viewing the call stack, viewing local variables, and so on.

Although you can set and remove breakpoints from the debugger window, it's easier to manage your breakpoints before you start debugging. To set a breakpoint, open the code editor for the source file in question and simply double-click in the gutter on the left side of the window. This

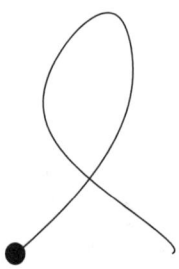

Figure 3.10 The Graffiti shortcut stroke.

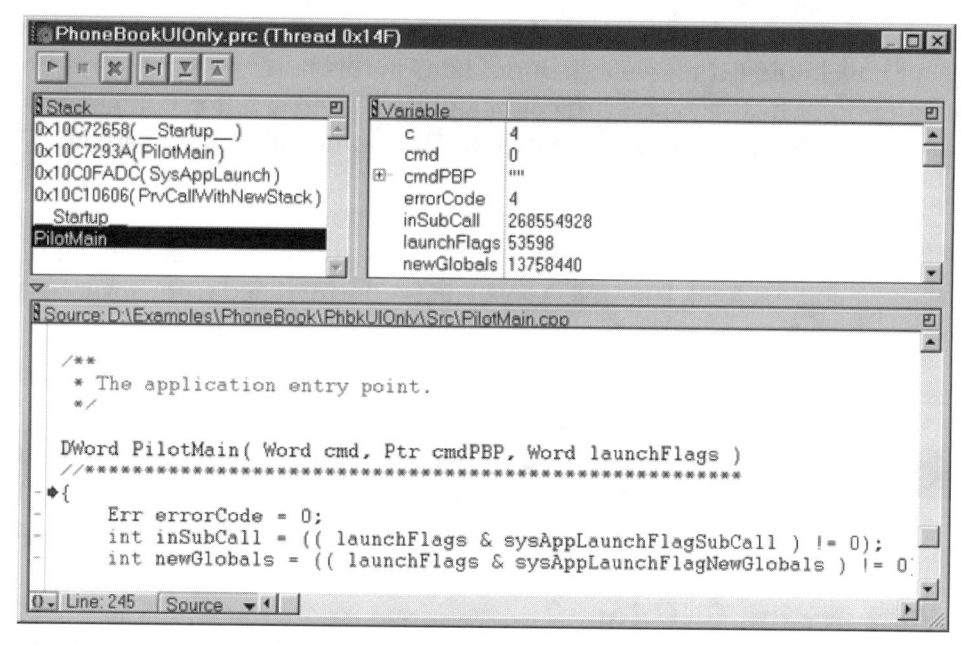

Figure 3.11 The CodeWarrior debugger window.

installs or removes a breakpoint at the given line. Breakpoints get saved with the project.

If you don't have any breakpoints installed, you can interrupt an application that is being debugged at any time with the following sequence of Graffiti characters: the Graffiti shortcut character, a period, and the number 1.

When you're done debugging, use the "Kill" menu item in the Debug menu to stop the debugger. This will also perform a soft reset of the device or the Emulator. The application is still installed and if it's crashing in its startup sequence, then you'll have to manually perform a modified soft reset (in the case of a real device) or else perform an Emulator recovery (discussed later in this chapter).

GCC and the GNU Tools

The second C/C++ development tool is GCC, part of a collection of free tools collectively known as the GNU tools (GNU stands for "GNU's not Unix"). Unlike CodeWarrior, the GNU tools are not officially supported by Palm Computing, and you may find that third-party tools and libraries may not support them either. For example, the Sybase UltraLite deployment technology that we talk about later in this book only supports CodeWarrior. The GNU tools are command-line based and don't come with a built-in integrated graphical user interface, either, although there are a couple of shareware IDEs that provide you with one. On the other hand, the GNU tools are currently the only way to do Palm development using the Unix/Linux platform. They're also a great way to explore Palm programming for free! The GNU tools can be downloaded from several sites and are also on the book's CD-ROM, in the GNU Tools folder.

The set of GNU tools for the Palm Computing platform is referred to as the prc-tools release. The current version of prc-tools is 0.5.0 and includes support for writing Palm OS 2.0 applications. To write Palm OS 3.0 applications, you'll have to download the latest Palm OS SDK from the Palm Computing Web site and install its files into the prc-tools directory.

What Are the GNU Tools?

The GNU tools are free development tools distributed under the terms of the GNU General Public License. Any program covered by the license must be distributed for free (apart from nominal copying charges, if any) with source code. Any modifications you make to such a program also fall under the terms of the license. A copy of the license is included with the GNU tools and is also available for reading online at the Free Software Foundation's Web site, *www.fsf.org*. Note that you can use the GNU tools to build programs that are *not* covered by the GNU Public License. Be sure to read both the GNU Public License and its sibling the GNU Library Public License before using any of the GNU tools or libraries.

The GNU project started in 1984 is one of the first serious attempts at open source code programming. The GNU project's goal is to develop a Unix-compatible software system that is freely available to anyone. The GNU tools in the prc-tools distribution are modified versions designed to build Palm Computing platform applications. The tools run on a number of platforms, including Windows and Linux, and the source is available for porting to any platform you desire, of course.

The GNU tools in the prc-tools distribution include the GCC C/C++ compiler and linker, the GDB line-oriented debugger, the PilRC resource compiler for creating resources from text files, a tool for converting object files into Palm resources, and the build-prc tool for combining all the resources into a Palm executable. The distribution also includes other tools you may find useful, such as a make tool for building projects. The documentation is quite light when compared to all the material available that covers development with CodeWarrior, so be sure to read the tutorial that is included with the pilrc-tools distribution.

Windows users can install the GNU tools using the installation program provided on the CD-ROM.

Starting and Building a Project

If you've only used IDEs like CodeWarrior or Microsoft Visual C++, the GNU tools will seem quite primitive. The tools have no graphical user interface, they're just invoked from the command line of a DOS prompt (Windows) or a shell (Unix/Linux). Make sure that the bin directory is in your search path so that the tools can be found.

In CodeWarrior, a project is a collection of files that are used to build a Palm application, together with the settings for compiling, linking, and processing those files into resources. With the GNU tools this is accomplished using a *makefile*. A makefile is a text file that is read by the *make* tool. It lists the series of commands necessary to build an application, such as compiling individual C/C++ files into object files. It also defines the *dependencies* between various files, so that if one file depends on a second file, changing the second file causes the first file to be rebuilt. Make uses these dependencies to determine the minimal set of operations that will create the application. If no files have changed, nothing is done. If only one C file has changed, then only it is compiled, not the others. A makefile isn't necessary to build an application, but the dependency checking is something a simple batch file or shell script can't easily do and it can save you time when working with large projects.

The easiest way to start a new project with the GNU tools is to simply clone an existing application and modify it. This is very similar to using project stationery in CodeWarrior. On the CD-ROM you'll find the skeleton for a Palm application, *GNUSample*, in the Samples directory. Create a new directory on your disk and copy the files from the GNUSample directory into it. Although there's a makefile, let's ignore it for now and build the various pieces by hand to understand how applications are created with the GNU tools.

The first step is to compile the two C files in the sample with the GCC compiler. You can do this with the following commands:

```
m68k-palmos-coff-gcc -O1 -c main.c -o main.o
m68k-palmos-coff-gcc -O1 -c other.c -o other.o
```

This compiles the main.c and other.c files to produce the main.o and other.o object files. If you had other C or C++ files to compile, you would compile each in a similar fashion. C files should have a .c extension, C++ files a .cc or .cpp extension. The -O1 option tells GCC to optimize the code.

A quick note about the tool names. Some of the GNU tools are unique to the pilrc-tools distribution and these have simple names like pilrc or build-prc. Other tools are common to several different platforms and have longer names. In this case the name m68k-palmos-coff-gcc refers to the version of GCC that generates Motorola 68000 code for the Palm Computing platform and uses the COFF format for object files and executables.

After compiling the files you should link them into an executable with the following command:

```
m68k-palmos-coff-gcc -O1 main.o other.o -o GNUSample.tmp
```

The object files from the previous step are combined with any library functions to form a COFF executable called GNUSample.tmp. This executable is *not* a Palm application, however, which is why we didn't call it GNUSample.prc. The executable must be converted into a set of resources that are later combined to form a Palm database:

```
m68k-palmos-coff-obj-res GNUSample.tmp
```

This produces a set of files with .grc extensions, each of which represents an individual code or data resource in the application database. The next step is to use the pilrc tool to convert the static user interface elements (discussed in the next chapter) defined in GNUSample.rcp into resources:

```
pilrc GNUSample.rcp
```

This produces a set of files with .bin extensions, one for each user interface element. These are combined with the code and data resources from the previous step to form a Palm application:

```
build-prc GNUSample.prc "GNU Sample" ERIC *.bin *.grc
```

The arguments to the build-prc tool are the name of the generated executable, the name of the application, the creator ID, and the set of resource files that combine to form the application. (The application icon is not one of the arguments, it's a static user interface element defined in the .rcp file we ran through pilrc.) The final .prc file can be installed and run on your Palm device or the Palm OS Emulator.

> **TIP**
> If when you link the COFF executable you get the message "relocation truncated to fit: DISP 16 *funcname*," that's usually GCC's obscure way of telling you it couldn't find the function *funcname*, which will occur if you've misspelled the function name. It can also occur, however, when one function calls another function and more than 32K of code sits between them—see the following section on building multisegment applications.

Unless you're a very skilled typist, you won't want to type all those commands every time you want to build a project. The sample project includes a makefile that performs these steps for you. To build the project you would simply type the following:

```
make GNUSample.prc
```

or even just:

```
make
```

If you add, remove, or rename files you'll have to modify the makefile appropriately. Read the comments in the file for instructions on how to do this.

Debugging with GDB

If your program crashes, you'll want to debug it. With the GNU tools this means using the GDB debugger. Unlike the CodeWarrior debugger, GDB does not have a graphical user interface, but instead responds to text commands that you type at the GDB command prompt. GDB does integrate somewhat with the Emacs text editor that comes with the GNU tools, however, so if you're an Emacs fan be sure to read through the tutorial that accompanies the pilrc-tools distribution for instructions on how to integrate the two.

Applications that are to be debugged must be compiled and linked with the -g option to gcc, as in:

```
m68k-palmos-coff-gcc -g -dDEBUG -c main.c -o main.o
m68k-palmos-coff-gcc -g -dDEBUG -c other.c -o other.o
m68k-palmos-coff-gcc -g main.o other.o -o GNUSample.tmp
```

For best results, turn off all optimizations when compiling the debugging version of your application.

To debug with GDB under Windows you need to use the Palm OS Emulator and a freeware tool called *gdbplug*, which acts as a relay between

GDB and the Emulator. Start the Emulator as discussed later in this chapter and load the application you just built. If the Emulator was launched by CodeWarrior, shut it and CodeWarrior down and start the Emulator separately—CodeWarrior will interfere with the debugging process otherwise. Now run the gdbplug application from a second DOS window:

```
gdbplug -port 2000 -enable
```

The relay opens a TCP/IP port that GDB will communicate with, so be sure to specify a port number that does not conflict with one already in use by another application. Once gdbplug is running, return to the main DOS window and start GDB with the COFF executable (not the final .prc file) as an argument:

```
m68k-palmos-coff-gdb GNUSample.tmp
```

After GDB starts you need to connect it to the gdbplug relay. Type the following command at the GDB prompt:

```
target pilot localhost:2000
```

Substitute the TCP/IP port you specified when you started gdbplug if it's different than 2000. At this point you should see a message that says remote debugging of the Palm OS Emulator is underway. Return to the Emulator and start your application. The application is stopped immediately by GDB, which prompts you for a command. Type the following:

```
help
```

This lists the complete set of commands that GDB supports. You can step in and over functions, set breakpoints, print the call stack, and so on. It's not as convenient or as simple to use as the CodeWarrior debugger, but it gets the job done.

C/C++ Programming Issues

This section lists a few of the limitations you have to be aware of when programming in C or C++ for the Palm Computing platform.

The C Runtime Library

The C programming language is very concise. Unlike other languages, there are no built-in functions in C. Instead, C (and C++) uses a set of standard routines referred to as the C *runtime library*, which defines familiar routines such as printf, strcpy, malloc, and so on. As of Release 5, however, CodeWarrior does not provide a standard C runtime library for use with Palm OS. The GNU tools do provide a standard library, but unless you're sure you'll never want to move your project to CodeWarrior, you're better off not using any of its functions.

Note that the C runtime library isn't required for C/C++ programming—you can program without the runtime library if the operating system provides the functions you need or you write your own functions. For example, the Palm OS String Manager has functions for comparing, copying, and converting strings that are very similar to the string functions in the C runtime library like strcmp, strcpy, and atoi. Instead of writing your own versions of functions, use the equivalent Palm OS functions whenever possible—since the Palm OS functions are in ROM, less RAM is required by the application. See Table 3.2 for a list of equivalent Palm OS functions.

Assertions and Error Messages

An *assertion* is a runtime sanity check often used when developing an application, used to ensure that specific conditions or assumptions hold true. If an assertion fails, a message is displayed with details about the failure, including the line number and filename of the failure. On most platforms, assertions are available via macros defined in the header file <assert.h>. On the Palm Computing platform, assertions are macros defined in the header file <System/ErrorMgr.h>.

The most basic macro is ErrDisplay, an unconditional assertion, which takes a string as its only parameter:

```
ErrDisplay( "Find is not yet supported" );
```

When ErrDisplay is encountered at run time, Palm OS displays a dialog similar to the one shown in Figure 3.12, replacing the message with the argument to ErrDisplay and adjusting the line number and filename to reflect the source of the message. The only way to dismiss the dialog is to reset the device, which of course stops the application. When running the application on the Palm OS Emulator, discussed later in this chapter, the dialog is as shown in Figure 3.13, and you're given the opportunity to debug the application or ignore the message instead of just resetting the (emulated) device.

Table 3.2 Selected Palm OS Equivalents to C Runtime Library Functions

C RUNTIME LIBRARY FUNCTION	PALM OS EQUIVALENT
atoi	StrAToI
bsearch	SysBinarySearch
clock	TimGetTicks
free	MemPtrFree
itoa	StrIToA, StrIToH
malloc	MemPtrNew
memcmp	MemCmp
qsort	SysQSort, SysInsertionSort
rand	SysRandom
realloc	MemPtrSize
sprintf	StrPrintF
strcat	StrCat
strchr	StrChr
strcmp	StrCompare
strcpy	StrCopy
strerror	SysErrString
stricmp	StrCaselessCompare
strlen	StrLen
strncat	StrNCat
strncmp	StrNCompare
strncpy	StrNCopy
strnicmp	StrNCaselessCompare
strstr	StrStr, FindStrInStr
strlwr	StrToLower
vsprintf	StrVPrintF

ErrDisplay is only enabled messages if the error-checking level, as defined by the ERROR_CHECK_LEVEL macro, is set to ERROR_CHECK_PARTIAL or ERROR_CHECK_FULL at compile time. The error-checking levels are defined as follows:

```
#define ERROR_CHECK_NONE     0
#define ERROR_CHECK_PARTIAL  1
#define ERROR_CHECK_FULL     2
```

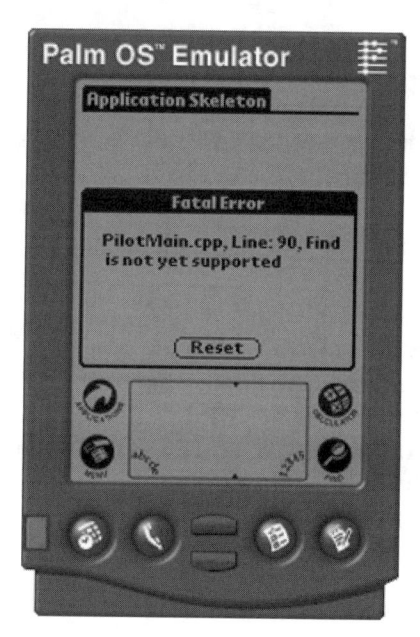

Development Tools and Software Development Kits

Figure 3.12 A fatal error message.

If not otherwise defined, ERROR_CHECK_LEVEL is set to ERROR_CHECK_FULL in <BuildRules.h>, which is called from <Common.h>, which is ultimately included from <Pilot.h>. To disable the ErrDisplay macro and other error checking, set ERROR_CHECK_LEVEL to 0 (ERROR_CHECK_NONE) before including <Pilot.h>.

Conditional assertions are done using the ErrFatalDisplayIf and ErrNonFatalDisplayIf macros:

```
#define ErrFatalDisplayIf( condition, message )
#define ErrNonFatalDisplayIf( condition, message )
```

Both macros take two arguments: a Boolean expression and a string. At run time the expression is evaluated and if the result is true the message

Figure 3.13 A fatal error message when using the emulator.

> ### Error Levels and Precompiled Headers
>
> CodeWarrior supports *precompiled* headers. A precompiled header is a header that is processed in a separate step and converted to a compact binary representation that can be quickly loaded by the compiler. Including precompiled headers (ending in .mch) in place of normal headers (ending in .h) greatly speeds the time required to compile most source files.
>
> The <Pilot.h> header file includes the precompiled header <Pilot.h.mch> (for C) or <Pilot.h++.mch> (for C++) unless the macro PILOT_PRECOMPILED_HEADERS_OFF is defined; so by default any macros you define before including <Pilot.h> have no effect on what's actually included by <Pilot.h>. To redefine the error level, for example, either define PILOT_PRECOMPILED_HEADERS_OFF in addition to defining ERROR_CHECK_LEVEL or else rebuild the precompiled header files by following the directions in the <Pilot.h> source and the CodeWarrior manual.

is displayed just as if ErrDisplay had been called. Note that this is different from a traditional assertion, where the message is displayed if the expression returns false. If you're used to the traditional form of assertions, you can easily define another macro:

```
#define assert(expr,msg) ErrFatalDisplayIf(!(expr),msg)
```

The difference between ErrFatalDisplayIf and ErrNonFatalDisplayIf is that ErrFatalDisplayIf is enabled if the error-checking level is ERROR_CHECK_FULL or ERROR_CHECK_PARTIAL, while ErrNonFatalDisplayIf is enabled only with the ERROR_CHECK_FULL level. Neither is enabled if the level is ERROR_CHECK_NONE.

ErrDisplay, ErrFatalDisplayIf, and ErrNonFatalDisplayIf all use the function ErrDisplayFileLineMsg to display the error dialog.

Palm OS 3.2 adds an ErrAlert function that displays a message from a predefined set of strings, and when dismissed allows the application to continue running. This kind of informational dialog is easily implemented on prior platforms using an alert resource, as described in Chapter 4.

Exception Handling

CodeWarrior implements full C++ exception handling, although it's off by default so you'll have to turn it on from the Target Settings window. The Error Manager also defines macros and functions in <System/Error-

Mgr.h> for implementing a restricted form of exception handling that can be used with C and C++, as demonstrated here:

```
ErrTry {
    VoidPtr p = MemPtrNew( 5000 );
    if( p == NULL ){
        // You can throw any long (32-bit) integer value
        // You can throw it from any function called within
        // the "try" block
        ErrThrow( memErrNotEnoughSpace );
    }
}
ErrCatch( err ) {
    // This code only executes if an exception is thrown.
    // It defines "err" as a long that holds the exception
    // value.
    if( err == memErrNotEnoughSpace ){
        ErrDisplay( "Memory allocation failed" );
    }
} ErrEndCatch
```

Refer to the *Palm OS Programmer's Companion* for details.

Callbacks and GCC

A *callback function* is a way for the operating system to call back into your application while performing an operation. For example, you can ask Palm OS to let you draw the individual items in a list. You do this by registering the callback function with Palm OS, which then calls the function as required.

Callback functions compiled with GCC require the use of special macros at the start and end of the function. These macros perform some internal housekeeping to ensure that the callback function can access global and static data. These macros are not required by programs compiled with CodeWarrior, just those compiled with GCC. You would use the macros like this:

```
void CallbackFunction()
{
    #ifdef __GCC__
        CALLBACK_PROLOGUE
    #endif

    ....

    #ifdef __GCC__
        CALLBACK_EPILOGUE
    #endif
}
```

Use the CALLBACK_PROLOGUE macro before attempting to access any global or static data. The macros are defined in the file Callback.h, which is not included with GCC but can be found on the CD-ROM and on the Web site for this book. Callback.h was written by Ian Goldberg, who has graciously allowed us to include it with this book. The code for Callback.h is shown in Figure 3.14.

C++ Programming Issues

C++ programmers have a few more issues to deal with than C programmers. The first question you should ask yourself is if you even need to use C++ to do your programming. C++ programs can be large if you're not careful about how you structure and use your classes.

```
#ifndef __CALLBACK_H__
#define __CALLBACK_H__

/* This is a workaround for a bug in the current version of gcc:

   gcc assumes that no one will touch %a4 after it is set up in crt0.o.
     This isn't true if a function is called as a callback by something
     that wasn't compiled by gcc (such as FrmCloseAllForms()). It may also
     not be true if it is used as a callback by something in a different
     shared library.

   We really want a function attribute "callback" which will insert this
     prologue and epilogue automatically.

     - Ian Goldberg
       iang@cs.berkeley.edu
       http://now.cs.berkeley.edu/~iang/
*/

register void *reg_a4 asm("%a4");

#define CALLBACK_PROLOGUE \
    void *save_a4 = reg_a4; asm("move.l %%a5,%%a4; sub.l #edata,%%a4" : :);

#define CALLBACK_EPILOGUE reg_a4 = save_a4;

#endif
```

Figure 3.14 The Callback.h header file for use with GCC.

Object Allocation

By default, the new operator allocates fixed blocks of memory from the dynamic heap and then invokes the constructor to initialize the newly created object. To use moveable blocks (to reduce heap fragmentation) or blocks allocated from a storage heap, overload the new operator as follows:

```
// Add this to a header file
extern void *operator new( unsigned long size, void *mem );

// Add this to a source file
void *operator new( unsigned long, void *mem )
{
    return mem;
}
```

This is the *placement* variant of the new operator. It doesn't actually allocate memory, it just returns the pointer that was passed to it as the second argument (the first argument to operator new is always the size of the memory block to allocate). If you look at the code that a C++ compiler generates, you'll see that immediately after a call to operator new the compiler invokes the constructor for the newly allocated object. Our overloaded operator doesn't allocate any memory, but the compiler still invokes the constructor. You use the placement variant like this:

```
char       memPtr[ sizeof( SomeClass ) ];
SomeClass *object = new( memPtr ) SomeClass();
```

Here's a more concrete example using some of the Palm OS Memory Manager APIs:

```
class MyClass {
    public:
        MyClass( int v ) : val( v ) {}

        int getValue() { return val; }

    private:
        int val;
};

// Allocate chunk to hold an instance
VoidHand hdl = MemHandleNew( sizeof( MyClass ) );
VoidPtr  mem = MemHandleLock( hdl );

// Invoke the constructor
MyClass *c = new( mem ) MyClass( 13 );
```

```
// Now unlock it...
MemHandleUnlock( mem );
```

When using the placement variant of new, don't delete the object with delete; instead invoke the destructor directly and then delete the memory as appropriate:

```
MyClass *c = (MyClass *) MemHandleLock( hdl );
c->~MyClass(); // invoke destructor
MemHandleUnlock( mem );
MemHandleFree( hdl );
```

For moveable blocks, always lock the block before accessing the object:

```
MyClass *c = (MyClass *) MemHandleLock( hdl );
int x = c->getValue();
MemHandleUnlock( hdl );
```

Be sure to use the correct sizes when allocating memory and don't forget to free the memory when you're done with it.

Virtual Function Strategies

In C++, virtual functions are implemented using dispatch tables, one table for each class that has virtual functions. These dispatch tables are considered to be global data, but global data is not always available, as we'll see in the next chapter. If you use virtual functions when global data is not available, your program will crash. You can try this for yourself quite easily by defining a simple class with a single virtual function:

```
class CrashMe {
    public:
        CrashMe() : v( 0 ) {}
        virtual void crash( int val ) { v = val; }
    private:
        int v;
};
```

Then add the following code to the PilotMain function of an application you're working with to create a new instance of the class and invoke the virtual function:

```
CrashMe *crashMe = new CrashMe();
crashMe->crash( 10 );
```

Compile and run the application. To make the crash occur you need to invoke the application without its global data: Switch to another application such as the Address Book and then perform a global Find with a random string of data. As part of its processing, the Find operation will briefly start the application, but without initializing any of its global data, causing a crash.

This restriction makes it hard to write base classes that define an interface (i.e., an abstract class) or some common behavior that is overridden by derived classes. You'll need to choose one of the following approaches.

1. **Avoid or limit the use of virtual functions.** Don't use any classes with virtual functions (including virtual destructors), or else limit their use to contexts where you know global data is available, as discussed in the next chapter. Unfortunately, this is quite limiting if you like to make extensive use of virtual functions, because it's not unusual for your application to be called without access to its global data.

2. **Simulate virtual functions with dispatch tables.** There's nothing particularly magic about virtual functions—with a bit of work you can simulate what the compiler does without relying on the global data block. First, though, you need to understand how virtual functions work.

   The compiler creates a virtual function dispatch table, or *vtable*, for each class that has virtual functions. The vtable is akin to static data, in that there is only one copy of the table per class. Each entry in a vtable points to one of the virtual functions in the class. The vtable of a derived class is based on the vtable of the base class, with additional entries for any new (noninherited) virtual functions. If a derived class does not override a particular virtual function, that function's entry in the vtable is copied from the base class's vtable, otherwise the address of the overriding function is stored in the vtable. When an instance of a class is created, the compiler silently adds a data member that points to the vtable for the class. When a virtual function is invoked, the correct function is located using an offset into the vtable.

   To simulate virtual functions without access to global data, you need a vtable allocated on the stack or in dynamic memory. We can't replace the real vtable that the compiler generates, so we remove any virtual functions and use our own dispatch table to achieve the same effect. It's easier to demonstrate this with an example. Consider the classes AV, BV, and CV defined in Figure 3.15, where BV derives from AV and CV derives from BV. AV defines two virtual functions, Func1 and Func2, and BV defines a third, Func3. BV overrides Func1 and CV overrides Func2 and Func3. We're going to convert these into classes A, B, and C, classes that use dispatch tables to simulate vtables.

The first step in transforming the AV class into the A class is to change each virtual function (for example, Func1) into two separate functions: a nonvirtual function (Func1) and a static function (virtFunc1). The A class is shown in Figure 3.16. The nonvirtual function is public and is declared identically to the original virtual function—it presents the public interface that other classes will invoke. The static function is protected and has an additional parameter to it and a different name, but is otherwise identical to the original virtual function. (Note

```
//
// Three simple classes with virtual functions.
//

class AV {
    public:
        AV() : value( 1 ) {}
        ~AV() {}

        virtual int Func1() { return value; }
        virtual int Func2( int val )
                            { return 2 * val; }

    protected:
        int value;
};

class BV : public AV {
    public:
        BV() { value = 2; }
        ~BV() {}

        int         Func1() { return 5 * value; }
        virtual bool Func3( int val1, int val2 )
                            { return val1 > val2; }
};

class CV : public BV {
    public:
        CV() { value = 3; }
        ~CV() {}

        int  Func2( int val ) { return 2 * val + 1; }
        bool Func3( int val1, int val2 )
                            { return !BV::Func3( val1, val2 ); }
};
```

Figure 3.15 A simple example of virtual functions.

that static functions and static data are stored in two different areas: static data is stored as part of the global memory block for the application, while static functions live with the rest of the code in the storage heap. Restrictions on accessing global and static data do not affect access to static functions.) The additional parameter ("self") is a pointer to an object of class A and takes the place of the "this" pointer that is implicit to member functions. The code that was in the definition of the original virtual function is moved into the new static function, altered suitably to use the "self" pointer.

The next step is to implement a dispatch table. A dispatch table is just a series of function pointers, easily represented by a structure. For convenience, we define typedef equivalents for the various function pointers; however, this isn't necessary. The important part is the definition of the dispatch table, DispatchTableA, and the addition of a reference to the dispatch table as member data. The dispatch table has an entry in it for each of the virtual functions originally defined in class AV. The code for each nonvirtual equivalent to the original virtual functions (i.e., the new Func1) uses the dispatch table to invoke the "real" virtual function. In Figure 3.16 the nonvirtual functions perform some error checking to ensure that the dispatch table entry they're using isn't null, but that isn't strictly necessary—you could replace that code with assertions.

The final step is to fill in the dispatch table and to modify the constructor for the original class. To fill in the dispatch table we define a static function called FillDispatchTable that takes a reference to a DispatchTableA. FillDispatchTable then fills it with the addresses of the static function equivalents to the original virtual functions. The constructor is modified to take a reference to a dispatch table and store it as member data. The transformation of class AV into class A is now complete.

Similar transformations are then used to convert class BV into B and class CV into C, as shown in Figure 3.17. Inheritance is respected, so B derives from A and C derives from B, just like BV derives from AV and CV from BV. B and C define new dispatch tables, DispatchTableB and DispatchTableC, which mirror the inheritance tree: DispatchTableB derives from DispatchTableA and DispatchTableC derives from DispatchTableB. However, only *new* virtual functions (as opposed to *overridden* virtual functions) are added to these dispatch tables. Class B defines a new virtual function Func3, so an entry is added to Dis-

```cpp
// Transform class AV into a class without virtual functions
// but that uses a dispatch table to achieve the same effect.

class A {
    protected:
        // Some typedefs, for convenience only.

        typedef int (*Func1Dispatch)( A *self );
        typedef int (*Func2Dispatch)( A *self, int val );

        // The dispatch table: one entry for each virtual
        // function.

        struct DispatchTableA {
            Func1Dispatch func1;
            Func2Dispatch func2;
        };

        // Member data: a reference to the dispatch table.

        const DispatchTableA & dispatchTable;

    public:
        // Constructor takes a reference to the dispatch table.

        A( const DispatchTableA & table );

        // Destructor is not changed.

        ~A() {}

        // Virtual functions become regular, nonvirtual functions.

        int Func1();
        int Func2( int val );

        // Function to fill the dispatch table.

        static void FillDispatchTable( DispatchTableA & table );

    protected:
        int      value;

        // Static equivalents of the original virtual functions.
        // Note the extra "self" parameter.

        static int virtFunc1( A *self );
        static int virtFunc2( A *self, int val );
};
```

Figure 3.16 Transforming class AV into class A.

```cpp
// Constructor changed to store away the reference to
// the dispatch table.

A::A( const DispatchTableA & table )
: dispatchTable( table )
, value( 1 )
{
}

// Places addresses of static functions into the
// dispatch table.

void A::FillDispatchTable( DispatchTableA & table )
{
    table.func1 = virtFunc1;
    table.func2 = virtFunc2;
}

// Originally a virtual function, now a nonvirtual function
// that uses the dispatch table to invoke the correct static
// equivalent, passing the "this" pointer as the first argument.

int A::Func1()
{
    return( dispatchTable.func1 != NULL ? (*dispatchTable.func1)( this ) : 0 );
}

// Ditto.

int A::Func2( int val )
{
    return( dispatchTable.func2 != NULL ? (*dispatchTable.func2)( this, val ) : 0 );
}

// The code for the original virtual Func1, transformed to use the
// "self" parameter in place of the implicit "this" parameter.

int A::virtFunc1( A *self )
{
    return self->value;
}

// The code for the original virtual Func2.

int A::virtFunc2( A *self, int val )
{
    return 2 * val;
}
```

Figure 3.16 *(Continued)*

```cpp
// Transform class BV into a class B that doesn't use virtual
// functions and inherits from class A instead of class AV.

class B : public A {
    protected:
        typedef bool (*Func3Dispatch)( B *self, int val1, int val2 );

        // Define a new dispatch table structure.  This one inherits
        // from the base class's dispatch table and adds a single
        // entry—overridden functions are not added, only new
        // virtual functions.

        struct DispatchTableB : public DispatchTableA {
            Func3Dispatch func3;
        };

    public:
        B( DispatchTableB & dispatchTable );

        ~B() {}

        // Func3 from class BV becomes a regular, nonvirtual function.

        bool Func3( int val1, int val2 );

        static void FillDispatchTable( DispatchTableB & table );

    protected:

        // Class BV overrides Func1, so class B defines a static
        // function but no regular, nonvirtual equivalent.

        static int  virtFunc1( B *self );

        // The code for the new Func3 function.

        static bool virtFunc3( B *self, int val1, int val2 );
};

// Constructor must pass the dispatch table back up to the
// parent. This works because DispatchTableB derives from
// DispatchTableA.

B::B( DispatchTableB & table )
: A( table )
{
    value = 2;
```

Figure 3.17 Transforming classes BV and CV into classes B and C.

```
    }

    // Fills in the dispatch table for class B.  First calls
    // the base class's routine, then overrides the Func1
    // entry and adds the new Func3 entry.

    void B::FillDispatchTable( DispatchTableB & table )
    {
        A::FillDispatchTable( table );
        table.func1 = (Func1Dispatch) virtFunc1;
        table.func3 = virtFunc3;
    }

    // The overridden version of Func1.

    int B::virtFunc1( B *self )
    {
        return 5 * self->value;
    }

    // The new Func3 dispatcher.

    bool B::Func3( int val1, int val2 )
    {
        DispatchTableB & d = *((DispatchTableB *) &dispatchTable);

        return( d.func3 != NULL ? (*d.func3)( this, val1, val2 ) : 0 );
    }

    // The code for Func3.

    bool B::virtFunc3( B *self, int val1, int val2 )
    {
        return val1 > val2;
    }

    // Transform class CV into class C in much the same way.

    class C : public B {
        protected:
            // Class CV does not add any new virtual functions,
            // so we don't need to add anything to the dispatch
            // table.  We could just use DispatchTableB, but this
            // is cleaner and makes it simpler to add virtual
            // functions later.
            struct DispatchTableC : public DispatchTableB {
            };
```

Figure 3.17   *(Continued)*

```
    public:
        C( DispatchTableC & dispatchTable );

        ~C();

        static void FillDispatchTable( DispatchTableC & table );

    protected:
        // Class overrides Func2 and Func3.
        static int  virtFunc2( C *self, int val );
        static bool virtFunc3( C *self, int val1, int val2 );
};

C::C( DispatchTableC & table )
: B( table )
{
    value = 3;
}

C::~C()
{
}

void C::FillDispatchTable( DispatchTableC & table )
{
    B::FillDispatchTable( table );
    table.func2 = (Func2Dispatch) virtFunc2;
    table.func3 = (Func3Dispatch) virtFunc3;
}

int C::virtFunc2( C *self, int val )
{
    return 2 * val + 1;
}

bool C::virtFunc3( C *self, int val1, int val2 )
{
    return !B::virtFunc3( self, val1, val2 );
}
```

Figure 3.17 *(Continued)*

patchTableB, but no virtual functions are defined in class C, so DispatchTableC does not include any additional members. New virtual functions are split into two functions as before, but overridden functions are just converted into static functions. Both classes define FillDispatchTable static functions to fill the dispatch table. Each FillDispatchTable first calls the base class's FillDispatchTable and then sets the values for each new or overridden virtual function, leaving the other entries untouched. Finally, the constructors for each class are modified to take a reference to a dispatch table and pass that reference along to the base class's constructor.

Virtual destructors can also be simulated with this code: Just move all the code from the destructors into separate routines that you call separately before deleting an object.

Using one of the classes A, B, or C is simple. First, you declare a variable to hold the dispatch table. You then initialize the dispatch table by calling FillDispatchTable for the appropriate class (for example, if you're using class B, you would declare a variable of type DispatchTableB and pass it as a parameter to B::FillDispatchTable). Then every time you create an instance of a class, you pass the initialized dispatch table as a parameter to its constructor. Then start using the object. A simple example is shown in Figure 3.18. If you run this code inside an application and step through it with the debugger you'll see that the classes behave exactly as if they had declared virtual functions.

It's certainly more work to define classes this way, but it allows you to obtain the benefits of virtual functions in situations where you normally can't use them. There is a bit more overhead than using compiler-generated virtual functions, but it's not substantial. This technique is used in Chapter 4 with the Phone Book sample.

3. **Simulate virtual functions with a cover class.** Alternatively, you can write a cover class that stores a pointer to an object of a known type. In effect, the cover class is a *proxy* for the "real" or *target* object. Function calls on the cover class are redirected to the appropriate function on the target object, as shown in Figure 3.19.

Writing a cover class is not difficult, but you have to manage the ownership of the target object quite carefully. The example in Figure 3.19 assumes that somebody else creates the target object and that the target object remains valid while the cover object is valid. A more typi-

```
// Declare space for the dispatch tables.
// You could store them in dynamic memory
// if necessary.

A::DispatchTableA tableA;
B::DispatchTableB tableB;
C::DispatchTableC tableC;

// Fill the dispatch tables. You have to
// do this for each class you're going to
// instantiate.

A::FillDispatchTable( tableA );
B::FillDispatchTable( tableB );
C::FillDispatchTable( tableC );

// Instantiate the classes, passing in
// the dispatch tables. Make sure the tables
// match the class, that is, class B uses
// DispatchTableB only.

A a( tableA );
B b( tableB );
C c( tableC );

// Refer to the classes through their
// base classes, to prove that the virtual
// functions are working.

A & afromb( b );
A & afromc( c );
B & bfromc( c );

int x;

x = a.Func1();           // returns 1
x = a.Func2( 2 );        // returns 4

x = afromb.Func1();      // returns 10
x = afromb.Func2( 2 );   // returns 4

x = afromc.Func1();      // returns 15
x = afromc.Func2( 2 );   // returns 5

x = b.Func1();           // returns 10
x = b.Func2( 2 );        // returns 4
x = b.Func3( 3, 4 );     // returns 0 (false)
```

Figure 3.18 Testing out the simulated virtual functions.

```
x = bfromc.Func1();        // returns 15
x = bfromc.Func2( 2 );     // returns 5
x = bfromc.Func3( 3, 4 );  // returns 1 (true)

x = c.Func1();             // returns 15
x = c.Func2( 2 );          // returns 5
x = c.Func3( 3, 4 );       // returns 1 (true)
```

Figure 3.18   (Continued)

cal scenario is to have the cover class create and destroy the target object, as shown in Figure 3.20.

No matter who manages the target object, be sure to define copy constructors and assignment operators in your cover classes to ensure that target objects are correctly copied when a cover object is itself copied.

4. **Relaunch the application.** The undocumented technique of relaunching the application using the SysAppLaunch function can be used in

```
class X {
    public:
        X() {}
        X( const X & ) {}
        int Func() { return 1; }
};

class Y {
    public:
        Y() {}
        Y( const Y & ) {}
        int Func() { return 2; }
};

class Z {
    public:
        Z() {}
        Z( const Z & ) {}
        int Func() { return 3; }
};

// Define a cover class for X, Y, and Z. The target
```

Figure 3.19   Using cover classes.

```cpp
// object is passed in as an argument to the constructor
// and must exist as long as the cover object exists.

class Cover {
    private:
        enum classType {
            TypeX, TypeY, TypeZ
        };
        classType  type;
        void      *obj;
    public:
        Cover( X & x ) : type( TypeX ), obj( &x ) {}
        Cover( Y & y ) : type( TypeY ), obj( &y ) {}
        Cover( Z & z ) : type( TypeZ ), obj( &z ) {}

        // Copy constructor just copies the pointer over

        Cover( const Cover & cov ) : type( cov.type ), obj( cov.obj ) {}

        // Assignment operator just copies the pointer over

        Cover& operator=( const Cover & cov ) {
            if( &cov != this ){
                type = cov.type;
                obj = cov.obj;
            }
            return *this;
        }

        int Func() {
            switch( type ){
                case TypeX:
                    return ((X *) obj)->Func();
                case TypeY:
                    return ((Y *) obj)->Func();
                case TypeZ:
                    return ((Z *) obj)->Func();
                default:
                    return 0; // shouldn't happen
            }
        }
};
```

Figure 3.19 *(Continued)*

```cpp
// Define a cover class for X, Y, and Z. The
// cover completely manages the creation of the
// objects.

class Cover {
    public:
        enum classType {
            TypeX, TypeY, TypeZ
        };
    private:
        classType  type;
        void       *obj;
    public:
        // Constructor creates a new object.

        Cover( classType type ) : type( type ) {
            switch( type ){
                case TypeX:
                    obj = new X();
                    break;
                case TypeY:
                    obj = new Y();
                    break;
                case TypeZ:
                    obj = new Z();
                    break;
                default:
                    // error, throw exception or assert
                    break;
            }
        }

        // Copy constructor invokes the target object's
        // copy constructor to create a new target object.
        // An alternative scheme would use reference counting
        // to keep track of how many cover objects hold a
        // reference to a particular target object.

        Cover( const Cover & cov ) : type( cov.type ) {
            switch( type ){
                case TypeX:
                    obj = new X( *((X *) cov.obj) );
                    break;
                case TypeY:
                    obj = new Y( *((Y *) cov.obj) );
                    break;
```

Figure 3.20 A cover class that manages the target object.

```
            case TypeZ:
                obj = new Z( *((Z *) cov.obj) );
                break;
            default:
                // error, throw exception or assert
                break;
        }
    }

    // Ditto for the assignment operator.

    Cover& operator=( const Cover & cov ) {
        if( &cov != this ){
            DeleteTarget();
            type = cov.type;
            switch( type ){
                case TypeX:
                    obj = new X( *((X *) cov.obj) );
                    break;
                case TypeY:
                    obj = new Y( *((Y *) cov.obj) );
                    break;
                case TypeZ:
                    obj = new Z( *((Z *) cov.obj) );
                    break;
            }
        }
        return *this;
    }

    // Destructor destroys target object as well.

    ~Cover() {
        DeleteTarget();
    }

    int Func() {
        switch( type ){
            case TypeX:
                return ((X *) obj)->Func();
            case TypeY:
                return ((Y *) obj)->Func();
            case TypeZ:
                return ((Z *) obj)->Func();
            default:
                return 0; // shouldn't happen
```

Figure 3.20 *(Continued)*

```
                    }
                }
        private:
                // To delete the target you have to cast
                // the generic pointer to a specific type so
                // that the compiler knows which destructor to call.

                void DeleteTarget() {
                    switch( type ){
                        case TypeX:
                            delete ((X *) obj);
                            break;
                        case TypeY:
                            delete ((Y *) obj);
                            break;
                        case TypeZ:
                            delete ((Z *) obj);
                            break;
                    }
                }
        };
```

Figure 3.20   *(Continued)*

some situations to "recover" the application's global data. This technique is not sanctioned by Palm Computing and should be used sparingly. The idea is quite simple: When an application first starts, it checks to see if its global data is available. If not, it uses SysAppLaunch to call itself recursively with globals enabled, returning immediately once the recursive call returns. The recursively called application can then use virtual functions because globals are enabled. The technique is described in more detail in Chapter 4.

You should carefully consider your other options before using this technique, because it's unsupported and decreases the amount of available dynamic memory. It may be the only way, however, to add support for some common Palm operations such as global Find to applications that use code developed for other systems. The UltraLite-based Phone Book sample discussed in Chapter 8 uses this technique precisely for that reason.

Of course, if your application doesn't use virtual functions, then none of these strategies are necessary.

Multisegment Applications

Palm applications are normally limited to a single 64K code segment. What's worse, no jumps of greater than 32K (backward or forward) are allowed in the generated code. If the code segment is greater than 32K in size, it's conceivable that a function near the start of the code segment could call a function near the end of the code segment and cause an error when your application was linked. While you can certainly write useful Palm applications in 32K or less, at some point you'll want to write a larger application.

With CodeWarrior it's fairly simple to avoid the 32K jump limit by using the segments view of the project window to control the object code linking order. You control the relative order of the files by dragging them into new positions in the view. Group the files that call each other close together to avoid the 32K jump limit. You can also use *pragmas* (compiler directives, see the CodeWarrior documentation) in your source files to indicate which functions are to be grouped together into segments. A third alternative is to use the "smart code" model (see the CodeWarrior documentation), which tells CodeWarrior to simulate jumps longer than 32K by using a series of jumps. This bloats the code, however, so use it only when necessary.

If your application requires more than a single 64K code segment, start your project using the "Palm OS Multi-Segment" project stationery and follow the directions in the Multi-Segment Read Me.txt file.

If you use the GNU tools, the situation is more complicated; refer to the CD-ROM for instructions.

Floating-Point Support

Palm OS 1.0 did not support floating-point computations. If applications required floating-point capabilities they had to link in a library of routines for performing basic floating-point arithmetic. With Palm OS 2.0 and higher those routines are now part of the operating system and are called automatically in the generated code when the CodeWarrior compiler is used. If your application requires floating-point numbers, be sure to check that you're running on a Palm OS 2.0 machine or higher—see the next chapter for the code to do this. If you want to support Palm OS 1.0 users, you can still link in the floating-point support manually; your application will just be a bit larger.

GCC supports floating-point with its own emulation software. There are ways to call the system routines instead; refer to the CD-ROM for details.

The Palm Operating System Emulator

Apart from your compiler, the Palm OS Emulator (usually referred to as POSE) is arguably the most useful tool in your programming arsenal. It lets you test and debug your applications on your desktop computer without having to install them on a Palm device, which is very useful when you only have one device on which you'd rather not install alpha-quality software. It's also faster than continually downloading applications to the device.

A version of POSE ships with CodeWarrior and is also included separately on the CD-ROM that accompanies this book, but check the Palm Computing Web site for the most recent version. At the time this book was written, version 2.0b3 is the latest official release, and version 2.1d26 is the latest stable release. Both versions are on the CD-ROM. You should use version 2.1d26 if possible, as it supports more features and has a number of fixes for bugs in 2.0b3.

History

Before the Emulator arrived, the only way to test a Palm application on a desktop computer was to link the source with the Simulator, a set of Macintosh-based libraries that simulated a Palm OS programming environment. The Simulator was far from perfect and only ran on the Macintosh.

Greg Hewgill wrote a Palm emulator called Copilot. Copilot was based on an existing emulator, the Unix Amiga Emulator (UAE), which allowed you to run Amiga software in a Unix environment. Both the Amiga and the Palm use the Motorola 68000 series chip as their central processing units, so the core of UAE could be used with some modifications to emulate a Palm device.

Copilot was so successful and useful that Palm Computing contacted the principal developers involved in its creation and took over development of the emulator for the Windows and Macintosh platforms. The renamed emulator is downloadable from the Palm Computing Web site. The original Copilot still exists and has been ported to other platforms such as Linux and OS/2.

Using the Emulator

POSE emulates a complete Palm Computing platform device. To do this it requires the Palm OS ROM image. The ROM image does not ship with POSE, nor is it found on the CD-ROM that accompanies this book. Instead, you must use a ROM transfer application to transfer the image from a Palm device onto your desktop computer. You can in fact download multiple images from different devices, so that you can use POSE to test your applications against different versions of the operating system. If you're serious about using POSE, you should also obtain the debug versions of the ROM images from Palm Computing. The debug versions perform extra sanity checking and inform you of potential problems that might cause you grief with future versions of the operating system. Information on how to obtain these images can be found on the Palm Computing Web site at www.palm.com/devzone/pose/pose.html.

Once you've transferred the ROM image, POSE looks and behaves like a real Palm device, as shown in Figure 3.21. You use the mouse to simulate pen strokes. This is more cumbersome than using a pen, so the desktop computer's keyboard can be used to enter characters directly instead of using Graffiti.

POSE has its own set of menus (under Windows, POSE does not have a menubar, so the menus are invoked with a right click on the POSE window) that allow you to reset the operating system, configure POSE (to locate the ROM image file and control how much RAM is installed on the "device"), load applications into the Emulator, perform Hot-Syncs (you'll need a null modem cable; see the POSE instructions), download ROM images, and run some random user interface tests. The user interface tests are referred to as Gremlins and are a good way to ensure your applications don't crash upon encountering unexpected user input.

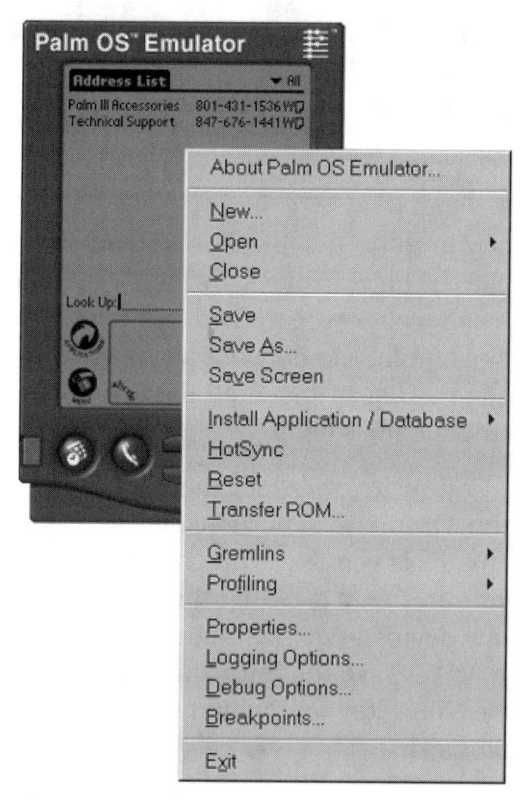

Figure 3.21 The Palm OS Emulator in action.

To load an application, make sure that the Launcher application (the one that lists all installed applications) isn't active by launching one of the standard applications such as the Memo Pad. This avoids a bug where the Launcher doesn't refresh itself properly when an application is installed or updated. Then select the "Load app" menu item to load the desired application. Return to the Launcher and tap on the application's icon to start it, just like you would on a real device.

If at some point your application crashes, POSE will offer you the opportunity to debug it or reset the device. With version 2.0b3, if the application crashes immediately when POSE is reset, you'll need to terminate POSE as you would any other misbehaving application (for example, by using the Task Manager under Windows NT). Before restarting POSE, delete any .RAM files from the POSE installation directory. This performs the equivalent of a hard reset. Version 2.1d26 users do not have to deal with this problem.

The Console

The Palm OS console allows you to do low-level debugging of a device, including the Palm OS Emulator. The console is a window on your desktop computer that you can use to interrogate the device and perform some basic operations. For example, the console allows you to download or update databases, see the list of installed databases (including applications), and examine the memory heaps.

To access the console with CodeWarrior, select the "Open Debug Console" menu item in the Palm OS menu. The console display window appears. If the Palm OS Emulator is running, you can immediately start typing some commands right into the text field; otherwise CodeWarrior will wait for you to place your device in debug mode. To get a list of the applications installed on the device, use the following command, ending the command by pressing the Enter key on the numeric keypad, not the Enter key on the regular keyboard:

```
Dir -t appl
```

To display the alarm table, type the following command:

```
SysAlarmDump
```

The Help command with no arguments lists all the commands that are available. To get help on a specific command, pass it as an argument to the Help command:

```
Help Dir
```

For more detailed information on the console commands that are available, consult the *Palm OS 3.0 Cookbook*.

The Conduit Development Kit

If you feel inclined to write your own conduits, you can download the Palm Conduit Development Kit (CDK) for free from the Palm Computing Web site at www.palm.com/devzone/conduits.html. The CDK comes in two flavors for Windows (C/C++ or Java) and a single version for the

Macintosh (C only). The Windows version requires Microsoft Visual C++ 5.0 (for the C/C++ version) or a Java 1.1–based development tool (for the Java version).

The CDK includes a tool, CondCfg, for installing and uninstalling conduits. We discuss the tool briefly in Chapter 8 when we discuss installing a conduit for UltraLite data synchronization.

CHAPTER 4

Writing Palm Applications

Now that you understand how a Palm device works and how to use the development tools, you're ready to start programming. In this chapter we discuss how to write Palm applications: what they are, how they're launched, how events are processed, how to create user interface resources, and how to build a user interface with those resources. This chapter is *not* a comprehensive guide to Palm programming, however, and you should consult the official Palm Computing documentation (included with the Palm OS SDK) or other books for more details. Rather, this chapter introduces you to Palm application development to enable you to write a basic application and to follow the examples in later chapters.

Applications

Before you can start building your own applications, it's important that you understand what an application is and how it gets started by the operating system.

What's an Application?

As mentioned in Chapter 2, an application is in fact a resource database. The resources in the database contain the compiled code, the initial values of global variables, and any user interface your application requires. Your development tool creates these resources for you. To launch the application, the system opens the database, jumps to a fixed address, and runs the compiled code.

Type and Creator ID

To identify a resource database as an application, Palm OS uses the database type "appl." Don't use this type for any database you create; it's reserved exclusively for applications.

Every application requires a unique creator ID. The creator ID identifies the application to the device. It also links all databases used by an application together as part of the HotSync process. To prevent conflicts, creator IDs are registered with Palm Computing. Registration can be done in a matter of minutes through the Palm Computing Web site at www.palm.com/devzone/crid/cridsub.html. Palm Computing reserves creator IDs that consist entirely of lowercase letters for its own use, so choose an ID that contains at least one uppercase letter or one nonalphabetic character. The creator ID is often the initials or an abbreviation of the developer's or company's name. In your planning for a new application, be sure to register a creator ID early on.

On the CD-ROM you'll find the source and executable for the Creator ID Viewer sample, which lists the creator IDs of all applications installed on your Palm device.

Why Register a Creator ID?

No two applications can have the same creator ID, because the two will conflict and overwrite each other when installed. That's why it's important to register your creator IDs with Palm Computing, since it guarantees uniqueness.

For testing purposes you can get away with reusing a creator ID or else using an unregistered ID. Use the sample Creator ID Viewer application to list all the creator IDs on the device and make sure your test programs don't conflict with an application you've already installed. But as soon as you start developing a "real" application that you plan to give or sell to others, you should register a creator ID for it.

All creator IDs used in this book have been registered.

The Flow of Control

Switching between applications is so fast that you might think that multiple applications are running simultaneously. In general, however, only one application runs at a time. When the user *launches* (starts) an application, Palm OS calls the application's entry point, its PilotMain function. The application runs until asked to quit, returning control back to the operating system when it exits the PilotMain function.

While the application is running, it calls Palm OS API (application programming interface) functions to do various things, such as drawing to the screen or processing user input. Sometimes other applications are launched on a temporary basis. But only a single application controls the user interface at any time. This application is referred to as the *active application*. In the next section, we discuss the various ways an application can be launched and how to determine if it's the active application.

The PilotMain Function

The PilotMain function is the entry point into your application. It serves the same purpose as the main function (or WinMain for Windows programmers) that you're already familiar with, but Palm applications receive a different set of arguments than a traditional C/C++ program. The prototype for PilotMain is as follows:

```
DWord PilotMain( Word cmd, Ptr cmdPBP, Word launchFlags )
```

The meanings of the parameters are as follows:

cmd is the *launch code* or *action code* that identifies how the application was started and what it is being asked to do

cmdPBP is a pointer to a parameter block whose contents depend on the launch code

launchFlags is a set of bit flags that provide additional information on the context of the application

We discuss these parameters and the whole launch process in the next section. The return value from PilotMain is the error status: A zero value means the application ran without error. Errors are returned as nonzero values, usually one of the system error codes.

> **Error Handling**
>
> The header file <System/SystemMgr.h> defines an *error class* for each Palm OS Manager. An error class is not a class in the C++ sense, it's simply a range of error codes that are reserved for a particular manager. Error classes start at 0x0100 and go up in increments of 0x0100, so the upper two bytes uniquely identify the error class. For example, the Memory Manager has the error class 0x0100 and the Data Manager has the error class 0x0200. Any errors reported by the Memory Manager fall in the range 0x0100 to 0x01FF, while Data Manager errors are in the range 0x0200 to 0x02FF. While the ranges are defined in <System/SystemMgr.h>, the actual error codes are defined in the header file for a particular manager.
>
> The set of error classes starting at 0x8000, defined by the appErrorClass macro, is reserved for application use.

How Applications Are Launched

A user often launches an application by selecting it from the Applications application, or by pressing one of the device's buttons (real or painted). As mentioned previously in the discussion of flow of control, however, applications can be launched in other circumstances. For example, when the Find button is pressed, each application in the system is invoked in turn and asked to search its data for the desired string. Or when data is being beamed to the device—for those devices that support infrared beaming—the application that handles the data is launched by the system.

The launch code parameter of the PilotMain function tells you how your application is being invoked, and many of the launch codes, in conjunction with the launch flags, place restrictions on what your application can do. Your PilotMain function can in fact be invoked by the system while you're already running, for example, so understanding the launching process is critical to writing well-behaved applications.

The Normal Launch

In a normal launch, the active application is first asked to quit and return control to Palm OS. The operating system then invokes the new application's PilotMain with the sysAppLaunchCmdNormalLaunch launch code. The skeleton PilotMain function looks like this:

```
DWord PilotMain( Word cmd, Ptr cmdPBP, Word launchFlags )
{
    Err errorCode = 0;

    if( cmd == sysAppLaunchCmdNormalLaunch ){
        // normal running of application
    }

    return errorCode;
}
```

In a normal launch you can ignore the parameter block pointer and the launch flags (although launch flags are set, as we'll see when we discuss initializing launches). Global and static variables are available and initialized. Your application runs until it decides to exit, usually in response to an externally generated event. Events and event processing are discussed later in this chapter. The launch process is shown in Figure 4.1.

The Subcall Launch

Sometimes your application's PilotMain function is called recursively. That is, your application is already up and running (usually through a normal launch), you call a Palm OS API function and the OS invokes (perhaps unexpectedly) your application's PilotMain function again. This is referred to as a *subcall launch*. In a subcall launch, the sysAppLaunchFlagSubCall bit of the launch flags parameter is set:

```
int inSubCall = ( ( launchFlags & sysAppLaunchFlagSubCall ) != 0 );
```

This bit is often set when PilotMain is called with the sysAppLaunchCmdGoTo launch code, which is sent after a Find operation. The

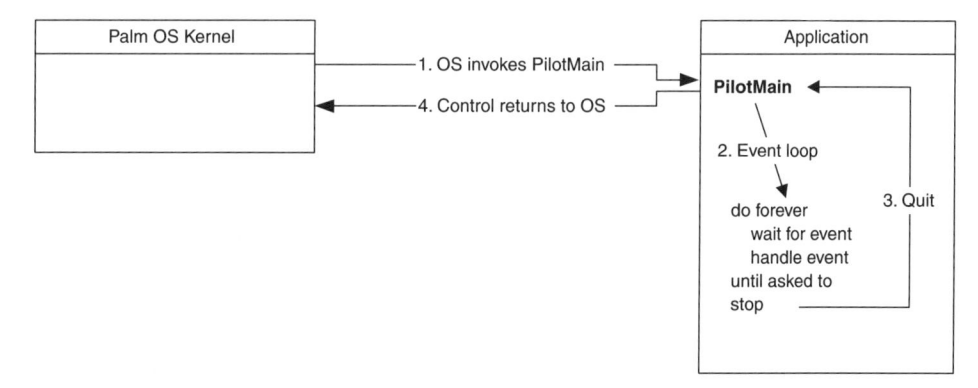

Figure 4.1 A normal launch.

sysAppLaunchCmdGoTo launch code instructs an application to display a particular piece of data, usually a record in a database that the application manages. If the user presses the Find button and selects data from the active application, then rather than ask the application to shut down and then restart, the system makes a subcall launch with the sysAppLaunchCmdGoTo launch code. In other words, the PilotMain function is called recursively:

```
extern Err ProcessGoToData( GoToParamsPtr goToData );

DWord PilotMain( Word cmd, Ptr cmdPBP, Word launchFlags )
{
    Err errorCode = 0;
    int inSubCall = ( ( launchFlags & sysAppLaunchFlagSubCall ) != 0 );

    if( cmd == sysAppLaunchCmdNormalLaunch ){
        // normal running of application
    } else if( cmd == sysAppLaunchCmdGoTo ){
        if( inSubCall ){
            #ifdef __GCC__
                CALLBACK_PROLOGUE
            #endif
            errorCode = ProcessGoToData( (GoToParamsPtr) cmdPBP );
            #ifdef __GCC__
                CALLBACK_EPILOGUE
            #endif
        } else {
            // not a subcall, handle differently...
        }
    }

    return errorCode;
}
```

When the launch code is sysAppLaunchCmdGoTo, the cmdPBP parameter can be cast to a GoToParamsPtr, which points to a structure describing the information the user wants displayed. In the preceding example, we call another function to process the data, the details of which we'll leave for later. The important thing is to note that after the data is processed, the PilotMain function is exited: Because a subcall launch calls PilotMain recursively, we can safely return right away and let the application continue running in the original PilotMain call. Figure 4.2 demonstrates the subcall launch process.

GCC users take note: When called recursively via a subcall launch, the PilotMain function needs to use the CALLBACK_PROLOGUE and CALLBACK_EPILOGUE macros discussed in Chapter 3 before accessing any

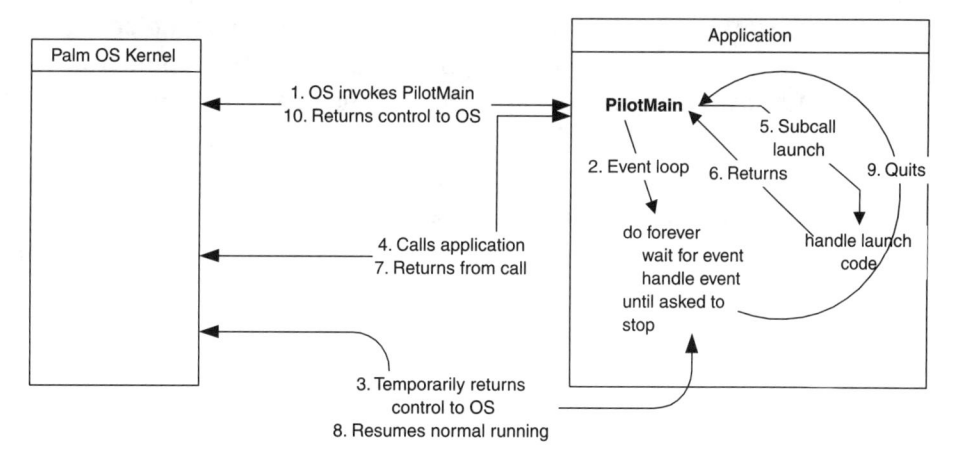

Figure 4.2 A subcall launch.

global or static data. The preceding example shows the proper use of the macros in a subcall launch.

In a subcall launch it's safe to access global and static data. After all, the application is already running and has effectively called itself as a subroutine. But what if the application wasn't already running?

The Initializing Launch

Another bit in the launch flags parameter indicates that a new block of global and static data has been allocated for the application:

```
int newGlobals = ( ( launchFlags & sysAppLaunchFlagNewGlobals ) != 0 );
```

When this flag is set it means the application was not active and is being launched as a new instance, and is referred to as an *initializing launch*. You should perform the same kind of processing you do for a normal launch. It's safe to access global and static data. In fact, a normal launch is also an initializing launch, because the sysAppLaunchFlagNewGlobals bit is always set during a normal launch. A normal launch is really just a special case of an initializing launch.

In addition to being an example of a subcall launch, the sysAppLaunch-CmdGoTo launch code is also an example of an initializing launch, as confusing as that might sound. The difference is which of the sysApp-LaunchFlagSubCall or sysAppLaunchFlagNewGlobals flags are set. If sysAppLaunchFlagSubCall is set, it's a subcall launch, meaning that during a Find operation the user chose data managed by the active applica-

PALM DATABASE PROGRAMMING

tion. If sysAppLaunchFlagSubCall is not set, the user selected data managed by another, nonactive application. The active application is asked to shut down and the new application, the one that manages the selected data, is launched with the sysAppLaunchCmdGoTo launch code instead of sysAppLaunchCmdNormalLaunch, and with the sysAppLaunchFlagNewGlobals flag set. As before, the cmdPBP parameter can be cast to a GoToParamsPtr to know what information to display when the application starts:

```
DWord PilotMain( Word cmd, Ptr cmdPBP, Word launchFlags )
{
    Err errorCode = 0;
    int inSubCall = (( launchFlags & sysAppLaunchFlagSubCall ) != 0);
    int newGlobals = (( launchFlags & sysAppLaunchFlagNewGlobals ) != 0);

    if( cmd == sysAppLaunchCmdNormalLaunch ){
        errorCode = RunApplication( NULL );
    } else if( cmd == sysAppLaunchCmdGoTo ){
        if( inSubCall ){
            errorCode = ProcessGoToData( (GoToParamsPtr) cmdPBP );
        } else if( newGlobals ){
            errorCode = RunApplication( (GoToParamsPtr) cmdPBP );
        } else {
            // this should never happen in the GoTo case!
        }
    }

    return errorCode;
}
```

Notice how we've defined a new function, RunApplication, that is called when an initializing launch is done using either the sysAppLaunchCmdNormalLaunch or sysAppLaunchCmdGoTo launch codes. It in turn calls StartApplication and StopApplication:

```
static Err StartApplication( GoToParamsPtr goToData )
{
    if( goToData != NULL ){
        // initialize based on goto data
    } else {
        // initialize based on normal launch
    }

    return 0;
}

static Err StopApplication()
{
```

```
    // Clean everything here
    return 0;
}

static Err RunApplication( GoToParamsPtr goToData )
{
    Err errorCode = StartApplication( goToData );

    if( errorCode == 0 ){ // everything is OK
        EventLoop();
        errorCode = StopApplication();
    }

    return errorCode;
}
```

When the sysAppLaunchFlagNewGlobals flag is set, the only difference between the two launch codes is that sysAppLaunchCmdNormalLaunch displays an initial user interface (usually returning to what the user was doing the last time the application was run) while sysAppLaunchCmd-GoTo displays a UI (user interface) based on the data in GoToParamsPtr. In both cases the application runs until asked to quit, and it's safe to access global and static data.

But what if an application is launched and neither the sysAppLaunchFlagSubCall nor the sysAppLaunchFlagNewGlobals bits are set?

The Notification Launch

There are over two dozen launch codes defined in the Palm OS header file <System/SystemMgr.h>. Most of them aren't used to "launch" applications in the traditional sense, but rather to notify an application about a system change (when the user changes the time, for example) or an event that needs immediate processing (such as when an alarm expires). Palm OS calls the application's PilotMain function directly without doing any initialization of the application. These are referred to as *notification launches*—the sysAppLaunchFlagNewGlobals flag is *not* set, and the application is expected to process the launch code as quickly as possible and then exit. In most cases it's not possible to interact with the user—no user interface calls are allowed. Figure 4.3 demonstrates the notification launch process. The next section summarizes the important launch codes.

When neither sysAppLaunchFlagNewGlobals nor sysAppLaunchFlagSubCall is set, don't use any global or static data, no matter what the

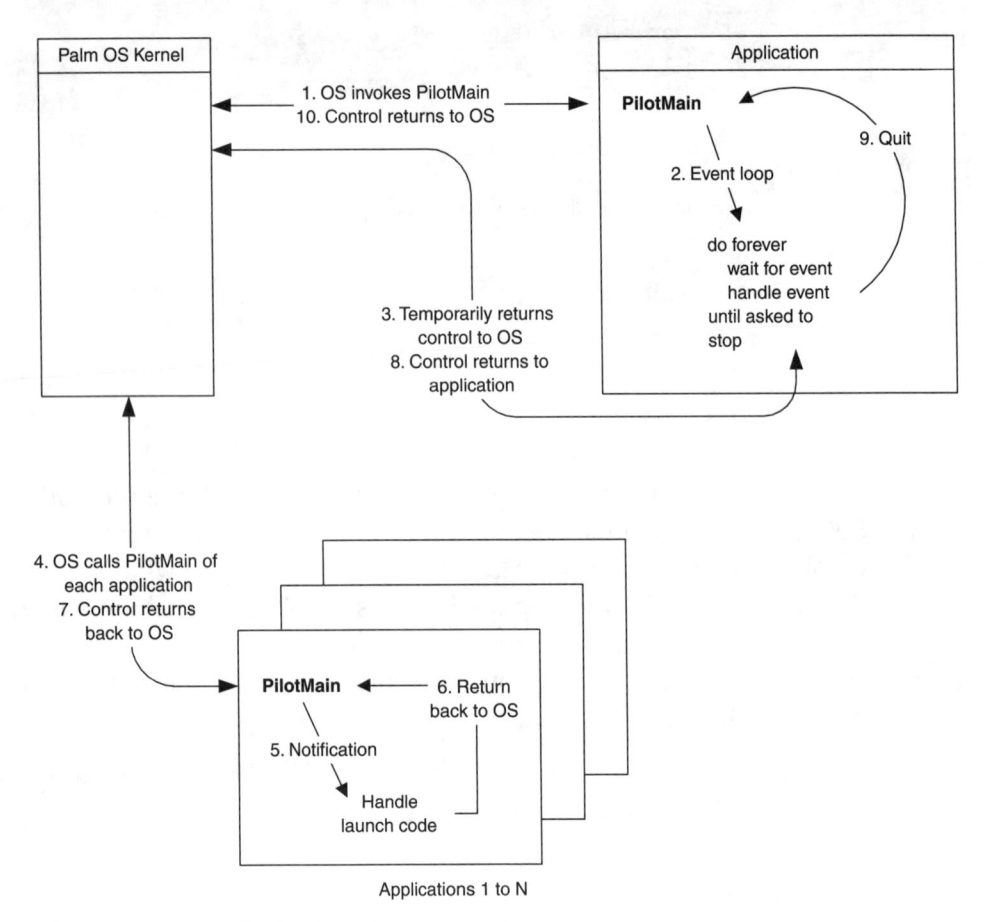

Figure 4.3 A notification launch.

launch code. If you're working in C++, this restriction also precludes invoking virtual functions or taking the address of a member function, because those operations both use global data. An explanation of why access to global data is restricted is found in the "How Applications Use Memory" section which follows. Without any global or static data, the application must load any data it requires from databases or from a storage area Palm OS provides for application preferences.

Restrictions on global data mean it's always important to test the sysAppLaunchFlagNewGlobals and sysAppLaunchFlagSubCall flags in the PilotMain of your application. Even if your application is already running, Palm OS might notify it from a background thread, leading to conflicts and even data corruption if both threads write to global data. If neither flag is set, don't access any global or static data.

Recovering Global Data

There is an undocumented technique that can be used in some circumstances to recover your application's global and static data within a notification launch. The technique involves relaunching the application using the SysAppLaunch function, as mentioned in Chapter 3. The idea is simple: When an application starts, it checks to see if global data is available, and if it isn't, the application calls itself recursively with globals enabled. The first copy of the application exits as soon as the second copy quits. The code to do this is defined in the RelaunchWithGlobals function as follows:

```
// Relaunches an application with globals enabled.
//    creatorID - the creatorID of the application
//    cmd       - the launch code
//    cmdPBP    - the launch parameter block
//    ret       - holds the return value after the launch
// Returns: nonzero if the launch failed

   Err RelaunchWithGlobals( ULong creatorID, Word cmd,
                            Ptr cmdPBP, DWord *ret )
   {
       UInt              card;
       LocalID           id;
       Err               err = sysErrNotAllowed;
       DmSearchStateType stateInfo;

       if( DmGetNextDatabaseByTypeCreator( true, &stateInfo,
                                           'appl', creatorID,
                                           true, &card, &id ) == 0 ){
           err = SysAppLaunch( card, id,
                               sysAppLaunchFlagNewGlobals, cmd,
                               cmdPBP, ret );
       }

       return err;
   }
```

RelaunchWithGlobals uses a function discussed in Chapter 5 to locate an application in storage memory. It then calls SysAppLaunch to start the application with the original launch code and parameter blocks. A sample PilotMain that uses RelaunchWithGlobals is as follows:

```
DWord PilotMain( Word cmd, Ptr cmdPBP, Word launchFlags )
{
    Err errorCode = 0;
    int inSubCall = ( ( launchFlags & sysAppLaunchFlagSubCall ) != 0 );
    int newGlobals = (( launchFlags & sysAppLaunchFlagNewGlobals ) != 0);
```

```
    if( cmd == sysAppLaunchCmdFind ){
        if( inSubCall || newGlobals ){
            errorCode = ProcessFindData( (FindParamsPtr) cmdPBP );
        } else {
            DWord ret;

            errorCode = RelaunchWithGlobals( 'ERIC', cmd, cmdPBP, &ret );
            if( errorCode == 0 ){
                // use error code returned by relaunched app
                errorCode = (Err) ret;
            } else {
                // relaunch failed, errorCode gives reason
            }
        }
    } else if( cmd == ...... ){ // handle other codes
        ......
    }

    return errorCode;
}
```

Because it's unsupported, you should only attempt this technique as a last resort. A better approach is to structure your application to avoid using global data. For example, define a structure to hold all your global variables and dynamically allocate the structure from inside the Pilot Main function. Pass a pointer to the structure as a parameter to any routine that requires access to global variables. This technique can be used even when global data is available.

Sometimes, though, there's no other choice than to relaunch the application. For example, the UltraLite-based applications discussed in Chapter 8 use global data in their custom databases and in the runtime support routines. Without relaunching the application there's no way to use an UltraLite database in any notification launch, including the Find operation.

Launch Code Summary

Palm OS defines over two dozen launch codes. Applications don't have to respond to every launch code, but they should immediately return 0 (no error) if a launch code is not handled. Failure to do so will cause the device to freeze or crash.

All system launch codes are defined in the <System/SystemMgr.h> header file. Comments in the header file describe what triggers each launch, what the application is expected to do, what the parameter block holds, and what launch flags may or may not be set. Here's a summary of the most important launch codes.

sysAppLaunchCmdNormalLaunch

This code is sent when the user requests the launch of an application. The application initializes itself and processes events until told to quit. The initial screen it displays is usually (but not always) the same screen that was displayed when the application was last run. The parameter block is not used. Global and static data is always available, and the application is the active application.

sysAppLaunchCmdFind

This code is sent when the user requests a Find operation. The parameter block points to a FindParamsType structure (defined in <UI/Find.h>) containing the search string and the starting position (usually a record number) for the search. The application loads its databases and searches for the string. Any matches are saved using the FindSaveMatch function and then displayed in the Find results dialog. Matching continues as long as there is space on the dialog to display results or the application finishes searching through its databases, at which point the application exits. Global and static data is only available within a subcall launch.

sysAppLaunchCmdGoTo

The code is sent after the user selects an item in the Find results dialog. The application initializes itself as with a normal launch and displays the selected data. The application then processes events until told to quit. The parameter block points to a GoToParamsType structure (defined in <UI/Find.h>), which holds the information about what the user selected (and was originally saved during a Find operation with the FindSaveMatch function). Global and static data is always available, and the application is the active application.

sysAppLaunchCmdSyncNotify

After a HotSync is complete, any applications whose databases have been changed are notified with this code. The application can make further changes to the databases, set alarms, or perform other necessary housekeeping tasks. The parameter block is not used. Global and static data is not available, and the application exits as soon as it's done processing the databases.

sysAppLaunchCmdTimeChange

When the user changes the device's time settings, each application is sent this notification. The application adjusts itself accordingly (perhaps by resetting alarm times) and exits. The parameter block is not used. Global and static data is not available.

sysAppLaunchCmdSystemReset

After a hard or soft reset, but not a modified soft reset, each application receives this notification. The application initializes or validates its settings and then exits. The parameter block points to a SysAppLaunchCmd-SystemResetType structure (defined in <System/SystemMgr.h>) that identifies the kind of reset that was performed (hard or soft). Global and static data is not available.

sysAppLaunchCmdAlarmTriggered

Applications can register an alarm with the operating system. When the alarm expires, the application is notified with this launch code. The application is *not* allowed to display anything on the screen and must exit as quickly as possible. The parameter block points to a SysAlarmTriggered-ParamType structure (defined in <System/AlarmMgr.h>). Global and static data is only available within a subcall launch.

sysAppLaunchCmdDisplayAlarm

After an alarm has been triggered, the application receives this separate notification. The application is allowed to display an alarm dialog if desired and wait until the user dismisses the dialog, after which the application exits. The parameter block points to a SysDisplayAlarmParam-Type structure (defined in <System/AlarmMgr.h>). Global and static data is only available within a subcall launch.

sysAppLaunchCmdSaveData

This notification is sent to the active application when a Find operation first starts to allow it to update its databases before the Find operation actually begins. The parameter block is not used. Global and static data is available.

sysAppLaunchCmdInitDatabase

This is sent after a HotSync when a new database (with a matching creator ID) is created. The parameter block points to a SysAppLaunchCmd-InitDatabaseType (defined in <System/SystemMgr.h>) that identifies the newly created database. The application performs any required housekeeping on the new database and then exits. Global and static data is not available.

Launch Flag Summary

In addition to sysAppLaunchFlagSubCall and sysAppLaunchFlagNewGlobals, Palm OS also defines the following launch flags in <System/SystemMgr.h>:

sysAppLaunchFlagNewThread. Application is being run on a new thread (implies sysAppLaunchFlagNewStack as well).

sysAppLaunchFlagNewStack. A new stack was created for the application.

sysAppLaunchFlagUIApp. Application is the active user interface application.

In general, only sysAppLaunchFlagSubCall, sysAppLaunchFlagNewGlobals, and perhaps sysAppLaunchFlagUIApp are of interest to an application.

How Applications Use Memory

When an initializing launch is performed, Palm OS allocates a block of memory from the dynamic heap to hold the global and static data the application requires. This is referred to as the *global data block*. One of the DragonBall processor's registers, the A5 register, holds a pointer to this data block. When you compile your application, all references to global and static data are transformed into references relative to the start of the data block. This is why you can't access global or static data if neither the sysAppLaunchFlagSubCall flag nor the sysAppLaunchFlagNewGlobals flags is set—the A5 register points to the active application's data block, not to yours. Reading global or static variables can cause your application to crash if the A5 register isn't set correctly, while writing those variables can cause a crash and/or corrupt the active application's data (remember, the dynamic heap isn't write-protected). These restrictions only apply to data, not to code.

TIP To the compiler there's almost no difference between global and static data, apart from compile-time limits on who can access static data. The compiler has to allocate space for both kinds of data at program start-up, though it may defer initialization of static data inside a function until the first call to that function.

The application's stack is also allocated from the dynamic heap. The stack size is fixed and is used to hold function parameters, local variables and function return addresses. As in any system where the stack cannot grow, if you declare large structures or arrays as local variables and/or call yourself recursively too many times, your application will use all its stack and crash. Note that with some launch codes you're not using your own stack but a stack supplied by the system or by another application. It doesn't matter whose stack you're using, always be frugal with it.

While running, an application can allocate memory from the dynamic heap for its own purposes. Because the dynamic heap is small, as discussed in Chapter 2, such allocations should be kept to a minimum and the memory should be deallocated as soon as possible. All memory allocated by an application is automatically freed when it terminates, but it's always good practice to explicitly deallocate the memory before exiting.

The storage heap holds the application's resources and its persistent data, stored in Palm databases. The application cannot allocate memory directly from the storage heap, it must use the database or application preferences APIs instead. The database APIs are discussed in Chapter 5, the application preference APIs are discussed later in this chapter. Temporary databases can be used to allocate large pieces of memory, but remember that even databases the size of any individual record or resource are limited to just under 64K. (Another option with Palm OS 3.0 or higher is to use the file-streaming APIs, which themselves use databases for storage but let you deal with data that is larger than 64K in size.)

Structuring an Application

The simplest of applications handles the sysAppLaunchCmdNormalLaunch launch code and defines functions to initialize the application, process events, and deinitialize the application. These functions are usually called StartApplication (or sometimes AppStart), EventLoop, and StopApplication (or AppStop), respectively. Using functions this way allows you to keep the PilotMain function uncluttered and makes it easier to add support later for different launch codes.

If your application allows the user to search through its data, you'll need to support the sysAppLaunchCmdSaveData, sysAppLaunchCmdFind, and sysAppLaunchCmdGoTo launch codes. Combine the processing for sysAppLaunchCmdNormalLaunch and sysAppLaunchCmdGoTo, as shown in the example for initializing launches.

Remember that with most launch codes global and static data is not available. To communicate between functions in such an environment it's simplest to define a structure to hold the data to share. If it's not large, define it on the stack, otherwise allocate some memory from the dynamic heap. Pass a pointer to the data when calling other functions. Adding a "don't use global data" comment to any function that can be called from outside an initializing launch is also a good idea.

Checking the Palm Operating System Version

If your application uses features that are not available in all versions of Palm OS, the first thing your application should do in its PilotMain function is check the Palm OS version number. If an incompatible version of the operating system is being used, the application should quit immediately by returning the sysErrRomIncompatible error code. For example, any application that uses the ROM-based floating-point emulation should ensure that Palm OS 2.0 or higher is being used.

As mentioned in Chapter 2, the Palm OS version number is obtained using the FtrGet function:

```
DWord romVersion;

FtrGet( sysFtrCreator, sysFtrNumROMVersion, &romVersion );
```

For an application that requires Palm OS 2.0 or higher, the version number must be equal to or greater than 0x02000000:

```
if( romVersion < 0x02000000 ){
    // version isn't recent enough!
    return sysErrRomIncompatible;
}
```

A well-behaved application will alert the user that a newer version of Palm OS is required to use the application. We'll see how to do this when we build the application's user interface later in this chapter. It's very important, however, to only notify the user during an initializing launch and when it's the active application:

```
if( romVersion < 0x02000000 ){
    if( ( launchFlags & sysAppLaunchFlagNewGlobals ) != 0 &&
        ( launchFlags & sysAppLaunchFlagUIApp ) != 0 ){
        // alert the user here!
```

```
        }

        return sysErrRomIncompatible;
}
```

Notice how the launch flags are checked to ensure that global data is available (an initializing launch) and that the application is the active application (and so can display a user interface). If neither of these conditions is satisfied, then the application should terminate quietly by immediately returning sysErrRomIncompatible.

The code to check the ROM version is usually packaged as the RomVersionCompatible function, found in CodeWarrior's project stationery and in the examples in this book. If your application doesn't require a specific version of Palm OS, you can make it a bit smaller by removing this function.

Event Processing

An *event* in Palm OS is a notification that something has occurred or is a request to perform a certain operation. Unlike notification launches, which make direct calls to the PilotMain function, events are queued and are retrieved by the application when it's ready to process them. Most events are queued by the operating system in response to user input, but the application can also add events to its own queue. If you're a Windows programmer, queuing an event is like posting a message to a window.

The Event Loop

After being launched with a normal or initializing launch, an application initializes itself and then enters an *event loop*, where it continuously checks the event queue for new events to process. The application processes events until it receives a stop event:

```
EventType event;

do {
    EvtGetEvent( &event, evtWaitForever );
    // process the event here....
} while( event.eType != appStopEvent ); // until told to stop
```

If you're a Windows programmer, this is very similar to processing the message queue using GetMessage and DispatchMessage.

The first parameter to the EvtGetEvent function (all event functions and structures are defined in the header file <UI/Event.h>) is a pointer to an

EventType structure, described in the following section. The function will copy the event information from the queue directly into this structure. The second parameter is a timeout value in *ticks*, the time to wait for an event to be queued if the queue is empty. A tick is a hundredth of a second. Use the function SysTicksPerSecond, defined in <System/SystemMgr.h>, to map ticks to seconds. If no event is available, the device is placed into doze mode until an event arrives or the timeout expires. If the timeout expires, a nilEvent is returned. Use the evtWaitForever macro if no timeout is required.

Your application must stop processing events whenever it receives an appStopEvent. If you don't, the user won't be able to start another application without first resetting the device.

The EventType Structure

The EventType structure includes members that identify the event, the pen state (up or down), the pen's position on the screen at the time of the event (if the pen is down), and a union of event-specific data:

```
typedef struct {
    enum events  eType;
    Boolean      penDown;
    SWord        screenX;
    SWord        screenY;
    union data {
        struct frmLoad {
            Word formID;
        } frmLoad;
        struct keyDown {
            Word chr;
            Word keyCodes;
            Word modifiers;
        } keyDown;
        ..... // etc. see <UI/Event.h> for the rest
    } data;
} EventType;
```

Event identifiers are members of the events enumeration and have such names as nilEvent and penDownEvent. Some events apply to the application as a whole, others are directed at specific user interface controls. The events defined in the Palm OS 3.0 SDK are summarized in Table 4.1. There are very few events compared to other systems such as Microsoft Windows.

Table 4.1 Palm OS Event Summaries

EVENT	MEANING
appStopEvent	The application is asked to stop.
ctlEnterEvent	A pen down occurred within the bounds of a control.
ctlExitEvent	The pen was lifted outside of a control, after a ctlEnterEvent.
ctlRepeatEvent	A repeating event, triggered by a repeat control while the pen is held down over the control.
ctlSelectEvent	The pen was lifted inside a control, after a ctlEnterEvent. Indicates a selection was made.
daySelectEvent	Private, used by the day selector object.
fldChangedEvent	The text of a field was scrolled as a result of drag selection.
fldEnterEvent	A pen down occurred within the bounds of a field object.
fldHeightChangedEvent	Private, used by the field object to change its height.
frmCloseEvent	A form is asked to close.
frmGotoEvent	A form is opened in response to a sysAppLaunchCmdGoTo launch code.
frmLoadEvent	The application is asked to load a form.
frmOpenEvent	A form is opened.
frmSaveEvent	A form is asked to save its data.
frmTitleEnterEvent	A pen down occurred within the title of a form.
frmTitleSelectEvent	The pen was lifted inside the title of a form, after a frmTitleEnterSelect.
frmUpdateEvent	A form is asked to redraw itself.
keyDownEvent	A Graffiti character was entered or a device button was pressed.
lstEnterEvent	A pen down occurred within the bounds of a list object.
lstExitEvent	The pen was lifted outside of a list object, after a lstEnterEvent.
lstSelectEvent	The pen was lifted inside a list object, after a lstEnterEvent. Indicates a selection was made.
menuEvent	A menu item was selected.
nilEvent	No event is available.
penDownEvent	The pen first touches the screen.
penMoveEvent	The pen moves while touching the screen.
penUpEvent	The pen is lifted from the screen.
popSelectEvent	An item was selected from a popup list object.
sclEnterEvent	A pen down occurred within the bounds of a scroll bar.
sclExitEvent	The pen is lifted from a scroll bar, after a sclEnterEvent.

Table 4.1 *Continued*

EVENT	MEANING
sclRepeatEvent	Tracks the scroll bar position as it changes, while the pen is down.
tblEnterEvent	A pen down occurred within the bounds of a table item.
tblExitEvent	The pen was lifted outside of the table item, after a tblEnterEvent.
tblSelectEvent	The pen was lifted inside a table item, after a tblEnterEvent.
winEnterEvent	A window is activated.
winExitEvent	A window is deactivated.

Event-specific data is defined for most events. If it is defined, the data union contains a structure member whose name is derived from the event name: For example, frmLoadEvent uses the frmLoad member, and penUpEvent uses the penUp member. Here's a simple example:

```
EventType event;

EvtGetEvent( &event, evtWaitForever );

switch( event.eType ){
    case frmLoadEvent: {
        Word id = event.data.frmLoad.formID;
        // do something...
        break;
    }
    case keyDownEvent: {
        if( event.data.keyDown.chr == 'A' ){
            // do something....
        }
        break;
    }
    ......  // etc. etc.
}
```

Most of the event-specific structures include a member identifying the object that is the source or target of the event.

Event Handling

Events occur for each pen stroke or button press and are queued for processing by the application. Most of these events are not of interest to the application, though, because they represent low-level operations. Instead of processing each pen stroke as it occurs, for example, the application lets the system process it to convert a sequence of pen strokes into a

Graffiti character. Similarly, when the user activates a menu, all your application cares about is which menu item the user finally chose, not the sequence of strokes that led to that choice.

Dealing with an event is referred to as *handling the event*. Palm OS provides functions that will handle many low-level events for you, leaving you free to deal only with the higher-level events. These functions are known as *event handlers*, and all take a pointer to an EventType structure as a parameter and return a Boolean value indicating whether the event has been completely handled. You call each event handler in sequence until one of them returns true. Note that event handlers may partially handle an event and still return false—some events are of interest to everyone. Let the event handler decide if an event has been completely processed or not, instead of calling an event handler in response to specific events. An event handler always returns false for any events it ignores.

Why isn't event handling automatically invoked when an event is fetched from the event queue? Some applications *are* interested in low-level events and may not want to pass them on to the built-in event handlers. If this is the case for your application, define your own event handler and call it first after fetching the event:

```
EventType event;

do {
    EvtGetEvent( &event, evtWaitForever );
    if( PreprocessEvent( &event ) ) continue; // optional
    // handle other events...
} while( event.eType != appStopEvent );

....

Boolean PreprocessEvent( EventTypePtr event )
{
    Boolean handled = false;

    ....   // handle events of interest, setting handled true

    return handled;
}
```

The next event handler to call, or the first event handler if you're not interested in low-level events, is the system event handler, SysHandleEvent. It takes an event pointer as its single argument. It translates pen strokes into Graffiti characters and handles button presses and other low-level processing. Call the system event handler before calling any of the other handlers.

After the system event handler comes the menu event handler, MenuHandleEvent. It takes three parameters, a pointer to a menubar, the event pointer, and a pointer for storing an error code. If you pass NULL for the first parameter, the current menubar is used. The error code is usually ignored. The menu event handler handles all low-level events within the menubar and its associated menus.

Any events that are unhandled by the system and menu event handlers are either meant for the application as a whole or for the active *form*, the user interface window that the user is currently dealing with. An example of an application-level event is the frmLoadEvent, which asks the application to load a form and make it the active form. Events such as frmOpenEvent, which notifies a form that it's being opened, or frmCloseEvent, which notifies a form that it's being closed, are form-level events. The application calls its own event handler first and passes any unhandled events to the form via FrmDispatchEvent. This is the completed event loop:

```
EventType event;
Word      error;

// Completed event loop...

do {
    EvtGetEvent( &event, evtWaitForever );
    if( PreprocessEvent( &event ) ) continue; // optional
    if( SysHandleEvent( &event ) ) continue;
    if( MenuHandleEvent( NULL, &event, &error ) ) continue;
    if( ApplicationHandleEvent( &event ) ) continue;
    FrmDispatchEvent( &event );
} while( event.eType != appStopEvent );

....

Boolean ApplicationHandleEvent( EventPtr event )
{
    Boolean handled = false;

    // handle "application-level" events here, returning
    // true as appropriate

    return handled;
}
```

When a form is created, the application registers its own event handler for the form. FrmDispatchEvent invokes the form's event handler first. If the event remains unhandled, FrmDispatchEvent then calls FrmHandleEvent to perform default handling. We'll explore this in some detail when we talk about forms. (The reason application-level and form-level events are separated this way is because sometimes Palm OS temporarily enters its own event loop but it still needs to have form-level events handled by the application. It also allows Palm OS to broadcast events to all open forms.) The bulk of your application's event handling is done in its form event handlers (you can have one for each form in your application) and not in its application event handler.

Keyboard and Pen Events

Most events are generated by the system in response to the user's pen strokes, and these are discussed later when we talk about building the application's user interface. The most basic events, the pen and keyboard events, are rarely handled by the application, but there's nothing preventing you from doing so if necessary.

A penDownEvent is queued when the user presses the pen on the device's screen. The screenX and screenY members of the EventType describe where the pen touched the screen:

```
// in an event handler somewhere
switch( event->eType ){
    case penDownEvent: {
        SWord x = event->screenX;
        SWord y = event->screenY;

        // do something
    }
}
```

The coordinates are relative to the top left corner of the window (typically, a form) in which the tap occurred. If the pen moves while it touches the screen, penMoveEvents are queued, and the screenX and screenY members describe the new position of the pen. When the pen is finally lifted, a penUpEvent is queued:

```
// in an event handler somewhere
switch( event->eType ){
    case penUpEvent: {
        PointType start = event->data.penUp.start;
        PointType end = event->data.penUp.end;
```

```
            // do something
        }
    }
```

PointType is a structure defined in <UI/Rect.h> to hold the x and y coordinates of a point. Note that unlike penDownEvent and penMoveEvent, the coordinates in the start and end members of the penUp structure (which list where the stroke started and where it ended) are relative to the origin of the display, not the window where the pen down occurred. However, the screenX and screenY members hold the window-relative position where the pen left the screen, so use the coordinates that are in the most convenient format.

The only keyboard event is keyDownEvent, queued when the user writes a Graffiti character, uses the system keyboard dialog, or presses one of the device's buttons. The event-specific data for keyDownEvent includes the ASCII or virtual keystroke value of the character as well as a set of flags referred to as modifiers:

```
    // in an event handler somewhere
    switch( event->eType ){
        case keyDownEvent: {
            Word asciiChar = event->data.keyDown.chr;
            Word virtualChar = event->data.keyDown.keyCode;
            Word modifiers = event->data.keyDown.modifiers;

            if( asciiChar == 'a' || asciiChar == 'A' ){
                // user typed in 'a' or 'A'
            } else if( asciiChar == 0 ){ // virtual key
                if( virtualChar == pageUpChr ){
                    // user pressed page up key on device
                } else if( virtualChar == pageDownChr ){
                    // user pressed page down key on device
                }
            }
            ..... // etc. etc.
        }
    }
```

If the chr member of the keyDown structure is nonzero, the keystroke corresponds to a regular ASCII character in the range 1 to 127. If chr is zero, however, then the key is a virtual key outside of the range of ASCII characters. A virtual key can be a hardware button (such as the page up and page down buttons shown in the example, or the power button), a painted button (such as the Find or Calculator buttons), a system command (for example, to toggle the state of the backlight), or just a character outside the ASCII range. Virtual keys are defined in the header

<UI/Chars.h>. Modifiers are bitmasks defined in <UI/Event.h>, such as shiftKeyMask or autoRepeatKeyMask. One modifier of particular interest is commandKeyMask, which indicates that the virtual key is actually a command. For example, if the commandKeyMask flag is set and the virtual key is backlightChr, it's the command to toggle the state of the backlight. Your application can intercept commands and substitute its own actions. For example, a space game might choose to remap the four hardware buttons to control the player's spaceship; it would do so by handling the hard1Chr, hard2Chr, hard3Chr, and hard4Chr virtual keys before the system had a chance to see them.

Performing Long Operations

As with any event-driven application on other platforms, it's important to process events on a regular and timely basis in order to keep the application responsive. An often-used rule of thumb is to always respond to user input within a tenth of a second. Any longer and the user gets impatient. (On the Palm Computing platform there is no hourglass cursor to indicate that the application is busy, so responsiveness is even more important than on a desktop platform.)

On other platforms you can offload long operations onto a separate thread, but Palm applications are single-threaded. To perform long operations and stay responsive you can use one of two techniques. The first technique is to check the event queue at regular intervals and process any waiting events. For example, consider the following program skeleton:

```
// Start the normal event loop

ProcessEvents( evtWaitForever, false );

....

// Perform a long operation

Boolean DoLongOperation()
{
    for( int i = 1; i <= 40000; ++i ){
        // Do something time-consuming here.
        // Then every once in a while check the event queue.

        if( ( i % 100 ) == 0 ) ){
            Boolean quit = ProcessEvents( 0, true );
            if( quit ){
                // application is quitting, stop
```

```
            return false;
        }
    }
}

    return true;
}

// Revised event loop

Boolean ProcessEvents( int timeout, Boolean stopOnNilEvent )
{
    EventType event;

    while( true ){
        EvtGetEvent( &event, timeout );

        switch( event.eType ){
            case nilEvent:
                if( stopOnNilEvent ){
                    return false;
                }
                break;
            case appStopEvent:
                return true;
            case .... // process other events
                ....
        }
    }
}
```

In this example the event loop has been revised to allow the caller to specify the timeout value and whether to stop when a nilEvent is read. A timeout value of 0 causes EvtGetEvent to return immediately if there are no events to process, returning a nilEvent.

The second technique is to split a long operation into several steps, each of which is triggered by an event. Your application can define its own event identifiers greater than or equal to firstUserEvent. To start the operation you add a user-defined event to the event queue that triggers the first step. Each step then adds another event to trigger the next step. The skeleton code for such a sequence might be as follows:

```
// Define the "user events" for this application

enum userEvents {
    firstStep = firstUserEvent,
    secondStep,
```

```
        thirdStep
};

....

// The event loop

EventType event;

do {
    EvtGetEvent( &event, evtWaitForever );

    switch( event.eType ){
        case firstStep:
            DoFirstStep();
            break;
        case secondStep:
            DoSecondStep();
            break;
        case thirdStep:
            DoThirdStep();
            break;
        case .... // other events
            ....
    }
} while( event.eType != appStopEvent ); // until told to stop

....

// At some point you start the operation

AddUserEvent( firstStep );

....

// Define a function to queue the user events

void AddUserEvent( userEvents eventID )
{
    EventType userEvent;

    userEvent.eType = eventID;
    EvtAddEventToQueue( &userEvent );
}

....

// The first step

void DoFirstStep()
{
```

```
        // do the first step...
        // at the end, post the event that starts the next one....

        AddUserEvent( secondStep );
    }

    // The second step

    void DoSecondStep()
    {
        // do the second step...
        // at the end, post the event that starts the next one...

        AddUserEvent( thirdStep );
    }

    void DoThirdStep()
    {
        // do the third step...
    }
```

Which approach to take depends on the nature of the operation. The first technique is best suited for operations that are hard to split into discrete steps, but watch out for recursive calls that start two or more long operations. The event loop will require special coding to cancel the operation or quit the application entirely. The second technique fits best with the event-driven paradigm because there's a single event loop, but it requires work in splitting the operation into steps and passing data between the different steps. On the other hand, at the start of each step it's easy to update the user about the state of the operation.

An Application Skeleton

Before proceeding any further, let's take a look at a simple application, AppSkeleton, which you'll find on the CD-ROM accompanying this book. AppSkeleton is the most basic well-behaved application you can write and includes the following features:

- A PilotMain that understands normal launches and includes the structure to support other launches.

- Resources that define a main form (the initial screen), an about form (to display information about the application), an alert (a dialog) for ROM version testing, a menubar, and the application icon.

- Code to display the main form and enter an event loop, and to display the about form when requested.

The code for the application is split across three C++ files: PilotMain.cpp, MainForm.cpp, and DialogUtils.cpp. The code for PilotMain.cpp is shown in Figure 4.4. Although it includes a few functions we have yet to discuss, PilotMain.cpp follows the basic application structure we've discussed so far. MainForm.cpp holds the event handler for the main form, while DialogUtils.cpp defines a utility routine (discussed later) for displaying the About form.

You can use AppSkeleton as a starting point for your own applications. It's not all that different from CodeWarrior's Starter application, but is slightly different in its structure. No matter which sample you start with, don't forget that your first step is always to change the name and creator ID of the application to avoid conflicts with other applications.

```
/**
 * A simple skeleton for a Palm OS application.
 */

#include <Pilot.h>
#include <SysEvtMgr.h>
#include "AppSkeleton.h"
#include "AppSkeleton_res.h"

/**
 * Handle application-level events.
 */

static Boolean ApplicationHandleEvent( EventPtr event )
//*******************************************************
{
    Boolean handled = false;

    if( event->eType == frmLoadEvent ){
        // Load the form and make it active
        Word formID = event->data.frmLoad.formID;
        FormPtr form = FrmInitForm( formID );
        FrmSetActiveForm( form );

        // Now set the event handler
        switch( formID ){
            case MainForm:
```

Figure 4.4 PilotMain.cpp from AppSkeleton

```
                    FrmSetEventHandler( form, MainFormEventHandler );
                    break;
        }

        handled = true;
    }

    return handled;
}

/**
 * Perform initialization on application start-up, when globals are enabled.
 */

static Err StartApplication( GoToParamsPtr gotoParms )
//******************************************************
{
    Word formID = MainForm;

    if( gotoParms != NULL ){
        // App was launched after a find operation, so the application
        // has to choose a new form to start with...

        // formID = ....
    }

    FrmGotoForm( formID );
    return 0;
}


/**
 * Perform cleanup when application quits, when globals are enabled.
 */

static Err StopApplication()
//**************************
{
    FrmCloseAllForms();
    return 0;
}

/**
 * Process a "goto" command when the application is already
 * running. This routine should just load and display the
 * requested data and immediately exit.
 */
```

Figure 4.4 *Continued*

```
static Err ProcessGoToData( GoToParamsPtr gotoParms )
//****************************************************
{
    return 0;
}

/**
 * Process a "find" command. Access to globals may not be
 * possible.
 */

static Err ProcessFindData( FindParamsPtr findParms )
//****************************************************
{
    return 0;
}

/**
 * Process a "save" command, which occurs before a find.
 */

static Err ProcessSaveData()
//*************************
{
    FrmSaveAllForms();
    return 0;
}

/**
 * Run the application. Called in response to a normal launch
 * or a "goto" launch, in either case globals are enabled and
 * the application runs until told to quit.
 */

static Err RunApplication( GoToParamsPtr gotoParms )
//****************************************************
{
    EventType event;
    Err       error;
    Word      menuError;

    error = StartApplication( gotoParms );
    if( error == 0 ){
        do {
            EvtGetEvent( &event, evtWaitForever );
            if( SysHandleEvent( &event ) ) continue;
```

Figure 4.4 *Continued*

```
                    if( MenuHandleEvent( NULL, &event, &menuError ) ) continue;
                    if( ApplicationHandleEvent( &event ) ) continue;
                    FrmDispatchEvent( &event );
                } while( event.eType != appStopEvent );

                error = StopApplication();
        }

        return error;
}

/**
 * Check to see if the ROM is Palm OS 2.0 or higher.
 */

#define version20    0x02000000

static Err RomVersionCompatible( DWord requiredVersion, Word launchFlags )
//***********************************************************************
{
    DWord romVersion;

    FtrGet( sysFtrCreator, sysFtrNumROMVersion, &romVersion );

    if( romVersion < requiredVersion ){
       if( ( launchFlags & sysAppLaunchFlagNewGlobals ) != 0 &&
           ( launchFlags & sysAppLaunchFlagUIApp ) != 0 ){
          FrmAlert( RomIncompatibleAlert );

          // Palm OS 1.0 requires you to explicitly launch another app

          if( romVersion < version20 ){
              AppLaunchWithCommand( sysFileCDefaultApp,
                                    sysAppLaunchCmdNormalLaunch, NULL );
          }
       }

       return( sysErrRomIncompatible );
    }

    return 0; // no error
}

/**
 * The application entry point.
 */
```

Figure 4.4 *Continued*

```
DWord PilotMain( Word cmd, Ptr cmdPBP, Word launchFlags )
//**********************************************************
{
    Err errorCode = 0;
    int inSubCall = (( launchFlags & sysAppLaunchFlagSubCall ) != 0);
    int newGlobals = (( launchFlags & sysAppLaunchFlagNewGlobals ) != 0);

    // Make sure Palm OS 2.0 or higher is being used

    errorCode = RomVersionCompatible( version20, launchFlags );
    if( errorCode != 0 ) return errorCode;

    // Handle the various launch codes...

    if( cmd == sysAppLaunchCmdNormalLaunch ){
        errorCode = RunApplication( NULL );
    } else if( cmd == sysAppLaunchCmdGoTo ){
        if( inSubCall ){
            errorCode = ProcessGoToData( (GoToParamsPtr) cmdPBP );
        } else if( newGlobals ){
            errorCode = RunApplication( (GoToParamsPtr) cmdPBP );
        }
    } else if( cmd == sysAppLaunchCmdFind ){
        errorCode = ProcessFindData( (FindParamsPtr) cmdPBP );
    } else if( cmd == sysAppLaunchCmdSaveData ){
        if( inSubCall ){
            errorCode = ProcessSaveData();
        }
    }

    return errorCode;
}
```

Figure 4.4 *Continued*

A version of AppSkeleton for use with the GNU tools is also found on the CD-ROM.

Building the User Interface

After the launch code is processed and before your application enters its event loop, it displays a user interface. That user interface is built from a series of static elements stored in resources. In this section we briefly go over the available resources and show you how they can be used to build

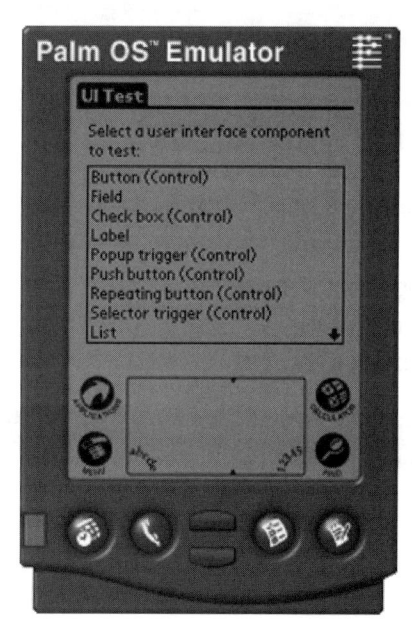

Figure 4.5 The UI Test application.

a user interface. On the CD-ROM you'll find an application called UI Test in the Sample folder that demonstrates each type of resource. Figure 4.5 shows UI Test in action.

Designing a User Interface

When it comes to user interfaces, the design stage is often more important than the implementation stage. The physical limitations of a Palm device place constraints on how much information you can display at any given time, so navigation between views has to be quick and obvious. You'll find a lot of information on good application design in the Palm OS documentation, but here are some general guidelines:

- Minimize the number of penstrokes required to perform an action and make the most common operations the quickest to access.

- Follow standard Palm user interface guidelines. For example, make your Options menu the last menu in the menubar. Study the extensive list of user interface design guidelines in the *Palm OS Programmer's Companion*.

- Whenever possible, model your applications after the built-in applications so that users can easily recognize and use your applications.

User Interface Resources

Applications are resource databases, and user interface elements are stored as separate resources in that database. Each resource in a resource database is uniquely identified by its type and its identifier. The type is a four-byte value such as tSTR or tFRM, while the identifier is a 16-bit numeric value. The resource types are predefined, but the identifiers are assigned by the developer. It's rare to actually refer to a resource by its type except when reading in string or string list resources. Common resource types are listed in Table 4.2.

As you've already seen, projects developed with CodeWarrior use the Constructor tool to define and edit user interface resources, including strings, storing them in .rsrc files. Constructor automatically generates a header file that defines preprocessor macros for each resource. The macros are formed from the name of the resource (stripped of any whitespace characters) and the kind of resource. For example, a form named "Address List" with a resource identifier of 1100 generates the following definition:

```
// Resource: tFRM 1100
#define AddressListForm        1100
```

You should include the header file that Constructor generates in your source files and refer to resources using the macros. If you'd rather define your own mappings, you can disable the automatic generation of the header file.

To create a resource with Constructor, open the .rsrc file for your project. The top half of the resource window lists the resource types that

Table 4.2 Common Resource Types

TYPE	MEANING
tSTR	String resource, holds a series of null-terminated characters.
tFRM	Form resource, defines a window and any controls on it.
Talt	Alert resource, defines a simple message box for alerting the user.
MBAR	Menubar resource, holds references to a number of menu resources.
MENU	Menu resource, defines a menu and the set of menu items on the menu.
tSTL	String list resource, holds an optional prefix string followed by a series of null-terminated strings.
tVER	Version resource, holds the version number for the application.

Constructor can create and edit, as shown in Figure 3.5 in the previous chapter. Each resource type has a sublist listing the individual resources of that type. If you've created the project using CodeWarrior's project stationery, there will already be several resources defined. To edit an existing resource, double-click its entry in the list, or select it and choose "Edit Resource" from the Edit menu. Click on the resource name to edit the name. The resource identifier can also be edited in this way. To add a new resource, there are a couple of approaches you can use. The first method is to deselect the selected item (if any—click on a blank area of the resource list) and then select "New Resource..." from the Edit menu. A dialog allows you to choose the type of resource to create as well as its initial name and identifier, as shown in Figure 4.6. The second approach is to select the resource type in the list and then select "New <type> Resource..." from the Edit menu.

If you use the GNU tools, you define user interface elements in text files using a simple resource definition language. The text files are passed through the PilRC tool to generate the resources for your application. You assign resource identifiers as part of the resource definitions. PilRC understands the include and define C preprocessor directives and can perform simple macro substitution, so the usual practice is to define a header file that maps macros to resource identifiers. You then include this header file in your source files.

No matter which tool you use, it's important to keep identifiers unique among resources of the same type. Constructor does this automatically. Resources of different types, though, can share the same identifier, which is a useful technique for linking related resources. For example, you can share a resource identifier between an alert and its help string.

Complete PilRC definitions for the various resources are not included here but can be found in the PilRC documentation available on the CD-

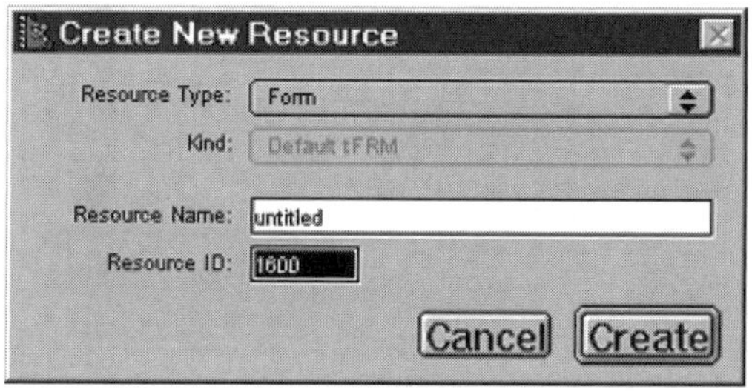

Figure 4.6 Creating a new resource.

ROM (in the GNU Tools folder), although a few short examples of PilRC definitions are used in the text to demonstrate how the resources are defined.

Alerts

Apart from demonstrating the proper structure for an application, the PilotMain.cpp code shared by both AppSkeleton and UI Test (refer back to Figure 4.4) also demonstrates the use of an *alert* user interface element in the RomVersionCompatible function. An alert is a modal dialog box that informs or asks a question. The alert has a title, an icon, some text, and one or more buttons. The icon must be one of four predefined choices—information, question, error, or warning—but the title, text, and button labels are all customizable. An alert is dismissed when the user taps one of its buttons. Because it is modal, the alert prevents the user from performing any other actions until the alert is dismissed.

Constructor's alert editor, shown in Figure 4.7, allows you to set the title, text, and icon for the alert. It can also set the optional help ID, which is the identifier of a string resource (see the next section) to display when the user requests help. It also lets you define the buttons that the alert displays in case the default OK button isn't enough. To add a new button,

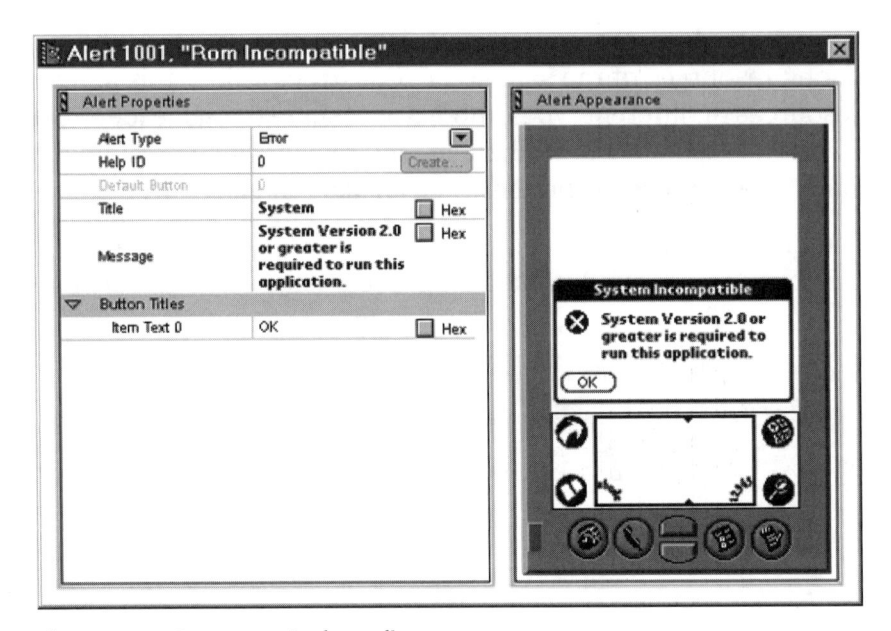

Figure 4.7 Constructor's alert editor.

select the "Button Titles" item or one of the existing button titles and then select "New Button Title" from the Edit menu.

The PilRC resource definition for alerts looks like this:

```
#include "AppSkeleton_res.h"    // include name-to-id mappings

ALERT RomIncompatibleAlert
HELPID RomIncompatibleAlertHelpID
ERROR
BEGIN
    TITLE "Version Error"
    MESSAGE "This application requires Palm OS 2.0 or higher to run."
    BUTTONS "OK"
END
```

The keywords INFORMATION, CONFIRMATION, or WARNING can all be used in place of ERROR to select the desired icon.

Whether Constructor or PilRC was used to define the alert, displaying it is just a matter of calling the FrmAlert function with the alert's resource ID:

```
#include "AppSkeleton_res.h"

int button = FrmAlert( RomIncompatibleAlert );
```

The return value identifies which button was pressed to dismiss the alert. The leftmost button is button 0, the next button is button 1, and so on. The application can perform different actions based on which button the user chose. Since FrmAlert does not return until the alert has been dismissed, no events are processed by your application's event loop. Instead, FrmAlert enters its own event loop, waiting for the user to tap a button.

To change the text in an alert from within the application, use a *custom alert*. A custom alert contains the sequences "^1," "^2," and "^3" in its message text (but not in the title or buttons—the text in titles and buttons is always fixed), which acts as a message template. Invoke a custom alert with the FrmCustomAlert function instead of FrmAlert:

```
int button = FrmCustomAlert( MyAlert, "first", "second",
                             "third" );
```

The last three arguments of FrmCustomAlert are substituted for the "^1," ^2," and "^3" sequences to form the actual message text. You can pass NULL for any sequence that isn't used in the message template; in other words if there is no "^3" sequence, then you can pass NULL for the third parameter. If a sequence is in the template, however, but you don't want to display a value, use an empty string ("") for Palm OS 3.0 and a single space (" ") for previous versions of the operating system.

Strings

Strings can be saved as resources. Help IDs, used in alerts and other user interface elements, refer to string resources. String resources make it easy to localize your application for use with different languages—a translator can work directly on the resources without requiring access to or modifying the application source code.

Constructor's string editor is shown in Figure 4.8. If you're using the GNU tools, the PilRC resource definition for strings looks like this:

```
#include "resources.h"

STRING SomeTextID "Sample sample text."
STRING RomIncompatibleAlertHelpID "Since this application uses "\
           "features unique to "\
           "PalmOS 2.0 or higher, it can only be installed "\
           "successfully on such a device."
```

You can include newline characters in a string: type it in directly with Constructor, or use the standard escaped newline character ("\n") with PilRC.

String resources are often used by other user interface elements, which refer to them by their identifier. To access a string resource programmatically you use the identifier to obtain a handle to the resource and then lock the handle:

```
VoidHand h = DmGetResource( 'tSTR', RomIncompatibleAlertHelpID );
CharPtr  str = (CharPtr) MemHandleLock( h );
.....  // do something with str
```

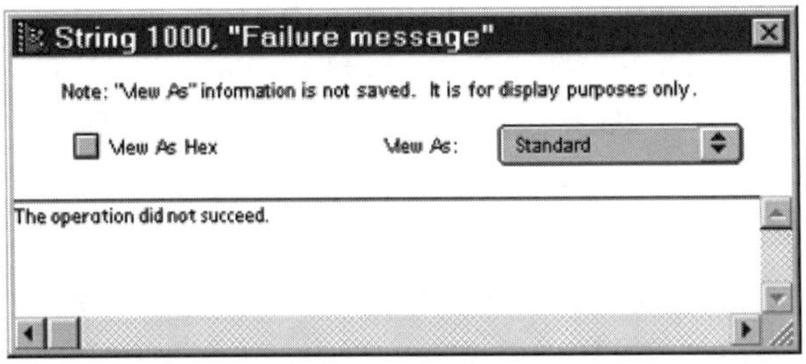

Figure 4.8 Constructor's string editor.

```
MemHandleUnlock( h );
DmReleaseResource( h );
```

Locking the handle returns a read-only pointer to the null-terminated string. When you're finished with the resource, unlock it and then release it. (You can use this technique with any resource, providing you know how the resources map into memory.) Once released, the pointer is no longer valid.

String Lists

A *string list* is a list of strings, together with an optional prefix, stored together as a single resource. Constructor's string list editor is shown in Figure 4.9. PilRC currently does not support the generation of string lists. There are two ways to retrieve a string from a string list: using SysStringByIndex or by directly reading the resource entry.

SysStringByIndex copies a string out of a string list into a user-supplied buffer:

```
Char buf[100];

// Copy second string, i.e. index = 1
SysStringbyIndex( MyStringListID, 1, buf, sizeof( buf ) );
```

The string is combined with the string list prefix (if defined) when copied.

To see the entire list of strings you can obtain and lock a handle to the resource, just like you do with individual string resources. The result of locking the handle, however, is not a simple, null-terminated string, but

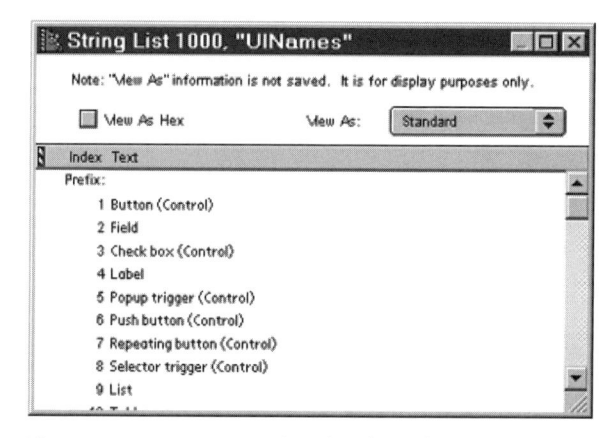

Figure 4.9 Constructor's string list editor.

a pointer to a structure describing the strings. Although the layout of the structure is not documented, a little sleuthing with the debugger yields the following information: A string list starts with the null-terminated prefix string, followed by two bytes holding the number of packed strings that follow, and ending with a series of null-terminated strings. Conceptually, the structure looks like this:

```
// Conceptual only, not legal C/C++!

#pragma pack(push,1) // 1-byte alignment
struct StringListType {
    Char prefix[ StrLen( prefix ) + 1 ];
    Byte count[2];   // N = count[0] * 256 + count[1]
    Char string1[ StrLen( string1 ) + 1 ];
    Char string2[ StrLen( string2 ) + 1 ];
    .....
    Char stringN[ StrLen( stringN ) + 1 ];
};
#pragma pack(pop)    // restore alignment
```

Of course, the structure is not legal C/C++ because it has a number of variable-length members. It's fairly easy to extract the strings from the locked resource once you understand the general structure, however. Given a locked string list resource:

```
VoidHand h = DmGetResource( 'tSTL', MyStringListID );
CharPtr  ptr = MemLockHandle( h );
```

The prefix string is simply the initial pointer value:

```
CharPtr prefix = ptr;
```

The count of nonprefix strings follows the prefix string:

```
ptr += StrLen( ptr ) + 1; // skip over prefix & null character
Word count = ptr[0] * 256 + ptr[1]; // avoids alignment problems
ptr += 2; // skip over the count
```

The remaining strings are packed together, one after the other:

```
for( Word i = 0; i < count; ++i ){
    CharPtr string = ptr;
    // do something with string
    ptr += StrLen( ptr ) + 1; // skip to next string
}
```

As with string resources, all strings should be treated as read-only, and you should unlock and release the resource handle when you're done with it:

```
MemHandleUnlock( h );
DmReleaseResource( h );
```

The StringListType class defined in Figure 4.10 is a convenient way to access a string list (see StringUtils.h and StringUtils.cpp in the UI Test source code). Its constructors take either a pointer to a string list structure or a resource identifier. If the former, the string list must be locked and stay locked until the object is destroyed; if the latter, the object obtains and locks the string list and releases it automatically upon destruction.

```
// A structure that defines the packed string
// format that follows the prefix string in
// a string list resource. We add a couple of
// convenience functions.

#pragma pack(push,1)

struct PackedStringListType {
    Byte count[2];
    Char strings[1];

    Word GetCount() const { return count[0] * 256 + count[1]; }
    CharPtr GetString( Word index ) const;
};

#pragma pack(pop)

typedef struct PackedStringListType *PackedStringListPtr;

// StringList resource handling

class StringListType {
    public:
        StringListType( VoidPtr stringResource );
        StringListType( Word resourceID );

        ~StringListType();

        // Returns true if valid
        Boolean IsValid() const { return _resData != NULL; }

        // Return a pointer to the prefix
        CharPtr GetPrefix() const { return (CharPtr) _resData; }

        // Return the number of non-prefix strings
        Word GetCount() const {
                return GetStringList()->GetCount();
```

Figure 4.10 The StringListType class.

```
            }

            // Return the given non-prefix string
            CharPtr GetString( Word index ) const {
                    return GetStringList()->GetString( index );
            }

            // Return a reference to the packed strings
            PackedStringListPtr GetStringList() const;

        private:
            // Disallow copying
            StringListType( const StringListType & );
            StringListType& operator=( const StringListType & );

        private:
            VoidHand _handle;
            VoidPtr  _resData;
};

CharPtr PackedStringListType::GetString( Word count ) const
{
    CharPtr ptr = (CharPtr) strings;

    if( count >= GetCount() ){
        ptr += StrLen( ptr ); // return nullchar
    } else {
        while( count-- > 0 ){
            ptr += StrLen( ptr );
            ++ptr;
        }
    }

    return ptr;
}

StringListType::StringListType( VoidPtr stringResource )
: _handle( 0 )
, _resData( stringResource )
{
}

StringListType::StringListType( Word resourceID )
: _handle( 0 )
, _resData( NULL )
{
    _handle = DmGetResource( 'tSTL', resourceID );
```

Figure 4.10 *Continued*

```
        if( _handle != 0 ){
            _resData = MemHandleLock( _handle );
        }
    }

    StringListType::~StringListType()
    {
        if( _handle != 0 ){
            MemHandleUnlock( _handle );
            DmReleaseResource( _handle );
        }
    }

    PackedStringListType *StringListType::GetStringList() const
    {
        CharPtr prefix = (CharPtr) _resData;
        PackedStringListPtr sl = (PackedStringListPtr) ( prefix +
                            StrLen( prefix ) + 1 );
        return sl;
    }
```

Figure 4.10 *Continued*

One useful addition to StringListType would be to add an iterator to quickly cycle through the strings in the list: The GetString method counts from the beginning of the string list each time it is called. Or StringListType could return an array of string pointers. This is easily done with the SysFormPointerArrayToStrings function—given a count and a set of packed strings, it allocates and initializes an unlocked array of pointers to those strings:

```
StringListType strList( MyStringListID );
VoidHand h = SysFormPointerArrayToStrings( strList.GetString( 0 ),
                    strList.GetCount() );
```

The array can be locked and passed to other functions for processing, as we'll see when we discuss list controls. The array remains valid only while the string list is valid. The handle returned by SysFormPointerArrayToStrings must be unlocked and freed (with MemHandleUnlock and MemHandleFree) when it's no longer needed.

If your application uses categories and you want to make use of the Category Manager functions that are described in Chapter 5, you'll have to create a special kind of string list called an app info string list, which is listed separately in Constructor's resource window. An app info string list has no prefix and consists of a series of category names. The string list should contain exactly 16 entries, even if they're just empty strings.

Forms and Dialogs

A *form* is a drawable window that can contain user interface objects such as buttons and menus. Each application will have at least one form. The form processes events sent from the system or from the objects it contains. Forms are the most common type of window, alerts and menus being other examples of windows.

Defining Forms

Constructor's form editor, shown in Figure 4.11, looks like the alert editor at first glance, but the properties are different. A form is also much more customizable. With the form editor active, select "Catalog" from the Window menu to bring up a list of user interface objects, referred to as catalog resources. See Figure 4.12 for an example of the catalog window. You can place any of these objects on the form by dragging them from the catalog window onto the form's drawing area. Each object you

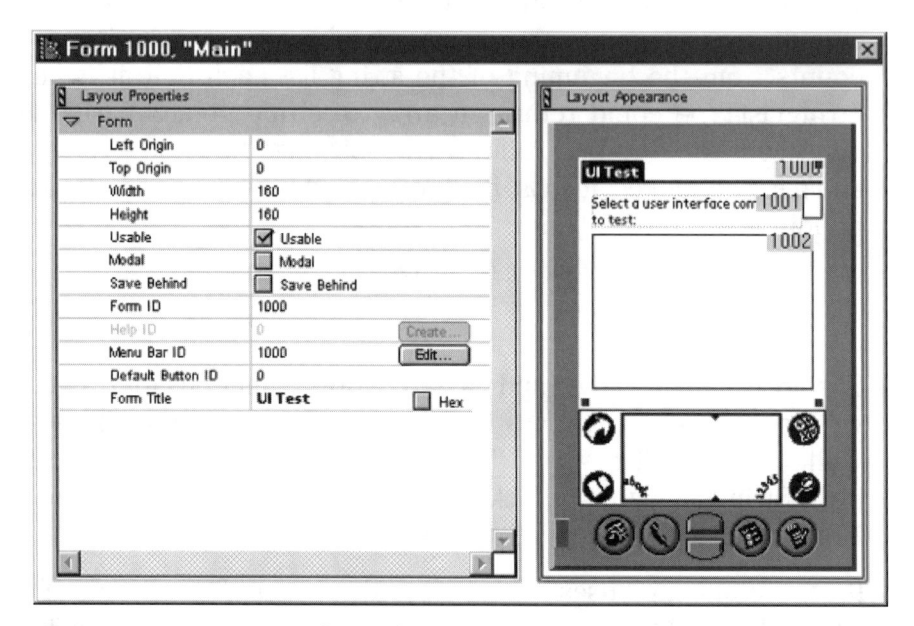

Figure 4.11 Constructor's form editor.

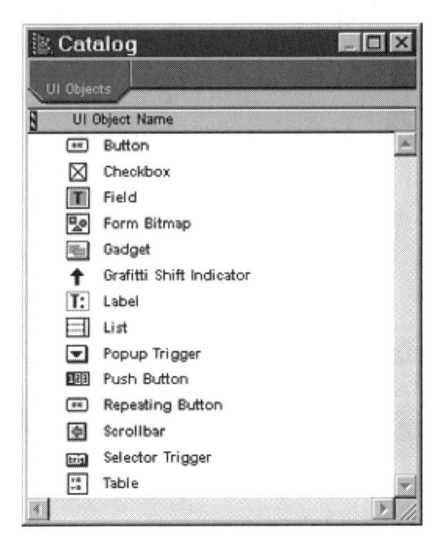

Figure 4.12 Constructor's catalog window.

add to a form is assigned a resource identifier based on the form's identifier, so keeping a large gap between each form ID (make the first form ID 1000, the second 1100, and so on) ensures that the IDs of any object you add to a form will not conflict with those on another form. By default Constructor shows you the ID of each object on a form, but you can turn this off. Selecting an object allows you to modify the properties for that object instead of the form's properties. If objects are close together, you can use the object hierarchy window, shown in Figure 4.13, to easily select the form or any object on the form.

A PilRC form definition is similar to an alert definition:

```
FORM MainFormID AT (0, 0, 160, 160)
HELPID MainHelpID
MENUID MainMenuID
BEGIN
```

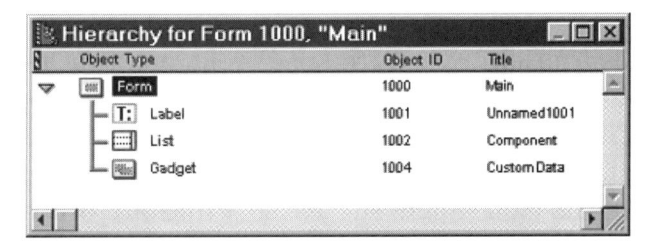

Figure 4.13 Constructor's object hierarchy.

```
        TITLE "Main Form"
        BUTTON "Exit" ID ExitButtonID (CENTER 140 AUTO AUTO)
END
```

In between the BEGIN and END statements are the definitions for the form title and its user interface objects. The syntax is quite complicated, refer to the PilRC documentation for details.

Loading and Unloading Forms

A form is *loaded* when it is copied from a resource into dynamic memory and added to the list of user interface objects managed by the operating system. To save memory, forms are loaded on demand and are unloaded when not active.

Loading a form is a five-step process:

1. Load the form with FrmInitForm.
2. Make it the active form with FrmSetActiveForm.
3. Set the form's event handler with FrmSetEventHandler.
4. Initialize the form's objects.
5. Draw the form with FrmDrawForm.

These steps are not executed together, but are in fact executed in response to two different events. The first three steps are performed when frmLoadEvent is received by the application-level event handler, as shown in Figure 4.14, which knows how to load a single form. Compare the code in Figure 4.14, which is taken from AppSkeleton, to the same code in UI Test: The only difference is that UI Test sets different event handlers for the different forms that the application loads. The last two steps are performed by the form itself, inside its event handler, as shown in Figure 4.15, in response to frmOpenEvent.

To start the loading process, use FrmGotoForm:

```
FrmGotoForm( MainForm );
```

FrmGotoForm adds frmCloseEvent, frmLoadEvent, and frmOpenEvent to the event queue. The first event, frmCloseEvent, is directed at the currently active form, if any. When a form receives this event, it deinitializes and disposes itself. The next two events load the new form as just described. (Although its name might suggest so, FrmGotoForm does not queue frmGotoEvent.)

```
Boolean ApplicationHandleEvent( EventPtr event )
{
    Boolean handled = false;

    if( event->eType == frmLoadEvent ){
        // Load the form and make it active
        Word formID = event->data.frmLoad.formID;
        FormPtr form = FrmInitForm( formID );
        FrmSetActiveForm( form );

        // Now set the event handler based on the form ID
        switch( formID ){
            case MainForm:
                FrmSetEventHandler( form, MainFormEventHandler );
                break;
        }

        handled = true;
    }

    return handled;
}
```

Figure 4.14 Handling frmLoadEvent in the application's event handler.

Once loaded, a form is referred to by a pointer of type FormPtr. The form pointer is returned by the call to FrmInitForm, but don't save this value: Call FrmGetActiveForm anytime you need the form pointer for the active form, as shown in Figure 4.15. Alternatively, you can call FrmGetFormPtr to obtain the pointer to a form by its resource identifier:

```
FormPtr form = FrmGetFormPtr( MainForm );
```

FrmGetFormPtr returns NULL if the form is not loaded. Once you have a form pointer, you can obtain the form's resource identifier with FrmGetFormId.

To unload a form, add frmCloseEvent to the event queue, initializing the formID member appropriately:

```
EventType event;

event.eType = frmCloseEvent;
event.data.frmClose.formID = MainForm;
EvtAddEventToQueue( &event );
```

```
Boolean MainFormEventHandler( EventPtr event )
{
    Boolean handled = false;
    FormPtr form;

    #ifdef __GCC__
        CALLBACK_PROLOGUE
    #endif

    switch( event->eType ){
        case frmOpenEvent:
            form = FrmGetActiveForm();
            InitializeForm( form ); // user-defined routine
            FrmDrawForm( form );
            handled = true;
            break;
        case frmCloseEvent:
            form = FrmGetActiveForm();
            DeinitializeForm( form ); // user-defined routine
            // don't set handled = true or else the form won't
            // be deleted...
            break;
    }

    #ifdef __GCC__
        CALLBACK_EPILOGUE
    #endif

    return handled;
}
```

Figure 4.15 Handling frmOpenEvent in the form's event handler.

FrmGotoForm is used in most situations, however, since it's unusual to close a form without opening another. Use FrmCloseAllForms to close all open forms, typically when the application is shutting down.

Handling Form Events

When we discussed event handling earlier in this chapter, we mentioned that forms have their own event handlers for processing form-specific events. A form event handler is a callback function with the following prototype:

```
Boolean FormEventHandler( EventPtr event );
```

As you can see, the prototype is identical to the application-level event handler shown in Figure 4.14. A form event handler is shown in Figure 4.15. If you're using C++, note that you can't use member functions, whether virtual or nonvirtual, as event handlers: Event handlers must be regular C functions or static C++ functions. GCC users take further note: Because form event handlers are callbacks (they're called indirectly from the application event loop when the application calls FrmDispatch Event), you must use the CALLBACK_PROLOGUE and CALLBACK_ EPILOGUE macros mentioned in Chapter 3.

Form event handlers process events destined for or generated by the form, as well as events generated by any objects on the form. (For Windows programmers, the form event handler is equivalent to a window procedure.) In general, any events that are not handled by the system, menu, or application event handlers are dispatched to the active form's event handler for further processing. There are a few exceptions to this rule: Events such as frmOpenEvent are dispatched to a specific form based on the identifier stored within the event structure. A single event handler can be shared by several forms, using the form identifier to handle any differences between the forms, but it's usual to provide separate event handlers for each form.

Form event handlers are called by FrmDispatchEvent, which itself is called from the application event loop to process nonsystem and nonapplication events. A form event handler returns a Boolean value to indicate if it's completely handled the event or not; if it hasn't, FrmDispatchEvent then calls FrmHandleEvent to finish the event processing. FrmHandleEvent performs a number of important tasks, such as converting low-level pen taps into higher-level events such as button presses. In general, a form should ignore any event that doesn't interest it and return false from the event handler to ensure that these tasks get done. In particular, a form should not return false when processing frmCloseEvent unless it wants to prevent the form from closing.

A well-written form event handler acts on these events:

- frmOpenEvent: initializes and draws the form. Allocates and initializes additional memory and resources needed by the form for its processing
- frmCloseEvent: deinitializes the form. Deallocates any memory or resources that were allocated in frmOpenEvent processing

The following form events can be considered optional:

- frmSaveEvent: saves the state of the form. For example, if the user has changed some text, the text is saved to whatever persistent storage the application uses. Saving usually happens just before a global Find operation is started, when an application calls FrmSaveAllForms in response to a sysAppLaunchCmdSaveData launch code. If there's no state to save, don't bother with this event.

- frmUpdateEvent: redraws the form. Although Palm OS tries to save the parts of a form that are obscured, for example, by a menu or a popup list, in low-memory situations the form is simply asked to redraw itself. If you don't handle this event, Palm OS calls FrmDrawForm for you. You need to handle this event if your form does any custom drawing.

- frmGotoEvent: initializes and draws the form and then sets its state based on data passed with the event. It usually occurs after a global Find operation and takes the place of frmOpenEvent.

Most of the code in a form's event handler deals with nonform events such as menuEvent or ctlSelectEvent, which is discussed later.

Drawing on Forms

If none of the predefined user interface objects fulfill your needs, you can always resort to drawing directly on the form. Palm OS provides a number of primitive drawing routines for drawing lines, rectangles, bitmaps, and strings. There are also routines to set clipping rectangles, erase areas, use fill patterns, and create offscreen drawing buffers. The drawing routines work on any window, not just forms, but applications typically don't draw on any other type of window, except perhaps the odd offscreen buffer.

Drawing routines work on the current *draw window*, which is usually the active form. There are routines to set and get the drawing window, but your applications don't need to call them—if you do your drawing in response to frmUpdateEvent or inside a callback routine (certain objects use callbacks to let the application draw into them), then the draw window is correctly set.

Drawing coordinates are always relative to the top left corner of the draw window. The header <UI/Rect.h> defines structures to represent points and rectangles:

```
typedef struct {
    SWord x;
    SWord y;
} PointType;

typedef struct {
    PointType topLeft; // x = left, y = top
    PointType extent;  // x = width, y = height
} RectangleType;
```

The header also defines functions such as RctPtInRectangle and RctGetIntersection for determining if a point is in a rectangle and the intersection of two rectangles, as well as other utility routines.

These are the prototypes for the basic drawing routines:

```
void WinDrawChars( CharPtr chars, Word len, SWord x, SWord y );
void WinDrawLine( short x1, short y1, short x2, short y2 );
void WinDrawRectangle( RectanglePtr r, Word cornerDiameter ); // filled
void WinDrawRectangleFrame( FrameType type, RectanglePtr r );
```

These draw characters, lines, filled rectangles, and frames. The functions WinEraseChars, WinEraseLine, and WinEraseRectangle erase what was drawn, while WinInvertChars, WinInvertLine, and WinInvertRectangle invert what was drawn. A WinDrawInvertedChars function is also available as a shortcut to calling WinDrawChars and WinInvertChars.

Characters are drawn in the current font, with or without underlining. The current font is set using FntSetFont:

```
FontID FntSetFont( FontID font );
```

The various fonts of the FontID enumeration (defined in <UI/Font.h>) are listed in Table 4.3. Palm OS 3.0 has the ability to define new fonts as

Table 4.3 Palm OS Fonts

FONTID	DESCRIPTION
boldFont	A bolded version of the standard font
largeFont	A large font
largeBoldFont	A bolded version of the large font (Palm OS 3.0 and up)
ledFont	Calculator font
stdFont	The standard font
symbolFont	Displays symbols instead of characters
symbol11Font	Larger version of the symbols
symbol7Font	Smaller version of the symbols

well. FntSetFont returns the previous font identifier. Character definitions for the various symbol fonts are found in <UI/Chars.h>.

To control the underlining, use WinSetUnderlineMode:

```
UnderlineModeType WinSetUnderlineMode( UnderlineModeType type );
```

The UnderlineModeType enumeration is defined in <UI/Window.h> and can be one of noUnderline, grayUnderline, or solidUnderline. WinSetUnderlineMode returns the previous underlining mode.

A number of functions are available to determine the height or width of character strings or to determine how many characters will fit entirely in a given width: FntCharHeight, FntCharsInWidth, FntCharWidth, and so on. If the version of Palm OS you're using supports the International Manager, you must worry about multibyte characters and use text manipulation functions such as TxtCharWidth instead. Consult the *Palm OS SDK Reference* for details on all these functions and how to determine whether the International Manager is present.

When drawing in response to frmUpdateEvent, don't forget to call FrmDrawForm after you're done with the custom drawing. This ensures that the form itself and any objects on it are also drawn.

Dialogs

Forms can be modal or nonmodal (modeless). A modal form ignores pen events outside its bounds and is often called a *dialog*. A dialog has to be dismissed by the user before the application continues and should have at least one button. A dialog is very similar to an alert, but is more flexible because it's not just a precanned form. The application's about box, shown in Figure 4.16, demonstrates a typical dialog. Unless otherwise noted, everything in this chapter that refers to forms also refers to dialogs.

To create a dialog, first create a form resource and mark it as modal. Resize the form if necessary: Unlike regular forms, dialogs should only be tall enough to display their contents and should be flush with the bottom of the screen. Then, when you're ready to display the dialog, use the DisplayDialog function shown in Figure 4.17, which you'll find in the DialogUtils.cpp file in the AppSkeleton and UI Test samples. The function takes two arguments, the resource identifier of the dialog and an optional event handler:

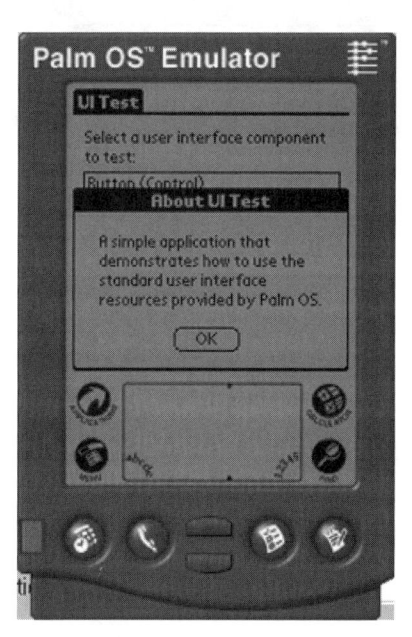

Figure 4.16 A dialog.

```
Word button = DisplayDialog( MyDialogID, NULL );
```

The return value is the resource identifier of the button that was tapped.

Menus

Menus allow the user to view and select commands with a few strokes of the pen and are a great way to maximize use of the limited screen space. Menus in Palm OS look and behave like menus in other operating systems, and shortcuts can be defined to allow quick access to individual commands. Every application should have at least one menu that displays information about the application, such as the version of the application and a copyright message, as shown in the AppSkeleton sample.

Designing Menus

What we generally refer to as a menu has three parts to it: a *menubar*, one or more menus, and one or more *menu items*. The menubar is the container for the menus, while the menus are containers for the menu items.

When designing menus, try to model your menus after the built-in applications whenever possible. The three common menus are Record, Edit,

```
//
// Displays a dialog, waiting for the first button
// press to occur. Returns the ID of the button that
// was pressed. Note that the event handler is optional.
//

Word DisplayDialog( Word formID, FormEventHandlerPtr handler )
{
    // Save current, load new...
    FormPtr active = FrmGetActiveForm();
    Word    activeID = ( active != NULL ) ? FrmGetFormId( active ) : 0;
    FormPtr dialog = FrmInitForm( formID );
    Word    buttonPressed = 0;

    FrmSetActiveForm( dialog );

    // handler is optional....
    if( handler ){
        FrmSetEventHandler( dialog, handler );
    }

    // send frmOpenEvent and then wait for it to close...
    FrmPopupForm( formID );
    buttonPressed = FrmDoDialog( dialog );

    FrmReturnToForm( activeID );

    return buttonPressed;
}
```

Figure 4.17 Displaying a dialog.

and Options. If all three are present, they should be present in that order. The Options menu is always present and has at least one item to bring up the application's about box. Use the same shortcut assignments as the built-in applications, otherwise you'll just confuse the user.

Creating Menus

To create menus in Constructor, you first create a menubar resource, which acts as a container for the menus. You can do this from the resource window or from the form editor. Once a menubar has been created, double-click on its entry in the resource window to bring up the menubar editor, shown in Figure 4.18.

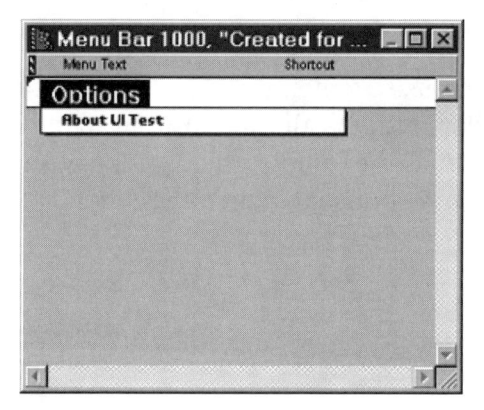

Figure 4.18 Constructor's menubar editor.

Returning to the resource window, create a menu resource. Then drag this resource onto the menubar editor to associate the menu with the menubar. To edit a menu, select it in the menubar editor and then use Constructor's menu to add new menu items or menu separators. You can edit the text for a menu item directly by clicking on it or by double-clicking on it to invoke a menu item editor. Although you can assign the menubar and menu identifiers, the menu item identifiers are automatically generated by Constructor based on the position of the menu item in the menu.

With PilRC, menubars, menus, and menu items are all defined using a single MENU resource:

```
MENU ID MainMenuID
BEGIN
    PULLDOWN "Edit"
    BEGIN
        MENUITEM "Undo" ID UndoID "U"
        MENUITEM SEPARATOR
        MENUITEM "Keyboard" ID KeyboardID "K"
    END
    PULLDOWN "Options"
    BEGIN
        MENUITEM "About This Application" ID AboutID "A"
    END
END
```

Associating a menubar identifier with a form loads the menubar whenever the form is active. The user can display the menubar by pressing the device's Menu button.

Handling Menu Events

When a menu is selected by the user, a menuEvent is sent to the active form. The form's event handler extracts the menu item identifier and performs the appropriate action. For example, the AppSkeleton sample displays the about box dialog in response to a menuEvent:

```
// In the form's event handler

switch( event->eType ){
    case menuEvent: {
        Word id = event->data.menu.itemID;
        if( id == OptionsAboutApplication ){
            DisplayDialog( AboutApplicationForm, NULL );
        }
        // other menu items would be handled here
        break;
    }
    .....   // etc. etc.
}
```

The identifier of the selected item is passed as event data.

Controls and Other Components

The user interface objects you place on a form are collectively referred to as *form objects* or *form components*. Because the term *object* is used for many different things, in this book we'll refer to them as components. In other systems they'd be called controls, but a control in Palm OS refers to a specific kind of form component.

Component Types

These are the types of form components that Palm OS supports:

- **Labels** display text and do not respond to the pen.
- **Controls** are tappable rectangular areas that display text. Buttons, check boxes, popup triggers, push buttons, repeating buttons, and selector triggers are all controls.
- **Fields** display editable text.
- **Lists** display lists of choices.
- **Tables** display values in rows and columns.
- **Scroll bars** select a range of values.

- **Form bitmaps** display bitmaps.
- **Graffiti shift indicators** display the current Graffiti shift state.
- **Gadgets** reserve an area of the form for custom drawing and event processing.

We explore each of these in some detail. See the UI Test sample for detailed examples.

Creating Components

In Constructor, components are added to a form by dragging them from the Catalog window, shown in Figure 4.12. In PilRC you define these objects within the BEGIN and END sections of the FORM definition. Refer to the PilRC documentation for syntax details.

Like other user interface objects, components have unique identifiers that are assigned by the developer when the components are created.

Finding Components

The application typically refers to a component by its identifier, but system routines refer to them by index or by pointer. The index of a component refers to its position in the form's internal data structures, while the pointer refers to the component's internal data structures. The following functions can be used to convert between identifier, index, and pointer:

```
VoidPtr FrmGetObjectPtr( FormPtr form, Word index );
Word    FrmGetObjectIndex( FormPtr form, Word identifier );
Word    FrmGetObjectId( FormPtr form, Word index );
```

For example, to cycle through the complete set of components on a form:

```
FormPtr form = FrmGetActiveForm();
Word    count = FrmGetNumberOfObjects( form );
for( Word i = 0; i < count; ++i ){
   VoidPtr object = FrmGetObjectPtr( form, i );
}
```

To map an identifier to a pointer, many applications define a convenience function:

```
VoidPtr GetObjectPtr( Word resourceID )
{
   FormPtr form = FrmGetActiveForm();
   return FrmGetObjectPtr( form, FrmGetObjectIndex( form, resourceID ) );
}
```

Never hang onto a pointer for longer than is absolutely necessary, because the pointer may become invalid as the system unlocks and moves components in memory. The index and identifier are always valid.

Common Properties

Components have the following properties in common:

- **Left origin.** The distance from the left side of the form to the left side of the component. Valid values are 0 to 159.
- **Top origin.** The distance from the top of the form to the top of the component. Valid values are 0 to 159.
- **Width.** The width of the component. Valid values are 1 to 160.
- **Height.** The height of the component. Valid values are 1 to 160.

At run time, these properties can be read using FrmGetObjectBounds and FrmGetObjectPosition and set with FrmSetObjectBounds and FrmSetObjectPosition.

Most components also have a Usable property that determines whether the object draws itself or not, analogous to a "visible" style in other environments. The Graffiti shift indicator and the table are exceptions to this. Use FrmHideObject or FrmShowObject to hide or show a component.

Labels

We'll start with labels, the simplest components, shown in Figure 4.19. Labels display one or more lines of text and do not respond to pen taps. The text of a label is usually fixed when the resource is created; however, if you want to read or write the text at run time use FrmGetLabel and FrmCopyLabel:

```
CharPtr FrmGetLabel( FormPtr form, Word resourceID );
void FrmCopyLabel( FormPtr form, Word resourceID, CharPtr string );
```

FrmGetLabel returns a pointer to the label's internal text buffer, while FrmCopyLabel copies a string into that buffer. The buffer size is fixed, so any strings copied into the label must be no longer than the length of the label's initial text. As with component pointers, the pointer returned by FrmGetLabel can be invalidated, so be sure to make a copy of the string if you want to hang onto it.

Figure 4.19 Labels.

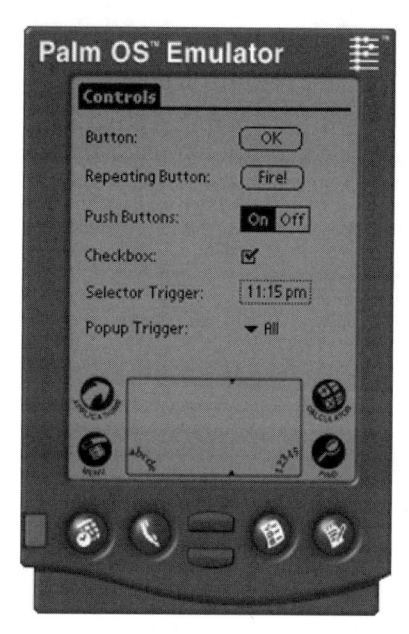

Figure 4.20 Controls.

Controls

Controls display text in various ways and also respond to pen taps. The six kinds of controls are shown in Figure 4.20. Each triggers an event when tapped, either ctlSelectEvent, ctlRepeatEvent, or popSelectEvent.

The most basic control is the button, which draws a rounded rectangle around some text. When tapped, a button queues ctlSelectEvent, which is processed like so:

```
// in the form event handler
switch( event->eType ){
    case ctlSelectEvent: {
        Word       ctrlID = event->data.ctlSelect.controlID;
        ControlPtr ctrlPtr = event->data.ctlSelect.pControl;

        if( ctrlID == MyButtonID ){
            // do something in response to tap
        }
        break;
    }
    ....
}
```

A button queues a single event every time it is tapped, even if the pen is held down for several seconds. To trigger events continuously while the pen is down, use a *repeating button* instead. Instead of ctlSelectEvent, a repeating button queues ctlRepeatEvent:

```
// in the form event handler
switch( event->eType ){
    case ctlRepeatEvent: {
        Word       ctrlID = event->data.ctlRepeat.controlID;
        ControlPtr ctrlPtr = event->data.ctlRepeat.pControl;
        DWord      timeofRepeat = event->data.ctlRepeat.time;

        if( ctrlID == MyButtonID ){
            // do something in response to continuous tap
        }
        break;
    }
    ....
}
```

Events are queued every half second or so while the pen remains down over the repeating button. For a squared button that toggles between on and off states every time it's tapped, use a *push button*. It queues a ctlSelect event like the button but in addition sets a flag that indicates the new state of the button:

```
// in the form event handler
switch( event->eType ){
    case ctlSelectEvent: {
        Word       ctrlID = event->data.ctlSelect.controlID;
        ControlPtr ctrlPtr = event->data.ctlSelect.pControl;
        Boolean    buttonIsOn = event->data.ctlSelect.on;

        if( ctrlID == MyButtonID ){
            // do something in response to tap
        }
        break;
    }
    ....
}
```

To get and set the push button state in your application, use CtlGetValue and CtlSetValue:

```
short CtlGetValue( ControlPtr ctrl ); // returns 0 (off) or 1 (on)
void  CtlSetValue( ControlPtr ctrl, short on ); // on = 0 or 1
```

When you create a push button, you can group it with other push buttons by assigning it a nonzero group ID. When the user taps a push button, the system ensures that all other push buttons in the same group are turned off, leaving one push button on at any given time. A push button is in effect a more compact representation of the radio button commonly seen on other platforms. Push buttons that are logically grouped should also be physically grouped together on the form. Push buttons with a zero group ID toggle their state independently.

A *check box* is also a kind of toggle button, only it draws a check mark when on and an empty box when off. An optional label is shown to the right of the box. The check box also triggers ctlSelectEvent. Use CtlGetValue and CtlSetValue to get and set its state.

A *selector trigger* is a button drawn with a dashed border. Tapping on it brings up a dialog that lets the user select a new value. When the dialog is dismissed, the selector trigger's label is adjusted to reflect the new selection. Like a button, a selector trigger queues ctlSelectEvent. Your application displays a dialog in response to this event. After the dialog is dismissed, the selector trigger's text is changed using CtlSetLabel:

```
void CtlSetLabel( ControlPtr ctrl, CharPtr newLabel );
```

CtlSetLabel just stores the pointer and does not copy the string, so you need to ensure that the pointer is valid while the form is loaded. The selector trigger is resized to fit the new label. To get the pointer to the label, use CtlGetLabel. CtlSetLabel and CtlGetLabel can be used with any control.

The final control is the *popup trigger*, which is similar to a selector trigger in that it lets the user select a new value from a list of values. Unlike the selector trigger, however, selection is handled automatically by the system. All you need to do is associate a list component (see the following) with the popup trigger. The system takes care of popping up the list and tracking the user's selection. When the user has made a selection, the popup trigger queues popSelectEvent describing which item was selected:

```
// in the form event handler
switch( event->eType ){
    case popSelectEvent: {
        Word       ctrlID = event->data.popSelect.controlID;
        ControlPtr ctrlPtr = event->data.popSelect.pControl;
        Word       listID = event->data.popSelect.listID;
        ListPtr    listPtr = event->data.popSelect.pList;
        Word       selection = event->data.popSelect.selection;
        Word       priorSelection =
                        event->data.popSelect.priorSelection;
```

```
      if( ctrlID == MyTriggerID ){
          // do something in response to selection
      }
      break;
   }
   ....
}
```

The popup trigger's label is automatically adjusted to reflect the new selection. To avoid some painting bugs, make sure that the list is always larger than the popup trigger. The list should be initialized and invisible (set its usable property to false) before the popup trigger is displayed.

A control can be prevented from responding to pen taps at run time by disabling it. CtlEnabled and CtlSetEnabled are used to get and set the enabled state:

```
Boolean CtlEnabled( ControlPtr ctrl );
void    CtlSetEnabled( ControlPtr ctrl, Boolean enabled );
```

A few other routines work with any control: To show or hide a control, use CtlShowControl and CtlHideControl, and to simulate a pen tap use CtlHitControl.

Field

A *field* displays editable text, as shown in Figure 4.21. It supports cut, copy, and paste operations, multiline text, scrolling, and automatic height expansion, which saves you a lot of coding.

Fields use memory handles to manage the text being edited. This allows the field to adjust the amount of memory it uses to accommodate the string as it is edited. The handle is obtained with FldGetTextHandle and set with FldSetTextHandle:

```
VoidHand FldGetTextHandle( FieldPtr field );
void FldSetTextHandle( FieldPtr field, VoidHand newHandle );
```

If the field is initially empty, you don't need to do anything: The field automatically allocates a handle when the user starts editing text. To set the initial text, allocate a handle, copy the text into the new memory block, unlock the handle, and assign the handle to a field:

```
// Initialize a handle
CharPtr  s = "Here's some text";
Word     l = StrLen( s );
VoidHand h = MemHandleNew( l + 1 );
CharPtr  d = MemHandleLock( h );
```

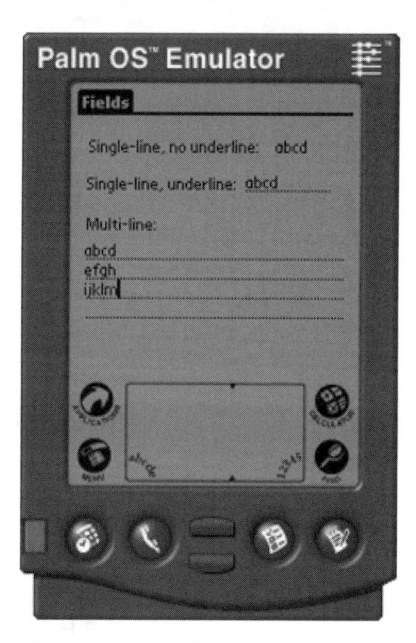

Figure 4.21 Fields.

```
    StrCopy( d, s );
    MemHandleUnlock( h );

    // Get the field's pointer
    FieldPtr field = GetObjectPtr( form, MyFieldID );

    // Get the old handle and set the new one
    VoidHand oldText = FldGetTextHandle( field );
    FldSetTextHandle( field, h );

    // Free old handle
    if( oldText != 0 ){
        MemHandleFree( oldText );
    }

    // Redraw field
    FldDrawField( field );
```

When setting a new handle with FldSetTextHandle, always free the old handle (*after* setting the new handle) to avoid leaking memory. You may find it useful to use the following convenience function:

```
    VoidHand ReplaceFieldHandle( Word fieldID, VoidHand newHandle,
                                 Boolean deleteOld )
    {
        FieldPtr field = (FieldPtr) GetObjectPtr( fieldID );
        VoidHand oldHandle = FldGetTextHandle( field );
```

```
        FldSetTextHandle( field, newHandle );
        if( oldHandle != 0 && deleteOld ){
            MemHandleFree( oldHandle );
            oldHandle = 0;
        }
        FldDrawField( field );
        return oldHandle;
}
```

By default a field frees its memory handle when the form it's on is closed, but you can prevent this by explicitly setting the field handle to 0 while processing frmCloseEvent.

If you just want to read the current text, FldGetTextPtr locks the field's handle and returns a pointer to the text, or NULL if there is no text. The pointer is only valid as long as the memory handle stays locked, and the field can unlock and move the memory block at any time, so don't hang onto the pointer longer than is absolutely necessary.

FldGetTextPtr locks the handle and returns a pointer to the text, but the next editing operation may unlock the handle, so don't hold onto the pointer for very long. Do not use this pointer to modify the text. To modify text, temporarily remove the handle, make the changes, then replace the handle:

```
VoidHand h = FldGetTextHandle( field );
FldSetTextHandle( field, 0 );
CharPtr string = MemHandleLock( h );
// modify the string....
MemHandleUnlock( h );
FldSetTextHandle( field, (Handle) h );
FldDrawField( field );
```

For simple editing, routines such as FldDelete and FldSetText can be used, but because each of these redraws the field, multiple changes are best handled as shown previously.

Text editing is handled automatically by the field. A text field receives input only if it has the *input focus*. Normally, the system automatically changes which component has input focus by tracking pen taps, but you can change the focus at any time with FrmSetFocus:

```
void FrmSetFocus( FormPtr form, Word index );
```

You might want to do this when the form first opens.

If a form has one or more fields, it should include an Edit menu that lets the user cut, copy, and paste text to or from the clipboard. Luckily, functions are provided that make this almost trivial:

```
void FldCopy( FieldPtr field );
void FldCut( FieldPtr field );
void FldPaste( FieldPtr field );
```

To select a range of text, use FldSetSelection. This selects all the text:

```
FldSetSelection( field, 0, FldGetTextLength( field ) );
```

The last operation on a field can be undone at any time by calling FldUndo.

NOTE

FldCopy, FldCut, FldPaste, FldSetSelection, and FldUndo implement the basic actions of the Edit menu. However, a good Edit menu also allows the user to open the on-screen keyboard, shown in Figure 4.22, or display the Graffiti quick reference dialog, shown in Figure 4.23. These are invoked using SysKeyboardDialog and SysGraffitiReferenceDialog:

   SysKeyboardDialog(kbdDefault); // invoke on-screen keyboard

   SysGraffitiReferenceDialog(referenceDefault); // invoke Graffiti reference

See the built-in Address Book for examples.

Other routines such as FldSetSelection and FldSetScrollPosition can be used to change the editing state of the field.

When you create a field, you indicate whether it has a scroll bar associ-

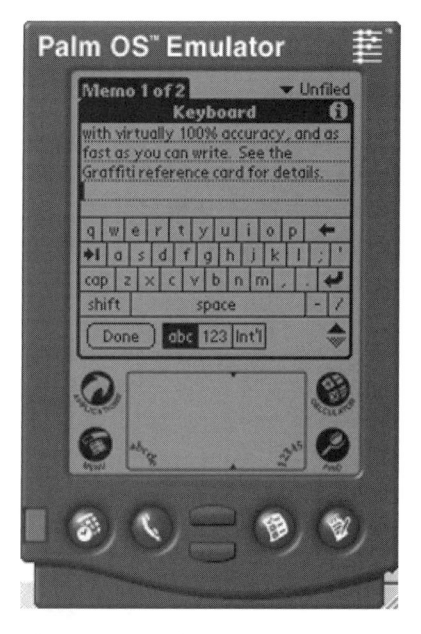

Figure 4.22 The on-screen keyboard dialog.

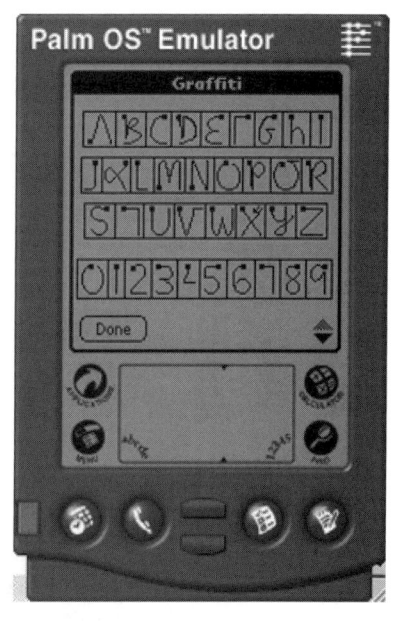

Figure 4.23 The Graffiti reference dialog.

ated with it. This doesn't actually create a scroll bar for you, but it does mean that the field queues fldChangedEvent whenever the number of lines it displays changes, so that you can update the scroll bar accordingly. Scroll bar creation is discussed subsequently.

Lists

A list displays a list of choices, with the current choice highlighted, as shown in Figure 4.24. A list displays a fixed number of items at any time. If there are more items than can be displayed, the list provides a way to scroll through the items. When an item is selected, the list queues lstSelectEvent:

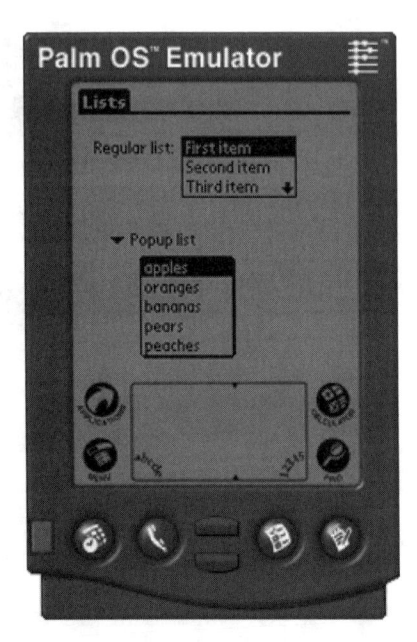

```
// in the form event handler
switch( event->eType ){
    case lstSelectEvent: {
        Word      listID = event->data.lstSelect.listID;
        ListPtr   listPtr = event->data.lstSelect.pList;
        Word      selection = event->data.lstSelect.selection;

        if( listID == MyListID ){
            // do something in response to selection
        }
        break;
    }
}
```

Figure 4.24 Lists

```
    ....
}
```

Item indexes are zero-based.

A list displays strings or custom-drawn items. To display a set of strings, use LstSetListChoices:

```
void LstSetListChoices( ListPtr list, CharPtr *strings, UInt numItems );
```

The second argument points to an array of strings, while the third argument is the number of strings in the array. The strings must remain valid as long as the list is using them, because the list does not make a copy of the strings. A typical strategy is to load a set of packed strings (null-terminated strings packed into a single memory block) and use SysFormPointerArrayToStrings to build an array:

```
CharPtr str = "First\0Second\0Third";
VoidHand h = SysFormPointerArrayToStrings( str, 3 );
LstSetListChoices( list, MemHandleLock( h ), 3 );
.....
// later, when done, remove choices and free handle
LstSetListChoices( list, 0, 0 );
MemHandleUnlock( h );
MemHandleFree( h );
```

If you use a string list, the StringListType class we previously discussed makes it easy to initialize a list:

```
StringListType *strList = new StringListType( MyStringListID );
VoidHand        h = SysFormPointerArrayToStrings(
                     strList->GetString( 0 ),
                     strList->GetCount() );
LstSetListChoices( list, MemHandleLock( h ), strList->GetCount() );
```

Remeπmber that the strings and the array of pointers must all remain valid while the list is in use. You can store them in global variables or you can use invisible gadgets to store them on a per-form basis. Gadgets are discussed shortly. When the form closes, be sure to free any handles or resources used by the list.

To display custom-drawn items, use LstSetListChoices to set the number of items in the list, passing NULL for the array of strings, and install a callback with LstSetDrawFunction:

```
LstSetListChoices( list, NULL, 10 );  // 10 items
LstSetDrawFunction( list, ListCustomDraw );
```

The callback function is invoked for each visible item whenever the list is redrawn and has the following prototype:

```
void ListCustomDraw( UInt itemToDraw, RectanglePtr itemBounds,
                     CharPtr *itemText )
{
    ListPtr list = GetObjectPtr( MyListID );
    CharPtr s = .... // get the string from somewhere
    WinDrawChars( s, StrLen( s ), bounds->topLeft.x,
                  bounds->topLeft.y );
}
```

Notice that the list pointer is not passed to the custom draw function, you have to obtain it yourself inside the function. As well, notice that the last argument points to the text of the item. If you don't set any text with LstSetListChoices, this will be NULL; otherwise, it will point to the appropriate string in the array.

Using a custom draw function is a bit more work, but it also offers more flexibility because you can draw the item yourself.

Use LstGetSelection and LstSetSelection to get and set the selected item, or LstGetSelectionText to get the selected item's text (if it has any). LstSetTopItem makes a specific item the topmost item, while LstMakeItemVisible ensures a specific item is visible.

You can display a list in a popup dialog using LstPopupList:

```
short LstPopupList( ListPtr list );
```

The index of the selected item is returned, or −1 if no item was selected. The popup trigger control uses this function to pop up its associated list.

Graffiti Shift Indicators

A *Graffiti shift indicator* displays the current Graffiti shift state. By convention, you place this object at the bottom right of a form with editable text. The system manages the object for you.

Form Bitmaps

A *form bitmap* displays an image stored in bitmap format. The bitmap itself is defined as a separate resource. There are no functions that deal specifically with form bitmaps, use the FrmShowObject and FrmHideObject functions to show or hide the bitmap at run time.

Gadgets

A *gadget* is a rectangular area on the form with which you can associate custom data. You are completely responsible for drawing the gadget in the form's frmUpdateEvent processing and for handling any key or pen strokes. The only functions that deal specifically with gadgets are FrmGetGadgetData and FrmSetGadgetData, which let you associate an arbitrary pointer with a particular gadget:

```
VoidPtr FrmGetGadgetData( FormPtr form, Word index );
void FrmSetGadgetData( FormPtr form, Word index, VoidPtr data );
```

One trick you may find useful is to define a structure or class to hold data specific to your form, such as memory handles that must remain locked while the form is being used, and use an invisible gadget to hold a reference to the data. Whenever you need the data you would call FrmGetGadgetData. When your form closes, be sure to free the data.

Scroll Bar

A scroll bar lets the user move between a range of values, as shown in Figure 4.25. Scroll bars are vertical. The moveable piece of the scroll bar

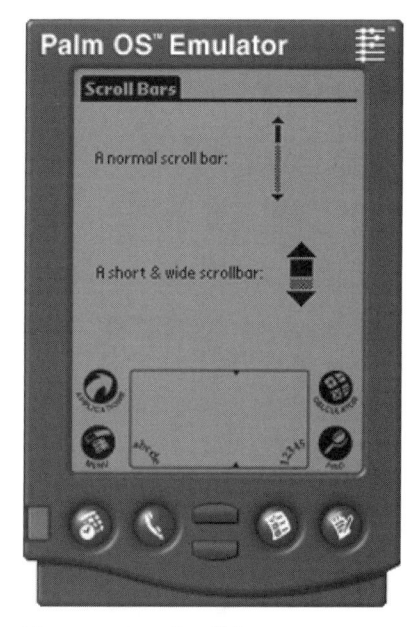

Figure 4.25 Scroll bars.

is referred to as the *scroll car* or *scroll thumb*. The range of the car is represented by two signed, 16-bit integers—the current value of the scroll bar is always in this range and determines the relative position of the car when the scroll bar is displayed. A page size determines how much the scroll bar value should change when the user moves the car in either direction.

Although the range, value, and page size settings can be set when the scroll bar resource is created, it's usual to get and set them at run time with SclGetScrollBar and SclSetScrollBar:

```
void SclGetScrollBar( ScrollBarPtr scrollbar, ShortPtr value,
                     ShortPtr min, ShortPtr max, ShortPtr pageSize );
void SclSetScrollBar( ScrollBarPtr scrollbar, Short value, Short min,
                     Short max, Short pageSize );
```

When pressed, the scroll bar queues sclEnterEvent, and as the user drags the car, it queues sclRepeatEvent. When the car is released, sclExitEvent is queued. Applications generally ignore sclEnterEvent but handle sclRepeatEvent and/or sclExitEvent:

```
// in the form event handler
switch( event->eType ){
   case sclRepeatEvent: {
      Word          scrollBarID =
                        event->data.sclRepeat.scrollBarID;
      ScrollBarPtr scrollBar =
            (ScrollBarPtr) event->data.sclRepeat.pScrollBar;
      Short         oldValue = event->data.sclRepeat.value;
      Short         newValue = event->data.sclRepeat.newValue;
      Long          timeOfScroll = event->data.sclRepeat.time;

      if( scrollBarID == MyScrollBar ){
         // update something based on new, interim value
      }
      break;
   }
   case sclExitEvent: {
      Word          scrollBarID = event->data.sclExit.scrollBarID;
      ScrollBarPtr scrollBar = event->data.sclExit.pScrollBar;
      Short         oldValue = event->data.sclExit.value;
      Short         newValue = event->data.sclExit.newValue;

      if( scrollBarID == MyScrollBar ){
         // update something based on new, final value
      }
      break;
   }
}
```

```
    ....
}
```

Applications that need to update data or other components as the user scrolls the car should handle sclRepeatEvent; otherwise, all they need to care about is sclExitEvent.

Scroll bars are rarely used by themselves and are usually associated with field or table components. The scroll bar should be placed next to the component. As the field or table is scrolled, the application adjusts the scroll bar to reflect the new state. Similarly, if the scroll car is moved, the application adjusts the state of the field or table to match.

To obtain the current scroll position of a multiline field, use FrmGetScrollValues:

```
void FldGetScrollValues( FieldPtr fld, WordPtr topMostLine,
                  WordPtr totalLines,
                  WordPtr visibleLines );
```

It returns the number of the topmost line, the total number of lines in the field, and the number of visible lines. The line number is indexed starting at 1, except for the first line, which always returns an index value of 0. (In other words, topMostLine will be 0, 2, 3, 4, etc.) Use these values to calculate a new range, position, and page size for the scroll bar:

```
Word overlap = 1; // how many lines of overlap
Word max = 0;

if( totalLines >= visibleLines ){
   max = totalLines - visibleLines;
} else if( topMostLine > 0 ){
   max = topMostLine;
}

SclSetScrollBar( scrollBar, topMostLine, 0, max,
              visibleLines - overlap );
```

It's common to leave an overlap of one or two lines. To scroll a field in response to sclRepeatEvent or sclExitEvent, use FldScrollField:

```
void FldScrollField( FieldPtr field, Word linesToScroll,
                  DirectionType direction );
```

Where the direction is one of the constants up (0) or down (1). Be aware that scrolling a field sometimes changes the number of lines displayed, so you should update the scroll bar with the new position after calling FldScrollField.

Tables

A table displays data in a row-column format similar to a spreadsheet, as shown in Figure 4.26. Tables are the most complicated user interface components to program, but they offer a lot of flexibility. A whole chapter could be written on table usage, but we'll just summarize the capabilities here. Again, refer to the UI Test application as well as the built-in applications (the source is included with the Palm OS SDK) for detailed examples.

Rows and Columns

A table has a fixed number of rows and columns. The values are set when the table resource is created and cannot be changed at run time. To scroll a table you must fill the rows with new data and redraw the table, which we'll discuss shortly. Any rows or columns that extend beyond the table's boundaries are clipped.

Like the table itself, a row or column has a usable state:

```
Boolean TblRowUsable( TablePtr table, Word row )
void TblSetRowUsable( TablePtr table, Word row, Boolean usable )
// no TblColumnUsable
void TblSetColumnUsable( TablePtr table, Word column, Boolean usable )
```

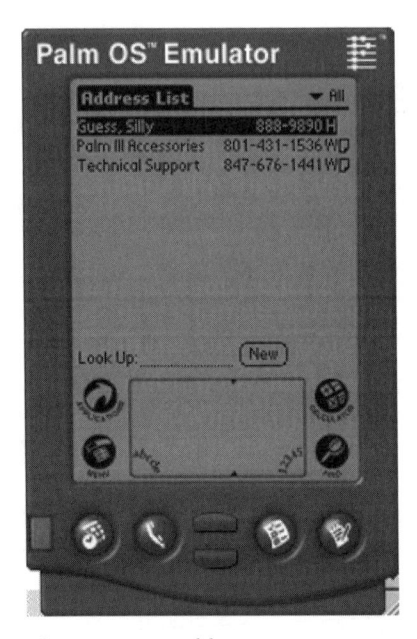

Figure 4.26 Tables.

Rows and columns have zero-based indexes. If a row or column is not marked as usable, it's not drawn.

The width of a column is set at run time, as well as the spacing between it and the next column:

```
Word TblGetColumnWidth( TablePtr table, Word column )
void TblSetColumnWidth( TablePtr table, Word column, Word width )
Word TblGetColumnSpacing( TablePtr table, Word column )
void TblSetColumnSpacing( TablePtr table, Word column, Word spacing )
```

The height of a row can also be set, although it will adjust itself dynamically as text is added or removed from a row:

```
Word TblGetRowHeight( TablePtr table, Word row )
void TblSetRowHeight( TablePtr table, Word row, Word height )
```

To prevent a row's height from changing, use TblSetRowStaticHeight:

```
void TblSetRowStaticHeight( TablePtr table, Word row,
                  Boolean staticHeight )
```

If the last parameter is true, the row's height stays fixed at its current value. A row can also be marked as selectable:

```
Boolean TblRowSelectable( TablePtr table, Word row )
void TblSetRowSelectable( TablePtr table, Word row, Boolean selectable )
```

If a row is selectable, the item that was tapped is highlighted. A row can also be assigned a 16-bit identifier:

```
Word TblGetRowID( TablePtr table, Word row )
void TblSetRowID( TablePtr table, Word row, Word id )
```

Given an identifier, use TblFindRowID to find the associated row index, if any:

```
Boolean TblFindRowID( TablePtr table, Word id, WordPtr rowIndex )
```

A row can also have a 32-bit value associated with it, separate from the 16-bit identifier:

```
ULong TblGetRowData( TablePtr table, Word row )
void TblSetRowData( TablePtr table, Word row, ULong data )
```

This value often stores a pointer to an application-defined structure.

Items

The intersection of a row and column is referred to as a table *item*. Although the height and width of the item depends on the height of the row and the width of the column, items have their own independent properties as well. The most important of these is the item's *style*, which determines what the item contains and how it draws itself. Item styles are members of the TableItemStyleType enumeration (see <UI/Table.h>) and are listed in Table 4.4. The style is set with TblSetItemStyle when the table is initialized:

```
void TblSetItemStyle( TablePtr table, Word row, Word column,
                      TableItemStyleType type )
```

Two values are also associated with each table item, an integer and a pointer:

```
Word TblGetItemInt( TablePtr table, Word row, Word column )
void TblSetItemInt( TablePtr table, Word row, Word column, Word value )
// no TblGetItemPtr
void TblSetItemPtr( TablePtr table, Word row, Word column, VoidPtr data )
```

These values are interpreted differently depending on the item's style:

- checkboxTableItem stores the state of its check box in the integer— 0 is unchecked, 1 is checked.
- dateTableItem stores the date in the integer. The date format is that of a DateType structure, defined in <System/DateTime.h>. A DateType stores year, month, and day values in a series of bitfields so that the size of the DateType structure is exactly one word (16 bits), so in general Word and DateType are interchangeable. (The year value is actually the number of years since 1904.) To set no date, use −1 as the value.

Table 4.4 Table Item Styles

STYLE	DESCRIPTION
checkboxTableItem	Displays a check box with no label
customTableItem	Custom-drawn item
dateTableItem	Displays a non-editable date
labelTableItem	Displays non-editable text with a colon appended
narrowTextTableItem	Displays editable text, reserving some space to the right of the text
numericTableItem	Displays a non-editable integer
popupTriggerTableItem	Displays a popup trigger
textTableItem	Displays editable text
textWithNoteTableItem	Displays editable text with a note icon to the right of the text

- labelTableItem references the label text via the pointer. The pointer must remain valid while the table is using it.
- narrowTextTableItem stores its spacing value in the integer.
- numericTableItem stores its value in the integer.
- popupTriggerTableItem references a list component via the pointer and stores the selected item in the integer. The list must remain valid while the table is using it.

Unlike labelTableItem, the three text styles—textTableItem, textWithNoteTableItem, narrowTextTableItem—use handles instead of pointers to store their text. When an item is displayed or edited, the handle is obtained. If the item is being edited, the handle is associated with a field component. A callback routine, referred to as the custom load routine, obtains this handle for each item and must be registered on a per-column basis with TblSetLoadDataProcedure:

```
void TblSetLoadDataProcedure( VoidPtr table, Word column,
                    TableLoadDataFuncPtr callback )
```

The custom load routine looks like this:

```
Err MyTableLoader( VoidPtr table, Word row, Word column,
                Boolean editable, VoidHand *handle,
                WordPtr offset, WordPtr size,
                FieldPtr fld )
{
    #ifdef __GCC__
        CALLBACK_PROLOGUE
    #endif

    // Initialize the field, if you omit this the field
    // defaults to a maximum of 255 characters

    if( fld != NULL ){
        #define MAXCHARS 40
        FldSetMaxChars( fld, MAXCHARS );
    }

    // Get the string to use... normally this would come
    // from a database record

    *handle = .... // obtain the handle somehow
    *offset = 0; // offset within handle
    *size   = MemHandleSize( *handle ); // max size of data

    #ifdef __GCC__
        CALLBACK_EPILOGUE
```

```
    #endif

    return 0;
}
```

The handle can be a database record handle, or it can be a handle you've allocated specifically to hold the data. Handles must remain valid while the table is using them, and you are responsible for freeing them when the form is unloaded. If desired, text style items can also install a custom save routine:

```
void TblSetSaveDataProcedure( VoidPtr table, Word column,
                    TableSaveDataFuncPtr callback )
```

The custom save routine can modify the text after it's been edited:

```
Boolean MyTableSaver( VoidPtr table, Word row, Word column )
{
    Boolean redrawTable = true;

    #ifdef __GCC__
        CALLBACK_PROLOGUE
    #endif

    FieldPtr field = TblGetCurrentField( table );
    // do something with the field's handle
    // call TblMarkRowInvalid if you make changes

    #ifdef __GCC__
        CALLBACK_EPILOGUE
    #endif

    return redrawTable;
}
```

The custom save routine is called while the table item still has the input focus. Use **TblGetCurrentField** to obtain the field component for the item.

Custom-drawn items, those with the customTableItem style, must install a callback routine to draw the item:

```
void TblSetCustomDrawProcedure( VoidPtr table, Word column,
            TableDrawItemFuncPtr callback )
```

The callback is invoked with the item bounds:

```
void MyDrawFunction( VoidPtr table, Word row, Word Column,
                    RectanglePtr bounds )
{
    #ifdef __GCC__
```

```
        CALLBACK_PROLOGUE
    #endif

    // draw the item here...

    #ifdef __GCC__
        CALLBACK_EPILOGUE
    #endif
}
```

Custom-drawn items can store whatever they please in the integer and pointer values.

Initialization

Table initialization is done when a form is first opened, and generally follows this pattern:

- Each row is marked usable or nonusable.
- Each column is marked usable or nonusable.
- For each row, set the style of each item in the row, and initialize the integer and pointer values for that item, if applicable.
- For each column, install custom load, save, or draw routines, as appropriate.

Events

In response to user input, a table queues tblEnterEvent, tblSelectEvent, and tblExitEvent. tblSelectEvent is queued when the user selects a row by tapping on it:

```
// in the form event handler
switch( event->eType ){
    case tblSelectEvent: {
        Word      tableID = event->data.tblSelect.tableID;
        TablePtr  table = event->data.tblSelect.pTable;
        Word      row = event->data.tblSelect.row;
        Word      column = event->data.tblSelect.column;

        if( tableID == MyTable ){
            // row has been selected...
        }
        break;
    }
}
```

The event data identifies the item (by row and column) that was tapped to select the row. The selected row is inverted. If you want to change the contents of an item in response to a tap, handle tblEnterEvent. The event-specific data (tblEnter and tblExit) for both events is identical to that of tblSelectEvent.

Scrolling

Scrolling a table is done by shifting rows in one direction, removing rows from one end, and adding them to the other end. This is done with TblInsertRow and TblRemoveRow:

```
void TblInsertRow( TablePtr table, Word rowIndex )
void TblRemoveRow( TablePtr table, Word rowIndex )
```

Even though their names suggest otherwise, TblInsertRow and TblRemoveRow do not change the number of rows in the table: TblInsertRow inserts a new, uninitialized row ahead of the specified row and at the same time removes the last row in the table, while TblRemoveRow removes the specified row and adds a new, uninitialized row to the end of the table. After either function is called, the application must initialize the new row and mark it usable if the row is to be displayed.

TblInsertRow and TblRemoveRow do not redraw the table. This lets you add or remove several rows at a time without excessive flicker. When you're done making changes, call TblMarkTableInvalid to mark all rows as invalid:

```
void TblMarkTableInvalid( TablePtr table )
```

Then call TblRedrawTable to redraw the invalid rows:

```
void TblRedrawTable( TablePtr table )
```

Whenever you make changes to a row you should also mark it as invalid using TblMarkRowInvalid so that it is redrawn the next time TblRedrawTable is called.

Bitmaps and Icons

A *bitmap* is an image displayed by the application as part of its user interface. An *icon* is the application's image as displayed in the application list. Palm OS 1.0 and 2.0 only recognize monochrome (black and white) images. Palm OS 3.0 supports 4-bit grayscale images as well as monochrome images.

The differences between bitmaps and icons are few but important. Bitmaps can be any size, but icons are limited to a size of 22 pixels wide by 22 pixels high for large icons and 16 pixels wide by 9 pixels high for small icons. Bitmaps can use any identifier, but assign 1000 to the large icon and 1001 to the small icon.

The Constructor bitmap editor, shown in Figure 4.27, and icon editor are very similar and should be familiar to anyone who has used a painting tool like Paint on Windows.

Monochrome bitmaps and icons are defined in PilRC as follows:

```
BITMAP ID MyBitmapID "thebitmap.bmp"
ICON "theicon.bmp"
SMALLICON "smallicon.bmp"
```

The images are Windows bitmaps stored in separate files that are converted to the Palm image format.

Miscellaneous Tasks

In this section we describe some common tasks your application may wish to perform.

Handling Find Requests

Your application should participate in global Find operations whenever possible. This requires handling three launch codes: sysAppLaunchCmdSaveData, sysAppLaunchCmdFind, and sysAppLaunchCmdGoTo.

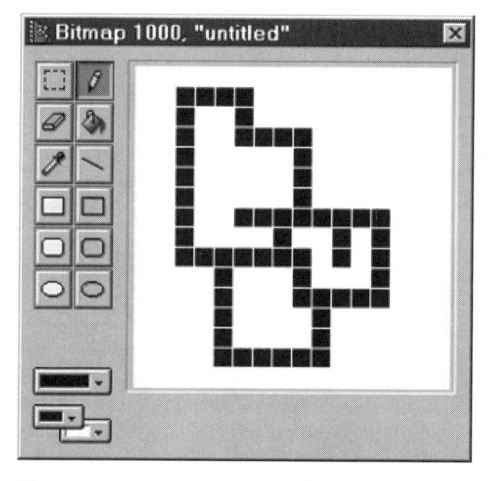

Figure 4.27 Constructor's bitmap editor.

How Global Find Works

To start a global Find operation, the user taps the Find button, enters the search text in the Find dialog, and presses the dialog's OK button. Palm OS then performs these steps:

1. sysAppLaunchCmdSaveData is sent to the active application to ask it to save its data. The application then asks any open forms to save their data by calling FrmSaveAllForms.

2. sysAppLaunchCmdFind is sent in turn to each application, starting with the active application. Each application searches its saved data for the requested string, reporting any successful matches into the Find results dialog shown in Figure 4.28. The search continues until there are no more applications or there is no more room on the Find results dialog to display any more matches. If the search stops because of lack of display space, the user is given the option to continue the search, at which point the search resumes where it left off.

3. If the user cancels the Find operation, the active application continues running as if nothing has happened.

4. If the user selects a match belonging to the active application, the system sends sysAppLaunchCmdGoTo as a subcall launch. The application queues a FrmGotoForm event to display the selected data.

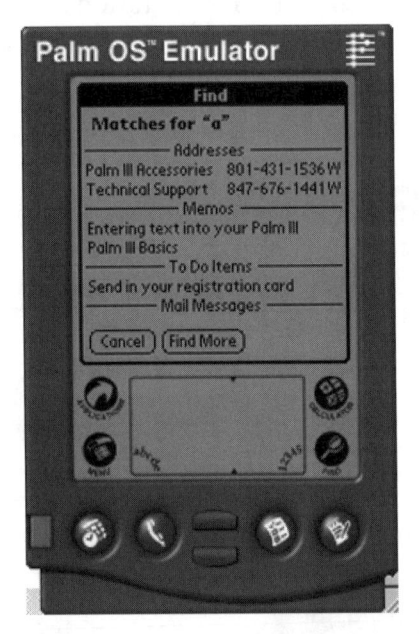

Figure 4.28 The Find results dialog.

5. Otherwise, the active application is stopped and a new application is launched with sysAppLaunchCmdGoTo, this time as an initializing launch. The new application immediately jumps to the correct form to display the selected data.

An application must be able to process sysAppLaunchCmdFind without access to its global data, or else relaunch itself to recover its global data.

Find Parameters

When your application is launched via sysAppLaunchCmdFind, the parameter block passed to PilotMain points to a FindParamsType structure, as defined in <UI/Find.h>, containing the following fields:

```
typedef struct {
    Word    dbAccesMode; // typo in header, note spelling!
    Word    recordNum;
    Boolean more;
    Char    strAsTyped[maxFindStrLen+1];
    Char    strToFind[maxFindStrLen+1];
    Word    lineNumber;
    Boolean continuation;
    // other private fields that are not to be accessed
} FindParamsType;
```

The search text as typed by the user is in the strAsTyped member, while a lowercase version of the search text is in the strToFind member. Searches are normally case insensitive, so most applications use the strToFind member as the search string.

One of the underlying assumptions of the global Find operation is that applications store their data in Palm record databases, with related data grouped into *records*. The dbAccesMode member is the access mode to use when opening the databases, while recordNum is the record index to start searching at. We discuss Palm databases in Chapter 5. There's nothing that says that you have to use a Palm database, however, and you can certainly interpret the record number differently.

The continuation member will be true if your application is being called yet again as part of the same Find operation. This happens when there are more matches in your application than can be drawn in the Find results dialog—if the user chooses to find more matches, your application is called again to continue its search.

The more and lineNumber members are modified by the application as part of the matching process. The application sets more to false when it starts the search, only setting it to true if it runs out of room on the Find results dialog, notifying the global Find that it's not done searching its data. The lineNumber member is incremented by the application each time a match is found and displayed in the Find results dialog.

Searching for Matches

The following pseudocode demonstrates how to handle a Find operation within your application:

```
draw header with FindDrawHeader
if FindDrawHeader returns true
    // no more room is available
    // more has been set to true by FindDrawHeader
    return
endif
set more = false
open database using dbAccesMode
set rec = recordNum
loop
    on occasion, check for pending events
    if pending events
        set more = true
        cleanup
        return
    endif
    find matching record starting at rec
    if not found
        set more = false
        cleanup
        return
    endif
    save record information with FindSaveMatch
    if FindSaveMatch returns true
        // no more room is available
        // more has been set to true by FindSaveMatch
        // record index of last match has been saved
        cleanup
        return
    endif
    draw record in Find results dialog
    set lineNumber = lineNumber + 1
endloop
cleanup
return
```

The first step is to draw the application's name as a header on the Find results dialog using FindDrawHeader:

```
Boolean FindDrawHeader( FindParamsPtr findParams, CharPtr title )
```

If true is returned, there is no more room left on the dialog and your application should abort the search and exit back to the system. FindDrawHeader sets the more member to true to ensure that the system calls the application again if the user continues with the search.

Otherwise, the search starts: initialize more to false, open the database, and perform any other initialization before the search actually begins. Then, starting with the record at index recordNum, search for a record that matches the string. Since the layout of your database is known only to your application, only your application can perform this search. You can use FindStrInStr to help with the search:

```
Boolean FindStrInStr( CharPtr strToSearch, CharPtr strToFind,
                      WordPtr position )
```

FindStrInStr assumes that the string to find is in lowercase and performs a case-insensitive search, returning true and an offset if a match was found.

If no match is found and there are no more records to search, set more to false and return to the system. If no match is found and there are more records to search, continue with the search.

If a match is found, call FindSaveMatch to save the record number, position within the record, and other pertinent information about the match:

```
Boolean FindSaveMatch( FindParamsPtr findParams, UInt recordNum,
                       Word position, UInt fieldNum, DWord customData,
                       UInt dbCardNum, LocalID dbID )
```

If FindSaveMatch returns true, there is no more room on the Find results dialog, so return to the system—FindSaveMatch has saved the record number and set more to true so that the Find operation will call your application again, this time with the number of the last matching record.

Otherwise, there is room to display a single line of data on the Find results dialog. Use FindGetLineBounds to get the drawing boundaries:

```
FindGetLineBounds( FindParamsPtr findParams, RectanglePtr r )
```

Once you have the bounds, use WinDrawChar to draw a string into the Find results dialog, being careful not to draw outside the rectangle boundaries. The string you draw is drawn from the matching record. Then, increment the lineNumber member and continue the search.

While searching, check to see if the user has pressed a button or tapped the screen by calling EvtSysEventAvail:

```
if( ( recordNumber & 0xff ) == 0 && EvtSysEventAvail( true ) ){
    findParams->more = true;
    // cleanup first, then leave
    return;
}
```

You don't need to check for events when processing each record. A common strategy is to check when searching every 16th record. Just be responsive to any user input.

Displaying the Selected Data

The system remembers which application drew which line in the Find results dialog. If the user selects a match, the system launches the appropriate application with the sysAppLaunchCmdGoTo launch code. The application is responsible for loading and initializing the appropriate form based on the data that was saved with FindSaveMatch. That data is passed back to the application via the PilotMain parameter block, which points to a structure of type GoToParamsType:

```
typedef struct {
    Word    searchStrLen;
    Word    dbCardNo;
    LocalID dbID;
    Word    recordNum;
    Word    matchPos;
    Word    matchFieldNum;
    DWord   matchCustom;
} GoToParamsType;
```

Often, the application just closes the active form and queues frmLoadEvent and frmGotoEvent to load and initialize the appropriate form:

```
Err ProcessGoToData( GoToParamsPtr goToData )
{
    EventType event;
    FormPtr   active = FrmGetActiveForm();

    MemSet( &event, sizeof( EventType ), 0 );

    if( active != NULL ){
        // Post a close event for the current form
        event.eType = frmCloseEvent;
        event.data.frmLoad.formID = FrmGetFormId( FrmGetActiveForm() );
        EvtAddEventToQueue( &event );
    }
    // Post a load event, substitute the appropriate form ID
    event.eType = frmLoadEvent;
    event.data.frmLoad.formID = EditFormID;
    EvtAddEventToQueue( &event );
```

```
    // Post a goto event, copy the data
    event.eType = frmGotoEvent;
    event.data.frmGoto.formID = EditFormID;
    event.data.frmGoto.recordNum = goToData->recordNum;
    event.data.frmGoto.matchPos = goToData->matchPos;
    event.data.frmGoto.matchLen = goToData->searchStrLen;
    event.data.frmGoto.matchFieldNum = goToData->matchFieldNum;
    event.data.frmGoto.matchCustom = goToData->matchCustom;
    EvtAddEventToQueue( &event );
}
```

If called as a subcall launch, the PilotMain should immediately exit after queuing these messages, otherwise it enters its event loop as it would if a normal launch occurred.

Multibyte characters complicate life somewhat, so refer to the chapter on building localized applications in the *Palm OS Programmer's Companion* for advice on responding to sysAppLaunchCmdGoTo in non-English locales.

A complete example of a Find operation that doesn't involve any database access is found in the UI Test application.

Saving and Restoring State

When closed, many applications save their current state, restoring it the next time the application is launched. The simplest way to save and restore state is to use the application preferences routines, PrefGetAppPreferences and PrefSetAppPreferences. First, define a structure to hold the application state:

```
struct AppPreferences {
    Word lastFormID;
};

AppPreferences Prefs;                // global variable to save state
#define CREATORID 'ERIC'; // replace with your creator ID
```

When your application is stopping, save the current state:

```
PrefSetAppPreferences( CREATORID, 0, 0, &Prefs, sizeof( Prefs ), true );
```

The last argument to PrefSetAppPreferences determines whether the preferences are saved when a HotSync is performed. If false, the preferences are saved to a different area that is not backed up. These are actually two different areas, meaning your application can have preferences that are backed up and preferences that aren't. You can also assign version and ID numbers to preferences in order to store multiple sets of preferences.

When your application starts, restore the state:

```
Word  size = sizeof( Prefs );
SWord rc = PrefGetAppPreferences( CREATORID, 0, &Prefs, &size, true );
if( rc != noPreferenceFound ){
    // initialize based on the stored preferences
} else {
    Prefs.lastFormID = MainFormID;
}
FrmGotoForm( Prefs.lastFormID );
```

If no preferences are found, be sure to initialize the state accordingly.

The Phone Book User Interface

We now know enough to develop a user interface for the Phone Book application we discussed in Chapter 1. The user interface is shown in Figure 1.1 and looks a lot like the built-in Address Book application. This is completely intentional—using the built-in applications as models for your own applications is generally a good design strategy. You'll find the source code for Phone Book on the CD-ROM, in the folder labeled Phone Book. The version discussed here is found in the PhbkUIOnly subfolder. Since we haven't discussed how to create or access data that persists beyond an application's lifetime, other than application preferences, this version uses hard-coded data to demonstrate the user interface. The data is actually compiled into the application as a set of string list resources. In the chapters that follow we'll modify Phone Book to use Palm databases and external databases to store its information. To end this chapter, we discuss how the Phone Book user interface was designed and how we'll be able to add database support in later chapters.

Application Design

Whether you're basing your application on a preexisting model or not, ask yourself a few questions in the design phase:

- **What's the purpose of the application?** The purpose must be clear and focused. If the application has no clear purpose, there's no point in writing it—it'll be hard to convince anyone to use it. If the purpose isn't focused on a single area, consider writing it as two or more separate applications, each focused on one part of the overall purpose.

The Unix philosophy of "do one thing well" is very applicable to the Palm Computing platform, because a narrow focus discourages you from bloating your application with more and more features.

- **Who will use it, how will they use it, and when will they use it?** Picture your typical users. An application used primarily at the office or at home has different requirements than an application used on the go by a busy traveler or outside in cold weather by a field engineer.

- **What features will it offer?** Avoid features that require too much memory or take too long to perform. A handheld is not a replacement for a desktop computer. Users might be willing to wait a bit while their desktop chugs away, but the responsiveness of their handheld devices can't be compromised.

- **Does it require data synchronization?** Decide where the data ultimately resides. Do your users just need to back up their data, or do they need to get it in and out of an external database?

The answers to these questions guide the overall design of your application. Here are the answers for the Phone Book application:

- **Purpose:** To display employee phone numbers.
- **Users:** Any employee about to phone or fax another employee.
- **Features:** Store employee name, department name, email address, various phone numbers. Quick number lookup, sorted names, participation in global Find.
- **Synchronization:** Yes. The data will reside (later on) in an external database of employee information.

With these answers in mind, we can start our user interface design.

The User Interface

User interface design is never easy: There are so many possible ways to present information, and the good ways are not always obvious. That's why using a built-in application as a model is helpful, because it immediately narrows the list of possibilities.

Whether you have a model or not, the purpose of your application should always guide its user interface design, particularly the design of the main form. If the main form doesn't make the purpose obvious, redesign the form or restate the purpose.

The purpose of Phone Book is to display employee phone numbers. Thus, the main form should display employee names and employee phone numbers, just like Address Book does. A table component is the natural choice to display two columns of information.

If the company is large enough, however, there is a chance that two employees have the same name, so we're going to display the employee's department name as well, on the theory that it's much less likely that two employees with identical names work in the same department. Showing the department name helps the user decide which employee is the one to contact, and a table certainly has no problem displaying a third column of information. The department name is less important than either the employee name or the phone number, though, so we're going to display an abbreviated department name—for example, *HR* instead of *Human Resources* or *Fin* instead of *Finance*—and we're going to provide an option to *not* display the department name in order to free up more space for the employee name.

The main form must also provide a way to quickly look up a particular name. The Address Book uses a lookup field: As the user enters characters, the Address Book selects the first record that matches. This seems like a reasonable feature, so we'll include a lookup field on the main form as well.

To change the sort order of the employee names, we'll provide a preferences dialog to choose between First Name, Last Name or Last Name, First Name formats. The dialog will also let the user select which phone number to display on the main form and whether the department name is displayed. We'll add an item to the Options menu to invoke the preferences dialog.

Finally, if the user taps a row in the table we'll bring up a dialog that displays detailed information about the employee, including the full name of the department and all the employee's phone numbers (fax, external, or extension).

This version of Phone Book is strictly read-only; we'll add the ability to modify the data later.

The Data Interface

A well-designed application separates the data from the user interface, so that changes to one don't necessarily affect the other. The user interface obtains the data it requires with a *data interface*, a set of functions or classes that hide the data model from the rest of the application.

Classes

The Phone Book application uses the PhoneData class. PhoneData is an abstract class that defines methods to access an abstract database. Concrete subclasses are defined to obtain the data from a variety of sources, whether it be from a string list, a Palm database, or an external database. This version of Phone Book defines the subclass StringListPhoneData to read the data from a set of string lists. Other subclasses are defined in later chapters.

The PhoneData class represents a particular employee using the PhoneEntry class. Each instance of PhoneEntry contains the complete information for a particular employee, stored as a series of strings. The strings are instances of the PString class, a utility class for dealing with reference-counted strings.

Virtual Functions Revisited

An abstract class defines virtual functions that are inherited and implemented by its subclasses, but virtual functions can only be used when global data is available. Since we want the Phone Book application to participate in the global Find operation, we have to work around the global data limitations using one of the strategies described in Chapter 3.

Because of restrictions beyond our control, the version of Phone Book we're going to build in Chapter 8 requires us to recover the global data block by relaunching the application, so we could use this strategy for all versions. It's certainly convenient, because relaunching allows us to use proper, compiler-generated virtual function tables. Still, the global data recovery technique is unsupported and should be avoided unless absolutely necessary, which means simulating virtual functions using dispatch tables or cover classes.

So what we're going to do is build two versions of our abstract class: one that uses virtual functions and one that simulates them with a dispatch table. A macro will select which version we want to use: The Phone Book we're building here uses the simulated virtual functions.

PART TWO

Databases

CHAPTER 5

Palm Databases

As you saw in Chapter 2, Palm OS organizes the storage heaps into databases. These databases are the only way to permanently store data on a Palm device, because there is no filesystem. This chapter introduces you to Palm databases and shows you how to create and use them in your own applications. You'll also be able to compare them to the relational databases discussed in the next chapter. An understanding of Palm databases is specifically required to use the Oracle Lite Consolidator, which we discuss in Part Three.

What's a Palm Database?

A *Palm database* is a set of memory blocks allocated from the storage heap. The memory blocks are linked together to form a single entity managed by the Palm OS Data Manager. The memory blocks do not have to be contiguous (next to each other) or be of equal size and can come from different storage heaps (Palm OS 1.0 and 2.0 only, in Palm OS 3.0 there is only a single heap), although they must all reside on the same memory card.

Records versus Resources

There are two kinds of Palm databases. A *resource database* manages a set of *resources*, which are memory blocks tagged with a resource type (a 4-byte unsigned value) and a resource ID (a 2-byte signed value). A *record database* manages a set of *records*, which are memory blocks tagged with a positional index (a 2-byte unsigned value) and a unique ID (a 3-byte unsigned value).

TIP The memory blocks in a database are allocated as handles, not as fixed blocks. This allows the records or resources in a database to be moved and resized as necessary by the application or the database. To read a record or resource, the handle must first be locked. Directly writing to a record or resource is not allowed because the storage heap is write-protected; system functions must be used instead, as we'll see later in this chapter.

The differences between a resource database and a record database are quite minor. Data Manager functions are used to manage these databases, and the internal database structures are almost identical. Certain Data Manager functions are only meant for use with one or either type of database, however, so be sure to use the correct functions. (It's easy to identify the functions, because they have *Record* or *Resource* in their names.)

Resources and records *are* treated differently in some respects. Records are ordered and are identified by index. Records also have a unique ID that is used for synchronization purposes, since the record's position can change. Resources are unordered and are identified solely by type and ID. When resources and records are treated identically, however, we'll refer to them generically as *database entries*.

All databases participate in the HotSync process. Resource databases are backed up to the desktop. Record databases are either backed up or else undergo record-by-record synchronization with an external data source. Part Three of this book discusses how to synchronize Palm databases with external databases.

The Database Header

A memory block called the *database header* maintains the list of entries (stored by local ID) in a database as well as additional information about the database. The database header is allocated when a database is created and defines the basic properties of the database:

- The creator ID and type of the database. The creator ID (a four-byte character value) identifies the application that "owns" the database; when an application is deleted from the system any databases with a matching creator ID are also removed. The type (also a four-byte character value) identifies the purpose of the database; DATA is a common choice as a type.
- The name of the database. The name must be unique among all installed databases and less than 32 characters long. As was mentioned in Chapter 2, include the creator ID (which is guaranteed to be unique if you've registered it with Palm Computing) in the database name to ensure uniqueness.
- Whether the database stores resources or records.

The header also includes information about the current state of the database (whether it's opened or closed) and optional fields for storing additional application-defined information. The database header is accessed using the DmDatabaseInfo and DmSetDatabaseInfo functions.

Basic Database Management

Databases are managed much like files are on other platforms: the Palm OS Data Manager provides functions to create, open, close, delete, describe, and enumerate databases.

Creating a Database

There are three ways to create a Palm database. The first way is to have users download a PDB file from the desktop using the Install Tool, the same way they install an application. It requires a bit of extra work on the part of the user, but it can be a convenient way to initialize an application. We don't discuss PDB files in this book other than to say this: If you want to create a PDB file, have your application create and populate a Palm database. Perform a HotSync and then look in the Palm Desktop backup folder for the PDB file that corresponds to the Palm database.

The other two ways are to use the Palm OS functions DmCreateDatabase and DmCreateDatabaseFromImage. The former creates an empty database, while the latter creates a new database from the in-memory image of a PDB file. The downside to creating a database from a memory image is that it bloats the size of your application unnecessarily, since the image is not used after the database is initialized. The image is usually stored as a resource so that it gets downloaded as part of the application. When the application runs, it gets the resource handle and locks the memory in place before calling DmCreateDatabaseFromImage.

The prototype for DmCreateDatabase is as follows:

```
Err DmCreateDatabase( UInt cardNo, const Char * const nameP,
                ULong creator, ULong type, Boolean resDB )
```

where *cardNo* is the memory card (this should always be set to 0 because there's only one memory card in the current devices), *nameP* is the unique name (no more than 32 characters, including the null byte) of the new database, *creator* is the creator ID of the application that owns the database, and *type* is the user-defined database type. The last parameter, *resDB*, determines the kind of database to create: If true, a resource database is created; otherwise, a record database is created. DmCreate Database returns a nonzero value if an error occurred, which usually occurs if a database with the same name already exists or if there isn't enough memory to create the database.

A common technique is to define preprocessor macros for the creator ID, database types, and database names for use with DmCreateDatabase and other system calls:

```
#define CREATORID  'ERIC'
#define DBTYPE     'DATA'
#define DBNAME     "MyData-Eric"

Err err = DmCreateDatabase( 0, DBNAME, CREATORID, DBTYPE, false );
if( err != 0 ){
    // handle creation error gracefully....
}
```

Be careful not to store any of these values in static or global data if your application needs to create or open databases when global data is not available, such as while processing a notification launch.

If your application uses more than one database, you should assign each database a different type, for example DAT1 and DAT2. Databases are generally found using the creator ID and the type, not by name.

Creating a database does not implicitly open it.

Opening a Database

You must open a database before accessing any of its records or resources, using one of these two functions:

```
DmOpenRef DmOpenDatabase( UInt cardNo, LocalID dbID, UInt mode )
DmOpenRef DmOpenDatabaseByTypeCreator( ULong type, ULong creatorID, UInt mode )
```

DmOpenDatabase is used when you know the memory card number (which currently is always 0) and the local ID (see Chapter 2) of the database header. DmOpenDatabaseByTypeCreator searches all installed memory cards for the database with the given type and creator ID. DmOpenDatabaseByTypeCreator is the function normally used by applications to locate and open a database.

The third parameter to both functions is the access mode, a combination of one or more of the flags listed in Table 5.1. The access mode indicates how the application is going to use the database: whether it's going to write or just read records, whether other applications are allowed to access the database while the current application is using it, and whether secret records (discussed later in this chapter) are to be shown.

Both functions return a reference to the database if the open succeeds, or null if the open fails. Use the DmGetLastErr function to obtain the reason for the failure. Failure usually occurs if the database can't be found or if it can't be opened with the desired access mode.

Most applications open databases as follows:

```
UInt                    mode = dmModeReadWrite;
DmOpenRef               dbRef;
```

Table 5.1 Database Access Mode Flags

FLAG	MEANING
dmModeReadWrite	Read-write access to the database.
dmModeReadOnly	Read-only access to the database.
dmModeWriteOnly	Write-only access to the database.
dmModeExclusive	Exclusive access to the database. The open fails if another application has the database open. No other application will be allowed to access the database once it is open.
dmModeShowSecret	Don't skip over secret records.
dmModeLeaveOpen	Don't automatically close the database when the application quits.

```
SystemPreferencesType prefs;

PrefGetPreferences( &prefs );
if( !prefs.hideSecretRecords ){
    mode |= dmModeShowSecret;
}

dbRef = DmOpenDatabaseByTypeCreator( DBTYPE, CREATORID, mode );
if( !dbRef ){
    // If error, assume database doesn't exist, so create it...
    Err err = DmCreateDatabase( 0, DBNAME, CREATORID, DBTYPE, false );
    if( err != 0 ){
        // handle error gracefully...
    }

    dbRef = DmOpenDatabaseByTypeCreator( DBTYPE, CREATORID, mode );
    if( !dbRef ){
        // should never happen, since we just created it, but
        // handle just in case...
    }

    // If the database requires any initialization, this is where
    // you do it, after it's been opened.
}
```

System preferences are checked to see if secret records should be shown or not, and the database is opened with nonexclusive, read-write access. If the database could not be opened, most applications assume it doesn't exist and create an empty database.

Closing a Database

As soon as an application is finished with an open database, it should close it using the DmCloseDatabase function:

```
Err DmCloseDatabase( DmOpenRef dbRef )
```

Further access to the database requires that the application reopen the database. Closing a database does not unlock any locked database entries. If there is a chance that database records are still in a locked or busy state, DmResetRecordStates can be called:

```
DmResetRecordStates( dbRef );
DmCloseDatabase( dbRef );
```

There is a performance penalty to calling DmResetRecordStates, however, and a well-written application that releases all its locks shouldn't have to call this function. The function is also documented as being for system use only, so avoid using it if you can.

If an application quits, any unclosed databases that weren't opened with the dmModeLeaveOpen access mode are implicitly closed by the system. Again, a well-written application shouldn't rely on this behavior.

Deleting a Database

Normally, applications do not delete their databases, relying on the system to do it for them when the application itself is deleted. If the application uses a database for temporary storage, however, it should delete the database when it's no longer needed. Deleting a database deletes the database header and all records or resources in the database and is accomplished using the DmDeleteDatabase function:

```
Err DmDeleteDatabase( UInt cardNo, LocalID dbID )
```

An open database cannot be deleted. You'll need the local ID for the database to delete it, which you can obtain in one of two ways. If you know the database name, use the DmFindDatabase function:

```
LocalID id = DmFindDatabase( 0, DBNAME ); // card, name
```

Alternatively, after you open the database use the DmOpenDatabaseInfo function to obtain its local ID:

```
LocalID id = 0;
DmOpenDatabaseInfo( dbRef, &id, NULL, NULL, NULL, NULL );
```

See the next section for details about DmOpenDatabaseInfo.

You can also prevent a database from being deleted with the DmDatabaseProtect function, which increments or decrements a protection count for the database:

```
Err DmDatabaseProtect( UInt cardNo, LocalID dbID, Boolean protect )
```

If the last parameter is true, the protection count is incremented; otherwise, it's decremented. The protection count of a database is always 0 right after a system reset.

Database Information

Information about the database is stored in the database header and is accessed via the DmOpenDatabaseInfo, DmDatabaseInfo, DmSetDatabaseInfo, and DmDatabaseSize functions. The DmOpenDatabaseInfo function returns basic information about an open database:

```
Err DmOpenDatabaseInfo( DmOpenRef dbRef, LocalIDPtr id,
                UIntPtr openCount, UIntPtr mode,
                UIntPtr cardNo, BooleanPtr resDB )
```

The first parameter is a reference to an open database. The remaining parameters are pointers to scalar (nonstructure) types. DmOpenDatabase Info is one of several Palm OS functions that return information via pointers instead of as return values. This lets you pass in NULL for the values that don't interest you. DmOpenDatabaseInfo returns the local ID of the database, the number of applications that currently have it open, the access mode used to open the database, the memory card it resides on, and whether it's a resource database or a record database.

DmDatabaseInfo and DmSetDatabaseInfo are used to read and write other database properties:

```
Err DmDatabaseInfo( UInt cardNo, LocalID id,
                CharPtr name, UIntPtr attributes,
                UIntPtr version, ULongPtr crDate,
                ULongPtr modDate, ULongPtr backupDate,
                ULongPtr modNumber, LocalIDPtr appInfoID,
                LocalID *sortInfoID, ULongPtr type,
                ULongPtr creator )
Err DmSetDatabaseInfo( UInt cardNo, LocalID id,
                CharPtr name, UIntPtr attributes,
                UIntPtr version, ULongPtr crDate,
                ULongPtr modDate, ULongPtr backupDate,
                ULongPtr modNumber, LocalID *appInfoID,
                LocalID *sortInfoID, ULongPtr type,
                ULongPtr creator )
```

The two functions have identical parameter lists: the card number and local ID of the database followed by a series of pointers. For DmDatabaseInfo, the pointers are used to return the information to the program. NULL pointers are ignored. For DmSetDatabaseInfo, the values of the non-NULL pointers become the new property values. The parameters are summarized in Table 5.2.

These functions are most often used to modify the database attributes and to access the custom information blocks. For example, this sequence marks a database as requiring backup:

```
LocalID id;
UInt    cardNum, attributes;

DmOpenDatabaseInfo( dbRef, &id, NULL, NULL, &cardNum, NULL );
DmDatabaseInfo( cardNum, id, NULL, &attributes, NULL, NULL, NULL,
                NULL, NULL, NULL, NULL, NULL, NULL );
```

Table 5.2 Parameters to DmDatabaseInfo/DmSetDatabaseInfo

PARAMETER	MEANING
name	The database name. For DmDatabaseInfo, must be an array at least 32 characters long.
attributes	Database attributes.
version	An application-defined version number. Functions such as DmOpenDatabaseByTypeCreator use this value to open the most recent version of a database.
crDate	The database creation date. Dates are represented as the number of seconds since January 1, 1904.
modDate	The date the database was last modified. This value is updated each time the database is closed. In Palm OS 3.0 and higher it is also updated when changes are made to a database, while the database is open.
backupDate	The date the database was last backed up.
modNumber	The modification number. This value is incremented each time a record is added, deleted, or modified.
appInfoID	The local ID of a custom application information block.
sortInfoID	The local ID of a custom sorting information block.
type	The type of the database.
creator	The creator ID of the database.

```
attributes |= dmHdrAttrBackup;
DmSetDatabaseInfo( cardNum, id, NULL, &attributes, NULL, NULL,
                  NULL, NULL, NULL, NULL, NULL, NULL );
```

Database attributes are summarized in Table 5.3. A general function for setting database attributes is as follows:

```
// Set database attributes:
//
//   dbRef   -- An open database.
//   bitmask -- The set of attributes to set or clear.
//   flags   -- The attributes to set, a subset of the bitmask.

void SetDBAttributes( DmOpenRef dbRef, UInt bitmask, UInt flags )
{
    LocalID id;
    UInt    cardNum, attributes;

    DmOpenDatabaseInfo( dbRef, &id, NULL, NULL, &cardNum, NULL );
    DmDatabaseInfo( cardNum, id, NULL, &attributes, NULL, NULL,
                    NULL, NULL, NULL, NULL, NULL, NULL );
    attributes &= ~bitmask;
    attributes |= flags;
```

```
        DmSetDatabaseInfo( cardNum, id, NULL, &attributes, NULL, NULL,
                    NULL, NULL, NULL, NULL, NULL, NULL, NULL );
}
```

The function uses masks to set or clear specific attributes:

```
// Set backup flag
SetDBAttributes( dbRef, dmHdrAttrBackup, dmHrdAttrBackup );

// Clear backup and appInfoDirty flags
SetDBAttributes( dbRef, dmHdrAttrBackup | dmHdrAttrAppInfoDirty, 0 );
```

Custom information blocks are discussed in the next section.

DmDatabaseSize returns the size of the database and the number of entries in the database:

Table 5.3 Database Attributes

ATTRIBUTE	MEANING
dmHdrAttrAppInfoDirty	The application information block has changed since the last HotSync.
dmHdrAttrBackup	Back up this database at the next HotSync, but only if there is no conduit defined for the application that owns the database, in which case the default backup conduit is used.
dmHdrAttrCopyPrevention	Prevent the database from being copied (such as by infrared beaming) onto another device.
dmHdrAttrHidden	Hide the database from being viewed. In Palm OS 3.2 or higher, applications with this bit set are not shown in the launcher.
dmHdrAttrLaunchableData	The database is not an application, but it can be launched—the launcher (Palm OS 3.2 or higher) starts the application that owns it, passing the database's local ID as a launch parameter.
dmHdrAttrOpen	The database is open. You cannot modify this attribute.
dmHdrAttrOKToInstallNewer	The backup conduit can install a newer version of this database, but with a different name.
dmHdrAttrReadOnly	The database is read-only.
dmHdrAttrResDB	The database is a resource database. If not set, the database is a record database. You cannot modify this attribute.
dmHdrAttrResetAfterInstall	Tells HotSync to reset the device after the database is installed.
dmHdrAttrStream	The database is a file stream (Palm OS 3.0 or higher).

```
ULong numRecords, totalBytesInDB, totalBytesInRecords;
DmDatabaseSize( cardNum, id, &numRecords, &totalBytesInDB,
                &totalBytesInRecords );
```

Custom Information Blocks

Two custom information blocks store information that doesn't belong in any record or resource but needs to be associated with the database. The information is considered part of the database and is used when processing the database. These blocks are allocated and initialized when the database is first created.

The first information block is referred to as the *application information block*, or appInfo for short, and is used to store general information about the database. To use the appInfo block, define a structure to hold the custom information:

```
struct MyAppInfo {
    AppInfoType categoryInfo;  // must be first
    UInt        size;          // size of structure
    UInt        someValue;
    Char        aString[20];
};
```

Since the appInfo block persists even when the application is not running, the structure must not contain any pointers or handles, as these may become invalid when the application quits or as memory blocks are moved or deallocated. Store variable-sized information at the end of the structure, and instead of pointers use offsets from the start of the structure. If you must refer to database entries, refer to them by their local IDs; the database itself tracks records and resources this way. We discuss obtaining local IDs for database entries later in this chapter.

If a record database uses the Category Manager functions to manage its categories, the first member of the appInfo block should be of type AppInfoType. This member maps category names to category identifiers. It must be initialized using the CategoryInitialize function when the appInfo block is created:

```
void CategoryInitialize( AppInfoPtr categoryInfo, Word nameList )
```

The first parameter is the address of the AppInfoType member, while the second parameter is the identifier of the app info string list resource that defines the category names. (Categories are introduced when we discuss record databases.) Remember that the app info string list must contain exactly 16 entries, even if most of those entries are empty strings.

If you think the structure will change as the application evolves, consider storing the size of the structure as a member, as shown in the preceding example. When the size of the structure changes, your application can check the stored size to determine whether an older or newer version of the structure is being used.

> **TIP**
> Application-defined information can be stored in two locations, either as part of the application's preferences or using the database application information block. Use application preferences to store information that is specific to the user of the device. Use the application information block if the information belongs with the data and you want others receiving a copy of the database—by infrared beaming or by installing a PDB file—to see the custom information, or you want the information available to the application's conduit.

Once the structure is defined, use DmNewHandle to allocate a memory block in the storage heap:

```
VoidHand appInfoHandle = DmNewHandle( dbRef, sizeof( MyAppInfo ) );
```

DmNewHandle takes a reference to an open database as its first parameter, to mark the block as belonging to the database. After allocating the block, assign it to the database header via DmSetDatabaseInfo:

```
LocalID appInfoID = MemHandleToLocalID( appInfoHandle );
DmSetDatabaseInfo( cardNum, dbID, NULL, NULL, NULL, NULL, NULL,
                   NULL, &appInfoID, NULL, NULL, NULL );
```

Note that you store the block in the database using its local ID, not its handle. The block is now part of the database. Next, initialize the structure. This is not as simple as it seems, however, because the storage heap is write-protected and the contents of a memory block can only be modified using the DmSet, DmStrCopy, or DmWrite functions:

```
Err DmSet( VoidPtr recordPtr, ULong offset, ULong bytes, Byte value );
Err DmStrCopy( VoidPtr recordPtr, ULong offset,
            const Char * const string );
Err DmWrite( VoidPtr recordPtr, ULong offset, const void *const src,
            ULong bytes );
```

So instead of initializing the structure directly, declare the structure as a local variable, initialize it, then copy it into the storage heap with DmWrite:

```
MyAppInfo  appInfo; // local copy
MyAppInfo *mem;     // copy in storage memory

// Initialize local copy
```

```
MemSet( &appInfo, sizeof( appInfo ), 0 );
appInfo.size = sizeof( appInfo );
appInfo.someValue = 99;
appInfo.aString[0] = 0;

// Copy local into storage memory
mem = (MyAppInfo *) MemHandleLock( appInfoHandle );
DmWrite( mem, 0, &appInfo, sizeof( appInfo ) );
CategoryInitialize( &mem->categoryInfo, CATEGORYLISTID );
MemHandleUnlock( appInfoHandle );
```

DmWrite copies a series of bytes into a memory block allocated from the storage heap. The memory block must first be locked, and DmWrite will not write outside the bounds of the block. CategoryInitialize is called after the storage memory is initialized, and it uses DmWrite to initialize the first member of the appInfo block. Don't call CategoryInitialize on the local copy of the appInfo block, as it will fail.

If the structure is large, your application may run out of stack space, so allocate a block of dynamic memory instead:

```
MyAppInfo *appInfo = MemPtrNew( sizeof( *appInfo ) );
MyAppInfo *mem;

if( appInfo ){
    MemSet( appInfo, sizeof( *appInfo ), 0 );
    appInfo->size = sizeof( *appInfo );
    appInfo->someValue = 99;
    appInfo->aString[0] = 0;

    mem = (MyAppInfo*) MemHandleLock( appInfoHandle );
    DmWrite( mem, 0, appInfo, sizeof( *appInfo ) );
    CategoryInitialize( &mem->categoryInfo, CATEGORYLISTID );
    MemHandleUnlock( appInfoHandle );
    MemPtrFree( appInfo );
}
```

The alternative is to initialize the members individually with DmWrite.

To recover the appInfo block at any time, use DmDatabaseInfo or DmGetAppInfoID to get its local ID and MemLocalIDToLockedPtr to obtain a pointer you can read from:

```
LocalID    appInfoID = 0;
MyAppInfo *appInfo = NULL;

// If you have a DmOpenRef, use:
//     appInfoID = DmGetAppInfoID( dbRef )
// instead of calling DmDatabaseInfo
DmDatabaseInfo( cardNum, dbID, NULL, NULL, NULL, NULL, NULL,
```

```
                NULL, &appInfoID, NULL, NULL, NULL );
appInfo = (MyAppInfo *) MemLocalIDToLockedPtr( appInfoID );

// Use it..

if( appInfo ){
    if( appInfo->someValue == 99 ){
        // do something...
    }

    MemPtrUnlock( appInfo );
}
```

As before, use DmSet, DmStrCopy, or DmWrite to modify the appInfo block. Call MemPtrUnlock to unlock the handle when you're done reading or writing the appInfo block.

The second information block is referred to as the *sorting information block*, or sortInfo for short, and stores data for sorting database entries. No Palm OS functions refer to the sorting information block, and very few applications use it. Define it just like you would the appInfo block, but use different parameters to DmDatabaseInfo and DmSetDatabaseInfo.

Enumerating Databases

There are two ways to enumerate the databases in the storage heap. The first is to get the local ID for each database in the memory card:

```
UInt count = DmNumDatabases( 0 ); // card 0
for( Int i = 0; i < count; ++i ){
    LocalID id = DmGetDatabase( 0, i ); // card 0

    // call DmDatabaseInfo or DmOpenDatabase using local ID
}
```

The second way is to use DmGetNextDatabaseByTypeCreator to return the databases that match a given type and/or creator ID:

```
Err DmGetNextDatabaseByTypeCreator( Boolean newSearch,
     DmSearchStatePtr searchInfoPtr, ULong type, ULong creator,
     Boolean onlyLatestVersion, UIntPtr cardNumber,
     UIntPtr localID );
```

For example, to search for all applications (databases of type appl) on the device:

```
DmSearchStateType searchInfo;
Boolean           newSearch = true;
```

```
UInt            cardNum;
LocalID         id;

for( newSearch = true;
    DmGetNextDatabaseByTypeCreator( newSearch, &searchInfo,
            'appl', 0, true, &cardNum, &id ) == 0;
    newSearch = false ){

    // call DmDatabaseInfo or DmOpenDatabase using local ID
}
```

Wildcards can be used to search for all database types and/or all database creator IDs (specify 0 for the type and/or creator ID), or the searching can be limited to a specific type and creator ID. DmGetNextDatabaseByTypeCreator can also ensure that the latest version of a database is returned.

Resource Databases

Resource databases are used to hold data that doesn't really fit into the linear model of a record database. Palm applications are resource databases: Each data or code segment generated by the compiler is a resource, as are the user interface elements. Resources usually store different kinds of data and are accessed randomly. Most applications just read resources, usually the application's own resources, rarely modifying or adding resources.

Reading Resources

A resource is tagged with both a type and an identifier. These values have no relationship to the type and creator ID of the database; they're simply used to classify resources within the database. When you design your user interface with Constructor, for example, the individual user interface elements are assigned types such as tFRM or tSTR, identifying the data structure stored in each resource. The identifiers are used to separate user interface elements of the same type.

Because reading resources is something every application does, Palm OS tracks all resource databases an application opens, including the application database itself, which is implicitly opened when the application is launched. To get a handle to a particular resource, call DmGetResource or DmGet1Resource:

```
VoidHand DmGetResource( ULong type, Int ID )
VoidHand DmGet1Resource( ULong type, Int ID )
```

Both functions return a handle to the given resource, or NULL if the resource wasn't found. The difference between the two is that DmGetResource searches all open resource databases while DmGet1Resource searches only the most recently opened resource database. To read the resource data, lock the handle and cast the pointer to the appropriate type:

```
VoidHand h   = DmGetResource( 'tSTR', MyStringID );
CharPtr  str = (CharPtr) MemHandleLock( h );
..... // do something with str
MemHandleUnlock( h );
DmReleaseResource( h );
```

To search for a resource in a specific resource database, use DmFindResource to find it and then call DmGetResourceIndex to obtain its handle:

```
Int      index = DmFindResource( dbRef, 'tSTR', MyResourceID );
VoidHand h     = DmGetResourceIndex( dbRef, index );
```

When done with the resource, be sure to unlock its handle with MemHandleUnlock and then release it with DmReleaseResource.

Creating Resources

To create a resource, call DmNewResource with the type, identifier, and size of the resource:

```
struct MyResource {
    .... // define as appropriate
};

VoidHand h = DmNewResource( dbRef, 'MYRS', 1000, sizeof( MyResource ) );
```

Alternatively, create a new memory block with DmNewHandle and then call DmAttachResource:

```
VoidHand h = DmNewHandle( dbRef, sizeof( MyResource ) );
DmAttachResource( dbRef, h, 'MYRS', 1000 );
```

Lock the handle and use DmSet, DmStrCopy, or DmWrite to initialize the new resource, just as we did with the appInfo block in the previous section.

Managing Resources

Palm OS provides other routines for managing resources, though it's rare for an application to use these functions. You can move a resource from one database to another by calling DmDetachResource and DmAttachResource:

```
Err DmAttachResource( DmOpenRef dbRef, VoidHand newData, ULong resType,
                ULong resID )
Err DmDetachResource( DmOpenRef dbRef, Int index, VoidHand *oldData )
```

Deleting a resource is done with DmRemoveResource:

```
Err DmRemoveResource( DmOpenRef dbRef, Int index )
```

Resources can be resized with DmResizeResource:

```
VoidHand DmResizeResource( VoidHandle handle, ULong newSize )
```

Information can be obtained about a resource, including its local ID, using DmResourceInfo:

```
Err DmResourceInfo( DmOpenRef dbRef, Int index, ULongPtr resType,
                IntPtr resID, LocalIDPtr localID )
```

There are also functions including DmNumResources and DmFindResourceType to enumerate resources.

Record Databases

Record databases are more common than resource databases. Records are ordered and categorized, and can be sorted and searched. A record has a unique identifier and some state flags for synchronizing with an external data source.

What's a Record?

Like a resource, a record is a memory block containing arbitrary data. Unlike a resource database, however, a record database tracks a number of things about each record it contains:

- The *order* of the record in the database, also referred to as its *index*. The index is a value from 0 to $N-1$, where N is the number of records in the database. Most Data Manager functions involving records use the index to identify the record.

- A *unique identifier* (a 3-byte integer) that never changes, also referred to as the *unique ID*. It uniquely identifies a record in the database, primarily for synchronization purposes.

- A *category* (a 4-bit integer, i.e., 16 possible categories) for classifying the record. Applications use categories to filter records for display.

- A *dirty* bit indicating the record has been modified.
- A *secret* bit indicating the record is a secret record. Secret records can be hidden from the user.
- A *delete* bit indicating the record has been deleted or archived but not yet removed from memory. The record information needs to remain in memory until the next synchronization so that the record can be deleted or archived on the desktop, but the record is skipped for all other operations.
- A *busy* bit indicating the record is locked for reading or writing.

This information, along with the local ID of the record, is managed by the database header and is not part of the actual record. The category value, dirty bit, secret bit, delete bit, and busy bit are collectively known as the *attributes* of the record and are packed together into a single byte.

The DmRecordInfo and DmSetRecordInfo functions are used to read and write the attributes and unique identifier of a record:

```
Err DmRecordInfo( DmOpenRef dbRef, UInt recordIndex,
                  UBytePtr attributes, ULongPtr uniqueID,
                  LocalIDPtr localID )
Err DmSetRecordInfo( DmOpenRef dbRef, UInt recordIndex,
                     UBytePtr attributes, ULongPtr uniqueID )
```

The two functions are almost identical, except that DmRecordInfo can return the local ID of a record as well as its attributes and unique ID. For DmRecordInfo, the pointers are used to return the information to the program (NULL pointers are ignored). For DmSetRecordInfo, the values of the non-NULL pointers become the new settings for the record.

Masks are defined for each attribute and are listed in Table 5.4. For example, to obtain the category number of a record and check if it's a secret record:

```
UByte    attributes;
UByte    category;
Boolean  isSecret;

DmRecordInfo( dbRef, index, &attributes, NULL, NULL );
category = ( attributes & dmRecAttrCategoryMask );
isSecret = ( ( attributes & dmRecAttrSecret ) != 0 );
```

To set a record's category, use the following:

```
Boolean SetCategory( DmOpenRef dbRef, UInt index, UInt category )
{
    UByte attributes;
```

Table 5.4 Record Attribute Masks

ATTRIBUTE MASK	MEANING
dmRecAttrBusy	If set, the record is busy. Can only be set by the system.
dmRecAttrCategoryMask	The category of the record, a value from 0 to 15.
dmRecAttrDelete	If set, the record has been deleted or archived.
dmRecAttrDirty	If set, the record is dirty.
dmRecAttrSecret	If set, the record is a secret record.

```
    if( category > 0x0F ) return false;

    DmRecordInfo( dbRef, index, &attributes, NULL, NULL );
    attributes &= ~dmRecAttrCategoryMask;
    attributes |= category;
    DmSetRecordInfo( dbRef, index, &attributes, NULL );
    return true;
}
```

Creating Records

To create a record, call DmNewRecord with the index and size of the record:

```
struct MyRecord {
    .... // define as appropriate
};

UInt     at = dmMaxRecordIndex; // add to the end
VoidHand h = DmNewRecord( dbRef, &at, sizeof( MyRecord ) );
.... // lock handle, call DmSet/DmWrite to initialize it, unlock it
DMReleaseRecord( dbRef, at, true ); // clears busy bit
```

Alternatively, create a new memory block with DmNewHandle and then call DmAttachRecord:

```
VoidHand h = DmNewHandle( dbRef, sizeof( MyRecord ) );
UInt     at = 0; // insert at the start
DmAttachRecord( dbRef, &at, h, NULL );
```

These functions are almost identical to those used to create resources, except that they insert a record at a specific index in the database. The second parameter of both functions points to an integer: On input it specifies the desired index, on output it holds the actual index of the new record. To insert a record at the beginning, use an index of 0. To insert a record at the end, use the constant dmMaxRecordIndex. If a record already exists at a given index, it and all the records that follow it are shifted up one position.

Newly created records are marked as dirty but have no other attributes set.

Accessing and Modifying Records

Reading a record is just a matter of calling DmQueryRecord to find a record by index and then locking the resulting handle:

```
VoidHand h = DmQueryRecord( dbRef, index );
MyRecord *rec = (MyRecord *) MemHandleLock( h );
.... // do something with the record
MemHandleUnlock( h );
```

Modifying a record requires a call to DmGetRecord instead of DmQueryRecord:

```
VoidHand h = DmGetRecord( dbRef, index );
MyRecord *rec = (MyRecord *) MemHandleLock( h );
DmSet( rec, sizeof( *rec ), 0 ); // modify it
MemHandleUnlock( h );
DmReleaseRecord( dbRef, index, true );
```

DmGetRecord sets the record's busy bit to prevent other applications from modifying it. After marking the record as busy and locking it, use DmSet, DmStrCopy, or DmWrite to modify it. When finished, unlock the handle and then clear the busy bit by calling DmReleaseRecord. Note that unlike DmReleaseResource, DmReleaseRecord refers to the record by its index, not its handle. If the last parameter to DmReleaseResource is true, the record's dirty bit is set after clearing the busy bit. The dirty bit identifies which records in a database have been modified and need to be synchronized at the next HotSync. After synchronization, the dirty bit is cleared automatically.

Always release a record as soon as possible once you're done modifying it.

Removing Records

Removing a record from a database isn't as simple as deallocating the record and removing all traces of its existence from the database header. If the database is synchronized with an external data source, the data source must be notified about the removal at the next HotSync so that it can perform the same operation on its own data. To do this, the database must carefully track record removals. On the other hand, your application may not care about synchronizing its data.

To handle these different requirements, there are four ways to remove a record from a database. The first way is to explicitly deallocate it using DmRemoveRecord:

```
Err DmRemoveRecord( DmOpenRef dbRef, UInt index )
```

DmRemoveRecord deallocates the record's memory block and removes its entry from the database's list of records. The indexes of the records that follow it are all decremented by one. Once released, a record is gone; the database cannot track its removal.

The second way is to *delete* the record using DmDeleteRecord:

```
Err DmDeleteRecord( DmOpenRef dbRef, UInt index )
```

When a record is deleted, its memory block is freed but the entry for the record is not removed from the database's list of records. The local ID stored in the entry is set to 0 and the entry's delete bit is set, indicating the record has been deleted and should be ignored by the application. The unique ID is left intact, however, and at the next HotSync the synchronization process uses the ID to delete the data from the external data source (if there is one). After a synchronization, the entries are removed from the database.

A third way is to *archive* the record using DmArchiveRecord:

```
Err DmArchiveRecord( DmOpenRef dbRef, Int index )
```

Archiving is similar to deleting except that the record's memory block is not deallocated and the local ID stored in the record entry is left intact, as is the unique ID. The delete bit is set, however. At the next HotSync the synchronization process archives the data before removing it from memory.

The final way is to *detach* the record using DmDetachRecord:

```
Err DmDetachRecord( DmOpenRef dbRef, Int index, VoidHandle *handle )
```

Once detached, a record can be attached to a database using DmAttachRecord, as was shown in the previous section. Detaching and attaching records is used primarily to move data between databases. A detached record has no entry in any database until it is reattached.

If the database is sorted, use DmMoveRecord to move deleted or archived records to the end of the database:

```
DmDeleteRecord( dbRef, index );
DmMoveRecord( dbRef, index, DmNumRecords( dbRef ) );
```

Search operations stop at the first record whose delete bit is set, which is why it's important to move those records to the end. Note that the sorting functions we discuss shortly also move these records to the end.

Finding Records

There are several ways to find the index of a record. If you know the unique ID of the record, you can use the DmFindRecordByID function:

```
Err DmFindRecordByID( DmOpenRef dbRef, ULong uniqueID, UIntPtr index )
```

If you have the handle to a block of memory, you can search all open record databases using DmSearchRecord:

```
Int DmSearchRecord( VoidHand recordHandle, DmOpenRef *dbRef );
```

DmSearchRecord returns –1 if the record was not found. If found, the second parameter returns the reference to the open database.

Both DmFindRecordByID and DmSearchRecord perform linear searches to find the record. If a database is in sorted order, a binary search can be performed using DmFindSortPosition, as described in the next section.

Sorting Records

Three functions are available to sort records. DmInsertionSort and DmQuickSort are used to sort records using the insertion or quicksort sorting algorithms, respectively:

```
Err DmInsertionSort( const DmOpenRef dbRef, DmComparF *compare,
                     Int other );
Err DmQuickSort( const DmOpenRef dbRef, DmComparF *compare,
                 Int other );
```

TIP The quicksort and insertion sort algorithms both sort data in place, which makes them very suitable for use on limited-memory systems such as the Palm. Use the insertion sort if the number of records is small (less than 15 or so) or only a few records are out of place; otherwise, use the quicksort algorithm.

Both algorithms move deleted or archived records (records with the delete bit set) to the end of the database before sorting the remaining records. Because records hold arbitrary data, you must define a function that compares two records to return their relative order. A pointer to the function is passed as an argument to the sorting functions, along with a user-defined integer value. The sorting algorithms call the comparison function whenever they need to compare one record to another, passing the user-defined value as an argument. The prototype for the comparison function is defined by the DmComparF type:

```
typedef Int DmComparF( void *rec1, void *rec2, Int other,
                SortRecordInfoPtr info1, SortRecordInfoPtr info2,
                VoidHand appInfo )
```

The first two arguments to the comparison function are the records to be compared (passed as pointers since the record handles have already been locked in place by the sorting function). The third argument is the user-defined argument that was passed to the sorting function. The fourth and fifth arguments point to a SortRecordInfoType structure, with the attributes and unique ID of each record. SortRecordInfoType is defined as follows:

```
typedef struct {
    Byte attributes;
    Byte uniqueID[3];
} SortRecordInfoType;

typedef SortRecordInfoType *SortRecordInfoPtr;
```

The last argument to the comparison function is the database's appInfo block handle, if defined. The comparison function returns an integer value indicating the relative order of the two records: 0 if the records are equal, a negative value if the first record is less than the second record, or a positive value if the first record is greater than the second record.

As an example, consider a database whose records are defined with the following structure:

```
struct Record {
    Int  value;
};
```

The comparison function is very simple:

```
Int CompareRecord( void *rec1, void *rec2, Int other,
                SortRecordInfoPtr info1, SortRecordInfoPtr info2,
                VoidHand appInfo )
{
    #ifdef __GCC__
        CALLBACK_PROLOGUE
    #endif
```

```
    Int sortOrder =
        ((Record *) rec1)->value - ((Record *) rec2)->value;

    #ifdef __GCC__
        CALLBACK_EPILOGUE
    #endif

    return sortOrder;
}
```

This is a more complicated comparison function that sorts by category and then by value within a category:

```
Int CompareRecord( void *rec1, void *rec2, Int other,
                   SortRecordInfoPtr info1, SortRecordInfoPtr info2,
                   VoidHand appInfo )
{
    #ifdef __GCC__
        CALLBACK_PROLOGUE
    #endif

    // Get categories

    Int cat1      = ( info1->attributes & dmRecAttrCategoryMask );
    Int cat2      = ( info2->attributes & dmRecAttrCategoryMask );
    Int sortOrder = cat1 - cat2;

    // If categories equal, break tie using value in record

    if( sortOrder == 0 ){
        sortOrder =
            ((Record *) rec1)->value - ((Record *) rec2)->value;
    }

    #ifdef __GCC__
        CALLBACK_EPILOGUE
    #endif

    return sortOrder;
}
```

Once the compare function has been defined, sorting the database is just a matter of invoking the correct sorting algorithm:

```
DmInsertionSort( dbRef, &CompareRecord, 0 );
```

After sorting a database, insert new records in sorted order whenever possible, using DmFindSortPosition:

```
UInt DmFindSortPosition( DmOpenRef dbRef, VoidPtr newRecord,
                         SortRecordInfoPtr newRecordInfo,
                         DmCompareF *compar, Int other )
```

You'll need to initialize a SortRecordInfoType with the attributes of the new record, if needed for comparison purposes. A pointer to this structure is passed to the DmFindSortPosition along with a pointer to the new record (which you haven't yet added to the database), the same record comparison function used to sort the database, and a user-defined integer value. The return value is the position at which to insert the new record. For example:

```
Record              newRecord; // on stack
SortRecordInfoType  info;
UInt                pos;
VoidHand            h;
Record              *ptr;
UInt                attributes;

newRecord.value = 100; // initialize new record
MemSet( &info, sizeof( info ), 0 );
info.attributes = 2;   // category 2, no other flags set

pos = DmFindSortPosition( dbRef, &newRecord, &info, CompareRecord, 0 );

// Now create new record at that position, then initialize
// it from the stack-based record

h = DmNewRecord( dbRef, &pos, sizeof( Record ) );
ptr = MemHandleLock( h );
DmWrite( ptr, 0, &newRecord, sizeof( Record ) );
MemHandleUnlock( h );

// Now initialize entry in database

DmRecordInfo( dbRef, pos, &attributes, NULL, NULL );
attributes &= ~dmRecAttrCategoryMask;
attributes |= ( info.attributes & dmRecAttrCategoryMask );
DmSetRecordInfo( dbRef, pos, attributes, NULL );
```

Alternatively, you can use DmNewHandle to create a new, unattached record, use DmFindSortPosition to find its insertion point, and then attach it using DmAttachRecord.

DmFindSortPosition can also be used to perform a binary search of a sorted database. Initialize a new record with the search values, then call DmFindSortPosition as if you want to insert it into the database. Interpret the return value p as follows, where n is the number of records in the database:

- If $p = 0$, the record doesn't exist in the database.

- If $p = n$, the record is the last record.
- If $1 <= p <= n - 1$, the record *may* exist in the database. Compare the search record with the record at position $p - 1$ to see if the two records are equal.

The following function encapsulates this logic:

```
//
// Generic function to search for a given record.  Returns
// true if found and sets *position to the record index.
// Assumes the comparison function ignores the
// SortRecordInfoPtr and AppInfo arguments.
//

Boolean BinarySearch( DmOpenRef dbRef, UIntPtr position,
                      VoidPtr newRecord,
                      DmCompareF *compar, Int other )
{
    Boolean             found = false;
    VoidHand            h;
    VoidPtr             rec;
    SortRecordInfoType  recInfo; // dummy, won't be initialized
    UInt                n = DmNumRecords( dbRef );
    UInt                p = DmFindSortPosition( dbRef, newRecord,
                                    &recInfo,
                                    compar, other );

    if( p == 0 ){
        return false;
    } else if( p == n ){
        return true;
    }

    // Possibly a match, have to compare to p-1

    h = DmQueryRecord( dbRef, p-1 );
    rec = MemHandleLock( h );

    found = ( (*compar)( newRecord, rec, other, NULL, NULL, NULL ) == 0
);

    MemHandleUnlock( h );

    if( found && position ){
        *position = p-1;
    }

    return found;
}
```

For simplicity, this function assumes that the SortRecordInfoType values and the appInfo block are not required to perform the comparisons.

Categories

As we've already seen, records can be grouped into up to 16 categories. The Data Manager includes functions to access records by category. To count the number of records in a given category, use DmNumRecordsInCategory:

```
UInt DmNumRecordsInCategory( DmOpenRef dbRef, UInt category )
```

Counting requires a linear search of the database. To return the record's position in its category, use DmPositionInCategory:

```
UInt DmPositionInCategory( DmOpenRef dbRef, UInt index, UInt category )
```

The record's position is always zero-based, just like the index, and also requires a linear search of the database. To search for the next record in a particular category, use DmQueryNextInCategory:

```
VoidHand DmQueryNextInCategory( DmOpenRef dbRef, UIntPtr index,
                                UInt category )
```

The second argument serves as both input and output: On input, it's the index at which the search should start; on output, it's the index of the next record in that category, if any. If a matching record is found, its handle is returned. To find the record at a certain offset from another record in the same category, use DmSeekRecordInCategory:

```
Err DmSeekRecordInCategory( DmOpenRef dbRef, UIntPtr index,
                            Int offset, Int direction, UInt category )
```

The meanings of the arguments are listed in Table 5.5. If the seek fails, a nonzero value is returned.

DmNumRecordsInCategory, DmPositionInCategory, DmQueryNextInCategory, and DmSeekRecordInCategory automatically skip deleted or archived records. As well, the constant dmAllCategories can be used as a category value to signify that any or all categories are to be searched or counted.

The final category-specific Data Manager function is DmMoveCategory:

```
Err DmMoveCategory( DmOpenRef dbRef, UInt toCategory, UInt fromCategory,
                    Boolean markAsDirty )
```

Table 5.5 Arguments to DmSeekRecordInCategory

ARGUMENT	MEANING
dbRef	Database reference
index	On input, the index at which to start the search. On output, the index of the matching record
offset	The offset within the category, a positive number
direction	The search direction, either dmSeekForward or dmSeekBackward
category	The category number

Use this function to move all the records from one category into another category, optionally marking the moved records as dirty.

The names of categories can be managed using the Category Manager routines. We've already encountered the CategoryInitialize function, which initializes the appInfo block with the names of categories drawn from a string list resource. This function must be called when the appInfo block is first created in order to prepare the database for use by the Category Manager. The first category should always be "Unfiled," and it's common to use "Business" and "Personal" as the next two categories.

To find the index of a category given its name, use CategoryFind:

```
Word CategoryFind( DmOpenRef db, CharPtr name )
```

To find the name of a category given its index and copy it into a buffer, use CategoryGetName:

```
void CategoryGetName( DmOpenRef db, Word index, CharPtr nameBuffer )
```

The maximum length of a category name is defined by the constant dmCategoryLength. To truncate the name to fit a certain pixel width, including adding an ellipsis to the name, use CategoryTruncateName:

```
void CategoryTruncateName( CharPtr name, Word maxWidth )
```

Note that the name is edited in place. To use the category name as the label of a control component, typically a popup trigger, truncating the name to fit the control, use CategorySetTriggerLabel:

```
void CategorySetTriggerLabel( ControlPtr ctrl, CharPtr name )
```

You can initialize a list component with the current category names using CategoryCreateList:

```
void CategoryCreateList( DmOpenRef db, ListPtr list,
                        Word currentCategory,
```

```
                        Boolean showAll, Boolean showUneditables,
                        Byte numUneditableCategories,
                        DWord editingStringID, Boolean resizeList )
```

This function fills the given list component with each category name, adding an "All" category if showAll is true, and selecting currentCategory as the current selection. If showUneditables is true, CategoryCreateList skips over the first numUneditableCategories when filling the list, which is why you define the "Unfiled" category as the first category. If editingStringID is nonzero, it identifies a string resource that is added to the end of the list to edit the categories, as in "Edit Categories…"; otherwise no string is added. If the list is a popup list, set resizeList to true to resize the list to fit the categories; otherwise, set it to false to leave the list size unchanged. When done with the list, call CategoryFreeList:

```
    void CategoryFreeList( DmOpenRef db, ListPtr list, Boolean showAll,
                        DWord editingStringID )
```

This removes the items that were added to the list and frees any memory allocated by CategoryCreateList. The values of showAll and editingStringID should match the values that were passed to CategoryCreateList. For example, here is a function that pops up a list that lets the user select a category:

```
Word SelectCategory( DmOpenRef db, ListPtr list,
                    Word currentCategory )
{
    Short   currSel, newSel;
    CharPtr name;

    CategoryCreateList( db, list, currentCategory, false, false,
                    0, 0, true );

    currSel = LstGetSelection( list );
    newSel = LstPopupList( list );

    if( newSel != -1 && newSel != currSel ){
        name = LstGetSelectionText( list, newSel );
        currentCategory = CategoryFind( db, name );
    }

    CategoryFreeList( db, list, false, 0 );

    return currentCategory;
}
```

The list must be invisible and correctly positioned before calling SelectCategory. To let the user add, delete, or rename categories, call CategoryEdit:

```
Boolean CategoryEdit( DmOpenRef dbRef, WordPtr lastSelected,
                      DWord titleStringID,
                      Byte numUneditableCategories )
```

CategoryEdit displays a category-editing dialog. The dialog title is specified by the string resource titleStringID, and defaults to "Edit Categories" if the resource ID is 0. The last parameter specifies the number of uneditable categories to skip. CategoryEdit returns true if any category names were changed, and lastSelected is the category that was selected when the dialog was dismissed. For Palm OS 2.0, CategoryEdit is defined to have three arguments instead of four—see the definition of CategoryEditV20 in the Palm OS 3.0 documentation.

Secret Records

When a record is marked *secret*, its contents are private and shouldn't be used or displayed unless the Security application allows private records to be shown. You can check the current security settings as follows:

```
SystemPreferencesType prefs;

PrefGetPreferences( &prefs );
if( prefs.hideSecretRecords ){
    // don't display
} else {
    // do display
}
```

If private records are to be shown, specify the dmModeShowSecret access mode when opening a database:

```
UInt                 mode = dmModeReadWrite;
SystemPreferencesType prefs;

PrefGetPreferences( &prefs );
if( !prefs.hideSecretRecords ){
    mode |= dmModeShowSecret;
}
```

If dmModeShowSecret is not specified when the database is opened, the category functions that skip over deleted records (DmNumRecordsInDatabase, DmPositionInCategory, DmQueryNextInCategory, DmSeekRecordInCategory) also skip over secret records.

Phone Book and Palm Databases

The Phone Book application is easily modified to use Palm databases instead of hard-coded data. All we need to do is define a new subclass of PhoneData called PalmDBPhoneData. Instead of creating an instance of StringListPhoneData on startup, Phone Book creates an instance of PalmDBPhoneData. No user interface changes are required, because we were careful to separate the user interface from the data interface. You'll find the code for the modified Phone Book on the CD-ROM, in the PhbkPalmDB subfolder of the Phone Book folder.

PalmDBPhoneData stores its information in a record database, modeled closely against the PhoneEntry class that Phone Book uses to extract the information for a particular employee from whatever data source it's using. Although much improved over its predecessor, this version of Phone Book is far from perfect: There's no synchronization with an external data source, which means all the information has to be entered by hand. This could be a very tedious operation, especially when you know the data is sitting in a corporate database, ready for downloading. If only you knew how to extract that data from the database....

CHAPTER 6

Relational Databases

Data that is stored externally from your Palm device is often stored in relational databases, which are quite different from the Palm databases we just discussed. Relational databases come in many different flavors, but the basic concepts are the same no matter who sells them. This chapter introduces you to relational databases, discussing how they work and how to use them. If you're already an experienced database programmer, you won't find anything that's new here, but it's important to get everyone on common ground before moving on to data synchronization.

Examples in this chapter use the sample database from Sybase's Adaptive Server Anywhere (ASA) relational database system. A fully functional evaluation version of ASA for Windows 95/98/NT is included on the CD-ROM, and installation and usage instructions can be found in Appendix B. The concepts apply to all relational databases unless otherwise noted. Note that the UltraLite deployment technology we discuss in Part Three, Data Synchronization, is included with ASA, so be sure to select the UltraLite option when installing ASA.

What's a Database?

A *database* stores and organizes information for use by applications. The Palm databases we discussed in Chapter 5 store and organize information using the storage heaps. Databases on other platforms use the filesystem as a storage medium. Either way, databases are used both to preserve and to share information.

There are many ways to store and access information in a database, but in general they fall into one of two groups. The first group provides applications with direct access to the data: The application understands and directly manipulates the internal structure of the database, as with Palm databases. The second group hides the internal structure of the database, forcing all access to occur through a published interface and leaving the database free to organize its data as it pleases.

Record-Oriented Databases

Direct access to the data has the advantage of providing quick retrieval of information, especially if indexes or other data structures can be used to quickly locate the desired information. Typically, a C structure is defined to group related data, just like we did with the Phone Book example in the previous chapter. An employee database, for example, might define the following structure:

```
struct Employee {
    int  ID;
    char firstName[50];
    char lastName[50];
};
```

Data is read from and written to the database using this structure, referred to as a *record* of information. For in-memory databases, it's just a matter of obtaining a pointer to the record, like we did for the Phone Book records; for file-based databases, it's locating the offset of the record in the file and reading or writing the record as a single block. These databases can be referred to as *record-oriented databases* (see Figure 6.1).

Although data retrieval is quick, there are also disadvantages to direct data access:

- The structure of a record is usually platform-dependent, because it depends on the how the compiler packs and aligns the structure

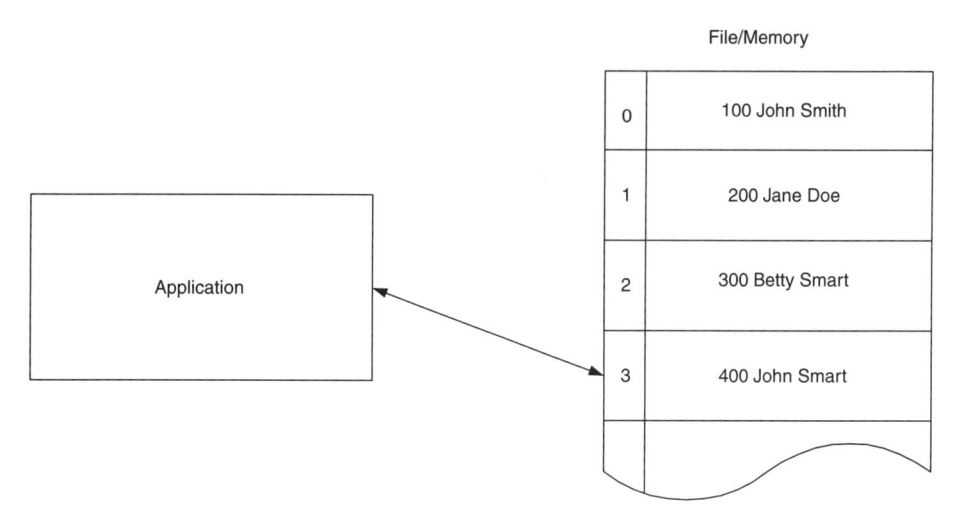

Figure 6.1 Accessing data in a record-oriented database.

members, the order in which the bytes in multibyte types are written (least significant byte to most significant byte or vice versa?), and the sizes of the types themselves (how big is an int in your compiler?).

- Keeping records in sorted order can be expensive, requiring many operations to move data in memory or on disk.
- Indexes or other data structures used for ordering records have to be updated whenever a record is updated, inserted, or deleted. Because a record is directly accessible, the programmer must remember to invoke functions to update the data structures whenever changes are made.
- Changes to the database's structure require the recompilation of all applications using the database and the reformatting of the data in the database.

To overcome or minimize these disadvantages, applications will use their own databases instead of sharing a single database. Data is then duplicated across different databases, wasting disk or memory space. Changes to data in one database are not automatically reflected in the other databases, which leads to inconsistencies.

Building and maintaining a record-oriented database can be a lot of work when done from scratch, but libraries are available to ease the programming burden. In some cases, the support is even built into the operating system, as is the case with Palm databases. Still, there are better ways to manage data.

Database Management Systems

Although record-oriented databases are appropriate for many purposes, the need to share data among different applications led to the development of *database management systems*. A database management system (DBMS) is a library or (more usually) a separate application (often referred to as a *database server*) that completely manages one or more databases. The data and the database server often run on a different machine, as shown in Figure 6.2. A DBMS hides the internals of a database from the applications that are using it: All access to the data occurs via the DBMS exclusively, never by direct access. The DBMS provides an interface for applications to use. If the interface is well designed, changes to the internal structure of the database do not generally affect the applications using the database.

The biggest disadvantage of a DBMS is the added overhead in terms of time and space. Database operations take longer because they must use the DBMS interface instead of directly accessing the data, especially if the DBMS runs as a separate application. And because a DBMS is a general-purpose data storage mechanism, it requires more space than a record-oriented database designed with a specific use in mind.

Generally, however, the advantages of a DBMS are seen to outweigh its disadvantages:

- Applications are insulated from changes to the structure of a database.
- The data is centralized, ensuring applications are always using correct data.
- Centralization also makes it easier to perform routine data management tasks, such as backups.
- Access to data is easily controlled by the DBMS. Roles can be assigned to users and privileges assigned to roles, limiting who can read or write data.

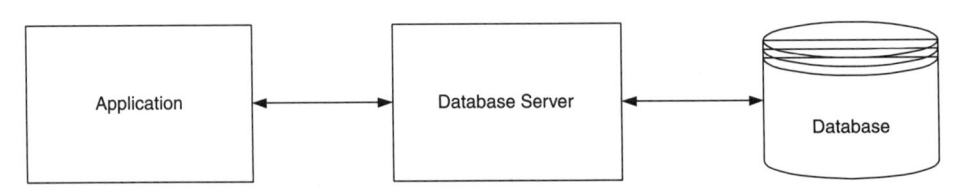

Figure 6.2 Accessing data with a database server.

- The DBMS can ensure the integrity of the data before it reaches the database by enforcing constraints on the data.
- Changes to the database can be applied together as a single *transaction*. Transactions are atomic, meaning that if any of the changes fail, the transaction stops and any changes that were applied as part of the transaction are *rolled back* to leave the database in the same state it was before the transaction started.

Although at first limited to large computers, database management systems are now found on all sizes of systems, although rarely on a system as small as the Palm Computing platform, at least up until now—Sybase's UltraLite technology, which we discuss in Chapter 8, is one of the first for handheld devices.

Database Management System Interfaces

The interface to a DBMS is almost as important as the DBMS itself, because it's the link between an application and its data. The interface of choice depends on the language the application is being written in, but in C/C++ there are three common approaches.

The first approach is the obvious one: provide a library of functions for communicating with the DBMS. Such a library is referred to as a native *call-level interface* (CLI). Using the CLI is a matter of linking the library with the application and making the appropriate API calls from within the application. If the DBMS runs as a separate application, the library uses a network protocol to communicate with the database server. The protocols are usually proprietary, meaning that only the vendor of the DBMS can provide a native call-level interface to its system. Sometimes, a set of C++ classes is provided as an interface, but unless the database is an object-oriented database (see the next section), these classes are layered on top of an existing call-level interface.

The second approach is really just a variant of the first, but it attempts to solve the major problem with native call-level interfaces: the lack of portability. Each DBMS vendor's interface is different from any other vendor's interface, making it hard to write portable code that runs on a number of systems. On the Windows platform, Microsoft developed the Open Database Connectivity (ODBC) interface to solve this problem. ODBC is a call-level interface that provides a single set of functions for applications to use. DBMS vendors and other third-party developers write libraries, called ODBC drivers, which adhere to this interface. The ODBC driver uses the native call-level interface or the proprietary network protocol to communicate with the DBMS. In theory, this prevents the application from being tied to a single DBMS. In practice, however, there are always differences between the various databases that can't be hidden, but ODBC does provide a high level of portability that would be hard to achieve otherwise. Although Windows-oriented, ODBC is available for use on other systems, most notably on Unix.

The last approach is to use an *embedded* interface. In an embedded interface, DBMS commands (for relational databases, these are written in a language referred to as SQL, which we explore later in this chapter) are actually inserted directly into the C/C++ source code. A special preprocessor is used to convert this mixture of DBMS commands and C/C++ code into pure C/C++ that communicates with the DBMS via a private, proprietary interface which may be different from any public call-level interface. There are several advantages to the embedded approach:

- DBMS commands are written in their native form, letting you deal with higher-level concepts instead of worrying about which functions to call in which order.
- The preprocessor can analyze and optimize the embedded DBMS commands in ways that a generic call-level interface cannot.

Embedded interfaces have their disadvantages, too. Building an application is more complicated due to the extra transformation step and may require special support by the development tools. Debugging the application may mean debugging the transformed source, not the original, unprocessed source. The preprocessing may place limitations on your coding style or the way you design your application.

On the Palm Computing platform you're unlikely to see any database that supports ODBC, simply because of the added overhead. Instead, any databases will use either a native interface or an embedded interface. Sybase's UltraLite technology, for example, uses an embedded interface.

Database Classifications

There are many ways a database (or, more accurately, a DBMS) can be classified, but current systems fall into one of two categories.

Relational Databases

In the 1960s a researcher named E. F. Codd decided to apply the concepts of relational algebra to databases. His work formed the basis for what we now refer to as *relational* databases, currently the most popular type of database.

In a relational database the data is organized into *tables* of rows and columns, with the data stored in the cells (the intersections of the rows and columns). Only one value can be stored in each cell. Columns are named (the names must be unique within the table) and define properties about the cells they contain. The most important properties are those that define the *domain* of allowable values—for example, any integer from 0 to 255, or any string of 10 characters. The domain also determines whether *null* values—values that are missing or unknown, separate from any other value in the domain—are allowed. Other properties define such things as whether case is to be respected when sorting and whether the values in the cell are modifiable. All cells in a single column share the same properties. See Figure 6.3 for an example of a relational table.

A table must have at least one column, but it can have zero rows (an empty table). Each row defines a set of related data. Unlike a spreadsheet, the position or *order* of the row in a table is irrelevant. Instead, each row has one or more columns that together form the *primary key* for the table—a set of values that uniquely identifies the row. (Some tables have one or more keys, in which case the designer of the table chooses one of them to be the primary key.) The primary key is all you need to perform operations on a row of data. For example, a table of employees would use the employee identification numbers as its primary key. Using the names of the employees as the primary key would not work because two or more employees may have the same name.

EMPLOYEE							
Name	Surname	Department	Email	Extension	External	Fax
John	Smith	Engineering	jsmith	374	NULL	NULL
Jane	Doe	Engineering	jdoe	375	NULL	NULL
Betty	Smart	Finance	bsmart	223	555-888-9223	555-767-2345
John	Smith	Finance	smithj	253	555-888-9253	555-767-2345
Robert	Desmits	Human Res.	desmits	112	555-888-9112	555-767-2344
Marg	Mathews	Reception	mathews	0	555-888-9000	555-767-2340

Figure 6.3 The EMPLOYEE relational table.

Tables can be related to each other using *foreign keys*. A foreign key links one row in a table with a row in another table (the *foreign* table) by storing the primary key of the foreign row as part of the first row. The employee table mentioned in the previous paragraph stores an employee's department identification number as well as the employee's name and employee identification number. The department identification number is the primary key of the table of departments, which lists information about each department in the company. When stored in the employee table, the department identification number is a foreign key linking each row in the employee table to a row in the department table. Linked rows do not have to have a one-to-one relationship: Several employees map into each department, as shown in Figure 6.4.

One of the important guarantees that relational databases provide is the guarantee of *referential integrity*, which ensures that related tables (linked by foreign keys) are always in a consistent and correct state. For example, if a database contains a table listing the organization's departments and another table listing the employees in each department, the database disallows removal of a department while there are employees in the department—the employees have to be removed from the department before the department can be deleted.

Relational databases are also *self-describing*, in that they hold tables (referred to as *system tables*) that describe the structure of the database. The information in the tables is referred to as the database *metadata*. If they know the structure of the system tables, applications can use the metadata to discover the structure of the database itself, such as the names of the tables and the columns in each table.

EMPLOYEE		
John Smith	100	jsmith
Jane Doe	100	jdoe
Betty Smart	200	bsmart
John Smith	200	smithj
Robert Desmits	300	desmits
Marg Mathews	400	mathews

foreign key links this table to the DEPARTMENT table

DEPARTMENT	
100	Engineering
200	Finance
300	Human Resources
400	Reception

primary key

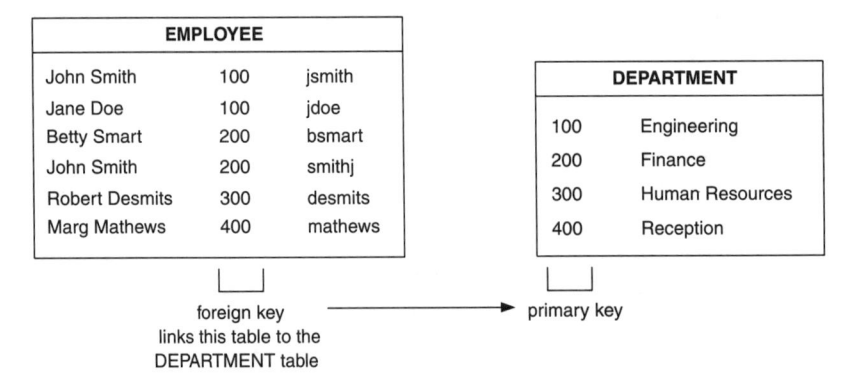

Figure 6.4 Linking tables by foreign keys.

Relational databases are the focus of this book; we won't be dealing with other database types, other than to briefly describe them.

Object-Oriented Databases

The growing popularity of object-oriented languages such as C++ and Java has led to the development of *object-oriented* databases. An object-oriented database is a database that stores actual objects instead of rows or records. The act of storing an object in the database is referred to as making the object *persistent*. Ideally, an application shouldn't know or care whether an object is in memory or in the database—the first attempt to use the object should cause it to be fetched from the database, sometimes referred to as object *materialization*. When the application exits, the state of each object is written back to the database.

Object-oriented databases appeal to programmers because implementing object persistence is nontrivial. Not only do you have to implement a way to efficiently store and retrieve objects, you also have to handle nested objects and references to other objects. For example, if your database holds objects for each employee in the company, each object can hold references to other employee objects to define supervisory or team relationships between the objects. Materializing the object representing a company-wide project could potentially cause all employee objects to materialize, which in most cases is not desirable. A good system will only materialize objects as they're actually used by an application, not just when they're referenced by an object.

TIP
An alternative to using object-oriented databases is to store objects in relational databases, using a technique referred to as *object-relational mapping*. In object-relational mapping, tables are used to store the state of an object. References to other objects become foreign keys. The storage process is quite complex, however, and requires special interfaces between the application and the database.

Apart from making object persistence easy, the usefulness of object-oriented databases for more traditional database operations—such as searching for objects that match certain criteria—is not well understood and is debated in the industry.

Because the focus is on relational databases, object-oriented databases are not dealt with in this book.

Other Classifications

Other common classifications for databases include:

Text databases. Databases optimized for storing and retrieving large amounts of text.

Multimedia databases. Databases optimized for storing and retrieving multimedia data including images, movies, and audio.

Distributed databases. Databases that are distributed across several machines but logically act as a single database.

For information on these and other types of databases, consult a recent book on general database theory. As with object-oriented databases, these database types are not dealt with in this book.

Database Design

Database design is the first step in writing a database application. Proper design ensures that the database accurately models an external world and captures the relationships between the various entities in that world. With relational databases there are two steps to the design process: mapping the data into tables and then normalizing and optimizing those tables.

Mapping Data into Tables

The primary goal of database design is simple: group raw data into tables that follow the relational database model. There are many ways to do this, ranging from informal groupings on a pad of paper to more formal methods developed with such tools as PowerDesigner and ER*win*. As you might expect, the more formal the method, the more time and effort it takes to develop the database, but formal approaches are better when dealing with complicated data groupings or to document a database model for use by several people.

A database model has two parts to it, an abstract model and a physical model. The abstract model describes the database at a high level, independent of any DBMS, and incorporates the business rules (rules that describe how operations are performed) related to the data. The physical model is the abstract model applied to a particular DBMS. Entire books have been written on database modeling describing how to build abstract and physical models, so what follows is a brief introduction to get you started.

The Abstract Model

The most common approach to building abstract models is to use the Entity-Relationship (E-R) model. An E-R model groups data into *entities* (things you want to model) and lists the *relationships* between those entities. A typical E-R model, referred to as an E-R diagram, is shown in Figure 6.5. As we'll see, E-R models are easily transformed into relational databases.

The first step in building an E-R model is to define the entities used by the model. Entities can be viewed as sets of attributes or properties that when grouped together define individual components of the model. When modeling a company, for example, each employee is an entity with such attributes as name, address, and birth date. Entities can refer to abstract concepts, not just physical objects: Company departments or divisions can be thought of as entities as well. Entities are object-oriented: An *entity class* defines the attributes or properties of a type of entity, while an *entity instance* refers to a particular entity in the class. The names of entity classes are usually written in uppercase letters, as in EMPLOYEE or DEPARTMENT, to distinguish them from the names of particular instances.

DIVISION
Division number
Division name
Division address

TEAM
Team number
Speciality

[1,n]

[1,n]

[0,n] is member of

[1,1]

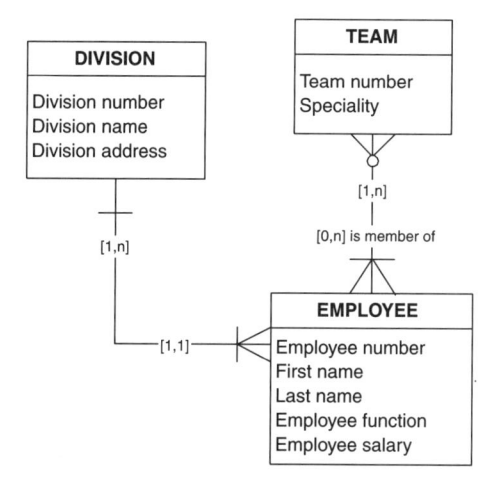

EMPLOYEE
Employee number
First name
Last name
Employee function
Employee salary

Figure 6.5 An E-R diagram.

When you design an E-R model, most of the entities are easily extracted from the external world that you're modeling. Look for the nouns in any description of the data. For example, "this data describes the relationships between employees and customers and allows us to track which departments are selling the most products" would immediately suggest the entity classes EMPLOYEE, CUSTOMER, DEPARTMENT, and PRODUCT. Other entities may not be as obvious, but can be discovered by listing actions that entities can perform, such as "for CUSTOMER to obtain PRODUCT they must place an ORDER." An iterative approach is often necessary to identify all the entities needed by the model.

Just like the entities themselves, the properties of an entity are usually quite obvious. Again, look for the nouns you use when describing an entity to someone else: "a CUSTOMER has a name, an address, and a telephone number," would suggest properties called Name, Address, and PhoneNumber. However, you might want to split some of the properties to provide further details: Address might become Street, City, and StateOrProvince, for example. Properties may have to be added for bookkeeping or other purposes. For example, it's common to assign a unique number to each instance of an entity class for identification purposes, especially if there's a chance (no matter how remote) that two or more identical entities would otherwise exist.

Make sure you note which properties, or combination of properties, uniquely identify an entity instance. These are the *entity identifiers*, and there may be several to choose from. Choose the one that seems the most obvious to understand and/or is the simplest to use; this will be your *primary* entity identifier.

Once you've defined the entities, the next step is to define the relationships between the entities, if any. If you were to describe the entities to someone, the relationships would be indicated by the verbs in the description. For example, "a department has a list of employees" or "a customer places an order and obtains product" would identify relationships between the DEPARTMENT and EMPLOYEE entities and the CUSTOMER, ORDER, and PRODUCT entities. Similarly, "each customer deals with several employees" defines a relationship between the EMPLOYEE and CUSTOMER entities. Relationships are referred to by the names of the tables involved, as in DEPARTMENT-EMPLOYEE or EMPLOYEE-CUSTOMER. Again, an iterative approach is often necessary to discover the important relationships in a model.

The final step in the E-R model is to determine the constraints on each relationship. For example, the DEPARTMENT-EMPLOYEE relationship has the following constraints:

- Each department has zero or more employees.
- Each employee is a member of exactly one department.

This constraint is referred to as a 1:N (one-to-N) relationship, because a single department instance is possibly referred to by several employee instances. A 1:N relationship is shown in Figure 6.6. Note that the order of the tables is important: The DEPARTMENT-EMPLOYEE relationship is 1:N but the EMPLOYEE-DEPARTMENT relationship is N:1. Other common relationships are 1:1 (one entity relates to at most one entity) and N:M (multiple entities relate to multiple entities). For example, the EMPLOYEE-CUSTOMER relationship in Figure 6.7 is an N:M relationship, because each customer can have several contacts within the organization (say, a contact in the sales department and a contact in the technical support department) and each employee can deal with several customers.

Constraints can also put limits on the minimum number of entities in a relationship, for example, by saying that one entity has to be related to exactly one other entity. Business rules are also part of the constraints. Note that the terminology and the notation used to describe relationships and constraints vary from one E-R system to another, but they all describe the same thing.

The Physical Model

The physical model applies the abstract model to a particular DBMS, in this case a relational database. This involves issuing commands to the database server to define the appropriate tables based on the entities, properties, relationships, and constraints developed in the abstract

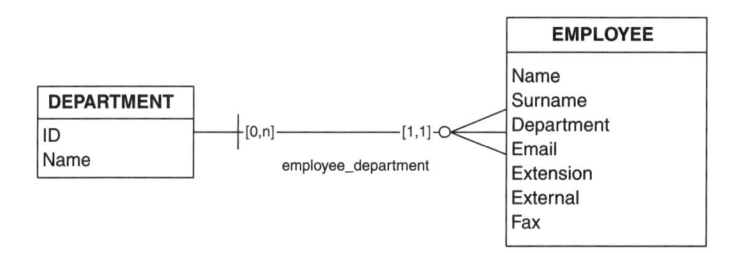

Figure 6.6 A 1:N relationship.

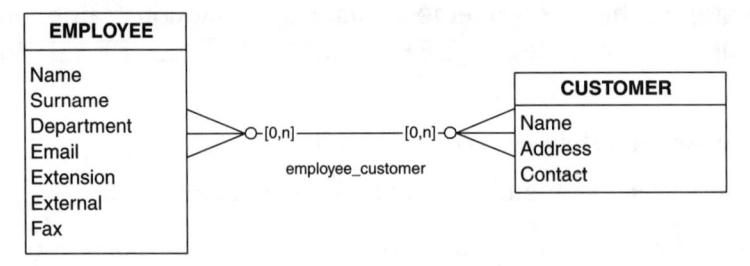

Figure 6.7 A *N:M* relationship.

model. Because different DBMS systems have slightly different syntax and support different feature sets, this step is quite system-dependent. Modeling tools are often able to target many different systems and greatly ease and speed the transition from the abstract model to the physical model.

In general, you build a physical model by applying the following rules:

- Each entity class defines a table.
- Each property of an entity class defines a column in the table, although you may have to compromise on the domain of a column if the DBMS doesn't support the type used in the abstract model. Choosing column types is discussed in the next section. Changes to the model may also be required for performance reasons.
- The primary entity identifier defines the primary key of the table.
- Each instance of an entity class defines a row in the table.

Mapping relationships onto the physical model is more difficult, however, because the only way to link two tables is to use foreign keys. A foreign key implies that one table row (entity instance) depends on a row in another table such that the database server guarantees referential integrity is always maintained, but it places no constraints beyond referential integrity. For example, consider the 1:*N* DEPARTMENT-EMPLOYEE relationship previously introduced. It's easily represented using two tables, with a foreign key in the EMPLOYEE table to link each employee to a particular department, as shown in Figure 6.8.

The foreign key is a one-way relationship: No department can be deleted while it has employees that refer to it, but any employee can be deleted at any time. (For the purposes of this example we're ignoring the fact that in a real employee database a foreign key also relates one employee

```
              EMPLOYEE
    EmployeeID      integer
    Name            char(50)
    Surname         char(50)
    Department      integer
    Email           char(50)
    Extension       char(50)
    External        char(50)
    Fax             char(50)
```

```
              DEPARTMENT
    DepartmentID    integer
    Name            char(50)
```

EMPLOYEE.DepartmentID = DEPARTMENT.DepartmentID

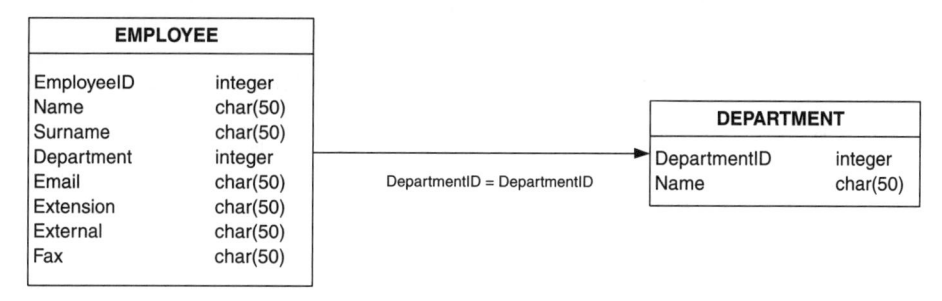

Figure 6.8 Physical model showing foreign key relationship.

to another to define the employee's manager, which requires reassigning employees to different managers before being able to delete the manager from the table.) Because many relationships are 1:N, linking two tables with a foreign key is often enough to represent the relationship. Consider, however, the N:M EMPLOYEE-CUSTOMER relationship. A single foreign key is inadequate, because each customer has two or more employee contacts. Adding more foreign keys is one solution, but it places absolute limits on how many contacts a particular customer has (which is not usually desirable) and also complicates the database structure, making it harder to write applications. A better solution is to store the relationships in a separate table called EMPCUST. Each row in the table represents a contact between an employee and a customer, as shown in Figure 6.9.

Each row in the EMPCUST table contains two foreign keys: one for the EMPLOYEE table and one for the CUSTOMER table. The EMPLOYEE and CUSTOMER tables are no longer directly linked to each other. In effect, we've replaced the EMPLOYEE-CUSTOMER relationship with EMPLOYEE-EMPCUST and CUSTOMER-EMPCUST relationships instead, as shown in Figure 6.10.

| EMPCUST ||
EmployeeID	CustomerID
1	1000
2	1000
3	1000
1	2000
3	2000
2	3000

Figure 6.9 The EMPCUST table.

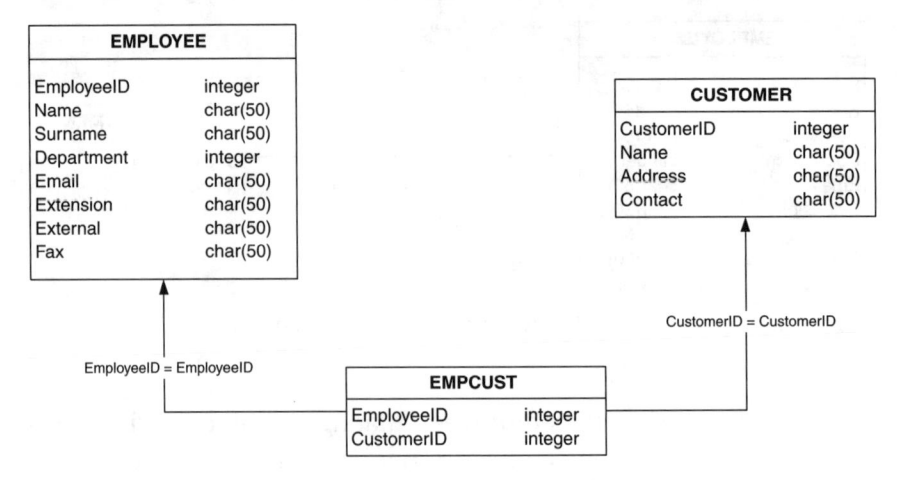

```
                    EMPLOYEE
        EmployeeID      integer                          CUSTOMER
        Name            char(50)
        Surname         char(50)          CustomerID      integer
        Department      integer           Name            char(50)
        Email           char(50)          Address         char(50)
        Extension       char(50)          Contact         char(50)
        External        char(50)
        Fax             char(50)

                                                        CustomerID = CustomerID
            EmployeeID = EmployeeID
                                    EMPCUST
                                EmployeeID      integer
                                CustomerID      integer
```

Figure 6.10 Mapping *N:M* relationships into three tables.

This allows us to store an unlimited set of employee-customer contacts. And referential integrity will ensure that no employee can be deleted without reassigning his or her contacts to someone else, and vice versa.

Constraints may or may not map directly from the abstract model to the physical model. Constraints on the domain of a column are usually supported. Other constraints have to be handled programmatically, either in the DBMS or by the application. If you can, centralize the logic in the database server, not the application, because this ensures that the logic is used by all applications. You can add logic to the database server by using *triggers*, which define code that is run automatically in response to certain events (such as updating a particular column), or by requiring applications to change the database by calling *stored procedures*, which group related DBMS commands into a single command. Triggers and stored procedures are written using a stored procedure language, and the syntax changes from DBMS to DBMS, so consult your system's documentation for details on how to use them. ASA supports both triggers and stored procedures, and also allows you to write stored procedures in Java.

Data Ownership

Relational database systems are designed for use in multiuser scenarios, with permissions to perform operations or access tables granted to users on a role basis by the DBMS. Most databases have at least two roles, that of a database administrator and an ordinary user. The database administrator has full access to the complete database and can create and modify tables, add users, and perform administrative tasks. Ordinary users are assigned permissions by the database administrator.

Applications using the DBMS identify themselves using a userid and password stored with the application or obtained from the system or by prompting the user. For Palm-based applications you can use the Palm device's user name to identify the user; however, you should restrict this use to low-security operations because it's quite simple to change the user name. A better solution is to have a password-based scheme. The Oracle Lite Consolidator, for example, which we discuss in Chapter 9, uses a separate password application to store a password on the device. When the Consolidator needs to perform an external database operation, it fetches this password from storage. A security-conscious user can easily enable or disable the password to limit access to the database.

Because permissions are important, when mapping the abstract model to a physical model, you have to consider who owns the data. The owner of a table is assigned when the table is created. Other users must be granted permissions to view or modify the data in the table.

Table Normalization and Optimization

Once the tables of a relational database have been defined, the next step is to *normalize* and *optimize* them. Normalization is the process of removing redundant information and avoiding table relationships that can lead to data errors or inconsistencies. Optimization is the process of reducing the amount of space used by a table or the amount of time required to perform operations on the table. Normalization is done once to ensure the physical model is accurate and consistent, but optimization is an ongoing process that often depends on how applications are using a particular table.

The Normal Forms

Unless you're careful, the tables you design can have what are called *modification anomalies*, which are flaws that either lead to loss of data or place unintended restrictions on the updating or insertion (adding) of data. To avoid these problems, researchers developed rules for classifying tables into groups referred to as *normal forms*. A table in a specific normal form is known to avoid one or more problems. What follows is a brief discussion of the most common normal forms and how to convert a table from one form to another. Converting a table to one of the normal forms is called *normalizing* the table.

The most basic normal form is referred to as *first normal form*, or 1NF. A table is in first normal form if it has no multivalued or repeating columns; in other words, each row only stores a single value for a particular column. In the *N:M* EMPLOYEE-CUSTOMER relationship discussed previously, for example, each customer can have several employee contacts. One possible solution was to store multiple references to the EMPLOYEE table as foreign keys in the CUSTOMER table, using several identical columns. That table would not be in first normal form. The solution we chose, storing the contact information in a separate EMPCUST table, ensures that EMPLOYEE and CUSTOMER are both in first normal form. To convert a table to 1NF, simply move all repeating data into separate tables.

Second normal form, or 2NF, requires that the table be in first normal form and that all nonkey columns (columns that are not keys of the table, whether primary or potential) depend on *all* of the primary key. If a table's primary key consists of a single column, which is most often the case, a table in first normal form is automatically in second normal form as well. Problems occur when a primary key spans several columns. Consider a table that combines the information in the EMPLOYEE and DEPARTMENT tables into a single table, using the employee's name and his or her department name as the primary key. Parts of the information (address, salary, etc.) depend solely on the employee name and other parts (building location, department manager, accounting information) depend solely on the department name. This table has modification anomalies that are avoided by second normal form: If you delete an employee and that employee happens to be the only member of a department, you delete all information about the department as well; similarly, you cannot create a new department without placing an employee in it. Another problem is that the information in the table is harder to update, because any changes to a department require changes to the rows for each employee in the department. To convert a table in 1NF to 2NF, identify the columns that depend entirely on a part of the primary key and move those columns and that part of the key into a separate table, linking the two tables via a foreign key. In this example, of course, this means using two separate tables to hold employee and department information.

Third normal form, or 3NF, requires that the table be in second normal form and that there are no transitive dependencies between columns. A *transitive dependency* is one that says "if column B depends on column A, and column C depends on column B, then column C also depends on column A." To illustrate, consider a company where an employee's salary depends solely on the department that employee is in, not on his or her length of service or position within the company. In the EMPLOYEE table this would mean that the Salary column depends on the DepartmentID column. But DepartmentID also depends on EmployeeID, since EmployeeID is the primary key for the table. This is a transitive dependency, and it has problems similar to the combined employee/department table we used to illustrate 2NF: For example, delete the only employee in a department and you lose all salary information for that department. To convert a table from 2NF to 3NF, split the columns that are part of a transitive dependency into other tables. Since we already have a DEPARTMENT table, we could transform EMPLOYEE into 3NF form simply by moving the Salary column into the DEPARTMENT table. Of course, in most companies the salary doesn't depend on the department, in which case Salary should remain in the EMPLOYEE table.

There are other normal forms beyond 3NF, but in most cases 3NF is all that is necessary. If you do encounter other modification anomalies with your tables, the rule is always the same: move the columns into separate tables and link the tables via foreign keys (if not to each other, then to a third table).

One problem with normalization is that it creates many tables. Each table adds overhead to the database server, and fetching information spread across multiple tables can be quite expensive, as you'll see later when we discuss the join operation. Don't create tables unnecessarily: They should reflect the entities in your abstract model or be a by-product of the normalization process.

Choosing Types and Indexes

Tables are optimized by carefully choosing the domains for the columns and by creating indexes to speed data searches. As is often the case, there are tradeoffs between optimizing for space versus optimizing for time: For example, indexes will use more space but can significantly increase the speed of certain operations. The challenge is to find a proper balance between the two. Necessary optimizations may not be apparent until after a database is already in use, so it's important to choose a DBMS that lets you easily change database characteristics in response to performance analysis.

The domain of a column specifies the allowable range of values for that column. The domain is commonly referred to as the *type* of the column. Although type names differ from system to system, all relational databases will have types equivalent to the following:

- INTEGER to represent 32-bit integral values. Other integer types are SMALLINT, TINYINT, or BIGINT.
- FLOAT, REAL, and DOUBLE to represent floating-point (approximate) values.
- CHAR(n) to represent fixed-length strings, where n refers to the length of the strings. Shorter strings are padded on the right with spaces until they're exactly n characters long. There is a maximum size to n, usually 255 or 32,767 characters.
- VARCHAR(n) to represent variable-length strings, where n refers to the maximum length of the strings. Unlike fixed-length strings, variable-length strings are not padded with spaces. There is a maximum size to n, usually 255 or 32,767 characters.
- BINARY(n) and VARBINARY(n) to represent fixed-length and variable-length binary data. These are very similar to CHAR and VARCHAR.
- NUMERIC(p,s) or DECIMAL(p,s) to represent fixed-point (exact) values, where p is the *precision* (the total number of digits) and s is the *scale* (the number of digits to the right of the decimal point). Other fixed-point types in common use are MONEY or SMALLMONEY, to represent monetary values.
- BIT to represent Boolean values.
- DATE, TIME, and TIMESTAMP to represent dates, times, and a combined date and time.
- LONG VARCHAR and LONG VARBINARY to represent arbitrary-length strings and binary data. Often referred to as TEXT and IMAGE types.

Constraints can be defined to further limit the domain of a column. The most common constraints are whether a column allows NULL values

(values of unknown type that do not match any other value) and whether the value of a column must be unique in each row in the table. Other constraints are supplied as expressions that the DBMS uses to check the data before allowing a new value to be written to the database.

As a general rule, the smaller the type, the less storage required by the database. Variable-length data, especially the LONG VARCHAR and LONG VARBINARY types, tend to be stored separately from the rest of a row in the database and can be more expensive to read or write.

An *index* is a data structure maintained by the DBMS to sort rows in ascending or descending order based on the values of one or more columns. Indexes are automatically created for primary key columns and can be explicitly created for other columns. Indexes greatly speed up searching and sorting, but involve extra overhead in terms of space (to store the index) and time (when changing, deleting, or adding a row, the index has to be updated as well).

If no index is available for a particular column, a *table scan* has to be performed for each searching or sorting operation involving that column. The DBMS reads the column values from every row in the table, which can be time-consuming on large tables. Consider defining indexes for these columns. Some systems keep statistics on access times for various operations, allowing you to tune your tables based on actual usage.

Database Design Is Hard Work

If it seems that there's a lot of work involved in designing a database, that's because it's true: Database design *is* hard work. The number of books on the topic and the number of (often expensive) tools available to help with the design process attest to that fact. There are highly paid professionals out there who do nothing but design and tune databases so that more applications and more users have quick access to the data they require.

That said, there's nothing that precludes the average programmer from designing a good database, and the more you do it, the easier it gets. And if you're writing handheld applications for an organization, chances are that the data you need already exists in a database, in which case it's more a matter of your understanding (and perhaps adjusting) an existing design, which is certainly a simpler proposition. However, even if you have to design a database from scratch, don't be put off by the work involved: As is usually the case, the initial design effort pays for itself later in the development process.

Structured Query Language

One of the benefits to using relational databases is that there is a fair amount of portability from one relational DBMS to another, so that the same concepts and techniques apply to products from different vendors. This is useful, because many organizations use several database systems for various purposes. If your organization uses Oracle databases and you choose to write UltraLite-based Palm applications, for example, you'll have to deal with two different database systems: a custom-built Sybase database on the handheld and an external Oracle database. It helps that both use a common database language, the Structured Query Language.

Structured Query Language, or SQL (pronounced as either S-Q-L or "sequel") for short, is an ANSI/ISO standard. The version in common use today is the 1992 standard, SQL92, although a newer version called SQL3 is now available that adds object-oriented extensions and other enhancements to the base language. SQL is not a general-purpose programming language, however, and any code that resides in the database server (in triggers or stored procedures, for example) tends to be non-portable because it uses DBMS-specific programming extensions. In this section we only discuss basic SQL syntax; consult your DBMS documentation for details on how to write server-based code. You can run the examples in this section against the Adaptive Server Anywhere (ASA) sample database using the Interactive SQL tool. Instructions for starting the database and the tool are found in Appendix B.

SQL Basics

SQL commands are grouped into SQL statements, separated by semicolons or some other separator. (The separator is usually optional if only one statement is being executed.) SQL statements are written as English phrases, starting with verbs such as CREATE, SELECT, or INSERT. White space is not significant, nor is the case of the words, but statement keywords are typically written in uppercase. Mathematical expressions are allowed in certain parts of a statement, and SQL supports a number of built-in functions for such calculations as computing the length of a string, the absolute value of a number, and so on.

Operations are performed on a relational database by forming a SQL command and submitting it to the database server, via one of the interfaces previously discussed. The database server parses the statements, forms an execution plan, and then performs the operation based on the plan. A good DBMS will optimize the execution plan as much as possible in order to reduce the amount of time required to perform the operation, but SQL statements should always be written as efficiently as possible to reduce the work involved. SQL commands that are executed frequently can be analyzed once and the resulting execution plan stored away for later reuse; this is referred to as *preparing* the command. Command preparation can be used by both embedded and call-level interfaces, although the preprocessor used for the embedded interface has the advantage of knowing exactly which SQL commands need to be executed and can use that information to better prepare the command.

SQL commands can be classified into two groups: commands that alter the structure of the database, and commands that manipulate the data in the database.

Data Description Language

The structure of the database is commonly referred to as the *schema* of the database, although the term sometimes refers to a subset of a database. A schema includes user-defined tables and data as well as the system-defined tables that describe the database. The subset of SQL commands that alter the schema is referred to as *data description language*, or DDL for short. Most DDL commands are not executed directly but are run using management tools such as Sybase Central, so we'll only consider some basic table manipulation commands here.

Tables are created with the CREATE TABLE statement, as in the following:

```
CREATE TABLE MyTable (
    id      INTEGER PRIMARY KEY,
    name    CHAR(40),
    address CHAR(100)
)
```

The statement assigns a name and a domain to each column. It also identifies the first column as the primary key. This table isn't related to any others. A more complicated example would create the EMPCUST table we discussed previously:

```
CREATE TABLE empcust (
    relationshipID INTEGER DEFAULT AUTOINCREMENT PRIMARY KEY,
    FOREIGN KEY employeeID REFERENCES employee,
    FOREIGN KEY customerID REFERENCES customer
)
```

This creates a table with three columns: relationshipID, employeeID, and customerID. The first column is the primary key for the table and is marked as an *autoincrement* column, which means that the database automatically assigns a value to the primary key when new rows are added to the table. The other two columns are foreign keys referencing the EMPLOYEE and CUSTOMER tables, which are already defined in the sample database. Once created, the structure of a table can be altered with the ALTER TABLE statement.

Permissions to read or modify a table are granted using the GRANT statement:

```
GRANT ALL ON empcust TO harry
```

This of course assumes that a use named "harry" exists in the system. Permissions can be revoked using the REVOKE TABLE statement.

Tables are deleted using the DROP TABLE statement:

```
DROP TABLE empcust
```

Of course, dropping or otherwise altering a table that is in active use is never a good idea.

Data Manipulation Language

The subset of SQL commands that actually add, update, or delete data from tables is referred to as *data manipulation language*, or DML for short. There are DML commands for selecting (often referred to as *querying* the database), inserting, updating, and deleting data from a table, as well as grouping changes into atomic transactions.

Single-Table Selection

The most basic DML statement is the SELECT statement, used to retrieve rows of data from a table. SELECT statements can be quite complicated or quite simple. To obtain the complete list of departments in the company, use this syntax:

```
SELECT * FROM department
```

The statement returns a result set with dept_id, dept_name, and dept_head_id columns:

```
100   R & D       501
200   Sales       902
300   Finance    1293
400   Marketing  1576
500   Shipping    703
```

The * (asterisk) selects all columns in the table, in the order they were created. A subset of the columns can be selected instead:

```
SELECT dept_name, dept_id FROM department

--- result set ---
R & D          100
Sales          200
Finance        300
Marketing      400
Shipping       500
```

Expressions can be used to return computed values. For example, to return a series of sentences:

```
select 'The ' || dept_name || ' department has ID ' || dept_id ||
       ' and is headed by ' || dept_head_id || '.' from department

--- result set ---
The R & D department has ID 100 and is headed by 501.
The Sales department has ID 200 and is headed by 902.
The Finance department has ID 300 and is headed by 1293.
The Marketing department has ID 400 and is headed by 1576.
The Shipping department has ID 500 and is headed by 703.
```

Or to return the number of departments in the DEPARTMENT table:

```
SELECT count(*) FROM department

--- result set ---
5
```

Unless a sort order is specifically mentioned, rows are returned in the order they're stored in the database. To ensure that rows are sorted, use the ORDER BY clause:

```
SELECT dept_name, dept_id FROM deparment ORDER BY dept_name

--- result set ---
Finance        300
Marketing      400
R & D          100
```

```
Sales        200
Shipping     500
```

Rows can also be sorted in descending order:

```
SELECT dept_name, dept_id FROM deparment ORDER BY dept_name DESC

--- result set ---
Shipping     500
Sales        200
R & D        100
Marketing    400
Finance      300
```

To remove duplicate rows, use the DISTINCT clause. For example, to get the list of managers run the following query on the EMPLOYEE table, which has a column called manager_id listing each employee's manager:

```
SELECT DISTINCT manager_id FROM employee ORDER BY manager_id

--- result set ---
 501
 703
 902
1293
1576
```

Not surprisingly, this is identical to the set of department heads listed in the DEPARTMENT table, which is not unusual for a small company with a flat management structure.

A subset of rows can be selected using a WHERE clause. For example, to list all employees who have a specific manager:

```
SELECT emp_lname, emp_fname FROM employee WHERE manager_id = 703

--- result set ---
Bertrand   Jeannette
Braun      Jane
Kuo        Felicia
Crowley    Charles
Barker     Joseph
Rebeiro    Anthony
Romero     Sheila
Lynch      Michael
```

You can combine several conditions together using AND and OR operations:

```
SELECT emp_id, emp_lname FROM employee
       WHERE ( emp_id > 100 AND emp_id < 110 ) OR emp_id > 1750
```

```
--- result set ---
 102  Whitney
 109  Cobb
1751  Ahmed
```

Apart from the usual comparison operators, you can also use operators like IS NULL, IN, LIKE, and BETWEEN to specify search criteria:

```
SELECT dept_name FROM department WHERE dept_name LIKE 'S%'

--- result set ---
Sales
Shipping
```

As you can imagine, search criteria can be quite complex.

Multitable Selection: Subqueries

A *subquery* is a SELECT statement that provides selection criteria to a second SELECT statement. Subqueries often (but not necessarily) involve two or more tables. For example, to select the names of the department heads use the following statement:

```
SELECT dept_id, emp_lname, emp_fname FROM employee
     WHERE emp_id IN
           ( SELECT dept_head_id FROM department )
```

When presented with this statement, the database server executes the inner SELECT first to obtain the list of department heads from the DEPARTMENT table:

```
SELECT dept_head_id FROM department

--- result set ---
 501
 902
1293
1576
 703
```

The result set is then substituted into the outer SELECT:

```
SELECT dept_id, emp_lname, emp_fname FROM employee
     WHERE emp_id IN ( 501, 902, 1293, 1576, 703 )

--- result set ---
100 Scott     David
200 Kelly     Moira
300 Shea      Mary Anne
400 Evans     Scott
500 Martinez  Jose
```

Subqueries can be nested to arbitrary depth; however, performance suffers the more complex the query gets.

Multitable Selection: Joins

While subqueries can be used to select data from one table based on data in another table, in many cases you want to select data from two tables and present them as a single result set. For example, you might want to list the names of the department heads along with the names of their departments, but this information is found in two separate tables, EMPLOYEE and DEPARTMENT. Because the normalization process encourages us to split data across tables, we need a way to recombine the data into a virtual table. This operation is referred to as *joining* the tables.

The simplest form of join is the *equi-join*, which is the cross product of two tables. The cross product is formed by taking each row of the first table and combining it with every row of the second table. If the first table has $c1$ columns and $r1$ rows and the second table has $c2$ columns and $r2$ rows, the result set formed by the cross product has $c1+c2$ columns and $r1*r2$ rows. For example, consider the following two tables, TableA and TableB:

```
TableA
id     first_name
100    John
200    Jane

TableB
id     last_name
100    Smith
200    Doe
300    Nobody
```

To perform an equi-join, simply refer to both tables in the FROM clause of the SELECT statement:

```
SELECT * from TableA, TableB

--- result set ---
100 John 100 Smith
100 John 200 Doe
100 John 300 Nobody
200 Jane 100 Smith
200 Jane 200 Doe
200 Jane 300 Nobody
```

Creating TableA and TableB

TableA and TableB are two very small tables used to keep the examples simple, but they don't exist in the ASA sample database. You can create them using the Interactive SQL tool with the following commands:

```
CREATE TABLE TableA ( id INTEGER, first_name CHAR(20) NULL );
CREATE TABLE TableB ( id INTEGER, last_name CHAR(20) NULL );
INSERT INTO TableA VALUES( 100, 'John' );
INSERT INTO TableA VALUES( 200, 'Jane' );
INSERT INTO TableB VALUES( 100, 'Smith' );
INSERT INTO TableB VALUES( 200, 'Doe' );
INSERT INTO TableB VALUES( 300, 'Nobody' );
```

The syntax for inserting data into tables is explained in the next section.

Notice that TableA and TableB have a column in common. If you remove the duplicate columns you end up with a *natural equi-join*:

```
SELECT TableA.id, first_name, last_name from TableA, TableB

--- result set ---
100 John Smith
100 John Doe
100 John Nobody
200 Jane Smith
200 Jane Doe
200 Jane Nobody
```

Because both tables share a column, the table name must be used to qualify identical column names so that the database server will select the correct column; otherwise, it will complain that the statement is ambiguous.

Equi-joins aren't very useful on their own because they produce very large tables with unnecessary and repeated data. What you really want, of course, is to only combine rows that are related in some way. You can do this by using a WHERE clause that places restrictions on the rows that participate in the join:

```
SELECT TableA.id, first_name, last_name FROM TableA, TableB
    WHERE TableA.id = TableB.id

--- result set ---
100 John Smith
200 Jane Doe
```

In effect, this performs a cross product of the two tables and then removes all rows from the cross product where the two id columns do not match. The term *natural join* typically refers to a restricted natural equi-join. Your DBMS may offer alternative ways to perform natural joins. For example, you can use a NATURAL JOIN clause with a join condition, naming a single table in the FROM clause and a second table after the JOIN clause:

```
SELECT TableA.id, first_name, last_name FROM TableA
    NATURAL JOIN TableB ON TableA.id = TableB.id
```

Or you can use a NATURAL JOIN clause by itself:

```
SELECT TableA.id, first_name, last_name FROM TableA
    NATURAL JOIN TableB
```

Note that without a join condition, the NATURAL JOIN clause only works when two tables have columns with the same names and the same meanings.

The term *key join* refers to a restricted equi-join where joined columns are related via a foreign key relationship instead of by name. Returning to the EMPLOYEE and DEPARTMENT tables in the ASA sample database, the dept_head_id column is a foreign key linking the DEPARTMENT table to the EMPLOYEE table, so getting the names of the department heads is easily done using a key join:

```
SELECT department.dept_id, emp_lname, emp_fname FROM employee, department
    WHERE employee.dept_id = department.dept_head_id

    --- result set ---
100 Scott     David
200 Kelly     Moira
300 Shea      Mary Anne
400 Evans     Scott
500 Martinez  Jose
```

The result of this join is identical to the one generated by the subquery example in the previous section—in many cases a join can be substituted for a subquery or vice versa. Just as with natural joins, there is an alternate syntax for key joins using the KEY JOIN clause; however, it can only be used if there is only one foreign key relationship linking the two tables. In our example the EMPLOYEE table has a foreign key (dept_id) linking it to the DEPARTMENT table, and the DEPARTMENT table has a foreign key (dept_head_id) linking it to the EMPLOYEE table, so the KEY JOIN clause cannot be used with these two tables because the database server cannot decide which foreign key to use—the join has to be performed with a WHERE clause.

The natural and key joins we just discussed are *inner* joins. Returning to first principles, an inner join only selects the rows from the initial equi-join (cross product) that satisfy the join condition. An *outer* join returns all the rows in an inner join as well as the rows from one of the tables (but not both) that are *not* included in the inner join because no row in the equi-join satisfies the join condition. In other words, an outer join lets you see which rows in a table match a join condition and which do not, and provides information about the matching row in the second table for the rows that do match. A *left outer join* returns all the rows from the table on the "left" (in the FROM clause), while a *right outer join* returns all the rows from the table on the "right" (in the JOIN clause).

Consider a natural right outer join performed on TableA and TableB:

```
SELECT * FROM TableA NATURAL RIGHT OUTER JOIN TableB

--- result set ---
100     John    100   Smith
200     Jane    200   Doe
(NULL)  (NULL)  300   Nobody
```

Notice how in contrast to an inner join, the row with id=300 from TableB is now included in the result set, since it has no matching row in TableA. NULL values are returned for the columns in TableA.

The order of the tables is important when performing outer joins:

```
SELECT * FROM TableB NATURAL RIGHT OUTER JOIN TableA

--- result set ---
100   Smith   100   John
200   Doe     200   Jane
```

Now all rows from TableA are being returned, and only the matching rows from TableB, because TableA is now the table on the "right."

Joins can be expensive operations to perform. A good DBMS can perform a number of optimizations that reduce certain joins to simpler operations without changing the results; however, not all joins can be optimized by the server, so it's best to use them judiciously.

Adding Rows

Rows are added to a table using the INSERT statement. The basic form of the statement requires you to specify values for each column in the table, in the order the columns were defined when the table was created:

```
INSERT INTO TableA VALUES ( 300, 'Toby' )
```

You can specify which columns you want to assign values to, and you can omit columns that were defined with a default value:

```
INSERT INTO TableB ( last_name ) VALUES ( Henrik' )
```

Since the id column of TableB is an autoincrement column, the database server assigns a new unique value to the newly inserted row. If you omit columns that do not have default values defined, an error occurs.

Inserted rows are not added to the table in any specific order. If you recently deleted some rows, for example, the DBMS may insert the row into one of the empty slots. To guarantee the order of rows on retrieval you have to use an ORDER BY clause in the SELECT statement.

Changing Rows

Rows are changed using the UPDATE statement. Several columns and one or more rows within a table can be changed at a time. For example, to change the names of all employees to Joe Smith use the following statement:

```
UPDATE employee SET emp_fname = 'Joe', emp_lname = 'Smith'
```

It's more typical, however, to update a single row or a small group of rows at a time, which is done by adding a WHERE clause to the UPDATE statement to identify the row(s) in question:

```
UPDATE TableB SET last_name = '' WHERE id = 300
```

Use the table's primary key in the WHERE clause to uniquely identify a row. The update count, a value returned by the DBMS describing the number of rows affected by the UPDATE statement, can be used to ensure that only one row was affected.

Some databases don't allow the primary key of a row to be changed with an UPDATE statement, in which case the only alternative is to insert a new copy of the row and delete the old row.

If many users are working with a table, changes made by one user may conflict with changes made by another. Conflicts are easily detected by modifying the WHERE clause to include the old value of a column:

```
UPDATE TableB SET last_name = '' WHERE id = 300 AND last_name = 'Nobody'
```

If no row meets the selection criteria, then someone else has already updated (or deleted!) the row. The conflict can be handled by the application or else reported back to the user as an error. This kind of update can be used as an alternative to locking other users out of the table in order to keep its state consistent and is referred to as *optimistic concurrency*, since it takes the optimistic approach in assuming that most updates succeed without a conflict arising.

Deleting Rows

Rows are removed from a table using the DELETE statement. Like the UPDATE statement, the DELETE statement can operate on groups of rows:

```
DELETE TableB WHERE id >= 200 AND NOT name IS NULL
```

Use the table's primary key in the WHERE clause to delete a single row:

```
DELETE TableB WHERE id = 100
```

As with UPDATE, a count of rows deleted is returned by the DBMS. You should also be prepared to handle referential integrity violations: The DBMS won't allow you to update a row that is referenced via a foreign key in another table, since that would leave the database in an inconsistent state. The only other acceptable alternative is to have the DBMS delete any referencing rows at the same time, an option which is referred to as a *cascading delete*. If supported, cascading deletes are enabled when the table is created. (A similar option called a *cascading update* automatically changes foreign keys to match the new value of a primary key.)

Transaction Processing

The final set of basic DML commands groups a series of SQL statements into a single transaction. Recall that a *transaction* refers to a set of changes that are applied to the database in an atomic operation—if any of the changes fail, the process stops and any changes made since the start of the transaction are rolled back. In other words, either all changes succeed, or none do.

Transaction boundaries are defined by the BEGIN TRANSACTION, COMMIT, and ROLLBACK statements. BEGIN TRANSACTION marks the start of a transaction. After executing other SQL statements that change the database (such as UPDATE statements), the changes are made permanent by the COMMIT statement, which marks the end of the transaction. If an error occurs at any point within the transaction, the

ROLLBACK statement can be used to end the transaction and restore the database to its state before the transaction started. Nested transactions are supported on most systems.

If transactions are not necessary, database servers support a mode of operation called *autocommit* mode. If autocommit is enabled, each statement starts an implicit transaction, which is committed when the statement succeeds or rolled back if an error occurs. The syntax to switch in and out of autocommit mode depends on the DBMS and the interface being used. The syntax for ASA is to use the SET OPTION statement, as shown here:

```
SELECT * FROM TableA

--- result set ---
100 John
200 Jane

SET OPTION AUTO_COMMIT = 'OFF'
UPDATE TableA SET first_name = 'Wiliam'
SELECT * FROM TableA

--- result set ---
100 William
200 Jane

ROLLBACK
SELECT * FROM TableA
--- result set ---
100 John
200 Jane
```

Whether autocommit is on or off by default is system-dependent.

Mapping Phone Book Data to the Relational Model

At the end of the previous chapter we discussed how useful it would be if we could extract data from an external database and download it into our Phone Book application. In other words, instead of laboriously entering the phone information for each employee, we would fetch it out of a central database. Say there is no such database, however, or the database is incomplete. How would we map the information we've been using—employee name, department name, email address, phone numbers—into the relational model? And once we've done that, how would we extract the data? Let's approach these two problems using the tech-

The Data

The first step is to describe the Phone Book data. The data was first described in Chapter 1 and is reproduced again in Table 6.1. There's nothing particularly unique or exciting about the data. Strings can represent each group of data, although we could also use integers for the extension numbers, and perhaps even the other phone numbers. For argument's sake, though, let's say that the extensions are represented by integers and the other values by strings.

The Abstract Model

The next step is to analyze the data and build an abstract model for it by creating an entity-relationship diagram. The goal is to discover the entity classes, properties, relationships, and constraints that best describe the data. Start the process by describing the data verbally, in as much detail as possible:

- The data lists the names of employees and their phone numbers.
- An employee has a name, a surname, an email address, a series of phone numbers, and a department.
- Each employee belongs to a department. Many employees belong to the same department.
- Names are not unique, but email addresses are.
- External and fax numbers have an identical format.

Table 6.1 Sample Phone Book Data

NAME	SURNAME	DEPARTMENT	EMAIL	EXTENSION	EXTERNAL	FAX
John	Smith	Engineering	jsmith	374	none	none
Jane	Doe	Engineering	jdoe	375	none	none
Betty	Smart	Finance	bsmart	223	555-888-9223	555-767-2345
John	Smith	Finance	smithj	253	555-888-9253	555-767-2345
Robert	Desmits	Human Resources	desmits	112	555-888-9112	555-767-2344
Marg	Mathews	Reception	mmathews	0	555-888-9000	555-767-2340

- Every employee has an extension, but not necessarily an external number or a fax number. The extension is unique.

From these statements we can deduce the following:

- There are two entity classes, EMPLOYEE and DEPARTMENT. Furthermore, there's an *N*:1 relationship between the two.
- EMPLOYEE has properties Name, Surname, Email, Extension, External, and Fax. Extension is an integer; the rest are all strings. Email and Extension are both entity identifiers.
- DEPARTMENT has a single property: Department, the name of the department. To avoid confusion with the entity class, we'll call the property DepartmentName instead. DepartmentName is an entity identifier.

This gives us the E-R diagram shown in Figure 6.11.

The Physical Model

Once the abstract model is defined, apply the rules to convert it to a physical model defining two tables: EMPLOYEE and DEPARTMENT. There is a foreign key relationship linking each row of EMPLOYEE to a row of DEPARTMENT.

Each table needs a primary key. The candidates are the columns that were entity identifiers: Email and Extension for EMPLOYEE, DepartmentName for DEPARTMENT. Extension isn't a good choice, because there's always the chance that two or more employees will be required to share a phone in the future. Also, if the employee leaves the company, the Extension value gets reassigned or added to a pool of free numbers, but the EMPLOYEE database will still need to track the employee for various reasons (to send tax slips at the beginning of the next year, for example).

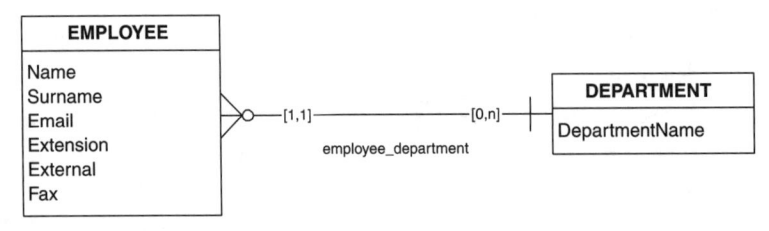

Figure 6.11 E-R diagram for Phone Book data.

This leaves us with Email and DepartmentName as our primary keys. There is one problem, however: Both values are strings. Searches could be performed more efficiently if the primary keys were integers instead of strings. Thus we define two new columns, EmployeeID and DepartmentID, to serve as the primary keys. The two tables are now linked by DepartmentID rather than DepartmentName.

Normalization is the next step. The DEPARTMENT table is already in third normal form: There are no repeating columns, the primary key is a single column, and there aren't enough columns to create a transitive dependency. However, a strong case can be made that the EMPLOYEE table is not in first normal form: The Extension, External, and Fax columns represent phone numbers and could be considered repeating values. The solution, of course, is to split EMPLOYEE into two tables: an EMPLOYEE table with EmployeeID, Name, Surname, DepartmentID, and Email columns; and a PHONE table with PhoneID, PhoneNumber, and PhoneType columns. PhoneID is an integer column to use as the primary key, PhoneNumber is the phone number stored as a string, and PhoneType is an integer identifying the type of phone number. A third table, EMPPHONE, links employees to phones by using EmployeeID and PhoneID as foreign keys. The final physical model is shown in Figure 6.12.

One advantage to having a separate table for phone numbers is that it's easy to add new phone number types without disturbing the structure of the database. For example, if the company starts issuing cellular phones, they can be added to the PHONE table simply by defining a new type.

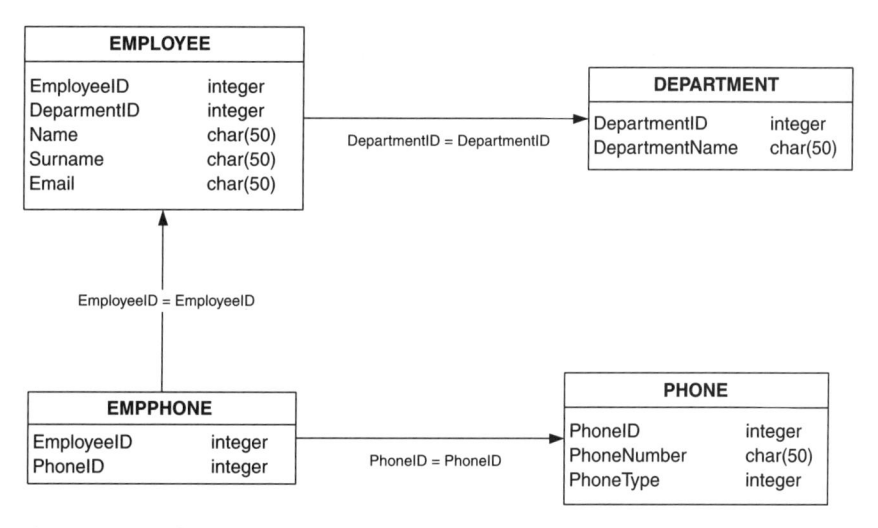

Figure 6.12 The final physical model.

The Database

The database is created from the physical model using the following SQL statements:

```
CREATE TABLE DEPARTMENT (
    DepartmentID   INTEGER PRIMARY KEY,
    DepartmentName VARCHAR(50) NOT NULL
);

CREATE TABLE EMPLOYEE (
    EmployeeID   INTEGER PRIMARY KEY,
    Name         VARCHAR(50),
    Surname      VARCHAR(50) NOT NULL,
    Email        VARCHAR(50),
    FOREIGN KEY DepartmentID REFERENCES DEPARTMENT
);

CREATE TABLE PHONE (
    PhoneID      INTEGER PRIMARY KEY,
    PhoneNumber VARCHAR(30),
    PhoneType    INTEGER NOT NULL
);

CREATE TABLE EMPPHONE (
    EmployeeID   INTEGER NOT NULL,
    PhoneID      INTEGER NOT NULL,
    FOREIGN KEY EmployeeID REFERENCES EMPLOYEE,
    FOREIGN KEY PhoneID REFERENCES PHONE,
    PRIMARY KEY( EmployeeID, PhoneID )
);
```

Alternatively, we can use database tools such as Sybase Central to create the database. (Note that the ASA sample database already contains tables called DEPARTMENT and EMPLOYEE, although they don't have the same columns.)

After creating the tables, we populate the database with the data from Table 6.1. First we fill the DEPARTMENT table:

```
INSERT INTO DEPARTMENT VALUES( 1, 'Engineering' );
INSERT INTO DEPARTMENT VALUES( 2, 'Finance' );
INSERT INTO DEPARTMENT VALUES( 3, 'Human Resources' );
INSERT INTO DEPARTMENT VALUES( 4, 'Reception' );
```

We've assigned an ID to each department. Next, we fill the EMPLOYEE table:

```
INSERT INTO EMPLOYEE VALUES ( 1, 'John', 'Smith', 'jsmith', 1 );
INSERT INTO EMPLOYEE VALUES ( 2, 'Jane', 'Doe', 'jdoe', 1 );
```

```
INSERT INTO EMPLOYEE VALUES ( 3, 'Betty', 'Smart', 'bsmart', 2 );
INSERT INTO EMPLOYEE VALUES ( 4, 'John', 'Smith', 'smithj', 2 );
INSERT INTO EMPLOYEE VALUES ( 5, 'Robert', 'Desmits', 'desmits', 3 );
INSERT INTO EMPLOYEE VALUES ( 6, 'Marg', 'Mathews', 'mmathews', 4 );
```

We've assigned an ID to each employee. Then we fill the PHONE table:

```
INSERT INTO PHONE VALUES ( 1, '374', 1 );
INSERT INTO PHONE VALUES ( 2, '375', 1 );
INSERT INTO PHONE VALUES ( 3, '223', 1 );
INSERT INTO PHONE VALUES ( 4, '555-888-9223', 2 );
INSERT INTO PHONE VALUES ( 5, '555-767-2345', 3 );
INSERT INTO PHONE VALUES ( 6, '555-888-9253', 2 );
INSERT INTO PHONE VALUES ( 7, '555-888-9112', 2 );
INSERT INTO PHONE VALUES ( 8, '555-767-2344', 3 );
INSERT INTO PHONE VALUES ( 9, '555-888-9000', 2 );
INSERT INTO PHONE VALUES ( 10,'555-767-2340', 3 );
INSERT INTO PHONE VALUES ( 11, '0', 1 );
INSERT INTO PHONE VALUES ( 12, '253', 1 );
INSERT INTO PHONE VALUES ( 13, '112', 1 );
```

We've assigned an ID to each phone number, and each phone type is one of the following values: 1 = extension, 2 = external, 3 = fax. For variety we've switched the order of a few entries to show that the table doesn't need to be in sorted order. Finally, we fill the EMPPHONE table:

```
INSERT INTO EMPPHONE VALUES ( 1, 1 );
INSERT INTO EMPPHONE VALUES ( 2, 2 );
INSERT INTO EMPPHONE VALUES ( 3, 3 );
INSERT INTO EMPPHONE VALUES ( 3, 4 );
INSERT INTO EMPPHONE VALUES ( 3, 5 );
INSERT INTO EMPPHONE VALUES ( 4, 12 );
INSERT INTO EMPPHONE VALUES ( 4, 6 );
INSERT INTO EMPPHONE VALUES ( 4, 5 );
INSERT INTO EMPPHONE VALUES ( 5, 13 );
INSERT INTO EMPPHONE VALUES ( 5, 7 );
INSERT INTO EMPPHONE VALUES ( 5, 8 );
INSERT INTO EMPPHONE VALUES ( 6, 11 );
INSERT INTO EMPPHONE VALUES ( 6, 9 );
INSERT INTO EMPPHONE VALUES ( 6, 10 );
```

Our database is now complete.

Sample Queries

Use this statement to get the list of employees and the names of their departments:

```
SELECT Name, Surname, DepartmentName FROM EMPLOYEE, DEPARTMENT
    WHERE EMPLOYEE.DepartmentID = DEPARTMENT.DepartmentID
```

```
--- result set ---
John    Smith   Engineering
Jane    Doe     Engineering
Betty   Smart   Finance
John    Smith   Finance
Robert  Desmits Human Resources
Marg    Mathews Reception
```

Or this statement to see the phone numbers assigned to an employee:

```
SELECT Name, Surname, PhoneNumber FROM EMPLOYEE, PHONE, EMPPHONE
    WHERE EMPPHONE.EmployeeID = EMPLOYEE.EmployeeID AND
        EMPPHONE.PhoneID = PHONE.PhoneID
```

```
--- result set ---
John    Smith    374
Jane    Doe      375
Betty   Smart    223
Betty   Smart    555-888-9223
Betty   Smart    555-767-2345
John    Smith    253
John    Smith    555-888-9253
John    Smith    555-767-2345
Robert  Desmits  112
Robert  Desmits  555-888-9112
Robert  Desmits  555-767-2344
Marg    Mathews  0
Marg    Mathews  555-888-9000
Marg    Mathews  555-767-2340
```

Our final statement uses two subqueries to list the employees that share phone numbers:

```
SELECT EmployeeID, Name, Surname FROM EMPLOYEE
    WHERE EmployeeID IN
        ( SELECT EmployeeID FROM EMPPHONE
            WHERE PhoneID IN
                ( SELECT PhoneID FROM EMPPHONE
                    GROUP BY PhoneID
                    HAVING Count(*) > 1 ) )
```

```
--- result set ---
Betty   Smart
John    Smith
```

We'll use queries like these when we link the Phone Book application to an external database.

PART THREE

Database Applications

CHAPTER 7

Data Synchronization

The key to the success of the Palm Computing platform is its support for seamless synchronization of data between the handheld device and a desktop computer. Synchronization allows a user to enter data once and have it appear on both machines, no matter where the data was input. In effect, both the handheld device and the desktop computer become extensions of each other. Data synchronization is not, however, a simple matter, and in this chapter we explore what data synchronization is, why it's difficult, and what strategies to use when synchronizing with external databases.

What Is Synchronization?

Generally speaking, data synchronization refers to the *exchange* and *transformation* of data between two applications that maintain separate data stores. The applications share data, although perhaps stored in different ways, and the synchronization process keeps each application's copy of the shared data current and up-to-date.

Two applications running against the same data store, such as a database server, don't require synchronization because a single copy of the data is used by both applications. Synchronization only comes into play when the same data is spread among two or more separate data stores. On the Palm Computing platform, data synchronization occurs between an application running on the Palm device and a desktop application called a *conduit*, which we discuss in more detail shortly.

Data synchronization is not new technology. Companies use one-way data synchronization, sometimes referred to as data *replication*, to mirror databases so that if a database server crashes, another is ready to takes its place with minimal loss of data. Some would argue that data replication is not the same as data synchronization and reserve the term *data synchronization* for a two-way exchange of information.

Data synchronization is also used in sales force automation, where field personnel with laptop computers run "personal" or "standalone" database servers that synchronize with the main corporate database servers. This allows field personnel to access and update customer information while disconnected from the corporate network. Any changes are uploaded and applied to the central database the next time the laptop connects to the network. Since data synchronization is usually a two-way process, any changes to the central database are also downloaded to the laptop and applied to the standalone database server. Field personnel are thus able to work whether they're connected to the network or not.

As you can see from the sales force automation example, synchronization is often used when a network connection isn't always available to connect to a particular data source. The application maintains a local copy of the data so that it can continue running without a network connection. This mode of operation is often referred to as *disconnected* or, more accurately, *occasionally connected* computing. Occasionally connected computing isn't limited to corporate applications—reading and writing electronic mail offline on your home computer is an example of occasionally connected computing. When the computer reconnects to the network—such as when your home computer connects to your Internet service provider—the local and remote copies of your mailbox are synchronized.

Even when a network connection is available, a local database can be used to provide faster response times and to avoid overwhelming a central database. Synchronization can be scheduled to occur when the database server isn't as busy or when the network is less congested.

Note that data synchronization refers to data *transformation* as well as data *exchange*. There's nothing that says that two synchronized data stores have to be mirror images of each other. One data store can hold a subset of the data in a second data store. This is often the case with Palm-based applications, for example, because the Palm device simply doesn't have the memory required to hold large amounts of data. The two data stores can also store their data in completely different formats. It's not uncommon, for example, for the standalone database server on a field employee's laptop computer to be from a different vendor than the central, corporate database server it synchronizes with. Synchronizing your Palm's Address Book application with the address lists held in your desktop computer's copy of Lotus Notes is another example of how data is transformed as well as exchanged, because the database used by Notes is quite different from the Address Book's database.

Although well understood, data synchronization can be complicated to code, and in the next section we'll run through an example that shows you why that's the case.

Why Synchronization Is Difficult

You could argue that data synchronization on the Palm Computing platform is actually quite simple: Create a database, set some flags, and the database will be backed up automatically at the next HotSync. But, as we just discussed, synchronization involves more than just backing up your data. Let's explore what synchronization means on the Palm Computing platform and the difficulties it poses.

The Learning Curve

Data synchronization with a Palm device is performed by a conduit. The conduit is an application that runs on the desktop computer, not on the Palm device, and is invoked automatically as part of the HotSync process. The conduit receives the modified data from the Palm device and updates the device with new data. Typically, the conduit is a gateway to another application, communicating directly with the application (which might be a database server) or else knowing how to read and write the application's data files. You can purchase conduits, for example, to synchronize data from the built-in Palm applications, including the

Address Book or the Date Book, to common desktop applications such as Lotus Notes or Microsoft Outlook.

When you're writing your own applications, however, it's unlikely that you'll find a suitable conduit to do the data synchronization for you. After all, the conduit has to know how data is laid out within the Palm database and how to communicate with the desktop application and/or convert the data to the appropriate desktop format. This then, is the first challenge to doing data synchronization on the Palm Computing platform: Unless you can find a suitable alternative, you're going to have to write your own custom conduit. This means learning another SDK (the Conduit SDK we mentioned in Chapter 3) and a new set of development tools, perhaps even a new language if you want to write a conduit in Java as opposed to C/C++.

Even after you learn all of that, the hardest part—the data synchronization itself—has to be written, and this requires even more knowledge. When you're synchronizing to a relational database, for example, you have to know how to interface to the database, how to extract the necessary data, and how to ensure data integrity. It's not a bad idea to learn all these things in the long run, but it's hard to get started when the learning curve is so steep, even if you split the tasks among two or more people.

Given these complexities, custom synchronization is not something you necessarily want to do, but can you avoid it?

A Database Synchronization Example

Let's stop for a moment and work our way through a simple synchronization example, which will allow us to identify the challenges involved in building a conduit to perform custom data synchronization. The example we'll use is an application called Time Book, which you'll find on the CD-ROM in the Samples folder. In this section, we use the Time Book application to identify the synchronization issues that need to be addressed as part of the development process. Although Time Book synchronizes with a relational database, the issues we identify apply to synchronization with other types of data sources as well.

Time Book Goals

Time Book is an application to track the time spent by a user on a project. Consultants and other professionals who bill clients on an hourly basis obviously need to keep accurate records of the time spent on each project, whether it be at their desks working at a computer or out visiting clients. Even workers who aren't billing clients need to keep track of their time, if only for calculating overtime pay or else keeping track of research activities that might qualify for tax credits or other government incentives. Almost any worker can use the Time Book application. And because projects can be shared among several people, a central data store is required to store the information, which means Time Book uses a relational database, running on a database server, as its data repository. Using a database has the added advantage of letting others—such as managers, team leaders, or accounting personnel—track the status of projects and prepare reports for various purposes from invoicing clients to filing for tax credits.

A desktop version of Time Book can be easily written using such popular development tools as Visual Basic or PowerBuilder—anything that lets you connect to a database server and write a GUI-based client. The Palm version of Time Book doesn't have direct access to the database server, however, so it must rely on data synchronization via a custom conduit.

TIP Strictly speaking, you could limit your application to running on newer Palm devices and use TCP/IP connections to perform its data synchronization, but the natural way to do synchronization with a Palm device is via the HotSync process.

Time Book Walk-Through

Let's say you're the developer who's been tasked to write the Palm version of Time Book, including the conduit. Your first step is to walk through the use of the Time Book application in order to identify the issues you'll need to address. The developer of the desktop version (which may be you) will need to perform a similar kind of walk-through (and hopefully you'll do it together if there are two or more of you working on the application), but you'll have additional problems to solve that the other developer won't run into, all related to the occasionally connected nature of your users.

The Time Book walk-through involves three users. John and Mary are coworkers who often work offsite at client locations. Sue is their manager, who also spends time away from her desk. Each uses the Palm and desktop versions of Time Book, but in this scenario we concentrate exclusively on their use of the Palm version.

The first step is to get the data out of the database and onto the devices. When the users HotSync their devices, the conduit is activated. The conduit interfaces with the database and pulls out the appropriate information. The information for John and Mary is limited to the projects they're working on or have recently worked on; Sue gets detailed information for all the projects she or her subordinates are working on. Once extracted, the conduit transforms the information into records that are then sent down to the device for storage in a Palm database. After the first HotSync, only changes to the data are downloaded to the device. See Figure 7.1.

The next step is to let users change the information. For example, John and Mary add new entries each day for the projects they're working on. They may also update data they've already entered. All these changes are recorded in the Palm database. At the next HotSync, the conduit receives the new and updated records and applies the changes to the database. Because John and Mary only have access to their own time records, there are no conflicts and everything proceeds smoothly. See Figure 7.2.

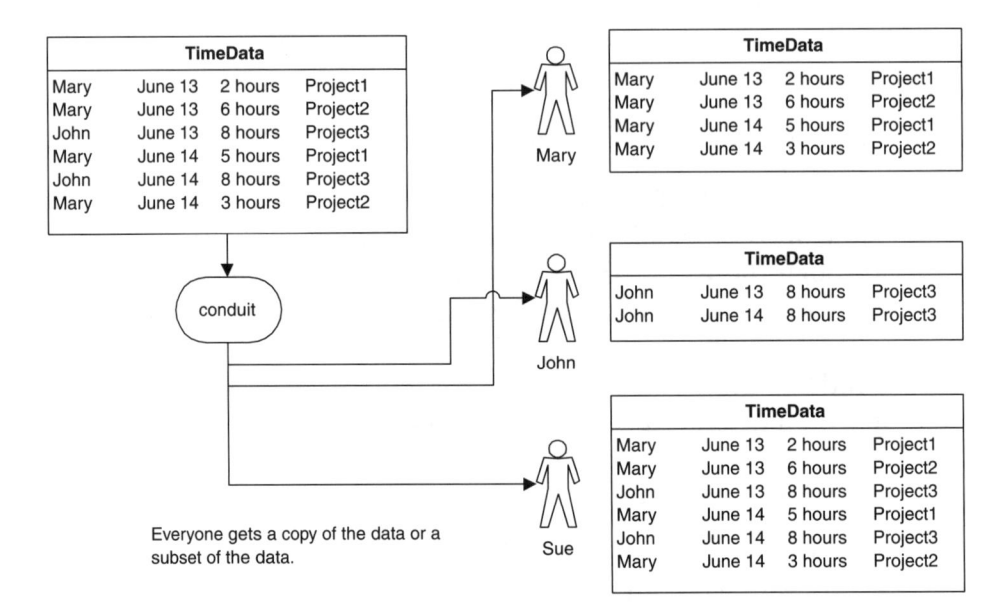

Figure 7.1 Time Book initialization.

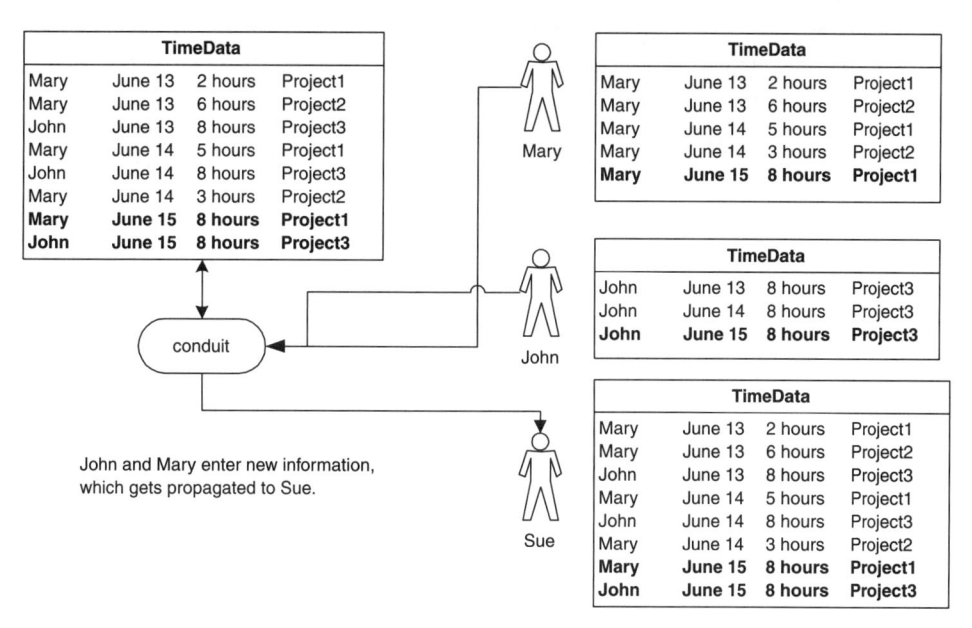

Figure 7.2 Uploading Time Book changes.

Sue can also change information, both for herself and for her subordinates. When she HotSyncs, the changes are also applied to the database. Sue also sees any changes that were made by John or Mary. As long as there are no conflicts, the next time John or Mary HotSyncs, the changes that Sue made that apply to them are downloaded to their devices. See Figure 7.3.

If John and Sue both change the same information, however, a conflict will occur when the second user performs a HotSync. The conduit notices that the information in the database has been updated since the last HotSync and that the information in the device has also been updated. The conduit then tries to resolve the conflict, using any of several schemes. For example, the conduit could let one update overwrite the other. Or it could determine that since Sue is John's manager, her changes should take precedence and report an error back to John along with the new data from Sue. Either way, the conduit has to ensure the integrity of the data in the database so that other users are always presented with the most consistent and correct data. See Figure 7.4.

Synchronization Challenges

User interface issues aside, the Time Book walk-through demonstrates the following synchronization challenges:

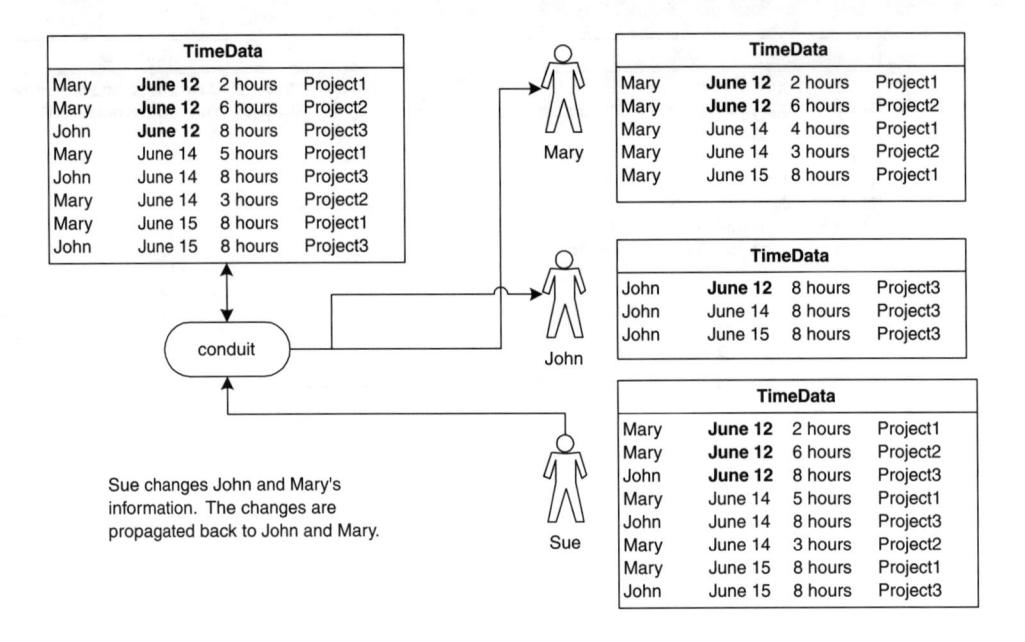

Figure 7.3 Manager updates to Time Book.

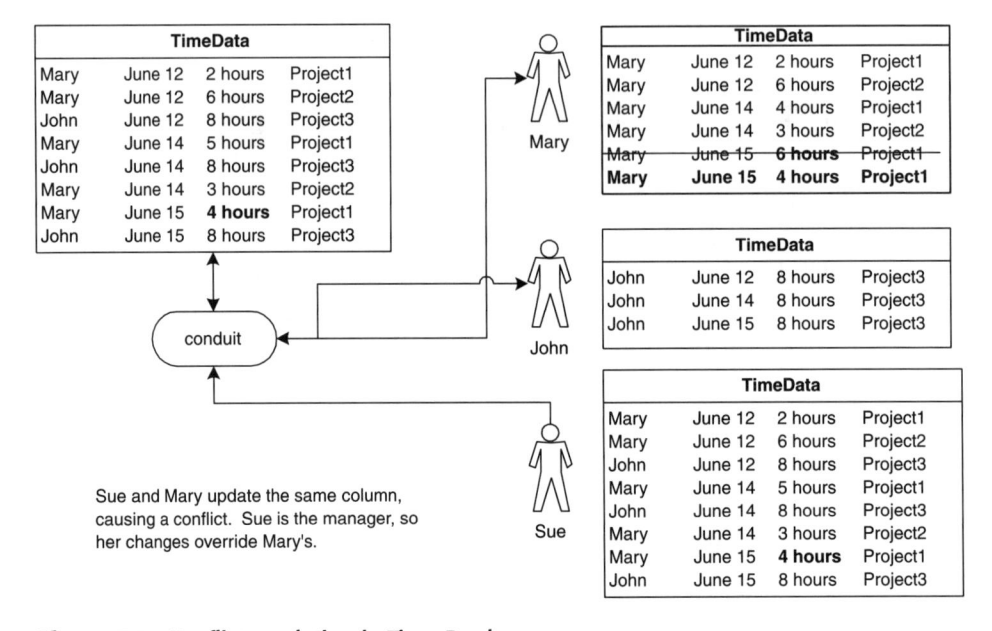

Figure 7.4 Conflict resolution in Time Book.

You have to understand the structure of the relational database and the data your application needs to extract from the database. This is true for any database application, of course, whether or not it runs on a Palm device. With Time Book, the database structure is fairly straightforward, consisting of a set of tables listing employees, clients, projects, and the time entries. If the database doesn't already have the information you need, you'll need to define new tables or modify existing tables to hold that information. If you're not using a relational database as the data source, you still need to understand how the data source is structured.

You have to know how to interface with the database. Your conduit needs to talk to the database server in order to read and write the data. It can do this through an ODBC driver (for C/C++ and other languages), a JDBC driver (for Java), or through a set of vendor-specific APIs or language extensions. The Time Book conduit knows where the database server resides and which interfaces it supports. If you're not using a relational database, you need to find similar ways of interacting with the data source, whether it be through a set of vendor-supplied library functions or through automation interfaces such as DDE or OLE.

You have to understand how to map that structure onto your Palm database. The database interfaces your conduit uses aren't available on the Palm device, so you have to map the data into Palm database records that the application can easily read and manipulate. The Time Book conduit maps each column it reads from the relational database into a specific offset inside the Palm database record. The Time Book application reads and writes data at those offsets.

You need to decide which subset of data is needed on the device. Memory and speed limitations make it impractical to load the complete set of data on the device. Security and confidentiality considerations also come into play. Time Book users only see the information that is relevant to their role within the company.

You have to ensure data integrity at all times, because the data is going to be used by many different users and/or applications. The Time Book data entered by Mary is used by the accounting department to bill her clients. Business rules in the database and in the Time Book application ensure that Mary enters data that is consistent, such as not billing the same time segment to two different customers. The

Time Book conduit ensures that if Mary aborts a HotSync, no incomplete data gets entered in the database.

You have to detect and resolve conflicts when synchronizing data with multiple clients. This problem exists in any multiuser system, but users who are directly connected to a database server are more likely to see up-to-date information and avoid conflicts than disconnected users. A Time Book user who doesn't HotSync for several days may have made changes based on old information (from the previous HotSync) without knowing that someone else made similar changes in the central database the day before. The Time Book conduit has to resolve those changes and ideally notify any users whose changes were rejected or modified.

When you think about it, however, most of these tasks are routine and could be automated to some degree: Interfacing with the database, mapping the data, ensuring data integrity, and detecting conflicts would differ very little in each conduit you write. In fact, you'd probably package these tasks as separate libraries or DLLs to be shared among your conduits. With a bit of work you could even make the code general enough to distribute to others outside your organization.

This, in fact, has been done by at least two database vendors, as we see in the next two chapters, who have developed conduits you can use with your own applications for transferring data to and from a relational database. These conduits drastically reduce the learning curve by taking care of routine synchronization tasks, leaving you to concentrate on your application's synchronization strategies. Instead of spending your time writing a conduit, you concentrate on the Palm application and the database configuration.

Strategies for Synchronization

The nonroutine synchronization tasks—data extraction and subsetting as well as conflict resolution—change from application to application depending on the application's requirements and your organization's business rules. Whether you're writing your own conduit or using someone else's, only you, the application developer, can decide which strategies to use. This section discusses the important issues when it comes to determining the strategies for each task.

Extracting and Subsetting Data

A relational database contains more data than your application requires. Even if the database is only used by your application, the self-describing nature of a relational database means that it includes system tables to hold database metadata in addition to the tables used by the application. Your first task is to subset the data so that you're only extracting data your application requires, in the format best suited to its purposes. Conceptually, this is done by writing a SELECT statement that defines the subset, although your synchronization software may present it differently. The following strategies are available.

> **TIP**
> If your synchronization software doesn't allow you enough control over the SELECT statement that defines the data subset, you might be able to achieve the same effect using views. A *view* is a virtual table, defined and managed by your database server. The columns in a view are defined by a SELECT statement. Tables and views can often be used interchangeably. Views may have limitations that real tables don't, however, so be sure to consult your database documentation for details on those limitations.

Incremental Synchronization

If possible, synchronization with a database should be incremental. In other words, only the rows in a database table that are new or have changed since the last synchronization should be downloaded to the device. The easiest way to do this is to insert a timestamp column into the table and to update the timestamp for a row each time the row is modified (use a trigger to automatically execute a SQL statement that updates the timestamp). The application stores the timestamp of its last update and uses that value to perform further row partitioning by excluding the rows with lesser timestamps. Note that the timestamp column does not need to be synchronized onto the device. See Figure 7.5 for an example.

If incremental synchronization is not used, then all rows that match the selection criteria participate in the synchronization process. This is sometimes referred to as *refreshing* the data or performing a *snapshot synchronization*. Small tables or tables with frequent changes are good candidates for refreshing as opposed to incremental synchronization.

ORDERINFO			
Order	Customer	Date	Timestamp
2383	100	Jun 3	Jun 3 12:34:56
2384	200	Jun 3	Jun 3 12:34:57
2385	100	Jun 3	Jun 4 09:45:87
2386	300	Jun 4	Jun 4 10:00:03

Only the rows that were new or updated since the last synchronization at 13:00:00 are selected for downloading.

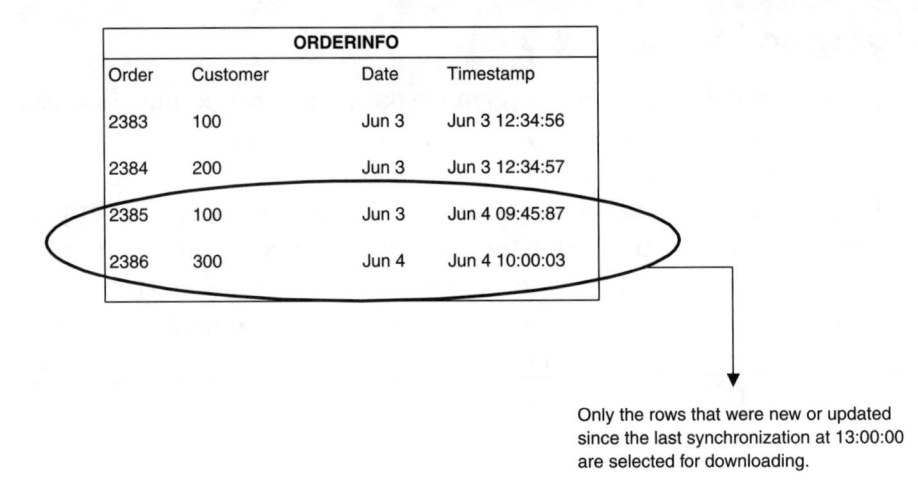

Figure 7.5 Incremental synchronization example.

While developing your application, you may also find it useful to include a way to perform snapshot synchronizations as you develop and test your data extraction and conflict resolution strategies.

Column Partitioning

Column partitioning means selecting only the columns in a table that are required by your application. The other columns are not synchronized. Note that you shouldn't just select the columns that are *displayed* by your application, although that's a good start—your application may require other columns for proper functioning. In particular, the primary key column (or columns) is almost always necessary, because it uniquely identifies each row in the table. See Figure 7.6.

ORDERINFO			
Order	Customer	Date	Timestamp
2383	100	Jun 3	Jun 3 12:34:56
2384	200	Jun 3	Jun 3 12:34:57
2385	100	Jun 3	Jun 4 09:45:87
2386	300	Jun 4	Jun 4 10:00:03

Only the columns that are needed by the application are downloaded.

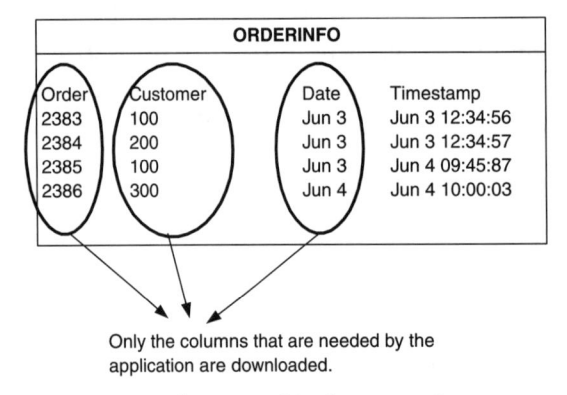

Figure 7.6 Column partitioning example.

Although it may surprise you, consider *adding* computed columns to the set of synchronized columns if the overhead of storing the computed values on the device is minimal when compared to the time to perform the same calculations inside your application.

Row Partitioning

Row partitioning is very similar to column partitioning, only it deals with the rows of a table instead of the columns. The premise is quite simple: select only the rows that are required by the user of your application. For example, the Time Book example uses row partitioning to ensure that John and Mary see only their own time entries, and not anyone else's. Row partitioning is done by adding a WHERE clause to the SELECT statement. See Figure 7.7.

Explicit Type Conversions

The data in the database isn't always stored in the format that is the most efficient or convenient for your application. You can explicitly convert data values to other types using the CAST function or its equivalent. It might make sense, for example, to convert a fixed-length character column to a variable-length character column to save some space on the device:

```
SELECT CAST( Address AS VARCHAR(100) ) FROM CUSTOMER
```

Explicit conversions on updateable columns must always be reversible. That is, the database server has to be able to implicitly convert any updated values to the correct type for the column if the update is to succeed.

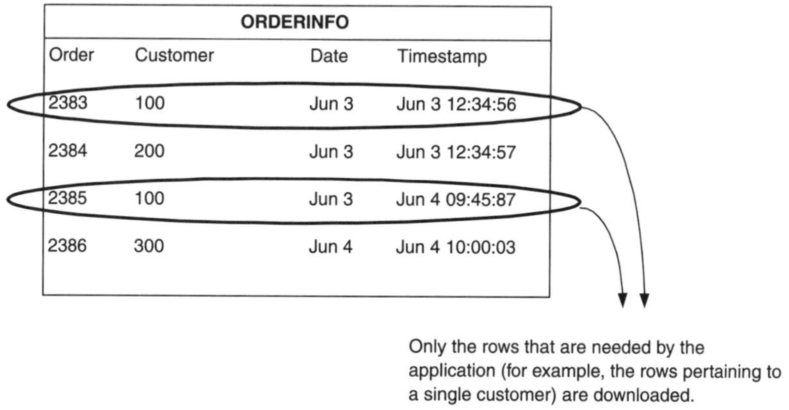

\multicolumn{4}{c}{ORDERINFO}
Order	Customer	Date	Timestamp
2383	100	Jun 3	Jun 3 12:34:56
2384	200	Jun 3	Jun 3 12:34:57
2385	100	Jun 3	Jun 4 09:45:87
2386	300	Jun 4	Jun 4 10:00:03

Only the rows that are needed by the application (for example, the rows pertaining to a single customer) are downloaded.

Figure 7.7 Row partitioning example.

Resolving Conflicts

A conflict occurs when two or more users modify the same piece of data independently. To detect conflicts, the application must store both the old and the new data values. When synchronization occurs, a conflict is detected by first comparing the old value stored by the application to the current value stored in the database. If the two are equal, no conflict occurs and the new value is stored in the database. Otherwise, another user or application has already modified the value in the database and a choice must be made as to which value to keep—the (already-modified) value stored in the database, the new value from the application, or perhaps a combination of the two values. No single conflict resolution strategy is appropriate for all applications, so your application must decide how conflicts are to be handled. What follows are some common strategies.

Conflict Avoidance

The simplest strategy is to avoid conflicts altogether. If users aren't allowed to make changes, no conflicts can occur, for example. Or you can define mutually exclusive data subsets for each user, so that no user can change another user's data.

One Side Always Wins

If conflicts can't be avoided, the next simplest strategy is that one side of the synchronization conflict always wins. In other words, either the new value from the device overwrites the current (already-modified) value in the database, or else the value in the database overwrites the value in the application. If the database always wins over the device, your application will need to inform the user that the update failed and perhaps give the user the opportunity to reapply the change if it makes sense.

Both Sides Win

Another strategy is to allow both changes to occur. The built-in Palm applications offer this choice, for example, ensuring that no changes are ever lost when a conflict occurs. However, when updating data in a relational database, this strategy rarely makes sense, because the synchronization procedure identifies the table rows to synchronize by their primary keys, and the primary key of a row must always be unique. For both sides to win, a copy of the row, identical except for the data in question, would have to be inserted into the table, and this would violate the uniqueness constraint. The only way for this to work would be to generate a new primary key for the copy to use. It's better to report an error than to have duplicate rows.

Custom Strategies

If none of the simpler strategies fits the bill, you can always implement your own custom conflict resolution rules. You could allow a manager's changes to always override those of his or her subordinates. You could merge two changes together. Or you can even send the conflict to a human for arbitration.

Primary Key Pooling

One situation where conflict avoidance is desired is in the assignment of primary keys. When the application adds data to the database, the synchronization process will assign primary keys for any new rows that are inserted into a table. For consistency, the primary key always has to be assigned by the database server; otherwise, two devices could choose the same primary key value and create an unexpected conflict.

Primary key conflicts are avoided by creating a pool of unused primary key values and assigning each device a unique range of values from the pool. The application uses primary key values from the device's pool wherever possible. At each HotSync, the primary key pool is updated to reflect any changes made by the application and to add new values if necessary.

While the assignment of new primary keys can be automated, the size of the pool and the ranges within the pool depend on the application. If the application runs out of primary key values, it should either prevent the user from entering new data (and tell the user to HotSync as soon as possible) or else explicitly handle primary key conflicts.

CHAPTER 8

Sybase UltraLite

Given the popularity of the Palm platform and the complexity of writing custom conduits, it was inevitable that prepackaged synchronization solutions appear in the marketplace. Database vendors are eager to expand the reach of their database systems, and occasionally connected computing is emerging as an important growth area in the fight for market share. This book discusses two prepackaged synchronization solutions for the Palm Computing platform, both from established database vendors. Although they won't eliminate all the work, both handle the more routine synchronization tasks for you and let you concentrate on implementing the application. This chapter discusses Sybase's UltraLite database deployment option.

What Is UltraLite?

UltraLite is an embedded, custom-built relational database with built-in synchronization capabilities. The database is part of your application, with an extremely small footprint that depends entirely on the capabilities and features your application requires. An UltraLite database synchronizes to an ODBC data source, which means it can be used with almost any database, not just databases from Sybase.

A Relational Database in Your Application

UltraLite differentiates itself from other synchronization solutions by moving the relational database onto the device. Instead of a standard record-oriented Palm database, the application deals with a fully relational data model, using SQL to select and update data and to commit and roll back changes. The application doesn't have to keep track of changes or worry about how the data is mapped into memory. Data synchronization becomes a peer-to-peer process, where one relational database synchronizes itself with another relational database. The application logic becomes more portable, since it doesn't depend on the specifics of the Palm Computing platform's data management APIs.

At this point you might be thinking that a Palm device is not a suitable platform for a relational database, and that an UltraLite database must either be very large or else of limited capability. In fact, UltraLite databases are very small, because they are custom-built for your application based solely on the features your application requires. In terms of capabilities, UltraLite databases have few limitations, the primary limitation being that only static SQL statements—SQL statements that are fully defined when the application is built, although with the ability to substitute values at run time—are allowed (see the following section for the full list of limitations). This limitation, which isn't a concern for most applications, and the exclusion of unnecessary features, such as support for files or for concurrent users, allow a database to be built with minimal overhead, usually in the 50K to 200K range (not counting data, of course). Thus UltraLite is a practical and powerful way to add the capabilities of a relational database to your application.

The impact of having a relational database on the device embedded within your application is greater than you think and can't be overemphasized. All the reasons that led application developers to embrace relational databases over flat-file databases are just as valid when writing applications for handheld devices.

MobiLink Synchronization

Although custom-built databases are the heart of UltraLite technology, they'd be useless without the ability to synchronize them to external databases. Just as with a regular Palm database, UltraLite synchronization depends on a conduit running on a desktop computer. This conduit interfaces to Sybase's MobiLink server to act as the gateway between an UltraLite database and an external database. (An UltraLite application can also bypass the conduit and connect directly to the MobiLink server using TCP/IP or the serial port.) The MobiLink server lets you define sophisticated data extraction and conflict resolution strategies. The conduit and the MobiLink server handle the whole synchronization process automatically.

The MobiLink server can synchronize to any ODBC-compliant relational database. UltraLite includes scripts to install the necessary tables and stored procedures into ASA, Sybase Adaptive Server Enterprise (formerly known as Sybase SQL Server), Microsoft SQL Server, and Oracle databases. Other databases can be supported by adapting these scripts.

Together, a custom-built UltraLite database and the MobiLink synchronization server make it easy to build complete database applications without writing custom conduits.

Supported Platforms

UltraLite applications can be deployed to the Palm Computing platform and the Windows CE platform. Support for more platforms is being planned as this book is being written; check the Sybase Web site for further details. Although it won't help you with the user interface, UltraLite does make it easy to port the data access parts of your application to other handheld platforms.

UltraLite application development is hosted on the Windows 95/98 or Windows NT operating systems. CodeWarrior is required to compile the applications for deployment to the Palm Computing platform; the GNU tools are not currently supported. UltraLite applications support Palm OS 2.0 or higher, while the MobiLink conduit requires HotSync Manager 3.0 or higher.

Limitations

In order to keep the custom database as small as possible, UltraLite deployment does limit what your application can do. The limitations are as follows:

No runtime schema changes allowed. An UltraLite application cannot alter the database schema in any way. Changes must be made at development time and a new version of the application must then be built to reflect the new schema.

No access to database metadata. An UltraLite custom database does not have any system tables and does not support system functions. The nonsystem built-in functions such as COUNT or CAST are supported, however.

No dynamic SQL. Only static (fixed) SQL statements are allowed in an UltraLite application. Parameterized statements are allowed, however, so that the value of a WHERE clause can be specified at run time.

These limitations are fundamental to the design of UltraLite. Other limitations are not fundamental and may be lessened or removed entirely in subsequent versions:

No interface other than embedded SQL. No other interfaces such as ODBC, OLEDB, or ADO are currently supported. Directly accessing the rows in memory is not allowed, either. (See Chapter 6 for more information on database interfaces.)

No support for other languages. C/C++ is the only language currently supported.

No reentrancy. Currently, the custom database generated by the UltraLite development process is not reentrant, because it uses global and static data. It's not possible to use the UltraLite database unless the application is started via a normal, initializing, or subcall launch, which are the only ones that have global data enabled. Among other things, this means that UltraLite applications cannot by default participate in global Find operations, since the whole point of a Find operation is to search through the database for records of interest. If you want to support global Find, you'll have to relaunch the application in order to recover its globals, as was discussed in Chapter 4. The Phone Book sample demonstrates how to do this.

No stored procedures, variables, triggers, or Java classes. These are all ways of moving logic from the application to the database, to increase performance or to centralize business logic. Given that the UltraLite database is embedded into the application, the same results are achieved by writing library routines that are linked into the application.

No sharing of data between applications. Each custom database is separate and self-contained. Even if two applications use the same tables, each requires its own database.

No floating-point, LONG VARCHAR, and LONG VARBINARY types. As well, support for CHAR(N), VARCHAR(N), BINARY(N), and VARBINARY(N) types is limited to the cases where $N <= 2048$.

No character set conversions. UltraLite assumes that all characters are represented using code page 1252, the Windows US code page, which is also supported by the Palm Computing platform.

Consult the UltraLite documentation for the full set of unsupported features. You should check the Sybase Web site regularly for information on upgrades to ASA and UltraLite.

Licensing

UltraLite is not sold as a separate product but instead comes as part of Sybase's Adaptive Server Anywhere (ASA) database system, which we used with our examples in Chapter 6. As part of ASA, UltraLite is positioned as deployment technology, a way to develop and deploy a custom database that is not ASA but uses ASA as a model. Although ASA is required to develop an UltraLite-based application, ASA is not in fact required for deployment because the MobiLink server works with other database systems.

The evaluation version of ASA that is included on the CD-ROM includes the UltraLite deployment technology. Although you're free to use the evaluation version to try the product, applications built with UltraLite technology require a license for distribution; contact Sybase for details.

Installation instructions for ASA are found in Appendix B.

How UltraLite Works

To understand how UltraLite works, you must understand what happens during the development and deployment phases of your application. During the development phase, the SQL statements and the database tables required by the application are analyzed to generate a custom database that becomes part of the application. Synchronization strategies are also developed. In the deployment phase, the custom database and the MobiLink server work together to manage and synchronize the application's data.

Development Phase

The first step in developing an UltraLite application is to define the *reference database*. A reference database is an ASA database used as the template for building the custom UltraLite database. The reference database is only used during the development phase and is not deployed with the application. When the application runs, it synchronizes itself with the *consolidated database*, which contains the tables and data used for synchronization. A single ASA database can be used both as the reference database and the consolidated database if so desired.

The reference database models a subset of the consolidated database. Typically this means that there is a one-to-one correspondence between the tables and columns in the reference database and a subset of the tables and columns in the consolidated database. The model does not have to be exact, however, and the reference database's schema can be different from the consolidated database's schema. Any differences in the schemas are handled by defining appropriate mappings as part of the synchronization process. The UltraLite documentation does recommend that the two schemas be as similar as possible, as shown in Figure 8.1.

In addition to modeling the structure of the consolidated database, the reference database can also hold data representative of the data in the

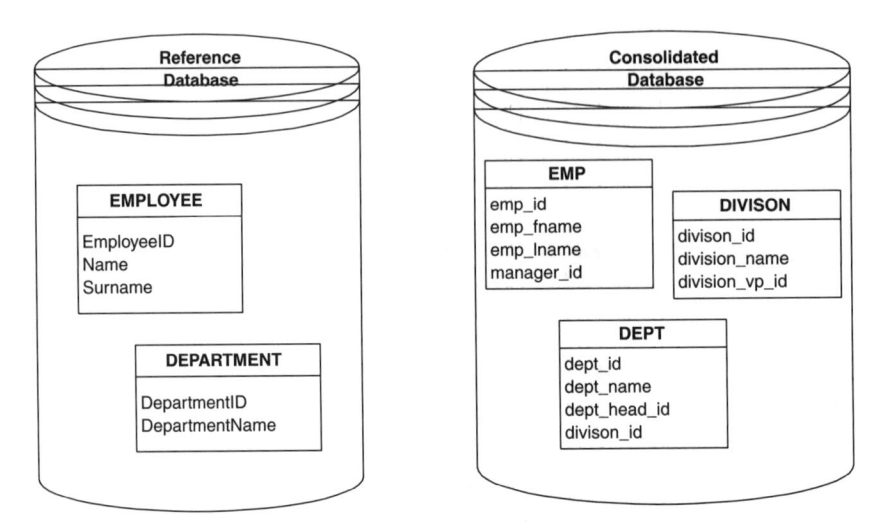

Reference database contains a subset of the tables in the consolidated database. Notice that the mappings don't have to be exact.

Figure 8.1 The reference and consolidated databases.

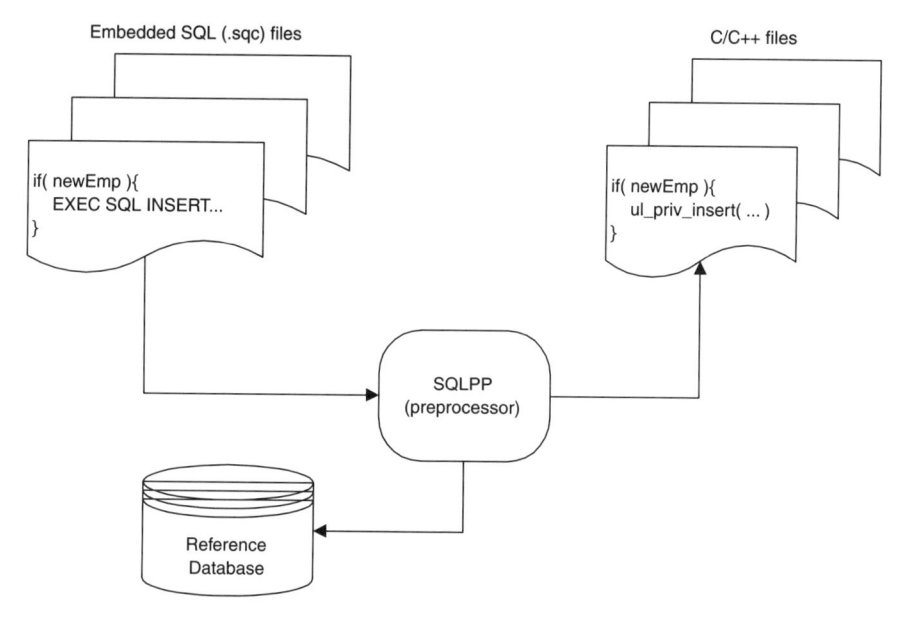

```
Embedded SQL (.sqc) files                    C/C++ files

if( newEmp ){                                if( newEmp ){
   EXEC SQL INSERT...                           ul_priv_insert( ... )
}                                            }

                        SQLPP
                     (preprocessor)

                    Reference
                    Database
```

Figure 8.2 Preprocessing the embedded SQL.

consolidated database. The data is not required, but if present, it is used to optimize the layout of an UltraLite database.

Once the reference database has been defined, the next step is to write the SQL statements required by your application. The SQL statements are added to your C/C++ source files, using the ASA embedded SQL syntax. These SQL statements operate against the schema of the reference database. The source files are then processed by the embedded SQL preprocessor. The preprocessor stores information about the SQL in the reference database. The preprocessor also transforms the embedded SQL into plain C/C++ code, replacing the SQL statements with calls into the UltraLite runtime library. The process is shown in Figure 8.2.

After the source files have been processed, the UltraLite analyzer is run. The analyzer is a Java program that runs inside the reference database using the ASA Java virtual machine. The analyzer uses the schema of the reference database and the information stored by the SQL preprocessor to create a custom database unique to the application. The analyzer generates a C source file that implements a custom database engine, as shown in Figure 8.3. The analyzer should be run every time the embedded SQL changes, or if the schema of the reference database changes.

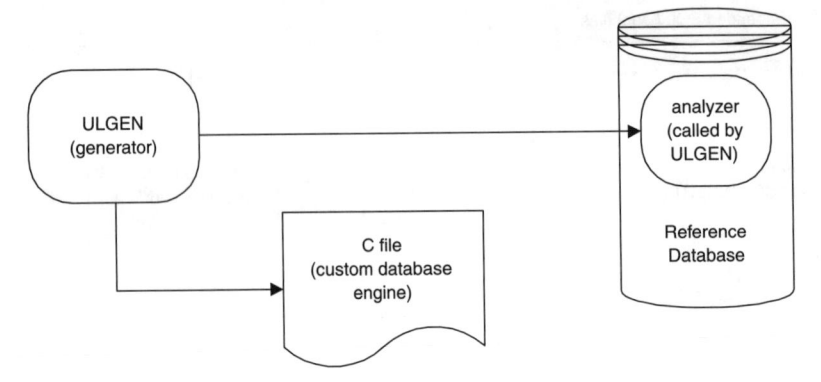

Figure 8.3 Analyzing the SQL.

Although the data in the reference database is used by the analyzer to optimize the custom database, the data is not used to populate the database with initial values. The synchronization process will populate the database later when the application is first run.

After the preprocessing and the analyzing, the generated files and any additional user-defined source files are compiled by the C/C++ compiler and linked against the UltraLite runtime library to form an UltraLite application, as shown in Figure 8.4.

Note that the size of the final database is proportional to the complexity of the database and the number of SQL statements the application executes.

Deployment Phase

Once built, the UltraLite application is deployed to the Palm device for execution. The application runs against the embedded database engine, reading and writing data to the in-memory database using the embedded SQL interface. The database uses the Palm storage heap to manage the data, but the details are completely hidden from the application because the application only deals with the database through the embedded SQL interface. Among other things, the database tracks changes that are made to the data it stores, for use when the next synchronization process starts.

Synchronization occurs whenever the user requests it. It can occur as part of a HotSync, using the MobiLink conduit to communicate with

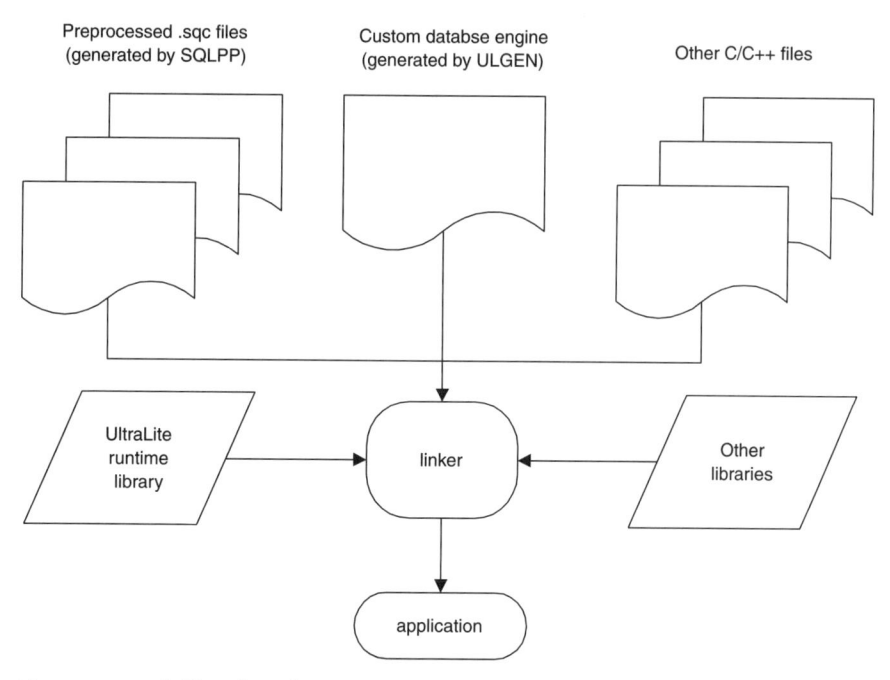

Figure 8.4 Linking the UltraLite application.

the MobiLink server, or it can occur independently, using either TCP/IP or the serial port to communicate directly with the MobiLink server. These modes of communication are referred to as synchronization *channels*, and apart from some simple initialization, the UltraLite database and the MobiLink server manage the channel without user intervention. The channels are shown in Figure 8.5. A HotSync operation is the preferred way of performing the synchronization on the Palm Computing platform, but the other channels may be useful to remote users who are away from their HotSync cradle for extended periods of time.

TIP

The more recent Palm devices such as the Palm III can communicate with each other through their infrared ports. Two UltraLite applications can (with some programming) exchange information via infrared beaming, but this is not data synchronization. Data exchanged in this fashion updates the application's custom database and can cause conflicts when synchronization does occur. If data exchange is allowed, you must adjust your conflict resolution strategies to account for these additional conflicts.

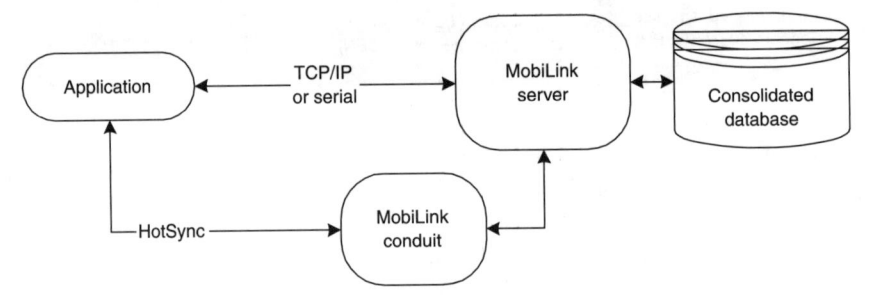

Figure 8.5 UltraLite synchronization channels.

Synchronization always takes place against the consolidated database; the reference database is only used during the development phase. The MobiLink server uses an ODBC connection to interface with the consolidated database.

The synchronization process involves a small number of steps to minimize the amount of data transferred between the handheld device and the desktop computer. Because communication between the device and the desktop is fairly slow, limiting the amount of data shortens the total synchronization time. You can shorten the time even more by careful data partitioning and by performing incremental synchronization, both of which we discuss later in this chapter.

The first step in the synchronization process is to upload changes made on the device to the MobiLink server, as shown in Figure 8.6. The server then applies these changes to the consolidated database. All changes are done within the context of a single transaction, including resolving any conflicts between uploaded data and the consolidated database.

Changes are uploaded as a series of rows, and the set of changes is referred to as the *upload stream*. The structure of a row in the stream is fixed and defined by the appropriate table schema in the reference database. Each uploaded row invokes a predefined *script* in the consoli-

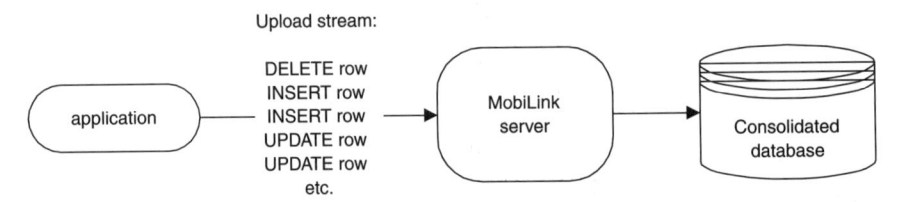

Figure 8.6 Uploading changes to the server.

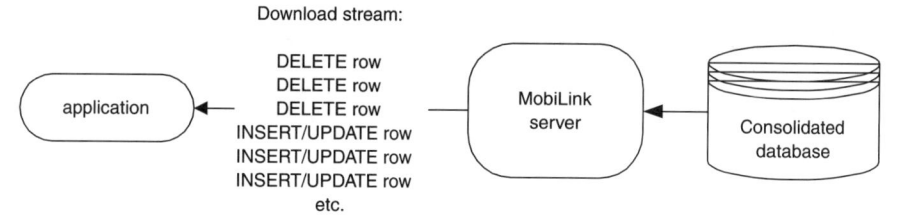

```
                Download stream:

                  DELETE row
                  DELETE row
  application    DELETE row           MobiLink
                  INSERT/UPDATE row    server         Consolidated
                  INSERT/UPDATE row                    database
                  INSERT/UPDATE row
                       etc.
```

Figure 8.7 Downloading changes to the device.

dated database to make the change. The script is a set of SQL statements that the MobiLink server invokes against the consolidated database to perform an operation. In this case, the script positions a database cursor using the row's primary key. Once positioned, the MobiLink server then inserts, updates, or deletes the row as appropriate.

After committing the uploaded changes, the MobiLink server then prepares the *download stream*, shown in Figure 8.7 The download stream is similar to the upload stream, consisting of the changes to the consolidated database that are to be applied to the UltraLite database. As with the upload stream, the download stream invokes a predefined script, but this script is invoked once per table to return a result set of changed rows. Each row in the result set is processed and applied to the UltraLite database. The changes are applied as a single transaction.

Once the upload and download streams have been processed, the UltraLite database and the MobiLink server each acknowledge the receipt of each stream, ending the synchronization process, as shown in Figure 8.8. If the connection is lost during a synchronization, have no fear—the UltraLite synchronization is very fault-tolerant. Uncommitted changes are not lost, they are simply reapplied at the next synchronization.

Every stage of the synchronization process is controlled by scripts in the consolidated database, and not by the application itself. All the application does is initiate the synchronization process.

```
                    -ack-
   application              MobiLink
                              server
                    -ack-
```

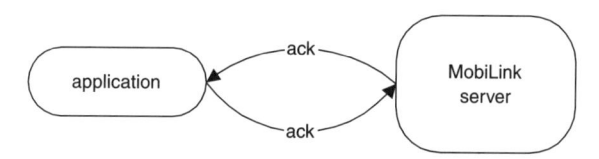

Figure 8.8 Acknowledging the changes.

Building and Deploying UltraLite Applications

Several steps are required to build and deploy UltraLite applications.

UltraLite Development

The steps required to build an UltraLite application for the Palm Computing platform are as follows:

1. Design the application
2. Start the CodeWarrior project
3. Create the reference and consolidated databases
4. Define the database schema
5. Write the embedded SQL to access the database
6. Write the user interface
7. Build and install the application

Each step is explained in the following sections.

Design the Application

As with any application, the first step is to decide what problem it will solve and determine the program's requirements. Refer back to the example at the end of Chapter 4 for design information.

Start the CodeWarrior Project

The following steps create a CodeWarrior project for building UltraLite applications.

1. **Create a new multisegment project.** Use the Palm OS Multi-Segment project stationery, or base the project on the AppSkeleton sample from Chapter 4. UltraLite applications are not excessively large, but they rarely fit into a single segment.

2. **Rename the project.** Follow the steps described in Chapter 3 to rename the project, assign a creator ID, and adjust the application name and icon.

3. **Change the compiler settings.** With the Target Settings window open, select the 68K Processor item in the left-hand pane and then

select the 4-Byte Ints option in the right-hand pane. The code generated by the UltraLite preprocessor and analyzer assumes that the int type is a 32-bit value. If you're going to use C++, select the C/C++ Language item in the left-hand pane and then select Activate C++ Compiler in the right-hand pane.

4. **Change the standard runtime library.** The default multisegment project includes MSL Runtime Palm OS (2i).Lib, the two-byte int version of the C/C++ startup code, as does the AppSkeleton project. Remove this library and add MSL Runtime Palm OS (4i).Lib, the 4-byte int version, in its place. You'll find the library in the Palm OS 3.0 Support/Runtime folder of your CodeWarrior installation.

5. **Adjust the access paths.** The source files that UltraLite generates require access to the UltraLite header files when compiled and to the UltraLite runtime library when linked. In the Target Settings window, select the Access Paths item in the left-hand pane. In the right-hand panel press the Add button. CodeWarrior asks you to select a directory from your hard disk. Select the path to the UltraLite header files, for example:

```
C:\Adaptive Server Anywhere 6.0\h
```

The actual path depends on where you installed your copy of ASA, of course. Before dismissing the dialog, select "Absolute Path" from the drop-down combobox at the top of the dialog. The path is treated as an absolute path instead of being relative to the project or compiler. Back in the Target Settings window, press the Add button again and select the path to the UltraLite runtime library:

```
C:\Adaptive Server Anywhere 6.0\ultralite\palm\68k\lib
```

Again, store this as an absolute path.

Create Your Own UltraLite Stationery

Use the newly defined project to create new CodeWarrior project stationery for building UltraLite applications. In your CodeWarrior folder you'll find a subfolder labeled Stationery. Create a folder called Palm OS UltraLite Application in the subfolder and copy your project into the new folder. The project then forms a template for building future UltraLite applications and saves you the hassle of going through the preceding steps each time you need to create a new UltraLite project.

6. **Add the UltraLite runtime library.** The support routines required by the custom database are found in the file:

    `C:\Adaptive Server Anywhere 6.0\ultralite\palm\68k\lib\ulrt.lib`

    Add this file to your project.

Build the project to make sure it compiles and links correctly. When run, the application does nothing except display a blank form.

Create the Databases

With the application skeleton in place, the next task is to create the consolidated and reference databases. We're going to use two different ASA databases as our consolidated and reference databases, although we could just as easily use a single database for both purposes. The CustDB sample that ships with ASA uses a single database for both, for example.

To create a database, start the Sybase Central tool. (Databases can also be created from the DOS prompt using the dbinit application.) Sybase Central allows you to manage all aspects of your databases using a graphical user interface. Note that there are two versions of Sybase Central: one written in C and one written in Java. The C version is used to create and manage ASA databases, while the Java version is used to create and manage the MobiLink synchronization process. The user interface is the same in both versions. At some point in the future the two versions will hopefully merge, in order to provide a single point of access for controlling all aspects of UltraLite deployment. Until that happens, you'll have to use both tools.

To start the C version of Sybase Central, use the Manage Adaptive Server Anywhere shortcut in the Sybase/Adaptive Server Anywhere 6.0 menu or folder. As you can see from the screenshot in Figure 8.9, Sybase Central uses a Windows Explorer–style metaphor, with a hierarchy of folders (including plug-in tools and databases) in the left-hand pane and the contents of the currently selected folder displayed in the right-hand pane.

To create a consolidated database, first select Adaptive Server Anywhere in the left-hand pane and then double-click on the Utilities folder. You'll see a list of operations in the right-hand pane, as shown in Figure 8.10. Double-click on the Create Database operation to invoke the wizard for creating a new database, shown in Figure 8.11. We're going to create the consolidated database for the Phone Book sample. Enter the path for the consolidated database on the first page:

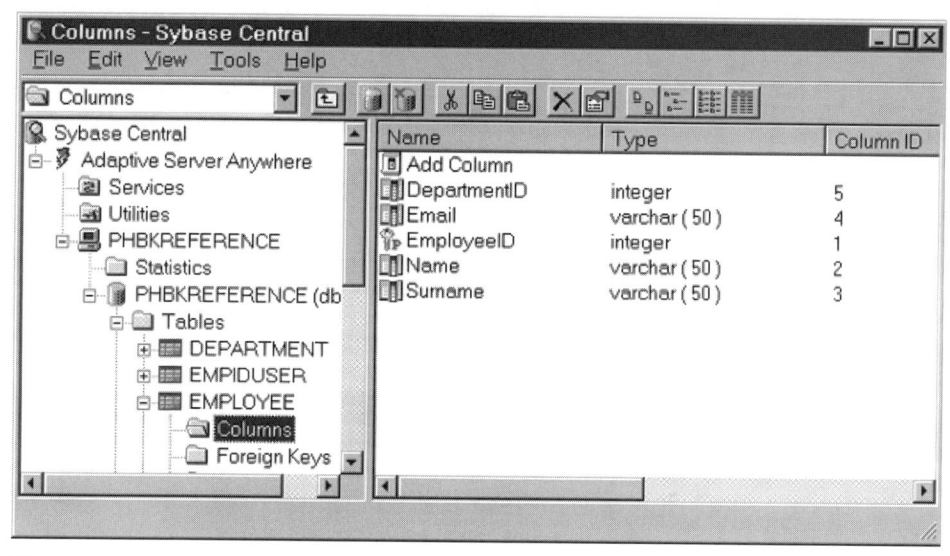

Figure 8.9 The C version of Sybase Central.

```
C:\Phone Book\PHBKConsolidated.db
```

Move through all the pages in the wizard, accepting the default values for each page, until the last page is reached. On the last page, choose to connect to the database after creation, as shown in Figure 8.12, and press the Finish button. Sybase Central creates the database and adds an entry for it in its left-hand pane.

Adding ASA to the Desktop

The ASA installation procedure does not install a folder on the desktop for accessing Sybase Central or any of the other tools or documentation. Instead, all access is done through the Start menu. It's easy to make the contents of the Start menu directly accessible from the desktop, however. Open the Start menu and select Settings -> Taskbar... → and then click on the Advanced... button in the Taskbar properties dialog. This opens the Explorer with the contents of the Start menu, which are really just regular folders and links stored in a user profile. Find the Adaptive Server Anywhere 6.0 folder (NT users note that the ASA folder is found in the All Users profile, not in the current user's profile) and do a drag-copy of it onto the desktop.

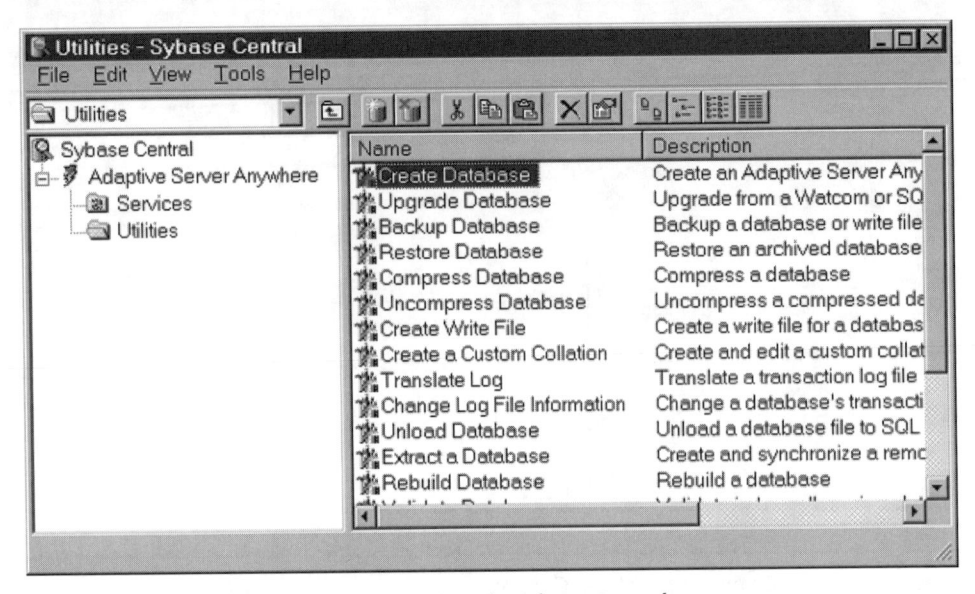

Figure 8.10 Available database operations in Sybase Central.

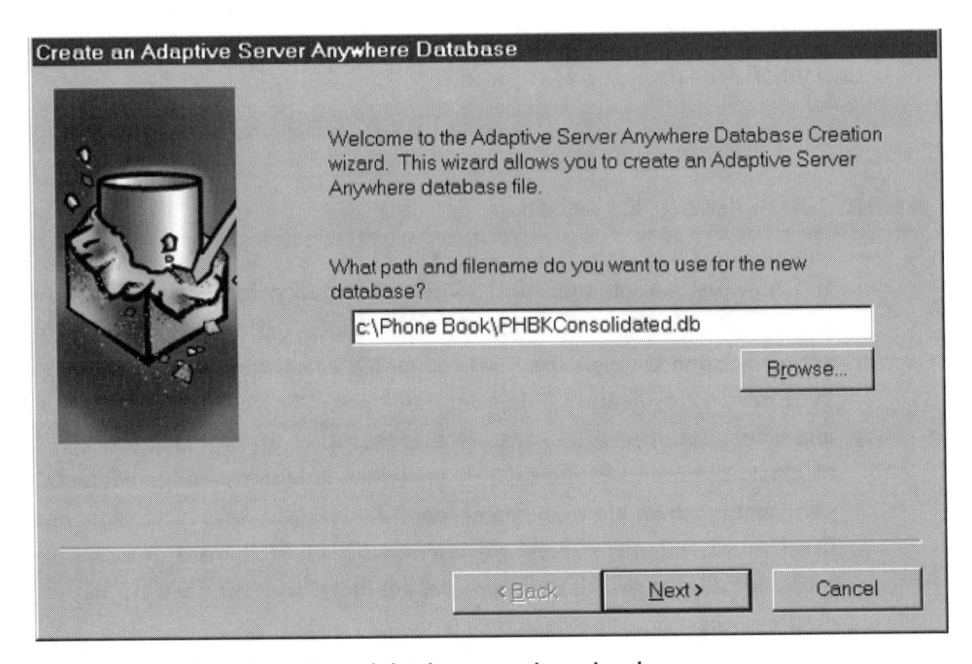

Figure 8.11 The Sybase Central database creation wizard.

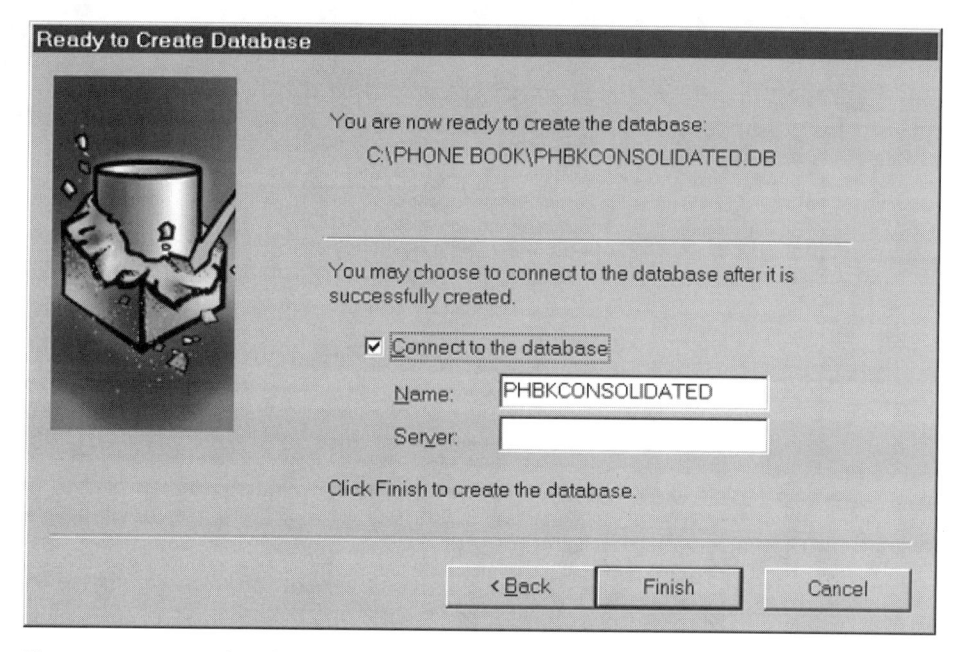

Figure 8.12 Creating the database.

Next, create a reference database in a similar manner, but using this path instead:

```
C:\Phone Book\PHBKReference.db
```

Again, ensure a connection is made after the database is created.

The next step is to define ODBC data sources for the new databases. This is done using a separate tool, the ODBC Administrator. You'll find a shortcut to the ODBC Administrator in the same menu or folder you used to start Sybase Central. Start the ODBC Administrator to see the list of currently installed data sources and database drivers, as shown in Figure 8.13. Your list may be different, of course, depending on what drivers and databases you already have installed on the system. Press the Add... button to add a new data source, and select the Adaptive Server Anywhere 6.0 database driver from the list of available drivers. You'll be presented with the configuration dialog shown in Figure 8.14. On the ODBC page of this dialog, enter *Phone Book Consolidated* as the name of the data source. Move to the Login page and enter *dba* and *sql* as the userid ID and password, respectively. Move to the Database page, press the Browse... button and select the PHBKConsolidated.db file you just created. Finally, return to the ODBC page and press the Test Con-

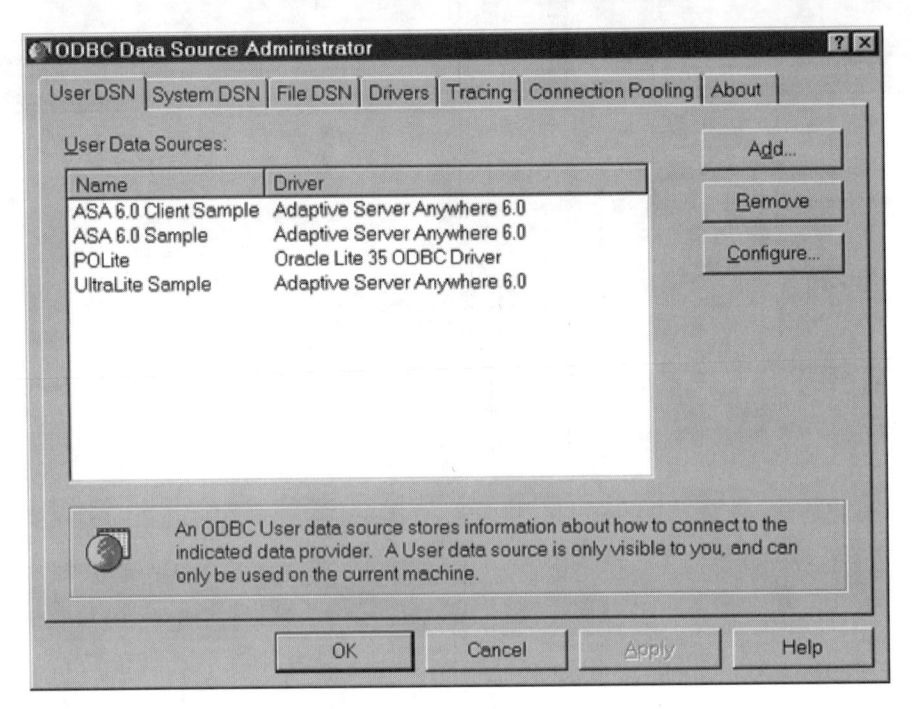

Figure 8.13 The ODBC Administrator.

nection button to ensure that a connection can be made. Then press OK to dismiss the dialog.

Repeat the procedure for the reference database, with Phone Book Reference as the data source name. The consolidated and reference databases are now ready for use by the Phone Book application.

In the future, you can start a database server by using this command:

```
dbeng6 -c 16m "c:\Phone Book\PHBKReference.db"
```

The -c option sets the server's cache size, which must be at least 16 Mb for the reference database. Refer to the ASA documentation for details on it and other options.

Define the Schema

The next task is to define the schema for each database, starting with the consolidated database. If you're using a preexisting database, of course, the schema may already exist, although it may require some modification. You may not have the access rights to make any changes, however,

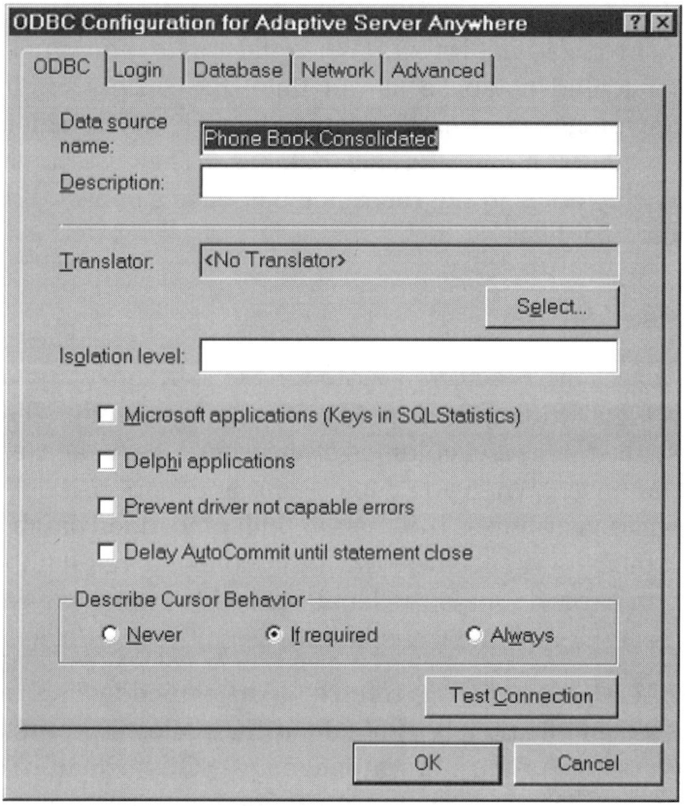

Figure 8.14 ODBC data source configuration.

and will have to coordinate any modifications with the group that runs and maintains the database.

You can use Sybase Central or other GUI tools to create the tables, or you can enter DDL commands using the Interactive SQL tool. In the Scripts folder on the CD-ROM you'll find the phbkref.sql and phbkcons.sql text files. These are scripts to install the Phone Book tables we discussed at the end of Chapter 6. Using the Interactive SQL tool, connect to the reference database and enter this command:

```
read "z:\Scripts\phbkref.sql"
```

Adjust the path according to your machine's configuration. Then connect to the consolidated database and apply the phbkcons.sql script in a similar fashion.

Remember, the schemas for the two databases do not have to be identical. During development, the UltraLite tools use the reference database's schema to build the memory layout of the custom database and to customize the synchronization protocol. When the application synchronizes with the consolidated database at run time, the scripts for handling uploads and downloads must handle data in formats that are identical or compatible to what is in the reference database. The easiest way to do this is to make the tables in the reference database a subset of those in the consolidated database.

Write the Embedded SQL

Once the databases are ready, you write the SQL statements your application requires, embedding them in C or C++ source code. These SQL statements use the tables and columns of the reference database, not the consolidated database. When you deploy your application, it doesn't use the reference database, it uses the custom-built embedded database, and the custom database synchronizes with the consolidated database. All your application cares about is the local, embedded database—the synchronization is automatic and transparent.

The mixture of C/C++ and SQL is referred to as embedded SQL and was briefly discussed in Chapter 6. Embedded SQL allows you to specify database operations in their natural language, SQL, instead of using a call-level interface. The SQL syntax for embedded SQL is a subset of what the database server understands, with a few extensions for interfacing with C/C++. The syntax of embedded SQL is discussed later in this chapter. Except for the SQL commands, embedded SQL source files look exactly like C or C++ source files, although they're commonly given the extension *.sqc* instead of *.c* or *.cpp*.

Editing .sqc Files with CodeWarrior

CodeWarrior's text editor can edit .sqc files, but you can't add .sqc files to a project unless you define a mapping for them. To do this, bring up your project's Settings window and select "File Mappings" in the left-hand pane. On the right side of the window you'll see the list of file types that CodeWarrior understands. To add an entry for .sqc files, type *TEXT* into the File text box, *.sqc* (with the period) in the Extension text box, and select "Ignored by Make" from the Flags drop-down list. See Figure 8.15. Then press the Add and Save buttons. You can now add .sqc files to your project. They will be ignored when CodeWarrior builds the project, but you can edit them by double-clicking on them just as you would for a .h or .c file.

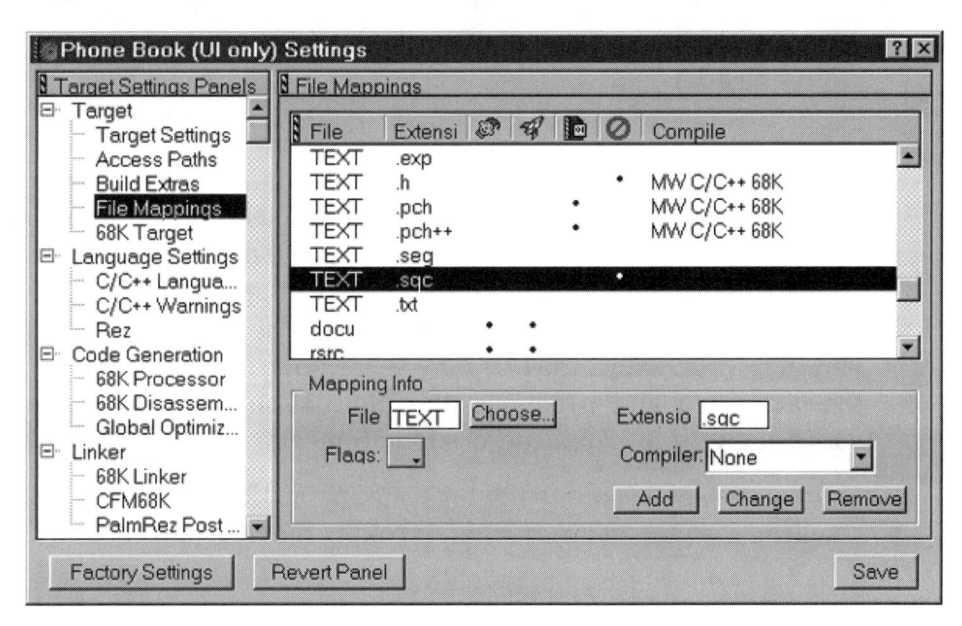

Figure 8.15 Enabling CodeWarrior to edit .sqc files.

Embedded SQL source files must be transformed into regular C or C++ source files before they can be compiled. This is done using the SQL preprocessor, one of the tools that ships with ASA. The SQL preprocessor replaces embedded SQL commands with C/C++ code, leaving the rest of the source code intact. The result is a C/C++ file devoid of any SQL syntax and suitable for compiling with a C/C++ compiler. To invoke the SQL preprocessor, use the sqlpp command:

```
sqlpp -c "dsn=Phone Book Reference;uid=dba;pwd=sql" -p MyProject
Source.sqc Source.cpp
```

The SQL preprocessor must connect to the reference database as part of the translation process, and the first argument specifies the connection parameters: data source name (dsn), user ID (uid), and password (pwd). While processing a source file, the SQL preprocessor stores information about its embedded SQL in the reference database, and the second argument is a project name used to store the information. The last two arguments are the name of the input and output files.

An application can use two or more embedded SQL files as long as the same project name is used when each file is transformed by the SQL preprocessor.

After processing each source file, the UltraLite generator is run to generate a custom database:

```
ulgen -c "dsn=Phone Book Reference;uid=dba;pwd=sql" MyProject customdb.c
```

The generator uses the information stored in the reference database by the SQL preprocessor to generate the database, so the first argument provides the appropriate connection information. The next two arguments identify the project and the name of the output file. The project name is the same name used to preprocess the embedded SQL files. As part of its processing, the UltraLite generator runs a Java program called the UltraLite analyzer that uses the information stored in the preprocessor to analyze your application's requirements.

If you use a single source file for your application's embedded SQL, you can drop the project name when invoking the SQL preprocessor:

```
sqlpp -c "dsn=Phone Book Reference;uid=dba;pwd=sql" Source.sqc Source.cpp
```

The preprocessor automatically invokes the UltraLite generator and combines the output of both tools into a single C/C++ source file.

Add the files output by the SQL preprocessor and the UltraLite generator to the CodeWarrior project. These files must be regenerated and recompiled each time you change a .sqc file or the schema of the reference database.

TIP CodeWarrior doesn't know about sqlpp or ulgen, so each time you run either tool you have to let CodeWarrior know that the generated C/C++ files have been modified by selecting "Synchronize Modification Dates" in the Project menu. Otherwise it won't notice that the files have changed and need to be recompiled. A better alternative is found on the CD-ROM: The author has written a CodeWarrior plug-in that lets you edit and compile .sqc files directly from CodeWarrior without the manual regeneration steps. The plug-in will be included with a later version of ASA, but you can find a beta of it on the CD-ROM in the "Plugins" folder.

Before using any routines or classes that access the custom database, your application must initialize the database using the routines ULPalmLaunch and db_init. When your application exits, it calls ULPalmExit to save the state of the database. If your application uses the TCP/IP or serial channels to perform its synchronization, it must call ULSynchronize to start the process, usually in response to a menu selection by the user. These routines are all discussed later in this chapter.

Design the User Interface

Using the information and techniques discussed in previous chapters, write a user interface for your application. Keep the user interface out of the embedded SQL, so that changes to the user interface don't require you to continually run the SQL preprocessor and UltraLite generator. In general, you'll find it easier to write your programs if you separate the user interface from the data access and use separate files for the embedded SQL. Otherwise, you'll be constantly regenerating the C or C++ source for all of your applications, and when you debug you'll be debugging the transformed source, which contains a lot of code you don't need (or want) to see.

Build and Install the Application

Compile and link the files to build an application. The result is a self-contained UltraLite application, ready for installation on a Palm device.

UltraLite Deployment

As with development, there are several steps required to deploy an UltraLite application:

1. Prepare the consolidated database
2. Install the MobiLink conduit
3. Run the MobiLink server
4. Run and synchronize the Application

Each step is explained in the following sections.

Prepare the Consolidated Database

A key feature of an UltraLite application is the seemingly transparent synchronization between the custom database embedded in the application and the external, consolidated database. The synchronization process involves the execution of a number of scripts by the MobiLink server. These scripts are the SQL statements executed by the server to update or query the consolidated database. The scripts are actually installed in the consolidated database along with other information, and this information is stored in a set of tables called MobiLink system tables.

MobiLink system tables are installed by default whenever an ASA database is created, but they must be explicitly created on other systems. Sybase provides SQL scripts to create the tables for three popular database systems: Sybase Adaptive Server Enterprise, Microsoft SQL Server, and Oracle. You can modify these scripts if you wish to install the tables on other database systems: The MobiLink server can use any ODBC-compliant database. MobiLink system tables only need to be installed once on any given database.

Once the tables are in place, you write the synchronization scripts. The scripts are accessed using the Java version of the Sybase Central tool, shown in Figure 8.16. To start Sybase Central, Java Edition, use the Manage MobiLink Synchronization shortcut in the UltraLite folder under the Sybase/Adaptive Server Anywhere 6.0 folder. To connect to the consolidated database, select the Tools/Connect menu item and enter the ODBC data source name for the database along with the userid and password, as shown in Figure 8.17.

Once connected to a database, Sybase Central lets you view the tables that are defined in the database, create and edit connection scripts, mark tables as being synchronizable, and view the UltraLite user names. We discuss each of these later in this chapter, but for now the key thing to remember is that for a table to be synchronizable it must be marked as such and it must have upload and download scripts defined. To mark a table as synchronizable, select the Synchronized Tables folder in the left-hand pane and double-click on the Add Synchronized Table item in the right-hand pane. Select the appropriate table from the list. Once a

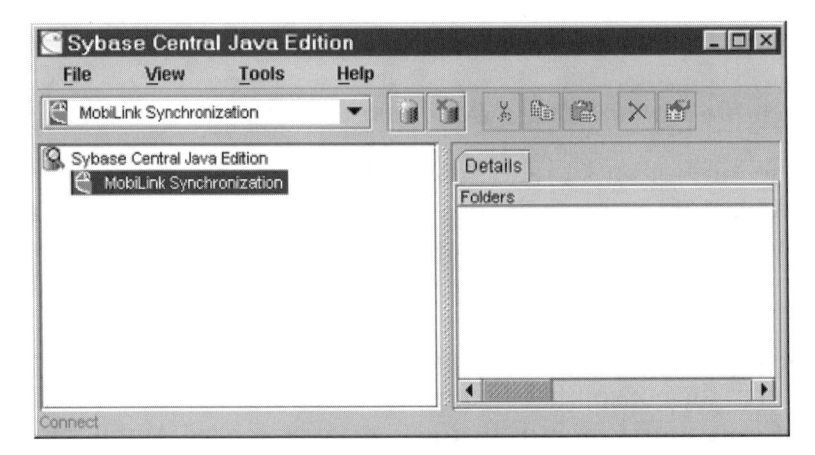

Figure 8.16 The Java version of Sybase Central.

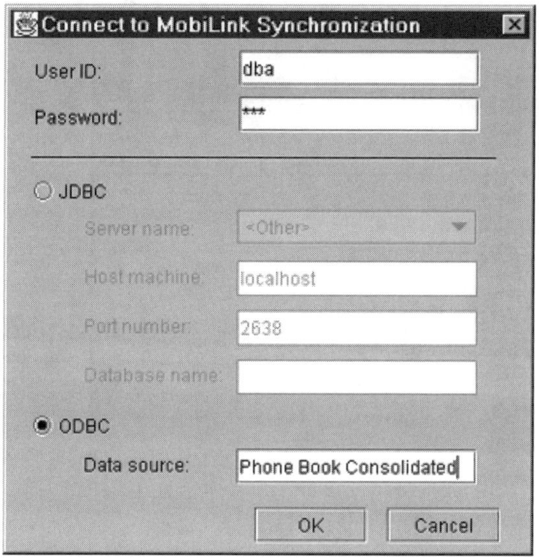

Figure 8.17 Connecting to a database with Sybase Central.

table has been marked as synchronizable, double-click on its new entry in the right-hand pane to view any scripts it has defined. Double-click on Add Table Script to add any of several scripts, including the scripts that upload and download data. Table scripts are discussed later in this chapter as well.

Install the MobiLink Conduit

After preparing the database, you'll need to install the MobiLink conduit on each user's desktop computer, unless you've decided against using HotSync to perform the database synchronization. The MobiLink conduit is a DLL (dynamic link library) supplied with ASA that must be in the system PATH or in the same directory as the HotSync application itself (usually C:\Pilot). Registry entries associate the conduit with a Palm application, identified by its creator ID. Multiple applications can use the MobiLink conduit as long as each application has its own set of registry entries.

The conduit registry entries are managed using a tool called CondCfg that ships as part of the Palm OS Conduit Development Kit (CDK). Instructions for obtaining the CDK are found in Chapter 3. When you run the CDK, you're presented with a list of all installed conduits on the system, as shown in Figure 8.18. To add a new entry for the MobiLink

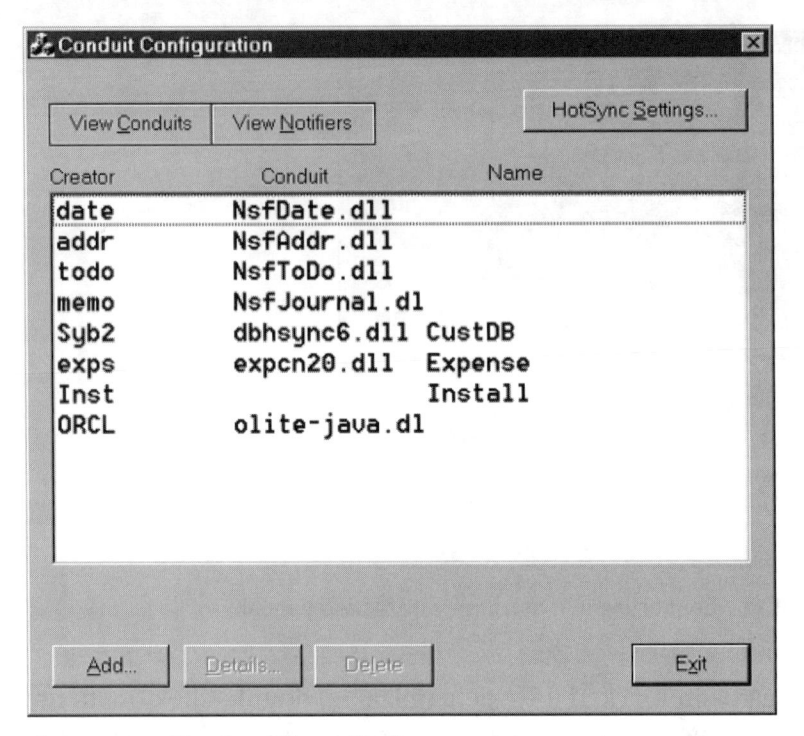

Figure 8.18 The CondCfg application.

conduit, press the Add button and then enter values for the following entries:

Conduit: The name of the MobiLink conduit DLL, dbhsync6.dll.

Creator ID: The four-byte creator ID of the application, entered in character form. The Phone Book application uses PHBK.

Directory: The name of the subdirectory to create in the user's HotSync directory. The HotSync log for the conduit will be created here. Usually the name of the application, as in Phone Book.

Name: The user-viewable name of the application, as in Phone Book.

Use the default values for the other entries, and be sure to select Application as the conduit type. The entries for the Phone Book application are shown in Figure 8.19. Press OK to save the values in the registry.

Unfortunately, CondCfg does not let you set an important registry entry, the connection string to connect to the consolidated database, which the conduit will pass as an argument to the MobiLink server. You can easily set this yourself, however, using the Windows registry editor. Run regedit.exe

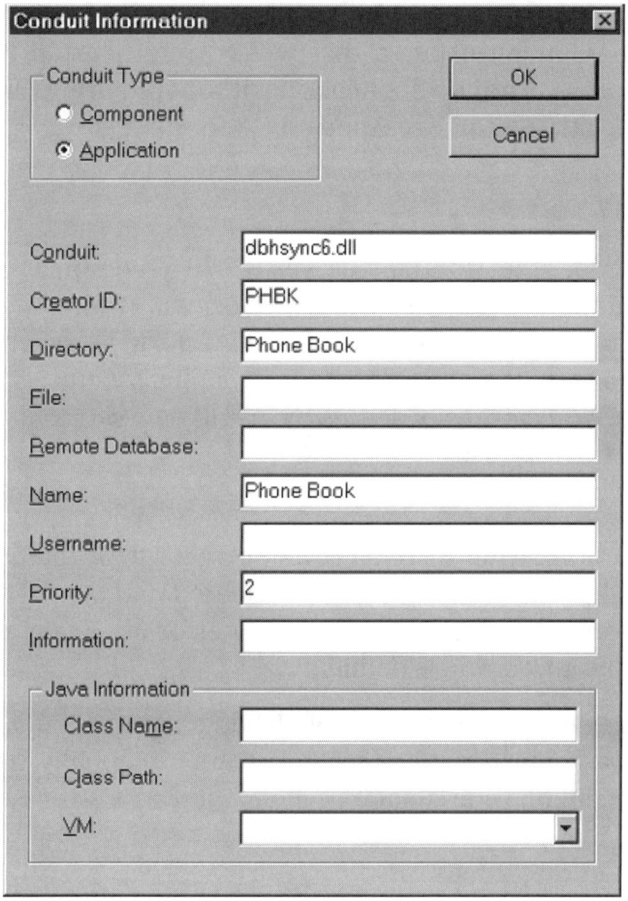

Figure 8.19 Installing the Phone Book conduit.

and look for the HKEY_CURRENT_USER\Software\U.S. Robotics\Pilot Desktop entry. (Alternatively, look for Palm Computing instead of U.S. Robotics.) You'll see a number of registry keys: Application0, Application1, Application2, and so on. One of these keys holds the registry entries you just created. Find it and then create two new string entries:

ConnectionString: The connection string to the consolidated database, in the same format used by the sqlpp or ulgen commands. For example, "dsn=Phone Book Consolidated;uid=dba;pwd=sql."

ConnectionType: Set this to "ODBC."

Other entries can also be set to control how much logging is done by the conduit during synchronization, which is useful for debugging synchronization problems. See the ASA documentation for details.

On the CD-ROM that accompanies this book you'll find a conduit installation program, MLConduitInstaller, that will correctly install or uninstall the conduit for an UltraLite application without requiring the use of CondCfg or the registry editor. See Appendix A for details.

Run the MobiLink Server

If not already running, the MobiLink server is started automatically by the MobiLink conduit when a HotSync is performed. If, however, your application is using TCP/IP or the serial port to perform its synchronization, you'll have to start the MobiLink server manually before synchronization can occur. You can easily do this by installing a shortcut on your desktop that runs the following command:

```
dbssrv6 -vcrs -c "dsn=Phone Book Consolidated;uid=dba;pwd=sql"
```

Adjust the connection string to reflect the correct ODBC data source name, user ID, and password for your consolidated database. The -vcrs option controls how much logging the server performs. Again, refer to the ASA documentation for more details.

If the database is not running and the ODBC data source is not configured to automatically start it, you'll have to start it manually. For ASA databases, use the dbeng6 command:

```
dbeng6 -c 16m "c:\Phone Book\PHBKConsolidated.db"
```

For other systems, consult the database server documentation.

Run and Synchronize the Application

With the deployment steps complete, you can now run your application. The custom database embedded inside your application is initially empty, so you'll need to synchronize to obtain the initial data, either by starting the HotSync or selecting the menu item that starts TCP/IP-based or serial-based synchronization.

Using UltraLite without Synchronization

Although synchronization with an external database is a key feature of UltraLite, you can build applications that use UltraLite without performing any synchronization. The primary reason for doing this is to test your application without having to configure the consolidated database or write synchronization scripts. On the other hand, you may just want the capabilities of a relational database on the Palm device without wanting to do more than just back it up.

When an UltraLite application is first installed, the application has no information in its database. Normally that information would arrive at the first synchronization with the MobiLink server. If there is no synchronization, you must code INSERT statements in your embedded SQL code to fill the tables with their initial data. Again, this is a good way to test your application without worrying about the deployment phase. Once your application is working you would remove the code that loaded the initial data and rely on synchronization to fill the tables.

If you plan on not using synchronization, be aware that by default the Palm databases that UltraLite uses to store its data are never backed up because their backup bit is not set. If you want to back them up, your application should set the backup bit on the databases when it exits, using the techniques discussed in Chapter 5:

```
UInt     appCard, dbCard;
LocalID appID, dbID;
ULong    creator;

// Get creator ID of current app
SysCurAppDatabase( &appCard, &appID );
DmDatabaseInfo( appCard, appID, NULL, NULL, NULL, NULL,
                NULL, NULL, NULL, NULL, NULL, NULL,
                &creator );

DmSearchStateType searchInfo;
Boolean           newSearch;
UInt              attributes;

// Search through all databases with this creator ID, skipping
// over the application's database
for( newSearch = true;
     DmGetNextDatabaseByTypeCreator( newSearch, &searchInfo,
                 0, creator, false, &dbCard, &dbID ) == 0;
     newSearch = false ){
    if( dbID == appID && appCard == dbCard ) continue;
    DmDatabaseInfo( dbCard, dbID, NULL, &attributes,
                    NULL, NULL, NULL, NULL, NULL, NULL,
                    NULL, NULL, NULL );
    attributes |= dmHdrAttrBackup;
    DmSetDatabaseInfo( dbCard, dbID, NULL, &attributes, NULL, NULL,
                       NULL, NULL, NULL, NULL, NULL, NULL, NULL );
}
```

At the next HotSync, the databases will be backed up by the default backup conduit. You'll find them as .PDB files in the Pilot\username\Backup folder—their names all start with "ultralite" and include the creator ID of the application in question. Note that for the backup to succeed, you must not associate any conduit with the application's creator ID.

A major problem with this approach is that installing a new version of an application wipes out all Palm databases with that application's creator ID. You could try reinstalling the backup copies, but if the schema has changed, the internal structure of those databases will not match what the UltraLite run time expects to find there and may cause your application to crash. The only way to get around this problem is to include code in your application that reads the data from the UltraLite database and saves it into a separate Palm database using a known format, which the application could later reread to refill the UltraLite database. You're probably better off getting your application to synchronize with an external database and letting MobiLink do the backups for you.

Embedded SQL

An application uses embedded SQL to communicate with the embedded UltraLite database. The syntax for embedded SQL is easy to understand if you're familiar with SQL. This section shows you how to use embedded SQL in your own code.

The SQL Preprocessor

The first step to understanding embedded SQL is to understand the role played by the SQL preprocessor. The SQL preprocessor reads input files and looks for lines that begin with the string EXEC SQL, as in the following:

```
EXEC SQL INCLUDE SQLCA;
```

EXEC SQL identifies the line as an embedded SQL statement. The statement ends with a semicolon and can be split across several lines for readability. You can even include C or C++ comments in the middle of a statement. The text in between the EXEC SQL and the semicolon identifies the SQL statement to execute. The statements can be normal SQL commands such as UPDATE, DELETE, SELECT, or INSERT, or they can be commands specific to embedded SQL, such as INCLUDE or WHENEVER.

An important thing to note is that the SQL preprocessor does *not* understand any C or C++ syntax other than comments. In particular, C/C++ preprocessor macros (#define) and conditional compilation directives (#if, #else, #endif, etc.) are ignored by the SQL preprocessor. Embedded SQL statements are processed in the order in which they're found in the source file.

The SQL Communications Area

The first embedded SQL command in a source file must define the *SQL communications area*, or SQLCA for short:

```
EXEC SQL INCLUDE SQLCA;
```

The SQL communications area defines a structure used to communicate errors and other information from the embedded database back to the C/C++ code. Place the INCLUDE SQLCA statement at the top of each embedded SQL file, after the header files:

```
// From ULPhoneData.sqc (before preprocessing)
#include <Pilot.h>
#include "ULPhoneData.h"

EXEC SQL INCLUDE SQLCA;
```

The SQL preprocessor transforms this statement into something like this:

```
// From ULPhoneData.cpp (after preprocessing)
#include <Pilot.h>
#include "ULPhoneData.h"

/* EXEC SQL INCLUDE    SQLCA; */
#include "ulglobal.h"

extern SQLCA sqlca;

....... // etc. etc.
```

The ulglobal.h header file, found in the h subdirectory of the ASA installation directory, defines types, global variables, and routines used by the generated code. A reference to the global variable sqlca of structure type SQLCA is then defined. At any point, the application can use sqlca to determine the status of the last SQL command. The most important field in the SQLCA is the sqlcode member, which returns the error code for the last SQL statement:

```
EXEC SQL UPDATE EMPLOYEE SET NAME = 'Test' WHERE EMPLOYEEID = 1
if( sqlca.sqlcode == 0 ){
    // no error or warning
} else if( sqlca.sqlcode > 0 ){
    // positive means warning
} else if( sqlca.sqlcode < 0 ){
    // negative means error
}
```

Error codes are defined in the header file sqlerr.h, included by and found in the same directory as ulglobal.h. Warnings are returned as positive values, while errors are returned as negative values. Zero is returned if there is no error or warning.

Because the SQL communications area and other generated code use global variables, an UltraLite database can only be used when the application's global data is available. To search an UltraLite database during a global Find operation, for example, you must first relaunch the application to recover its global data, as described in Chapter 4.

Error Handling

After defining the SQL communications area, define error handlers. An *error handler* is just code that the SQL preprocessor automatically inserts after each SQL statement to check for and handle error conditions. It's no different than checking the error code value yourself. The most basic error handler is the GOTO handler:

```
EXEC SQL WHENEVER SQLERROR GOTO label;
```

Whenever an error occurs (the error code is negative), execution jumps to the given label. Each function or method with embedded SQL commands must then define such a label. Alternatively, you can specify some C/C++ code to execute instead of a goto:

```
EXEC SQL WHENEVER SQLERROR { if( !handleError( &sqlca ) ) return; };
```

You can also trap warnings by using SQLWARNING in place of SQLERROR.

An error handler affects the code generation for SQL statements that follow it. You can change an error handler at any time in the source file.

The SQLCODE macro can be used in your error-handling code to obtain the error code from the SQL communications area instead of directly referencing sqlca.sqlcode.

Initialization and Deinitialization

The INCLUDE and WHENEVER statements are declarative statements and can occur anywhere within the source file. Executable statements, those that generate code that accesses the embedded database, can also occur anywhere within a source file, but at run time none of the code must execute before the database is initialized. On the Palm, the embedded database is initialized using ULPalmLaunch and db_init:

```
if( ULPalmLaunch( &sqlca, ULPalmDBStream() ) ){
    db_init( &sqlca );
}
```

ULPalmLaunch and db_init are not embedded SQL commands; they're routines from the UltraLite runtime library, but they're mentioned here because they're so important. db_init must only be called if ULPalmLaunch returns true. The second parameter to ULPalmLaunch specifies the synchronization channel that's being used, which in this example is HotSync. We discuss db_init, ULPalmLaunch, and related routines in a later section.

After initialization, use a CONNECT statement to connect to the embedded database:

```
EXEC SQL CONNECT "dba" IDENTIFIED BY "sql";
```

The userid and password are ignored, but the CONNECT must run before any other executable statement. If CONNECT returns an error code of 0, the database is ready to use.

When your application is shutting down, it must disconnect from the database:

```
EXEC SQL DISCONNECT;
```

After disconnecting, the application calls ULPalmExit to clean up:

```
ULPalmExit( &sqlca, "User Name", ULPalmDBStream() );
```

Again, ULPalmExit is discussed in a later section. Note when porting an UltraLite application to other platforms, the db_fini function must be called instead of ULPalmExit, but never call db_fini on the Palm platform.

If you're using C++, it's common to write a class that encapsulates all database access and to write connect and disconnect methods to perform the database initialization and deinitialization for you. For example, you could define a Database class in Database.h as follows:

```cpp
// Database.h

class Database {
    public:
        Database() {}
        ~Database();

        Boolean Connect();
        Boolean Disconnect();

        Int GetErrorCode();

        ...... // other methods
};
```

You would define the class in Database.sqc:

```cpp
// Database.sqc

#include <Pilot.h>
#include "Database.h"

EXEC SQL INCLUDE SQLCA;

EXEC SQL WHENEVER SQLERROR { return false; };

Boolean Database::Connect()
{
    if( ULPalmLaunch( &sqlca, ULPalmDBStream() ) ){
        db_init( &sqlca );
    }

    EXEC SQL CONNECT "dba" IDENTIFIED BY "sql";
    return true;
}

Boolean Database::Disconnect()
{
    EXEC SQL DISCONNECT;
    ULPalmExit( &sqlca, GetUserName(), ULPalmDBStream() );
    return true;
}

Int Database::GetErrorCode()
{
    return SQLCODE;
}
....... // other methods
```

Your application would then define a global variable of type Database and call its Connect method in the StartApplication routine and Disconnect in the StopApplication routine:

```cpp
// PilotMain.cpp

Database TheDatabase;

......

Err StartApplication()
{
    if( !TheDatabase.Connect() ){
        // handle error
    }

    ..... // other initialization as normal
}

Err StopApplication()
{
    TheDatabase.Disconnect();
    ..... // other deinitialization as normal
}
```

These examples all assume you're using the HotSync synchronization channel. The code for the serial and TCP/IP cases is very similar, as we'll see later.

Executing Simple SQL Statements

Once connected, you can start executing SQL statements against the embedded database. You can use any SQL statement that doesn't use features not supported by UltraLite. For example, to insert a new row, use the following:

```
EXEC SQL INSERT INTO EMPLOYEE ( EmployeeID, Name, Surname )
        VALUES ( 99, 'Wayne', 'Gretzky' );
```

Or to delete all rows with null values:

```
EXEC SQL DELETE FROM EMPLOYEE WHERE Name IS NULL OR Surname IS NULL;
```

Remember that the SQL must refer to the tables and columns in the reference database, not the consolidated database. Statements that alter the database schema (DDL commands) are not allowed.

If a SQL statement uses features not supported by UltraLite, or tables and columns not in the reference database, the SQL preprocessor will report an error when the source file is processed.

UltraLite only supports *static* SQL statements. A SQL statement is static if the tables and columns it affects are completely defined when compiled by the SQL preprocessor. In other words, the following is *not* allowed:

```
CharPtr str;

if( insertJoe ){
    str = "INSERT INTO EMPLOYEE ( EmployeeID, Name, Surname )" \
          "VALUES ( 200, 'Joe', 'Black' )";
} else {
    str = "DELETE FROM EMPLOYEE WHERE EmployeeID = 200";
}

EXEC SQL str;   // not allowed!
```

Code it instead as:

```
if( insertJoe ){
    EXEC SQL INSERT INTO EMPLOYEE ( EmployeeID, Name, Surname )
             VALUES ( 200, 'Joe', 'Black' );
} else {
    EXEC SQL DELETE FROM EMPLOYEE WHERE EmployeeID = 200;
}
```

Nonstatic statements are referred to as *dynamic* statements.

At first glance, this seems to be a serious limitation. What if the user selects a row to delete based on its primary key? If UltraLite supported dynamic statements, you could perhaps code it like this:

```
Int  key = GetKeyFromUser();
Char sqlStatement[200];
Char buf[10];

StrCopy( sqlStatement, "DELETE FROM EMPLOYEE WHERE EmployeeID = " );
StrCat( sqlStatement, StrIToA( buf, key ) );

EXEC SQL sqlStatement; // not allowed!
```

So it would seem that you have to code it instead like this:

```
Int key = GetKeyFromUser();

switch( key ){
   case 1:
        EXEC SQL DELETE FROM EMPLOYEE WHERE EmployeeID = 1;
```

```
        break;
    case 2:
        EXEC SQL DELETE FROM EMPLOYEE WHERE EmployeeID = 2;
        break;
    // etc. etc.
}
```

Not only does this seem inefficient, but there's simply no way to cover all the possible conditions that the application might require. To rectify this, Embedded SQL provides a way to substitute runtime values into a SQL statement. These values cannot be used to change the table or columns that are affected by the statement, so the statement is still considered to be a static statement. Values are substituted using host variables.

Host Variables

A *host variable* is a C/C++ variable that can be used in a SELECT, UPDATE, INSERT, or DELETE statement wherever a string or a number is allowed. When the SQL preprocessor encounters a statement with a host variable, it replaces the host variable with a placeholder. At run time, the variable's value is substituted for the placeholder.

Declaring Host Variables

Host variables must be declared before they can be used:

```
EXEC SQL BEGIN DECLARE SECTION;
Int key;
EXEC SQL END DECLARE SECTION;

key = GetKeyFromUser();
EXEC SQL DELETE FROM EMPLOYEE WHERE EmployeeID = :key;
```

Notice how the name of the variable is preceded with a colon (:) in the SQL statement. This marks it as a host variable. Host variables must be declared before they can used, however, and this is done by enclosing a set of C/C++ variable declarations within BEGIN DECLARE SECTION and END DECLARE SECTION statements:

```
EXEC SQL BEGIN DECLARE SECTION;
    short id;
    char  name[51];
    char  surname[51];
EXEC SQL END DECLARE SECTION;

id = 100;
StrCopy( name, "Kelly" );
```

```
StrCopy( surname, "McMastrad" );

EXEC SQL INSERT INTO EMPLOYEE ( EmployeeID, Name, Surname )
        VALUES ( :id, :name, :surname );
```

The code within a DECLARE SECTION is the only C/C++ code in the source file that the SQL preprocessor scans. It scans the code in order to determine the types of the host variables.

Supported Types

The SQL preprocessor supports a limited number of basic C types for host variables:

- short, unsigned short, int, unsigned int, long, and unsigned long: 16-bit and 32-bit integer values.
- char[n]: null-terminated, fixed-length strings, equivalent to CHAR(n–1) in the database.
- char *buf: buf is assumed to point to a buffer that can hold at least 2048 characters plus a null terminator.

The SQL preprocessor also implicitly understands the following types for host variables:

- DECL_FIXCHAR(n): A fixed-length string, equivalent to CHAR(n) in the database. The string is *not* null-terminated.
- DECL_VARCHAR(n): A variable-length string, equivalent to VARCHAR(n) in the database. The string is optionally null-terminated.
- DECL_BINARY(n): For variable-length or fixed-length binary data, equivalent to BINARY(n) or VARBINARY(n) in the database.
- DECL_DECIMAL(p,s): For fixed-precision values, equivalent to NUMERIC(p,s) or DECIMAL(p,s) in the database. Values are stored in a packed format.
- DECL_DATETIME: For date- or time-related values, equivalent to DATE, TIME, or TIMESTAMP in the database.

The C/C++ compiler also understands these types because they're defined as macros in the sqlca.h header file. For example, DECL_VARCHAR has a length field that must be set when initializing a variable:

```
EXEC BEGIN DECLARE SECTION;
    DECL_VARCHAR(30) country;
```

```
EXEC END DECLARE SECTION;

StrCopy( country.array, "Canada" );
country.len = StrLen( country.array );
```

DECL_BINARY, DECL_DECIMAL, DECL_FIXCHAR, and DECL_VARCHAR all declare structures with an array member called array, while DECL_BINARY and DECL_VARCHAR also define a length member called len:

```
#define DECL_VARCHAR( size )   \
        struct { unsigned short int len; \
                 unsigned char array[size+1]; \
        }

#define DECL_BINARY( size )   \
        struct { unsigned short int len; \
                 unsigned char array[size]; \
        }

#define DECL_DECIMAL( prec, scale )   \
        struct { char    array[ ((prec)/2) + 1 ]; \
        }

#define DECL_FIXCHAR( size )   \
        struct { char    array[ size ]; \
        }
```

DECL_DATETIME is just a synonym for the SQLDATETIME type:

```
#define DECL_DATETIME   \
        struct sqldatetime

typedef struct sqldatetime {
    unsigned short   year;         /* e.g. 1992                      */
    unsigned char    month;        /* 0-11                           */
    unsigned char    day_of_week;  /* 0-6   0=Sunday, 1=Monday, ... */
    unsigned short   day_of_year;  /* 0-365                          */
    unsigned char    day;          /* 1-31                           */
    unsigned char    hour;         /* 0-23                           */
    unsigned char    minute;       /* 0-59                           */
    unsigned char    second;       /* 0-59                           */
    a_sql_uint32     microsecond;  /* 0-999999                       */
} SQLDATETIME;
```

Any values returned from or sent with a SQL statement must map onto one of these types.

Restrictions

Host variables must be simple variables. They can't be expressions or function calls, nor can they refer to structure/class members. This is not allowed:

```
EXEC BEGIN DECLARE SECTION;
    struct MyData {    // not allowed
        int              id;
        DECL_VARCHAR(51) name;
    };
EXEC END DECLARE SECTION;

struct MyData data;

data.id = 50;
StrCopy( data.name.array, "Janice" );
data.name.len = StrLen( data.name.array );

// this is not allowed!
EXEC SQL UPDATE EMPLOYEE SET Name = :data.name
    WHERE EmployeeID = :data.id;
```

However, repositioning the declaration block and clever use of the C/C++ preprocessor can make this work:

```
// These declarations are processed by the SQL preprocessor
// but ignored by the C/C++ compiler
#if 0
EXEC BEGIN DECLARE SECTION;
    int              data_id;
    DECL_VARCHAR(51) data_name;
EXEC END DECLARE SECTION;
#endif

// Declare our real structure/class with the same types
// but different names
struct MyData {
    int              id;
    DECL_VARCHAR(51) name;
};

struct MyData data;

data.id = 50;
StrCopy( data.name.array, "Janice" );
data.name.len = StrLen( data.name.array );

// Define a mapping from the simple names to the
// member-based names
```

```
#define data_id data.id
#define data_name data.name

// this is OK
EXEC SQL UPDATE EMPLOYEE SET Name = :data_name
        WHERE EmployeeID = :data_id;
```

The key is to use the C/C++ preprocessor to map complex names into simple names and to declare types for those simple names. The SQL preprocessor understands the simple names and generates code using them. When the C/C++ compiler processes the source file, it will replace those simple names with the macro values that we've defined.

Another important restriction to keep in mind is that the SQL preprocessor considers host variables to be global to the file, so you can't declare the same host variable twice in the same file.

NULL Values

A NULL SQL value does not have a direct representation in C/C++, so a second variable called an *indicator* is used along with a host variable to set or get NULL values. An indicator is a signed integer variable declared along with host variables:

```
EXEC SQL BEGIN DECLARATION;
    int             id;
    DECL_VARCHAR(51) name;
    int             name_indicator;
EXEC SQL END DECLARATION;
```

An indicator is used by appending a colon (:) and the name of the indicator to a host variable, as in the following:

```
:name:name_indicator
```

To set a value to NULL, set the indicator to −1. The value of the host variable will be ignored:

```
id = 50;
name_indicator = -1;
EXEC SQL UPDATE EMPLOYEE SET Name = :name:name_indicator
        WHERE EmployeeID = :id;
```

If you supply an indicator when fetching a value into a host variable (discussed shortly), the indicator will be set to −1 if the value was NULL (in which case you should ignore the host variable) or to 0 if the value in the host variable is non-NULL. Note that you must always provide an indicator if you are fetching values from a column that can return NULL values, otherwise an error will occur if a NULL value is fetched. When setting values, the indicator is not necessary if non-NULL values are being set.

Fetching Data

Data is fetched using the SELECT and FETCH statements.

Single Row of Data

To fetch a single row of data, use the SELECT statement with the INTO clause:

```
EXEC SQL BEGIN DECLARE;
    int              id;
    DECL_VARCHAR(51) name;
    DECL_VARCHAR(51) surname;
    int              name_indicator;
EXEC SQL END DECLARE;

id = 50;

EXEC SQL SELECT Name, Surname INTO :name:name_indicator, :surname
         FROM EMPLOYEE WHERE EmployeeID = :id;
```

The INTO clause specifies the host variables that will receive the data values, with optional indicators to mark NULL values. The INTO clause is a syntax extension specifically for embedded SQL and occurs before the FROM clause. The SELECT statement must return exactly one row of data, otherwise an error (either SQLE_TOO_MANY_RECORDS or SQLE_NOTFOUND) occurs.

Multiple Rows of Data

If a SELECT statement can return zero or more rows instead of exactly one row, you must declare a *cursor* for the statement. A cursor is a way of navigating through a result set. Conceptually, if you think of a result set as an array of structures, with one array element for each row, the cursor is a pointer into the array. Unlike regular arrays, however, there are markers at either end of the array and the cursor can also point to one of those markers. Thus, the cursor is said to be positioned *before* the result set, *in* the result set, or *after* the result set. The *current* row is the row that the cursor currently points to.

Use the DECLARE CURSOR statement to declare a cursor:

```
EXEC SQL DECLARE MyCursor CURSOR FOR
    SELECT EmployeeID, Name, Surname FROM EMPLOYEE
        WHERE EmployeeID >= :id;
```

The cursor is given a name, in this case MyCursor, and a SELECT statement. The SELECT statement is not executed when the cursor is declared, but only when the cursor is opened:

```
EXEC SQL OPEN MyCursor;
```

When the OPEN statement returns, the SELECT statement has been executed and the cursor is positioned before the result set. To move the cursor to the next row and read the values, use the FETCH statement:

```
EXEC SQL FETCH MyCursor INTO :empID; :name:name_indicator, :surname;
```

FETCH sets the error code to SQLE_NOTFOUND when there are no more rows to read, after which you should close the cursor:

```
EXEC SQL CLOSE MyCursor;
```

Although the four statements do not need to be together, you'll often see them grouped in a single function:

```
void IterateNames()
{
    EXEC SQL BEGIN DECLARE SECTION;
        int  id;
        char name[51];
        char surname[51];
    EXEC SQL END DECLARE SECTION;

    EXEC SQL DECLARE Iterate CURSOR FOR
        SELECT EmployeeID, Name, Surname FROM EMPLOYEE;

    EXEC SQL OPEN Iterate;

    while( 1 ){
        EXEC SQL FETCH Iterate INTO :id, :name, :surname;

        if( SQLCODE == SQLE_NOTFOUND ) break;
        if( SQLCODE < 0 ) break; // error

        // do something with id, name & surname
    }

    EXEC SQL CLOSE Iterate;
}
```

Note that the DECLARE CURSOR statement must appear in the source file ahead of any OPEN, FETCH, or CLOSE statement that refers to it.

Don't forget to close a cursor when you're done with it; otherwise, your application will leak memory.

Although the default is to advance to the next row, the FETCH statement can also move the cursor back to a previous row or even move to a specific row in the result set. Moving the cursor is referred to as *scrolling* the cursor. Here are some examples of scrolling:

```
EXEC SQL FETCH FIRST Iterate INTO :id, :name, :surname;
EXEC SQL FETCH NEXT Iterate INTO :id, :name, :surname;
EXEC SQL FETCH PREVIOUS Iterate INTO :id, :name, :surname;
EXEC SQL FETCH RELATIVE 5 Iterate INTO :id, :name, :surname;
EXEC SQL FETCH ABSOLUTE 20 Iterate INTO :id, :name, :surname;
EXEC SQL FETCH LAST Iterate INTO :id, :name, :surname;
```

To refetch the current row, use FETCH RELATIVE 0.

Transactions

To end a transaction and commit any changes, use the COMMIT statement:

```
EXEC SQL COMMIT;
```

To end a transaction and rollback any changes, use the ROLLBACK statement:

```
EXEC SQL ROLLBACK;
```

A new transaction is started after each commit or rollback.

Note that any pending changes must be committed or rolled back before synchronization is attempted; otherwise, an error occurs. For HotSync synchronization, this means committing any changes before calling ULPalmExit, while for the other synchronization channels it means committing any changes before calling ULSynchronize. See the next section for details on the synchronization channels.

Synchronization Channels

UltraLite offers three synchronization channels: HotSync, TCP/IP, and serial. You select a channel by passing different parameters to the ULPalmLaunch, ULPalmExit, and ULSynchronize functions. This section describes how to use each channel and how to choose the channel that best fits your needs.

User Identification

Each device must pass a user name to the MobiLink server when synchronizing. The user name is a string up to 128 characters long. The server in turn passes the user name as a parameter to the synchronization scripts, making it possible to vary what the scripts do based on who is performing the synchronization. You might use this feature, for example, to determine whether someone is a manager and whether their changes take precedence over someone else's whenever a conflict is detected.

The user name you pass to the MobiLink server should identify the user and the application, because only one set of synchronization scripts can be associated with a particular table in the consolidated database. A user name that includes information about the application performing the synchronization lets two different applications running on the same device use the same tables, yet allows the scripts to select different behaviors based on the application. One way to identify the user is to use the HotSync user name:

```
#include <Pilot.h>
#include <DLServer.h>

.....

char userName[ dlkMaxUserNameLength + 1 ];

DlkGetSyncInfo( NULL, NULL, NULL, userName, NULL, NULL );
```

DlkGetSyncInfo is an undocumented function found in <DLServer.h>. Combine this with the application's creator ID to form the synchronization user name:

```
#include <Pilot.h>
#include <DLServer.h>

// Combine the the creator ID + user name to form
// a name for synchronization. The first argument must
// point to a buffer at least 50 characters long,
// to account for max length of DB name + creator ID.
// The second argument determines whether spaces should
// be converted to underscores.
//
// Returns: creatorID (4 characters) + space/underscore +
//          user name

void GetULSyncName( Char *nameBuffer, Boolean noSpaces )
```

```
    {
        UInt    card;
        LocalID appID;
        ULong   creator;

        // Get creator ID of current app
        SysCurAppDatabase( &card, &appID );
        DmDatabaseInfo( card, appID, NULL, NULL, NULL, NULL,
                        NULL, NULL, NULL, NULL, NULL,
                        &creator );

        // First part of name is the creator ID
        nameBuffer[0] = (Char) ( ( creator & 0xff000000 ) >> 24 );
        nameBuffer[1] = (Char) ( ( creator & 0x00ff0000 ) >> 16 );
        nameBuffer[2] = (Char) ( ( creator & 0x0000ff00 ) >> 8 );
        nameBuffer[3] = (Char) ( creator & 0x000000ff );
        nameBuffer[4] = ' ';
        nameBuffer[5] = 0;

        DlkGetSyncInfo( NULL, NULL, NULL, &nameBuffer[5], NULL, NULL );

        if( noSpaces ){
            while( ( nameBuffer = StrChr( nameBuffer, ' ' ) ) != NULL ){
                *nameBuffer = '_';
            }
        }
    }
```

Of course, for added security you might consider including some kind of password or digital signature as part of the user identification string. Your synchronization scripts would be responsible for parsing the string and validating the user, rejecting the synchronization attempt for invalid users.

HotSync Synchronization

In HotSync synchronization, there is no direct communication between the application and the MobiLink server. Instead, the application writes an upload stream to a Palm database whenever it exits. At the next HotSync, the Palm database is passed to the MobiLink conduit, which extracts the upload stream and passes it on to the MobiLink server for processing. The MobiLink server returns a download stream to the conduit, which converts it to a Palm database and installs it on the device. The next time the application is started, the UltraLite run time notices that a download stream is available and integrates it into the embedded database.

To use HotSync synchronization, call ULPalmLaunch and ULPalmExit as follows:

```
// HotSync: on startup....

if( ULPalmLaunch( &sqlca, ULPalmDBStream() ) ){
    db_init( &sqlca );
}

......

// HotSync: on exit...

char userName[50];
GetULSyncName( userName, true );
ULPalmExit( &sqlca, userName, ULPalmDBStream() );
```

Both functions take a pointer to the SQL communications area as their first argument. The last parameter to both functions is a call to ULPalmDBStream, which returns a virtual stream that maps the upload and download streams to Palm databases. The second parameter to ULPalmExit is the user name, which we obtain from the GetULSyncName function we defined previously.

ULSynchronize is not called when using HotSync synchronization.

To reduce the application startup time after a HotSync, consider trapping the sysAppLaunchCmdSyncNotify launch code, which is sent at the end of the HotSync process to all installed applications. Your application can simply initialize and deinitialize the database to integrate any downloaded data. Note that during a sysAppLaunchCmdSyncNotify you don't have access to global data, so the first thing you'll need to do is recover your globals by relaunching the application.

TCP/IP Synchronization

In TCP/IP, the user initiates the synchronization while the application is running. The user must be using a Palm device that supports TCP/IP (a PalmPilot Professional or a device running Palm OS 3.0 or higher). The synchronization is done through the cradle or through a modem. See the UltraLite documentation for details on how to configure your device to use TCP/IP.

To use TCP/IP synchronization, call ULPalmLaunch and ULPalm Exit with NULL for all parameters except the SQL communications area:

```
// TCP/IP: on startup...

if( ULPalmLaunch( &sqlca, NULL ) ){
    db_init( &sqlca );
}

......

// TCP/IP: on exit...

ULPalmExit( &sqlca, NULL, NULL );
```

In the application's user interface, add a way for the user to start a synchronization session, via a menu item, for example. When the user indicates that he or she wants to synchronize the database, call ULSynchronize:

```
char userName[50];
GetULSyncName( userName, true );
ULSynchronize( &sqlca, userName, ULSocketStream(),
               "host=myserver.mycompany.com;port=2439" );
```

The first parameter to ULSynchronize is the SQL communications area, the second is the user name, the third is the value returned by ULSocketStream, and the last parameter identifies the machine and port of the MobiLink server. You can omit the port specification if the server is using the default port (2439). The server must be running before synchronization is attempted.

Serial Synchronization

Serial synchronization uses the Palm cradle to directly link the application to a MobiLink server running on the desktop computer. The MobiLink server listens on the appropriate COM port (the one the cradle is attached to), waiting for a synchronization request. To specify a serial connection to the COM1 port, for example, use this command to start the server:

```
dbsserv6 -x serial{port=1}
         -c "dsn=Phone Book Consolidated;uid=dba;pwd=sql"
```

Set port=2 to use COM2, port=3 to use COM3, and so on. Note that only a single application can use the serial port at any given time, so be sure to shut down the HotSync Manager before you start the MobiLink server.

The application calls ULPalmLaunch and ULPalmExit with NULL parameters except for the SQL communications area, just as with TCP/IP:

```
// Serial: on startup...

if( ULPalmLaunch( &sqlca, NULL ) ){
    db_init( &sqlca );
}

......

// Serial: on exit...

ULPalmExit( &sqlca, NULL, NULL );
```

When synchronization is required, call ULSynchronize as follows:

```
char userName[50];
GetULSyncName( userName, true );
ULSynchronize( &sqlca, userName, ULSerialStream(),
               "timeout=60" );
```

The difference compared to TCP/IP synchronization is that ULSerialStream is used in place of ULSocketStream, while the last parameter specifies a timeout value in seconds. You can omit the timeout specification and pass NULL to use the default timeout of 30 seconds.

Which Channel to Use?

Which channel you choose to use depends on what's most convenient for your users. Serial synchronization is the fastest, but it requires a direct serial connection to the MobiLink server running on the desktop, while TCP/IP synchronization can communicate with a server anywhere on the network or even on the Internet. Configuring the device and server for serial synchronization is very simple, but configuring the device for TCP/IP access and installing the appropriate remote access server (used to connect to your corporate network from a dial-up line—see the UltraLite documentation for setup details) can be quite complicated.

The most natural synchronization method for Palm users, however, is via the HotSync process, because it's something they're already familiar with and do regularly. The downside to HotSync synchronization is that it requires the application to possibly write an upload stream when it exits, in case the user initiates a HotSync, and possibly read a download stream when it starts, if a HotSync did occur. Reading and writing these streams takes time and delays the starting and stopping of the application. Display a message asking the user to wait before calling either ULPalmLaunch or ULPalmExit, so they know that something is happening.

No matter which channel is being used, however, once synchronization starts there is no way to cancel it other than by removing the device from the cradle or severing the network/serial connection.

Synchronization

The whole synchronization process is controlled by scripts you write and install in the consolidated database. The scripts are written in the SQL dialect used by the database and can be simple DML (Data Manipulation Language) statements or calls to stored procedures that perform more complicated actions.

Understanding UltraLite Synchronization

The first key to understanding UltraLite synchronization is that it doesn't really involve the application at all. The synchronization occurs between the embedded custom database and the external consolidated database. The application uses the data in the custom database without knowing or caring where it came from. That's why you can develop the application separately without worrying about the synchronization aspects. (A good design should always account for the synchronization right from the start, but the implementation can be left to later.)

The second key is to realize that although the synchronization is between the custom and consolidated databases, conceptually you're synchronizing the reference database with the consolidated database. The custom database is derived from the reference database, but its internal structure is completely hidden. When you write your embedded SQL, you use tables and columns from the reference database, so when you write the synchronization scripts, you map data from the reference database to tables in the consolidated database.

A note on terminology: When discussing synchronization, the *remote* database is always the database that is being synchronized with the consolidated database. Synchronization occurs at the consolidated database, so everything about the process is relative to the consolidated database.

Scripts and Events

When the MobiLink server is started, it establishes one or more connections with the consolidated database and locates the UltraLite system tables. The synchronization scripts are stored in the system tables, and not in the MobiLink server. The server fetches the scripts from the system tables in order to execute them. That's why you use Sybase Central to install the scripts in the consolidated database. You can also insert scripts directly into the system tables if that's more convenient—instructions for how to do this are found in the UltraLite documentation.

Once a connection is established and the scripts are located, synchronization can occur. The synchronization process is divided into a number of steps, each of which triggers an *event* or notification. When an event occurs, the MobiLink server looks in the system tables for a synchronization script associated with the event. If a script is found, it executes it; otherwise, it proceeds to the next step in the synchronization process. Executing a script in response to an event is referred to as handling the event. Although there are many events, most of them are optional, and only a few have to be explicitly handled. The large number of events lets you control every aspect of the synchronization process, if so desired.

Two events actually occur outside the synchronization process. The begin_connection event is triggered immediately after the MobiLink server connects to the database, but before any synchronization starts. The end_connection event occurs just before the MobiLink server disconnects from the database. These events are triggered for each connection a server makes to the database.

Event Types and Script Parameters

Apart from begin_connection and end_connection, events fall into one of three categories:

- A *cursor event* occurs when a cursor needs to be opened. The associated script is a SELECT statement that defines the cursor.
- A *table event* occurs at various stages. The associated script returns synchronization logic for a specific remote table.
- A *connection event* also occurs at various stages. The associated script returns synchronization logic for the connection as a whole.

The type of the event determines the type of the script. Thus, a connection event triggers a connection script, a table event triggers a table script, and a cursor event triggers a cursor script. A few events have the same name but have different types, so be sure about which event you're handling.

Of the three events, cursor events must be handled to perform even the most basic synchronization. Connection and table events are used for conflict resolution and complex synchronization strategies and are not required for simple synchronization.

When a script is executed in response to an event other than begin_connection or end_connection, the script is passed one or more parameters. The script uses these parameters to customize its logic. Almost every script, for example, receives the user name (the user identification passed by the application to ULSynchronize or ULPalmExit) as a parameter. Any placeholders (question mark characters) in the script are replaced with the parameter values before the MobiLink server executes the script. For example, you might use the begin_synchronization connection event to track synchronizations by having it trigger the following script:

```
INSERT INTO LastSyncAttempt ( UserName ) VALUES ( ? )
```

The MobiLink server replaces the question mark with the user name and actually executes this script:

```
INSERT INTO LastSyncAttempt ( UserName ) VALUES ( 'PHBK_Eric_Giguere' )
```

When describing events, we list the event parameters using the same syntax as the UltraLite documentation:

```
begin_download_deletes( userName, tableName )
```

If an event has two or more parameters, the order of the parameters determines the order of the placeholder substitutions. Most scripts can ignore the parameters if they want to simply by omitting any placeholders, although for a few events the placeholders are not optional.

Connection events have a single parameter, the user name. Table events have two parameters: the user name and the name of the remote table. Cursor events get either the user name or a list of primary keys.

The Synchronization Process

The synchronization process begins when a device directly (with TCP/IP or serial connection) or indirectly (via HotSync and the MobiLink conduit) requests a synchronization.

Overview

At an abstract level, this is what happens during synchronization:

1. The application prepares an upload stream consisting of the rows that are new or have changed and the rows that have been deleted.
2. The MobiLink server receives the upload stream and applies the changes, detecting any conflicts when updating rows.
3. The MobiLink server then prepares a download stream of new, updated, or deleted rows.
4. The application receives the download stream and applies the changes to its embedded database.
5. Acknowledgments are sent to terminate the process.

Of course, the details are more complicated. The various steps in a complete synchronization can be grouped into general steps, upload steps, and download steps.

General Steps

The following general steps occur during synchronization:

1. Trigger begin_synchronization(userName).
2. For each remote table being synchronized, trigger begin_synchronization(userName, tableName).
3. Execute a COMMIT.
4. Process the upload stream using the upload steps.
5. Execute a COMMIT.
6. Prepare the download stream using the download steps.
7. Execute a COMMIT.
8. For each remote table being synchronized, trigger end_synchronization(userName, tableName).
9. Trigger end_synchronization(userName).
10. Execute COMMIT.

Notice how the MobiLink server commits pending changes at various points throughout the synchronization process. To ensure the integrity of the data, no script should perform a commit or rollback operation. The only exception to this is the script that handles errors.

None of the events triggered by these steps has to be handled.

Upload Steps

The following steps occur when processing the upload stream:

1. Trigger begin_upload(userName).
2. For each remote table, trigger begin_upload(userName, tableName).
3. For each remote table:
   a. Trigger begin_upload_rows(userName, tableName).
   b. For each new or changed row uploaded from the remote table:
      - Open the cursor defined by upload_cursor(pk1, ..., pkn), where pk1 to pk*n* are the primary keys used by the cursor, searching for an existing row with matching primary key values.
      - If the row is new, insert it using this cursor.
      - If the row is changed and there are no conflicts, update the row.
      - Otherwise, handle the conflict by opening two new cursors, old_row_cursor(pk1, ..., pk*n*) and new_row_cursor(pk1, ..., pk*n*), and inserting the old row (the row as it currently stands in the database) using old_row_cursor and inserting the new row (the changed row) using new_row_cursor. Then trigger resolve_conflict(userName, tableName) to resolve the conflict.
   c. Trigger end_upload_rows(userName, tableName).
4. For each remote table, in reverse order:
   a. Trigger begin_upload_deletes(userName, tableName).
   b. For each row deleted from the remote table:
      - Open the cursor defined by upload_cursor(pk1, ..., pk*n*).
      - Delete the row using this cursor.
   c. Trigger end_upload_deletes(userName, tableName).
5. For each remote table, trigger end_upload(userName, tableName).
6. Trigger end_upload(userName).

As you can see, processing the upload stream is a much more complicated set of steps. However, the only event you're required to handle is the upload_cursor event, although you should also handle old_row_cursor, new_row_cursor, and resolve_conflict in order to handle conflicts.

Download Steps

The following steps occur to produce a download stream:

1. Trigger begin_download(userName).
2. For each remote table, trigger begin_download(userName, tableName).
3. For each remote table:
   a. Trigger begin_download_deletes(userName, tableName).
   b. Open the cursor defined by download_delete_cursor(userName) and add the resulting rows to the download stream. These rows will be deleted from the remote table when the device processes the download stream.
   c. Trigger end_download_deletes(userName, tableName).
   d. Trigger begin_download_rows(userName, tableName).
   e. Open the cursor defined by download_cursor(userName) and add the resulting rows to the download stream. These rows will be inserted or updated in the remote table when the device processes the download stream.
   f. Trigger end_download_rows(userName, tableName).
4. For each remote table, trigger end_download(userName, tableName).
5. Trigger end_download(userName).
6. Wait for the device to receive and apply the download stream.
7. If the download stream was successfully applied, execute a COMMIT and send an acknowledgment to the device.
8. Otherwise, execute a ROLLBACK to roll back any changes made to produce the download stream.

Producing the download stream is also a complicated set of steps, but the only scripts you're required to write are the download_delete_cursor and download_cursor events.

Synchronization Examples

If you're having a hard time understanding the synchronization process, don't be alarmed. A few examples of some basic synchronization will help clear things up. We'll use the tables we defined in Chapter 6 for the

Phone Book application. Remember, it's not necessary to define scripts to handle every event.

Note that the examples assume that each remote table has a corresponding table in the consolidated database. This isn't necessary, of course, but it makes the examples simpler to understand and explain. With MobiLink you can define arbitrary mappings between a remote table and one or more tables in the consolidated database.

One-Way Complete Snapshot

Our first example copies a table from the consolidated database to the remote database. If no changes to the remote table are allowed, this is referred to as *one-way complete snapshot* synchronization. It's one-way because data flows in only one direction (consolidated to remote), complete because all the rows in the consolidated table are copied to the remote table, and snapshot because every row is copied even if it's already in the remote table.

To perform this synchronization, you define two scripts: download_delete_cursor to clear out the remote table and download_cursor to fill it. Filling the table is easy; just define download_cursor as follows:

```
SELECT EmployeeID, Name, Surname FROM EMPLOYEE
```

Because this is a complete snapshot synchronization, the download_cursor script ignores the user name parameter passed to it.

You might be wondering how we knew which columns to include in our SELECT statement. When the UltraLite analyzer is run against the reference database, it actually inserts a sample download_cursor script called default_download_cursor into the UltraLite system tables. (The reference database has its own copy of the UltraLite system tables, but they're not used for synchronization unless the reference database and the consolidated database are the same database.) Using the Java version of Sybase Central, you can connect to the reference database and examine this script. Copy it over to the consolidated database and use it as the basis for your download_cursor script.

Although filling the table is easy, clearing it is harder: The download_delete_cursor script has to select all the rows currently in the remote table. When the result set is sent to the device, any row in the remote database that matches a row in the result set (the primary keys are equal) is removed from the remote table. The problem, of course, is that if you delete a row from the consolidated database, how then do you select it for deletion in the remote database?

As it turns out, there are at least three ways to handle this problem:

- Assume that no rows are ever deleted from the consolidated table and don't define a script for download_delete_cursor.
- Never delete a row from the consolidated table. Instead, add a status column to the consolidated table (leave the remote table unchanged) and simply *mark* the row as deleted. Change the download_cursor script to return all rows that haven't been deleted:

    ```
    SELECT EmployeeID, Name, Surname FROM EMPLOYEE WHERE Deleted = 0
    ```

    Then define the download_delete_cursor script to return all rows that have been deleted:

    ```
    SELECT EmployeeID, Name, Surname FROM EMPLOYEE WHERE Deleted = 1
    ```

- Install a trigger on the consolidated table that is invoked whenever a row is deleted from the table. The trigger copies information about the row (the primary keys) to a *shadow table* that is not directly involved in the synchronization. The download_cursor remains unchanged, but the download_delete_cursor forms a result set from the shadow table.

The download_delete_cursor script must return a result set with the same set of columns as the download_cursor script.

Two-Way Complete Snapshot

The second example modifies the first example to allow changes to the remote table. In other words, the application is allowed to insert, update, or delete rows from its copy of the table. This is the *two-way* variation of the complete snapshot. The download_cursor and download_delete_cursor scripts are defined as in the one-way case, since we're always making a complete copy of the consolidated table. What's different is that we need to define an upload_cursor script as follows:

```
SELECT EmployeeID, Name, Surname FROM EMPLOYEE WHERE EmployeeID = ?
```

Recall that the upload_cursor event passes the script a number of parameters, one parameter for each primary key in the remote table. These values are used to form a WHERE clause that restricts the output of the SELECT statement. For each new or changed row received from the remote table, the MobiLink server uses this script to see if there is a matching row in the consolidated table. If there is, the row is updated, or a conflict is detected. Conflict resolution is discussed later. If there is no matching row, a new row is inserted into the consolidated table.

TIP The difference between the download_cursor and the upload_cursor scripts often confuses first-time UltraLite users. The download_cursor script selects zero or more rows that are to be downloaded to the remote database. The upload_cursor script locates a row in the consolidated database whose primary key values match the primary key values of the uploaded row.

Just as with the download_cursor, the UltraLite analyzer generates a default_upload_cursor script for you in the reference database which you can use as the basis for your consolidated table's upload_cursor script.

Partitioned Snapshots

Partitioned snapshots are similar to complete snapshots but return a subset of the rows in a table instead of all the rows. This process is what we referred to as row partitioning in Chapter 7. Column partitioning—returning a subset of the columns in a table—is done for you automatically when the UltraLite analyzer examines your SQL to build the custom database.

To partition the result set, define criteria to restrict the results of the SELECT statement used by the download_cursor script. The restrictions are usually based on the user name parameter passed by the download_cursor event. For example, say we had a table called EMPIDUSER that mapped employee IDs to synchronization user names. EMPIDUSER is defined as follows:

```
CREATE TABLE EMPIDUSER (
    EmployeeID INTEGER NOT NULL,
    UserName VARCHAR(128) NOT NULL PRIMARY KEY,
    FOREIGN KEY EmployeeID REFERENCES EMPLOYEE
);
```

We could restrict an employee to viewing information about himself or herself by defining the download_cursor script with a subquery as follows:

```
SELECT EmployeeID, Name, Surname FROM EMPLOYEE
    WHERE EmployeeID IN (
        SELECT EmployeeID FROM EMPIDUSER
            WHERE EMPIDUSER.UserName = ? )
```

Or alternatively using a join:

```
SELECT EMPLOYEE.EmployeeID, Name, Surname FROM EMPLOYEE, EMPIDUSER
    WHERE EMPLOYEE.EmployeeID = EMPIDUSER.EmployeeID AND
        EMPIDUSER.UserName = ?
```

A different query would allow employees to see information about themselves and anyone in their department:

```
SELECT EmployeeID, Name, Surname FROM EMPLOYEE
    WHERE DepartmentID IN (
        SELECT DepartmentID FROM EMPLOYEE
            WHERE EmployeeID IN (
                SELECT EmployeeID FROM EMPIDUSER WHERE
                    UserName = ? ) )
```

The download_delete_cursor would of course resemble the download_cursor script but with additional restrictions to select the rows to delete. Some additional work would be required to track rows that move from one partition to another. For example, if an employee transferred to a different department, that employee's information would have to be deleted in the remote databases of his or her former coworkers.

The upload_cursor script doesn't need to change, but the application logic should ensure that the user can't add new rows outside his or her own partition.

Incremental Synchronization

One problem with snapshots is that they generate a lot of traffic on the download stream: Rows that haven't changed are still deleted from the remote table and new rows with identical values are downloaded to take their place. On the other hand, the upload stream only sends the application's changes up to the server. Ideally, the server should download only the changes to the consolidated table to the device. This is the incremental synchronization we referred to in Chapter 7.

The easiest way to implement incremental synchronization is to use *timestamps*. A timestamp combines date and time values to record exactly when something occurred. By keeping track of when each row of the consolidated table was last modified and when the remote table was last synchronized, you can easily determine which rows in the consolidated table need to be downloaded to the device. The UltraLite documentation refers to this method of incremental synchronization as *timestamp synchronization*.

To track changes to the consolidated table, add a column to the table to store a timestamp. Add triggers that update the timestamp each time a row is updated or inserted. You'll also use timestamps to track deleted rows, whether they be deleted by setting a status field or by adding them to a shadow table. Add a timestamp column to the table that tracks user names. Change the download_cursor script to select only those rows whose timestamps are larger than the timestamp of the last synchronization for the given user name. Change the download_delete_cursor in a similar fashion. At the end of the download process, update the user name's timestamp to reflect the new synchronization time.

For a detailed example of this, refer to the UltraLite documentation and the CustDB sample.

Conflict Resolution

When a row is updated in a remote table, the device sends two copies of the row to the MobiLink server: One copy has the old values of the row prior to the update, while the second copy has the new values of the row after the update. When the server receives these rows, it compares the old values with the row values stored in the consolidated tables. If they're the same, the row in the consolidated table is updated with the new values from the remote table and no error occurs. If they're not the same, another application has already updated the row and a conflict is detected.

The MobiLink server resolves conflicts by invoking three scripts: old_row_cursor to store the old row values, new_row_cursor to store the new row values, and resolve_conflict to actually resolve the conflict. Both old_row_cursor and new_row_cursor define cursors similar to that defined by upload_cursor, passing the primary keys for the rows as parameters. There are no default behaviors defined for any of these scripts, because there's no way that the MobiLink server or even the UltraLite analyzer can determine the correct conflict resolution strategy. The simplest strategy is to let one side win, as discussed in Chapter 7: Either the new values from the remote table overwrite what's already in the consolidated table, or the new values are ignored and the current values in the consolidated table are prepared for downloading back to the remote table. More complicated strategies would use the user name or some other logic to determine which side wins.

For an example of conflict resolution in action, study the scripts for the ULOrder table in the CustDB sample. It defines two global temporary tables—tables whose rows are visible only to the connection that added them and that are automatically deleted when the connection is closed—to store the new and old values for a row. When resolve_conflict is called, it uses one of the new row values to determine whether new row values should overwrite what's in the consolidated table. The global temporary tables are then cleared, leaving them empty for use with the next conflict on the same connection.

Primary Key Pooling

Conflicts also occur if two remote tables insert new rows with identical primary keys. This is easily avoided with primary key pooling, as discussed in Chapter 7. A primary key pool is a table that assigns a fixed number of unused primary key values to each user. The pool table is synchronized using a partitioning strategy, so that each application has access to its unused primary key values. When the application inserts a new row, it obtains a primary key from the pool table. The primary key is no longer unused, so the appropriate row is deleted from the pool table. At the next synchronization, scripts in the consolidated database check to see whether the pool needs to be topped up with primary key values.

Again, refer to the CustDB sample for a good example of how to implement primary key pooling.

Error Handling

If an error occurs while the MobiLink server is executing a script, it invokes the handle_error script, passing it four values: the SQL error code (an integer), the error message, the synchronization user name, and the table name (which may be NULL if no table name was passed to the original script). The handle_error script then invokes a stored procedure to handle the error, as follows:

```
CALL MyErrorProcedure( ?, ?, ?, ?, ? )
```

The first parameter to the stored procedure is an output parameter of integer type, used to return an action code to the MobiLink server. An alternate way to call the stored procedure is also supported:

```
? = CALL MyErrorProcedure( ?, ?, ?, ? )
```

In this case, the first placeholder indicates that the return value of the stored procedure is the action code.

The MobiLink server currently understands three action codes:

1000 means ignore the current row and continue processing with the next row.

3000 means roll back the current transaction and cancel what's left of the synchronization.

4000 means roll back the current transaction and shut down the MobiLink server.

The default action if no script is defined is 3000. (Note that 2000 is currently unused.)

If your script wishes to record information about the error in the consolidated database before returning either 3000 or 4000, it must first roll back the current transaction, make the changes, and then commit the transaction. Otherwise, the information it recorded will be rolled back when the error handler returns its action code.

Debugging UltraLite Applications

Debugging the database code in an UltraLite application can be frustrating for two reasons:

- You don't debug the original embedded SQL, you debug the source generated by the SQL preprocessor. Not only does the SQL preprocessor convert embedded SQL into rather cryptic code, it's also easy to fall into the trap of making changes to the C/C++ source file and losing those changes the next time you run the SQL preprocessor.

- The HotSync manager and the CodeWarrior debugger both need to use the serial port to the device, which means shutting down CodeWarrior to synchronize the database or shutting down HotSync to debug the application.

There's no real way to solve the first frustration, you just need to get in the habit of debugging through the transformed source and of only making changes to the .sqc files, not the generated .c or .cpp files. The second problem can be avoided if you use the Palm OS Emulator and

TCP/IP synchronization to do your debugging. The Palm OS Emulator has a property that lets it map TCP/IP calls that a Palm application makes directly to the TCP/IP support on your desktop computer, with no need to configure the TCP/IP settings of the emulated device. TCP/IP-based UltraLite synchronization is then a snap to use and is great for testing the synchronization while simultaneously debugging the application. When you're ready to test your application on a real device, you can simply switch from TCP/IP to serial or HotSync synchronization if that's what's going to be used.

Phone Book and UltraLite

On the CD-ROM you'll find a version of the Phone Book application modified to use an UltraLite database, in the PhbkUltraLite subfolder of the Phone Book folder. Just as we did with the Palm database version of the application, all we really do in this version is define a new subclass of PhoneData called ULPhoneData, which uses embedded SQL to access a custom database. The application was also modified slightly to relaunch itself in order to recover its global variables while processing a global Find operation or after a HotSync has occurred.

To use and compile this version of Phone Book, you'll have to define ODBC data sources called Phone Book Reference and Phone Book Consolidated. Phone Book Reference should refer to the PHBKReference.db file and Phone Book Consolidated to the PHBKConsolidated.db file. Both database files are found on the CD-ROM in the same folder as the UltraLite version of Phone Book.

CHAPTER 9

Oracle Lite Consolidator

Although you can use UltraLite to synchronize to an Oracle database, you should also check out Oracle's current synchronization solution for the Palm Computing platform, the Oracle Lite Consolidator. This chapter introduces you to the Oracle Lite Consolidator and shows you how you can use it to build a synchronization solution that is different from UltraLite.

Oracle is also working on a version of Oracle 8i Lite for the Palm Computing platform; however, that product wasn't yet available as this book was written. It should be out by the time this book is published, though, so be sure to check the book's Web site for more details on it and other recently announced handheld database products from IBM and Microsoft.

What Is the Consolidator?

The Oracle Lite Consolidator allows you to map Oracle Lite tables into Palm databases. Unlike UltraLite, it doesn't embed a relational database in your application, nor does it provide complete control over the synchronization process. It does provide a way to get data from Oracle Lite onto the Palm and to keep that data up to date without writing your own conduit.

Oracle Lite

The Consolidator ships with Oracle Lite 3.5, a single-user relational database compatible with the larger Oracle7 or Oracle8 database servers. An evaluation copy of Oracle Lite can be downloaded free of charge from the Oracle Web site, www.oracle.com. A copy of Oracle Lite is *not* included on the CD-ROM that accompanies this book.

Oracle Lite is a small-footprint database meant to run on Windows 95/98, Windows NT, and Windows CE platforms. It supports the replication of tables from Oracle7 or Oracle8 servers. Like Sybase's Adaptive Server Anywhere, Oracle Lite is primarily aimed at mobile users who require a local database they can use when disconnected from the corporate network but can easily synchronize with the master data server.

The Consolidator

The Oracle Lite Consolidator is a way of extending the reach of Oracle Lite to the Palm Computing platform by providing a conduit and a runtime library that allows Palm databases to be synchronized with Oracle Lite tables. Multiple Palm devices can synchronize with a single copy of Oracle Lite.

The Consolidator offers partitioned synchronization (snapshot or incremental) with the most basic conflict resolution (one side always wins). Data is stored on the device in Palm databases, one Palm database per synchronized Oracle Lite table. The rows of a table are stored as records in the corresponding Palm database. Functions are provided to read and write data to and from a record, because the format of the data depends on the columns in the originating table. Apart from these functions, the application deals with the tables using the usual Palm Data Manager routines.

Consolidator documentation is found in a PDF file installed with Oracle Lite called "Oracle Lite for Handheld Devices." The documentation is a bit thin on details, so you have to glean many important facts from the sample applications.

Requirements

Oracle Lite requires Windows 95/98 or Windows NT. The examples listed here assume that you're using Windows NT and hence refer to the c:\orant installation directory; however, the process is the same for the other systems.

The Consolidator is installed when Oracle Lite is installed. In addition, the Consolidator requires the installation of the Java Runtime Environment (JRE) or the Java Development Kit (JDK), versions 1.1.5 or higher. Either of these can be obtained from Sun Microsystems' Java Web site, http://java.sun.com.

Consolidator applications run on Palm Computing platform devices supporting Palm OS 2.0 or higher. The conduit requires HotSync Manager 2.1 or higher.

Consolidator Samples

The Consolidator includes a version of the built-in Address Book application modified to use a Consolidator database synchronized with an Oracle Lite database. The sample is quite complex, however, and if you're unfamiliar with the inner workings of the Address Book to begin with, you'll find the sample hard to follow.

A better, more recent sample called FixIt can be downloaded from the Oracle Web site. Go to www.oracle.com/search and search for it there. FixIt is a job ticket application used by fictional maintenance workers to track the calls for help that they answer every day based on data extracted from an Oracle Lite database. You'll find that it's a much easier sample to learn from.

How the Consolidator Works

As with UltraLite, the workings of the Consolidator are best understood by walking through what happens during the development and deployment phases of an application.

Development Phase

The first step is to prepare the Oracle Lite database by defining the tables to be used by your application. Unlike UltraLite, there is no separation of reference and consolidated database: The Oracle Lite database acts as both.

Once the tables are defined, you generate the *metadata* for the tables. The metadata is a structure that defines how the columns of a table map into the records of a Palm database. The metadata is generated by code within the Oracle database, similar to how the UltraLite analyzer runs within the database. Unlike UltraLite, however, the metadata generator does not analyze the application's data requirements to determine which set of columns is actually needed by the application—you must explicitly determine the columns that are to be downloaded.

With metadata in hand, you write a Palm application as you normally would, except that whenever you need to access the data inside a record you use the metadata structure in conjunction with the Consolidator runtime library. Apart from that, the usual Palm database behaviors apply: set the dirty bit to mark updated records, use DmDeleteRecord to delete a record, and use DmAttachRecord to add a new record.

Deployment Phase

The application is installed on the Palm device and a HotSync operation is initiated. The Consolidator conduit synchronizes each Consolidator database with its corresponding Oracle Lite table. Partitioning can be used to control which data in the Oracle Lite table is copied down to the client. Conflicts are detected and resolved either in favor of the client or the Oracle Lite database.

A password application is also installed on the device during the deployment phase. This application lets the user of a device assign a password to use during the next Consolidator HotSync. The password provides basic security to allow only authorized users to make changes to data.

Building and Deploying Consolidator Applications

Although not as complicated or complete a solution as UltraLite, several steps are still required to build Consolidator applications.

Consolidator Development

The steps required to build an Oracle Lite Consolidator application are as follows:

1. Design the application
2. Start the CodeWarrior project

3. Create the Oracle Lite database and tables
4. Generate the metadata
5. Write the code to access the database
6. Write the user interface
7. Build and install the application

Each step is explained in the following sections.

Design the Application

As before, spend time on the application design, using the information you learned about in Chapters 4 and 5.

Start the CodeWarrior Project

The steps used to create an UltraLite-based CodeWarrior project can also be used to create a Consolidator-based project with the following changes:

You don't need multisegment support. Because Consolidator is just a way to map Oracle database tables into Palm databases, there's no custom database generated and so the application will usually fit in a single segment. The downside, of course, is that you have to handle all the database access yourself.

Default compiler settings. Two-byte or four-byte ints can be used, so choose the setting that makes the most sense for your application.

Different runtime library. Link the Consolidator runtime library olrl4p.lib with your application. You'll find the file in the C:\orant\Consolidator\SDK\lib directory. You should add SDK\lib and SDK\inc directories to the access paths for the project.

As always, be sure to assign a unique creator ID to your application.

Create the Database and Tables

The next task is to create the Oracle Lite database on the desktop computer. Alternatively, you can just reuse the sample database that Consolidator installs. If you want to create a new database, in the Start menu you'll find a submenu for Oracle Lite. One of the tools that ships with Oracle Lite is the Oracle8 Navigator, a tool for creating and examining Oracle databases. Start the tool. Select File/New/New Oracle Lite Data-

PALM DATABASE PROGRAMMING

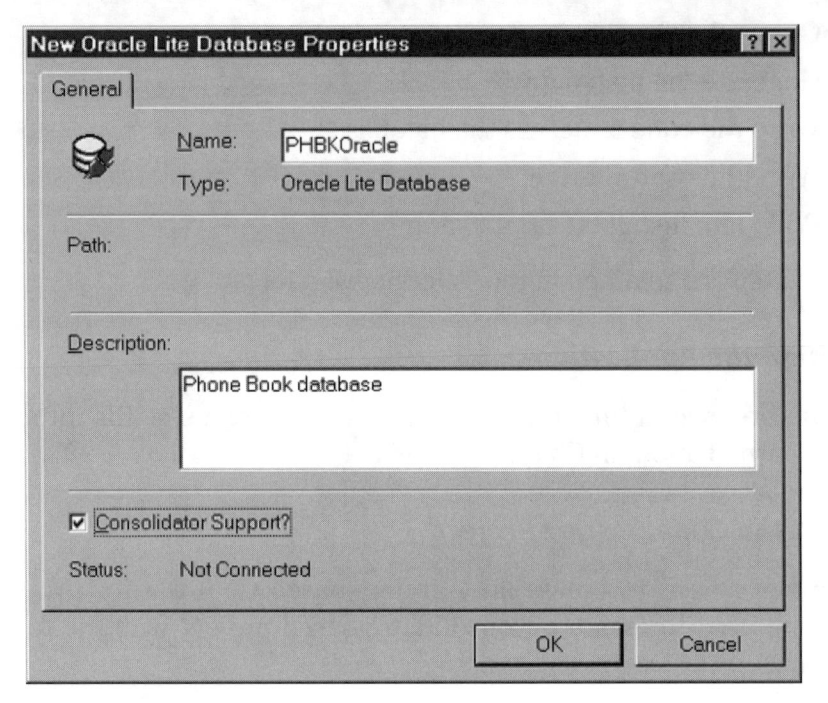

Figure 9.1 Creating an Oracle Lite database.

base to create a new database, as shown in Figure 9.1. Type in the name of the new database, for example, OracleTest. Make sure Consolidator support is enabled before pressing OK to create the database. The new database is then created as c:\orant\OLDB35\OracleTest.odb.

If you've created a new database, you'll need an ODBC data source for it, so invoke the ODBC Administrator and create a new data source using the Oracle Lite 35 Driver. Configure the new entry using an appropriate data source name (with no spaces), c:\orant\OLDB35 as the directory name, and the database name, as shown in Figure 9.2.

Use the Oracle8 Navigator to create the tables. You can do this quite simply by selecting the Table folder for the database you're using and selecting New from the popup menu to display a property sheet. In the property sheet, type the name of a table, say EMPLOYEE, and select an owner, say SAMPLE1 (assuming you're using the sample database). Then flip to the Design page, create the columns, and press OK. Select the table you just created and choose Open from the popup menu to edit and add data to the table. Enter some values to populate the table.

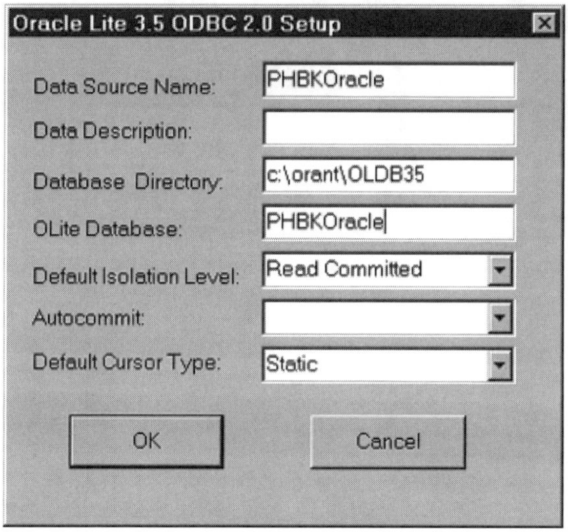

Figure 9.2 Configuring an Oracle Lite ODBC data source.

Generate the Metadata

Once the ODBC data source is ready, you need to generate the Consolidator metadata that describes the table. You can do this from the Oracle8 Navigator, but first you have to create a publication and at least one subscription

A *publication* is the set of columns from a table that are to be downloaded to a client, while a *subscription* is a set of rows from a publication. Together, a publication and a subscription perform vertical and horizontal partitioning of the table to minimize the data that is downloaded to the client.

To create a publication, open the Consolidator folder in the Oracle8 Navigator, select the Publication item, and then select New from the popup menu, to view the property sheet shown in Figure 9.3. Give the new publication a name, say, P_EMPLOYEE, and then select the columns from the table you want to publish. This defines the vertical partitioning of the data. In the bottom half of the dialog there's a checkbox labeled Where. Check this and type a SQL condition that will be used in a WHERE clause to perform horizontal partitioning. The condition should include a placeholder character, the question mark (?). The placeholder will be replaced later with a value you assign to a particular subscription. Press OK to finish.

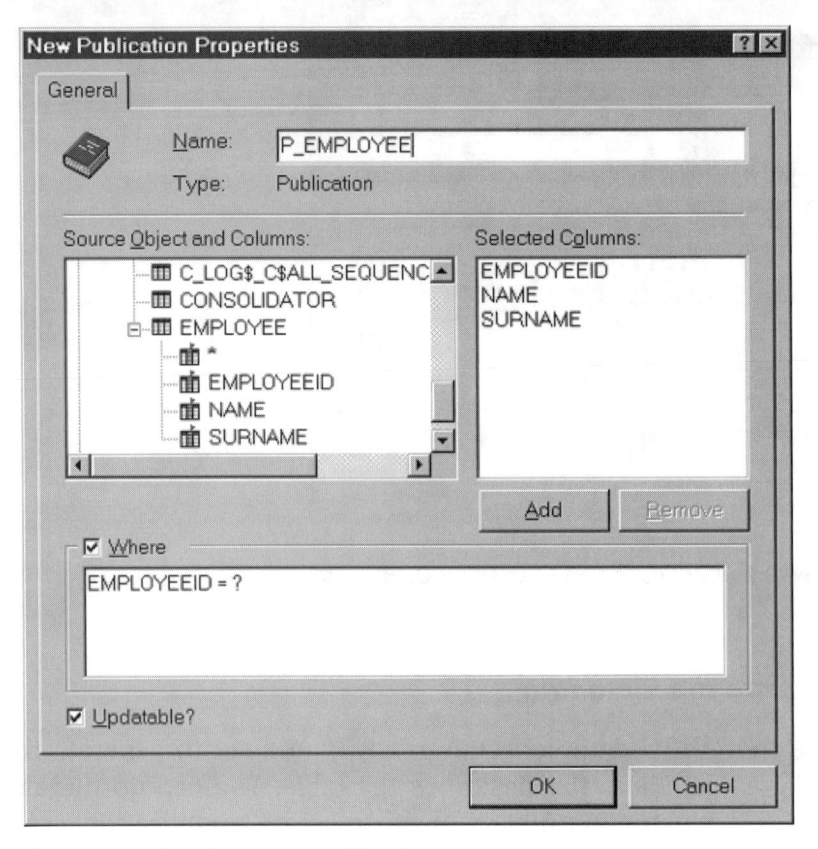

Figure 9.3 Creating a new publication.

To create a subscription, first select the Client item in the Consolidator folder and create a client. The client is the name of a Palm device as used by the HotSync Manager to identify the device during synchronization. You need to create a client for each device that's going to use the Consolidator. If a device name includes one or more space characters, you'll have to rename the device to remove the spaces. Clients are created by selecting New from the popup menu and then typing the name of the client and a password for the client as shown in Figure 9.4. Once a client has been created, reselect it and select Properties from its popup menu to bring up the property sheet shown in Figure 9.5. The second page on this sheet lets you create a subscription for the client to any of the available publications. Select the publication name, the conflict resolution rule (which side wins when conflicts are detected), and enter a parameter value. The placeholder in the publication's WHERE condition is replaced with this value to determine the set of rows that are downloaded to the client. Press the Create button to create the new subscription.

Figure 9.4 Creating a new client.

With a publication and a subscription created, return to the Publication folder and select the publication. From its popup menu, select the item Generate Metadata. Navigator will generate the metadata for the publication, storing it in a file of your choice, usually as a header file. The header file is to be included by your application, as it defines structures and arrays used by the Consolidator runtime routines to access the application's data.

Generate metadata for each publication used by your application.

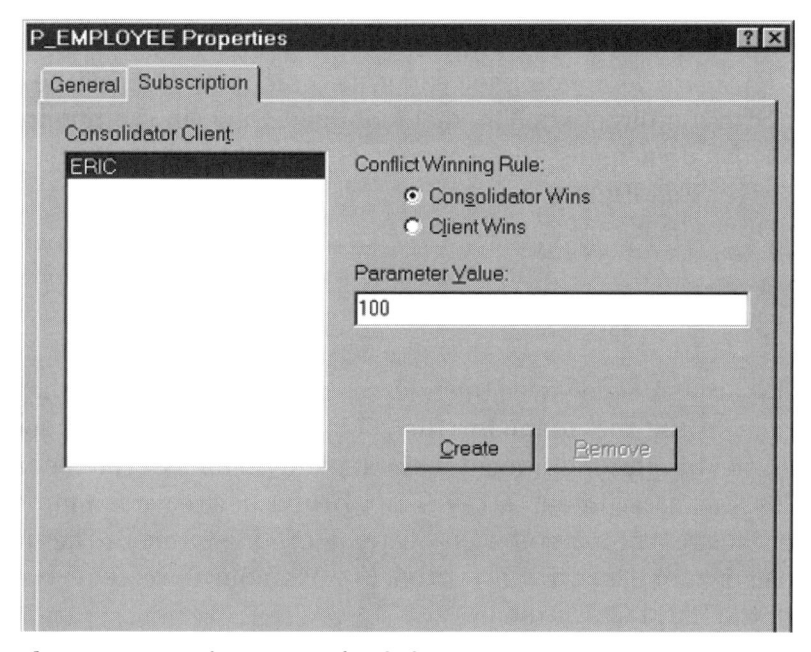

Figure 9.5 Creating a new subscription.

Write the Database Code

Next, write the code that accesses the database or databases used by your application. This is the most complicated part of the process, because the format of the databases is determined by the Consolidator.

The first step is to open the databases. Unlike databases your application would normally create, Consolidator databases use the ORCL creator ID and the DATA resource type. To open a specific database, cycle through all ORCL/DATA databases (using DmGetNextDatabaseByType-Creator) and look for the desired database by its name, which will be the name of the table it represents. If the database doesn't exist, you can actually create it yourself using the metadata; see the samples for examples of this.

Once the databases are open, you access the records in the normal fashion using such routines as DmQueryRecord. To read or write data from a particular record, however, you must use routines defined by the Consolidator run time. These routines read or write individual column values from/to a pointer that you allocate. The Consolidator run time defines type mappings for the common SQL types, as in the following:

```
typedef signed short olrl4p_tSMALLINT;
typedef float olrl4p_tFLOAT;
```

These types are defined in the header file <olrl4p.h>, part of the Consolidator SDK\Inc directory. The metadata generated in the previous step defines the data using these types. The routine to read the data is olrl4p_fGet_FieldByIndex:

```
int olrl4p_fGet_FieldByIndex( const void **fieldData,
                              const olrl4p_tTable_MD *tableMetaData,
                              const void *rawRecordData,
                              int columnIndex )
```

The first argument receives the address of the desired data; the second argument is the metadata for the table, as defined in the generated header file; the third argument is the locked pointer to the record data; and the fourth argument is the index of the desired column, less one (these indexes are zero-based instead of one-based). The function returns nonzero if an error occurred. For example, to read the Name column of the EMPLOYEE table:

```
VoidPtr  data = .....; // locked pointer to raw record data
CharPtr  name = NULL;
int      rc;

rc = olrl4p_fGet_FieldByIndex( &name, olrl4p_cp_EMPLOYEE_md, data,
olrl4p_tEMPLOYEE_Fields::ix_Name );
if( rc != 0 ){
   // error....
} else if( name == NULL ){
   // column value is NULL
} else {
   // name is a valid string
}
```

Note that olrl4p_cp_EMPLOYEE_md is a pointer to the metadata for the EMPLOYEE table and olrl4p_tEMPLOYEE_Fields::ix_Name is the index of the Name column. Both values are defined in the generated metadata for the table.

The routine to write the data is as follows:

```
int olrl4p_fSet_FieldByIndex( DmOpenRef dbRef, void **recordData,
                              olrl4p_tINT *recordLen, const void *field,
                              olrl4p_tVARFIELDLENGTH len,
                              olrl4p_tTable_MD *tableMetaData,
                              int columnIndex )
```

The first argument is the database reference; the second argument points to the locked pointer of raw record data; the third argument is the length of the record; the fourth argument is the data to copy into the record; the fifth argument is the length of the data for variable-size types; the sixth argument is the table metadata; and the seventh argument is the column index, less one. For fixed-size types, use 0 as the length; for strings use –1 and the length is calculated automatically:

```
VoidPtr     data = ....; // locked pointer to raw record data
olrl4p_tINT len; // ignored
int         rc;

rc = olrl4p_fSet_FieldByIndex( dbRef, &data, &len, "John", -1,

olrl4p_cp_EMPLOYEE_md,

olrl4p_tEMPLOYEE_Fields::ix_Name );
if( rc != 0 ){
   // error
} else {
   // unlock record
}
```

To create a new record, pass in a pointer to a NULL pointer as the second argument. The routine will allocate a new record of the correct size and return a locked pointer to the record in the second argument. You then pass this value on to subsequent calls to fill in the remaining fields. When you're done, you call MemPtrRecoverHandle to recover the record handle associated with the locked pointer, unlock the record, and then associate it with the database by calling DmAttachRecord.

It's recommended that you separate the data access into separate C or C++ files so that the user interface doesn't directly deal with any of the Consolidator runtime routines.

Write the User Interface

Nothing unusual here.

Build and Install the Application

Build and install the application like any other.

Consolidator Deployment

The steps to deploy the application are as follows:

1. Prepare the database
2. Install the Consolidator conduit
3. Run the message generator and processor
4. Synchronize and run the application

Each step is explained in detail in the following sections.

Prepare the Database

There's nothing more to do to the database other than to fill it with data and/or create any required subscriptions.

Install the Consolidator Conduit

Oracle Lite automatically installs the Consolidator conduit for you. A single conduit synchronizes all the databases, which is why the Palm databases all use the ORCL creator ID.

Note that if you want to let your users dial in to synchronize with the server, the Consolidator documentation includes detailed steps on how to do this using Network HotSync.

Run the Message Generator and Processor

Periodically run the Message Generator and Processor (MGP) to process uploaded data and prepare data for downloading. The MGP is run using the MGP.bat file:

```
c:\orant\Consolidator\MGP.bat
```

Once started, MGP continues running until you interrupt it by pressing Ctrl-C.

Synchronize and Run the Application

Perform a HotSync to copy the data from the publications down to the client, then run the application. After you make any changes, perform a HotSync to upload those changes to the database.

If a client's subscription is password protected, that client has to install the passwd.prc application on the device and use it to set the password before each HotSync; otherwise, no synchronization occurs.

Conflict Resolution

Unlike UltraLite, the Consolidator does not provide much choice in conflict resolution strategies. The only available approaches are that the client wins (client's values overwrite what's in the database) or the Consolidator wins (updated values in the database overwrite what's in the client). You set the strategy per subscription, however, so some users (managers, for example) can overwrite what's in the database while others cannot.

Primary Key Pooling

The Consolidator lets you define sequences of integers as primary key pools. You assign a range of integers to each client using the Sequence folder in the Oracle8 Navigator. The clients then use the olrl4p_fGet_

SeqCurrVal and olrl4p_fGet_SeqNextVal functions to obtain a value from the pool to use when creating their records.

Phone Book and the Consolidator

On the CD-ROM you'll find a version of the Phone Book application modified to use the Oracle Lite Consolidator, in the PhbkOracle subfolder of the Phone Book folder.

CHAPTER 10

Conclusion

This book has presented you with enough information to get you well on your way to writing sophisticated and useful applications for the Palm Computing platform. Even if you don't use either UltraLite or the Consolidator and decide instead to take the plunge and write your own conduit, you now have a much better understanding of the challenges you'll face and what you can do to overcome them. Learning to use new routines is not hard—it's understanding the concepts behind those routines that can be elusive. This book provides you with a firm foundation to use as you further explore the Palm Computing platform and perhaps even other handheld platforms such as Windows CE.

Although we've covered a lot of material in this book, there is also a lot that hasn't been covered. The Palm OS APIs for beaming, network access, serial line access, and alarm management haven't been discussed, to name a few. You'll find detailed documentation on all of this in the Palm OS SDK, however, and once you understand the basics that we have covered—how applications work, how to build user interfaces, how to manage data—the rest falls into place quite easily.

Study the examples on the CD-ROM carefully, as they cover everything discussed in this book in even more detail. Consult Appendix A for a list of what's found on the CD-ROM.

No book is ever error-free, so be sure to check the book's Web site (www.ericgiguere.com/palm) for corrections and additional information. Also, visit the Palm Computing Web site regularly, especially the Development Zone area (www.palm.com/devzone), to ensure you keep up to date with the latest developments on the Palm Computing platform. The book's Web site also has links to other valuable Web sites that you should explore.

APPENDIX A

CD-ROM Contents

This appendix describes what's on the CD-ROM that accompanies this book. Note that in most folders on the CD-ROM you'll find an index.html file describing the contents of that folder and any special installation or usage instructions. Use your Web browser to view these files. The root directory of the CD-ROM also includes an index.html file that links into these other files.

CD-ROM Layout

The CD-ROM includes the following folders:

Evaluation Software. Evaluation copies of CodeWarrior Lite Release 5 and Adaptive Server Anywhere 6.02.

Palm Computing. Software, documentation, and SDKs from the Palm Computing Web site, licensed for inclusion in this book. Please check the Palm Computing Web site (www.palm.com/devzone) regularly for updated versions.

GNU Tools. The PilRC distribution of the GNU Tools described in Chapter 3.

Samples. Sample applications discussed in the book, each in its own folder. Includes AppSkeleton, UI Test, GNUSample, Phone Book, and Time Book. Phone Book is further divided into subfolders, one for each variant of the Phone Book application.

Scripts. Database scripts for creating and populating the databases used by the Phone Book and Time Book samples.

Windows. The MLConduitInstaller application for installing the MobiLink conduit used for HotSync-based synchronization of UltraLite programs.

Plugins. Beta copies of CodeWarrior plug-ins for editing and compiling UltraLite source files as part of your CodeWarrior projects.

Except for GNUSample, all applications in the Samples folder require CodeWarrior or CodeWarrior Lite.

Please check the book's Web site (www.ericgiguere.com/palm) for updates and corrections to software written exclusively for this book.

User Assistance and Information

The software accompanying this book is being provided as is without warranty or support of any kind. Should you require basic installation assistance, or if your media is defective, please call the Wiley product support number at (212) 850-6194 weekdays between 9 A.M. and 4 P.M. Eastern Standard Time. You can also contact product support via email at: wprtusw@wiley.com.

To place additional orders or to request application information about other Wiley products, please call (800) 879-4539.

APPENDIX B

Sybase Adaptive Server Anywhere

On the CD-ROM that accompanies this book you'll find an evaluation version of Sybase's Adaptive Server Anywhere (ASA), a relational DBMS. ASA is actually one part of a software suite referred to as SQL Anywhere Studio and has been known previously as SQL Anywhere or Watcom SQL. The version of ASA included with this book is version 6.0.2 for Windows 95/98/NT, which is the first version that includes the Ultra-Lite deployment technology discussed in Chapter 8. This appendix covers the basic installation and use of ASA. For more details on ASA, of course, consult the online documentation that accompanies the product.

Installing ASA

To install ASA on your system, load the CD-ROM and open the folder titled Adaptive Server Anywhere Installation, and then run the SETUP.EXE program to start the ASA installation. Be sure to install the UltraLite deployment option. Note that UltraLite requires you to run Hot-Sync Manager 3.0 or higher on your desktop, so if you're running an earlier version of the HotSync Manager, download the latest version from the Palm Computing Web site and install it before installing ASA.

Running ASA

ASA includes a sample database, which includes tables and data that might be used by a small company to maintain internal and external information—lists of employees, departments, customers, orders, and so on.

Starting the sample database is very simple. Once ASA has been installed, use an entry in the Start menu to run the sample database: select Start, then Sybase, then Adaptive Server Anywhere 6.0, then Personal Server Sample. This runs the personal form of the ASA database server, which is used if the application and the database are on the same machine—use the network version to run the database server on a different machine. Note that in ASA, the database server is often referred to as the database *engine*. To start a database engine from a DOS prompt you would use the dbeng6 command—refer to the ASA documentation for more details.

After starting the database server, you'll see a window much like the one in Figure B.1, which we'll refer to as the *server window*. The window will disappear after a few seconds, but can be opened at any time by double-clicking on the ASA icon in the taskbar, shown in Figure B.2. The icon remains in the taskbar as long as the engine is running.

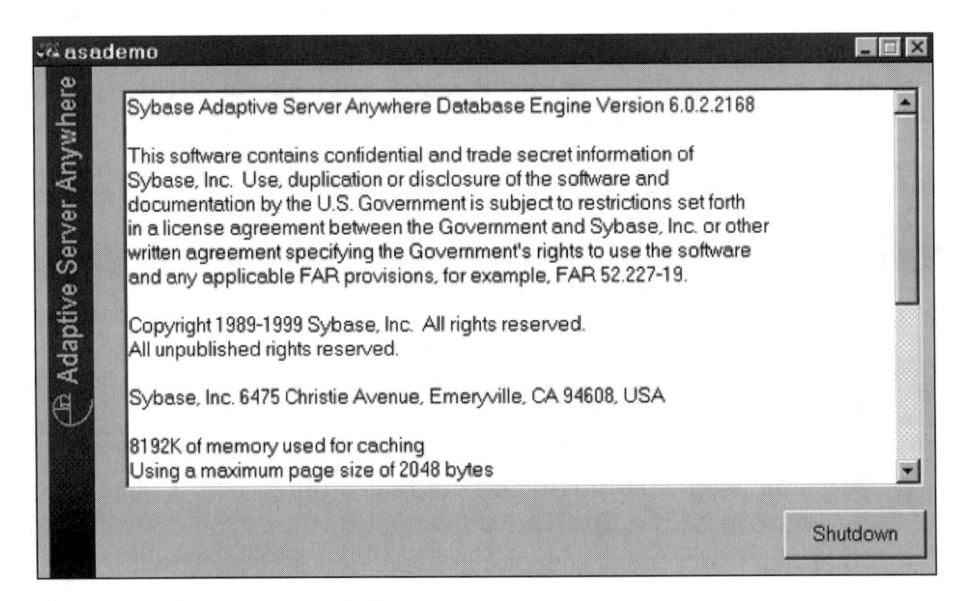

Figure B.1 The ASA server window.

Figure B.2 The ASA taskbar icon.

To shutdown the database server, open the server window and press the Shutdown button.

ASA Tools

ASA comes with a number of tools for creating and maintaining databases. The two we use in this chapter are the Interactive SQL and the Sybase Central tools. Both are run by selecting the appropriate entry on the Start menu: select Start, then Sybase, then Adaptive Server Anywhere 6.0, then either Interactive SQL or Manage Adaptive Server Any-

Figure B.3 ASA connection dialog.

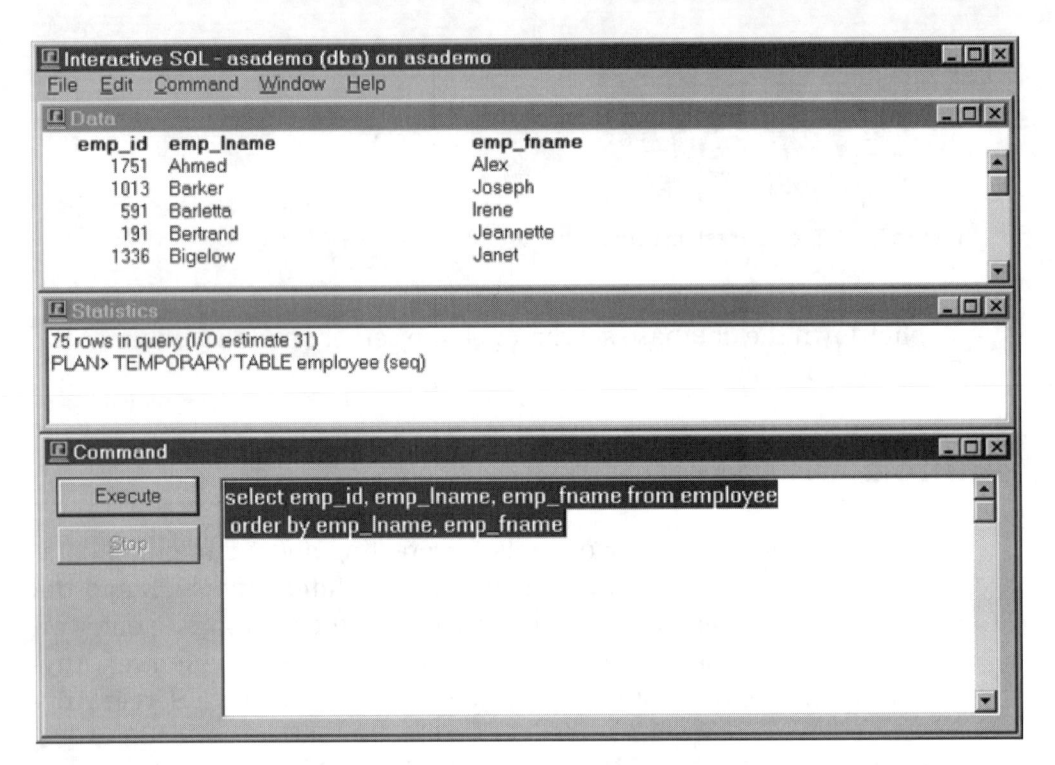

Figure B.4 The Interactive SQL tool.

where. Before running either tool, make sure the sample database is running. When the Interactive SQL tool starts, it displays the connection dialog shown in Figure B.3. Enter *dba* in the User ID field and *sql* in the Password field. This connects the tools to the sample database using the role of a database administrator. To use the Sybase Central tool with the sample database, select the Tools menu, then select Connect to display the same connection dialog. Enter *dba* and *sql* here as well.

The Interactive SQL tool allows you to interactively query a database using SQL. The tool consists of three subwindows, as shown in Figure B.4: The top window (titled "Data") lists the results of a database command; the middle window (titled "Statistics") lists statistics gathered when running a command; and the bottom window (titled "Commands") is the command input area. To enter a command, type it into the input area and then press either the Execute button or else F9.

The Sybase Central tool allows you to create and manage databases, as shown in Figure B.5. It uses the Windows Explorer metaphor, with a tree view in the left side of the window and a list view in the right side of the

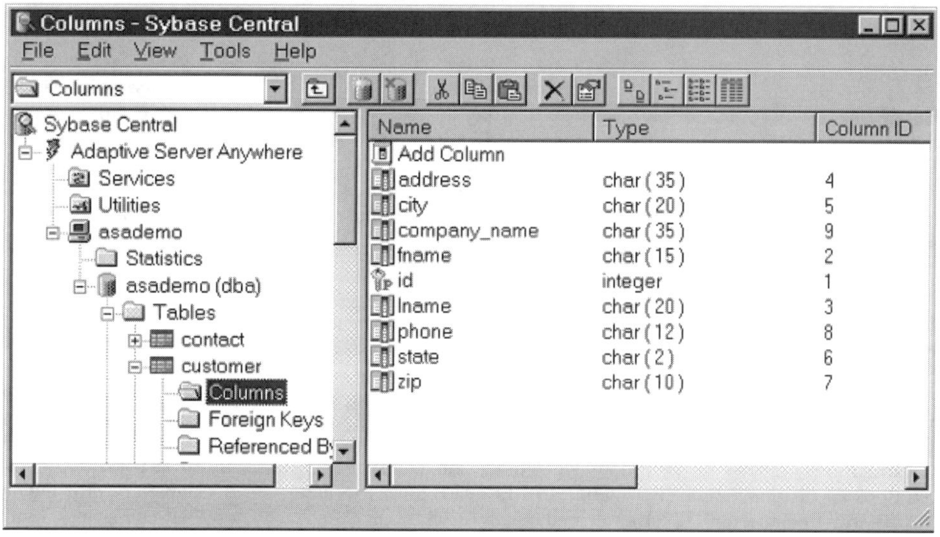
Columns - Sybase Central
File Edit View Tools Help
Columns
Sybase Central
Adaptive Server Anywhere
Services
Utilities
asademo
Statistics
asademo (dba)
Tables
contact
customer
Columns
Foreign Keys
Referenced By
Name
Type
Column ID
Add Column
address char (35) 4
city char (20) 5
company_name char (35) 9
fname char (15) 2
id integer 1
lname char (20) 3
phone char (12) 8
state char (2) 6
zip char (10) 7

Figure B.5 The Sybase Central tool.

window. The list view shows the details of the currently selected tree view item, such as the tables in a database. The list view also shows any commands that are available related to the current entry, such as adding a new table. Double-clicking on a command invokes a wizard or an editor to make the appropriate changes.

INDEX

A

Abstract models
 of databases, 212–215
 of Phone Book application, 237–238
Access mode flags, for databases (table), 175
Action code, with PilotMain function, 79
Active applications, 79
Adaptive Server Anywhere (ASA) system
 installing, 343
 relational databases with, 203
 running, 344–345
 tools in, 345–347
 with UltraLite, 274–278
Address Book application, 327
Alert editor, with Constructor, 114–115
Alerts
 custom, 115–116
 in user interfaces, 114–116
ALTER TABLE statement, 226
AND operation, in SELECT statement, 228–229
appInfo block, 181–184
AppInfoType, in custom information blocks, 181
appl database type, 78
Application information blocks, 181–184
Application names, changing, 33–34
Applications, 77–167
 active, 79
 checking Palm OS versions for, 93–94
 described, 77–79
 designing user interfaces for, 110–157, 164–167
 error handling for, 80
 event processing for, 94–105
 launching, 79, 80–91
 memory allocation for, 91–92
 miscellaneous tasks for, 157–164
 multisegment, 70
 relaunching, 65–70
 skeletons for, 105–110
 structuring, 92–93
Application skeletons, 105–110
AppSkeleton, 105–110
AppStart function, 92–93
AppStop function, 92–93
Archiving records, 189
ASA connection dialog, 345
ASA server window, 344
ASCII characters, 101

B

Assembly language, 14
<assert.h> file, 47
Assertions, 47
Asterisk (*), in SELECT statement, 227
Attribute masks, for records, 188, 189
Attributes. *See also* Database attributes
 of records, 188
Autocommit mode, 236
Autoincrement columns, 226
autoRepeatKeyMask, 102

Batteries
 for Palm devices, 13
 sleep mode and, 15
BEGIN DECLARE SECTION statement, 297–298
BEGIN TRANSACTION statement, 235–236
BETWEEN operator, in SELECT statement, 229
.bin files, 44
Bitmap editor window, for Constructor, 36, 37, 157
Bitmaps, form, 135
Blocks. *See also* Custom information blocks; Memory blocks
 allocating, 23, 91–92
 with applications, 91–92
 locking and unlocking memory, 22
 in object allocation, 53–54
Breakpoints, setting for debugging, 40–41
Build-prc tool, 42–45
Busy bits, in records, 188
Buttons, as controls, 137–138

C

Callback functions, 51–52
Callback.h header file, 52
CALLBACK_PROLOGUE macro, 52
Call-level interface (CLI), 207
Cards, memory, 20–21
Cascading deletes, in tables, 235
Cascading updates, in tables, 235
Catalog window, for Constructor, 122–123
Categories, of records, 187, 197–200
CategoryCreateList function, 198–199
CategoryEdit routines, 18, 19, 199–200
CategoryEditV10 routines, 19
CategoryEditV20 routines, 18, 19
CategoryFind function, 198
CategoryFreeList function, 199
CategoryGetName function, 198

CategoryInitialize function, 198
 with custom information blocks, 183
Category Manager routines, 198–200
CategorySetTriggerLabel function, 198
CategoryTruncateName function, 198
C/C++ languages, 4, 5
 CodeWarrior and, 30
 embedded SQL and, 280–283, 298–299, 300–301
 GNU tools with, 41–46
 Palm Computing platform and, 46–71
 UltraLite and, 264
CD-ROM, contents of accompanying, 341–342
Channels, synchronization, 269, 304–310
Characters, drawing on forms, 129
Character strings, functions for, 130
Character types, 29
Check boxes, as controls, 137, 139
Classes, for Phone Book application, 167
Closing databases, 176–177
CodeWarrior, 30–41
 building projects with, 38
 C/C++ languages and, 46–71
 CodeWarrior Lite versus, 31
 Consolidator and, 329
 Constructor tool for, 35–37
 debugging with, 38–41
 editing .sqc files with, 280
 error handling in, 47–50
 exception handling in, 50–51
 floating-point support with, 70–71
 GNU tools and, 41–46
 history of, 30–31
 launching new projects with, 32–34
 multisegment applications with, 70
 Palm OS and, 30
 Palm OS console and, 74
 Palm OS Emulator with, 71–74
 SQL preprocessor and, 282
 with UltraLite applications, 272–274
 UltraLite generator and, 282
CodeWarrior dialog, 31
CodeWarrior Lite, CodeWarrior versus, 31
COFF format, 44, 45
Column partitioning, in data synchronization, 256–257
Columns
 autoincrement, 226
 retrieving from tables, 226–229
 in table normalization, 221
 in tables, 150–151, 209
 types of, 222–223

348

Index

commandKeyMask, 102
COMMIT statement, 235–236, 304
<Common.h> header file, 28
Communication managers, 16
Comparison functions, in sorting, 193–194
Components
　common properties of, 136
　controls, 137–140
　creating, 135
　finding, 135–136
　labels, 136–137
　types of, 134–135
　in user interfaces, 134–136
Computed values, in SELECT statement, 227
CondCfg tool, 75, 285–288
Conduit Development Kit (CDK), 74–75
Conduits, 3, 4, 247–248
　in data synchronization, 246
　MobiLink, 283–288
　for Time Book application, 249–251, 251–254
　with UltraLite databases, 262–263
Conflict resolution
　in Consolidator, 337
　in data synchronization, 258–259, 320–321
Connection events, in UltraLite synchronization, 311–312
CONNECT statement, in SQL, 293
Console, 74
Consolidated databases
　for Phone Book application, 274–278
　with UltraLite applications, 266–268
Consolidator, 325–337
　applications with, 328–336
　deploying, 336–337
　described, 326
　samples of, 327
　system requirements for, 326–327
Constructor tool, 34, 35–37
　alerts with, 114–116
　creating components with, 135
　creating menus with, 132–133
　creating resources with, 112–114
　forms with, 122–130
　string lists with, 117–122
　string resources with, 116–117
Controls, 134
　kinds of, 137
Coordinates, in drawing on forms, 128–129
Copilot emulator, 71–72
Cover classes
　in relaunching applications, 65–70

simulating virtual functions with, 63–65
CREATE TABLE statement, 225–226
Creating databases, 173–174
　with Consolidator, 327–336
　with UltraLite, 274–278, 278–280, 280–283
Creating records in databases, 189–190
Creating resources in databases, 186
Creator ID
　for applications, 78
　in database headers, 173
　for databases, 24
　for new projects, 33
　registering, 78
C runtime library, 46–47
CtlEnabled function, 140
CtlGetLabel function, 139
CtlGetValue function, 138, 139
ctlRepeatEvent function, 138
ctlSelectEvent function, 137, 139
CtlSetEnabled function, 140
CtlSetLabel function, 139
CtlSetValue function, 138, 139
Cursor events, in UltraLite synchronization, 311–312
Cursors, in fetching multiple rows of data, 302–304
Custom alerts, 115–116
Custom-drawn items, in tables, 154–155
Custom information blocks, databases and, 181–184
Custom load routine, with table items, 153–154
Custom save routine, with table items, 154
Custom strategies, for conflict resolution, 259

D

Data, Palm platform and, 3
Database administrators, 218–219
Database applications
　for Palm platforms, 8–9
　with UltraLite, 272–290
Database classes, 294–295
Database entries, 172. *See also* Records; Resources
Database headers, 172–173
Database.h file, 294
Database information, in database headers, 177–181
Database management systems (DBMSs), 206–207
　abstract database models and, 212–213
　classification of, 208–212

interfaces for, 207–208
　physical database models and, 212–213, 215–218
Database models, 212–218
Database programming, for Palm platforms, 4, 171–201
Database programming, for Palm platforms, 8
Databases. *See also* Oracle Lite databases; Palm databases; Phone Book application; Record databases; Relational databases; Resource databases
　administrators of, 218–219
　applications as, 77–78
　classification of, 208–212
　defined, 24, 204
　designing, 212–224
　distributed, 212
　engines of, 344
　Find requests with, 157–163
　management of, 173–185
　management system interfaces for, 207–208
　management systems for, 206–207
　metadata in, 210, 328
　multimedia, 212
　names of, 173
　object-oriented, 211
　ordinary users of, 218–219
　ownership of data in, 218–219
　for Phone Book application, 240–241
　querying, 226–236
　record-oriented, 204–205
　records in, 159
　relational, 203–242
　self-describing, 210
　storage heaps and, 23–24, 171
　structured query language for, 224–236
　text, 212
Database servers, 206
Database.sqc file, 294
Data description language (DDL), 225–226
Data interfaces, 207–208
　for Phone Book application, 166–167
Data Manager API, 23–24, 172
Data manipulation language (DML), 226–236
Data ownership, 218–219
Data retrieval
　with database management systems, 206–207
　from record-oriented databases, 204–205

Data synchronization, 165, 245–259
  conflict resolution in, 258–259
  described, 245–247
  difficulty of, 247–254
  incremental, 255–256
  primary key pooling in, 259
  strategies for, 254–259
db_init routine, 284, 293
Deallocating records, 191
Debugger, 38–41
  configuring, 39
  console mode for, 39–40
  exiting, 41
  window for, 40–41
Debugging UltraLite applications, 322–323
DECLARE CURSOR statement, 302–304
Declaring host variables, 297–298
Delete bits, in records, 188
DELETE statement, 235
  host variables in, 297
Deleting databases, 177
Deleting records, 191
Deleting resources, 187
Deleting tables, 228
Dependencies, between files, 43
Desktop computers, Palm platform and, 3
Detaching records, 191–192
Dialogs, 122, 130–131, 132
DialogUtils.cpp, from AppSkeleton, 106
Direct data access, via record-oriented databases, 204–205
Dirty bits
  in records, 188
  in synchronizing records, 190
Disconnected mode, data synchronization and, 246
Dispatch tables, 19
  for virtual functions, 54–70
DisplayDialog function, 130, 132
DISTINCT clause, in SELECT statement, 228
Distributed databases, 212
DlkGetSyncInfo function, 305–306
DmArchiveRecord function, 191
DmAttachRecord function, 189, 191
DmAttachResource function, 186, 187
dmCategoryLength constant, 198
DmCloseDatabase function, 176–177
DmComparF type, 193
DmCreateDatabaseFromImage function, 173–174
DmCreateDatabase function, 173–174
DmDatabaseInfo function, 177–181
  with custom information blocks, 183
  parameters to (table), 179

DmDatabaseSize function, 177–181
DmDeleteDatabase function, 177
DmDeleteRecord function, 191
DmDetachRecord function, 191–192
DmDetachResource function, 187
DmFindResource function, 186
DmFindSortPosition function, 194–197
DmGet1Resource function, 185–186
DmGetAppInfoID function
  with custom information blocks, 183–184
DmGetNextDatabaseByTypeCreator function, 184–185
DmGetRecord function, 190
DmGetResource function, 185–186
DmGetResourceIndex function, 186
DmInsertionSort function, 192–193
dmModeShowSecret, 200
DmMoveCategory function, 197–198
DmMoveRecord function, 191–192
DmNewHandle function, 186, 189
  with custom information blocks, 182
DmNewRecord function, 189
DmNewResource function, 186
DmNumRecordsInCategory function, 197
DmOpenDatabase function, 175–176
DmOpenDatabaseInfo function, 177–181
DmPositionInCategory function, 197
DmQueryNextInCategory function, 197
DmQueryRecord function, 190
DmQuickSort function, 192–193
DmRecordInfo function, 188
DmReleaseRecord function, 190
DmReleaseResource function, 186
DmRemoveRecord function, 191
DmRemoveResource function, 187
DmResetRecordStates function, 176
DmResizeResource function, 187
DmResourceInfo function, 187
DmSeekRecordInCategory function, 197
DmSetDatabaseInfo function, 177–181
DmSet function, with custom information blocks, 182, 184
DmSetRecordInfo function, 188
DmStrCopy function, with custom information blocks, 182, 184
DmWrite function, with custom information blocks, 182–183, 184
Domains, of values in tables, 209
Download stream, in UltraLite synchronization, 271, 315
Doze mode, 15
DragonBall processor, 13–14
Draw functions, 145–146

Drawing on forms, 128–130, 145–146
Draw window, 128
DROP TABLE statement, 226
Dynamic heap, 21
  allocating from, 23, 91–92
  hard reset and, 26
  modified soft reset and, 25
  soft reset and, 25
Dynamic SQL statements, 296

E

EasySync, 4
Edit menu, 131–132
  for fields, 143
Embedded interfaces, 208
Embedded SQL, for UltraLite databases, 280–283, 290–304
END DECLARE SECTION statement, 297–298
Engines, of databases, 344
Entities, in databases, 213–215
Entity classes, in databases, 213, 216
Entity identifiers, in databases, 214
Entity instances, in databases, 213, 216
Entity-Relationship (E-R) models, 213–215
Enumerating databases, 184–185
Enumerating resources, 187
Equi-joins, in relational databases, 230–231
ErrDisplay macro, 47–50
ErrFatalDisplayIf assertion macro, 49–50
ErrNonFatalDisplayIf assertion macro, 49–50
Error classes, for applications, 80
Error codes, 79, 80
  with AppSkeleton, 108–112
Error handlers, with SQL, 292
Error handling
  by embedded SQL, 292–293
  by MobiLink, 321–322
Error messages
  from compiler, 38
  at runtime, 47–50
Error status, with PilotMain function, 79
Event handling, 97–100
EventLoop function, 92–93
Event loops, 94–95
Event processing, 94–105
  event handling during, 97–100
  event loops in, 94–95
  EventType structure in, 95–97
  of keyboard events, 100–102
  long operations in, 102–105
  of pen events, 100–102

Index

Events, 94
  form, 126–128
  low-level, 98
  menu, 134
  with tables, 155–156
  in UltraLite synchronization, 310–311, 311–312, 313–315
Event-specific data, 97
Event types, in UltraLite synchronization, 311–312
EventType structure, 95–97
EvtGetEvent function, 94–95, 98–100
EvtSysEventAvail function, in Find requests, 161–162
evtWaitForever macro, 95
Exceptions, 50–51
Exchange of data, in data synchronization, 245, 247
EXEC SQL command, 290–291
Explicit type conversion, in data synchronization, 257
Extracting data, in data synchronization, 254–257

F

Fetching data, 302–304
FETCH statement, with UltraLite, 302–304
Fields, 134, 140–144
  text editing in, 142–143
FindDrawHeader function, 160–161
FindGetLineBounds function, 161
Finding records, 192
Find requests
  in applications, 157–163
  displaying selected data with, 162–163
  parameters for, 159–160
  searching for matches in, 160–162
Find results dialog, 158
FindSaveMatch, 161
FindStrInStr function, 161
First normal form (1NF), of tables, 220
FixIt sample, 327
FldDelete function, 142
FldGetTextHandle function, 140
FldGetTextPtr function, 142
FldScrollField function, 149
FldSetScrollPosition function, 143
FldSetSelection function, 143
FldSetText function, 142
FldSetTextHandle function, 140–142
Floating-point computations, 70–71
FontID enumeration, 129–130
Fonts, in forms, 129–130
Foreign keys
  in databases, 216–217
  in tables, 210
Foreign tables, 210

Forks, in Macintosh files, 35
Form bitmaps, 135, 146
Form components. *See* Components
Form editor, with Constructor, 122–124
Form editor window, for Constructor, 36, 37
Form event handlers, 126–128
Form events, 126–128
Form objects. *See* Components
Forms, 122–130
  drawing on, 128–130
  event handling and, 99–100
  loading and unloading, 124–126
  modal, 130
  modeless, 130
  nonmodal, 130
Frames, in forms, 129
FrmAlert function, 115
FrmCloseAllForms function, 126
frmCloseEvent function, 99, 125, 127
FrmCopyLabel function, 136
FrmCustomAlert function, 115–116
FrmDispatchEvent function, 100, 127
FrmGetActiveForm function, 125
FrmGetFormPtr function, 125
FrmGetGadgetData function, 147
FrmGetLabel function, 136
frmGoToEvent function, with Find requests, 162
frmGoToForm function, 124, 126, 128
FrmHandleEvent function, 127
FrmHideObject function, 146
frmLoadEvent function, 99, 124
  with Find requests, 162
frmOpenEvent function, 99, 124, 126, 127
frmSaveEvent function, 128
FrmSetGadgetData function, 147
FrmShowObject function, 146
frmUpdateEvent function, 128
FROM clause, in SELECT statement, 230, 232
FtrGet function, 17

G

Gadgets, 135, 147
GCC compiler
  callback functions and, 51–52
GNU tools with, 41–46
GDB debugger, 42, 45–46
Gdbplug tool, 45–46
GetString method, 121
Global data
  memory management for, 91–92
  in notification launches, 87–88
  virtual functions and, 54–55
Global data block, 91

Global Find operations, in applications, 157–163
GNU General Public License, 42
GNU Library Public License, 42
GNUSample template, building projects with, 43–45
GNU tools, 41–46
  building projects with, 43–45
  compiling with, 43–44
  debugging with, 45–46
  defining user interface elements for, 113
  history of, 42–43
  names for, 44
Graffiti reference dialog, 143
Graffiti shift indicators, 135, 146
Graffiti shortcut sequences, for debugger, 40, 41
GRANT statement, 226
Graphical user interfaces (GUIs), 5.
  See also User interfaces
  Palm platform and, 2
.grc files, 44

H

Handles, 22, 172
  dynamic heap allocation and, 23
  with string lists, 117–118
  with strings, 116–117
Hard resets, 26
Header file directory, 28
Header files
  precompiled, 50
  in Software Development Kit, 28–30
Headers, database, 172–173, 177–181
Heaps, 21–22
Height
  of components, 136
  of rows, 151
Host variables, with UltraLite, 297–302
HotSync channels, 304
HotSyncs
  hard resets and, 26
  resets and, 25
  with UltraLite, 268–269, 306–307, 309

I

Icons, 156–157
IDE (integrated development environment), for CodeWarrior, 30
Idle mode, 15
INCLUDE statement, in SQL, 293–295
Incremental synchronization, 255–256, 319–320
Indexes, 223
  for categories, 198
  for record databases, 172, 189–190
  table optimization with, 221–222

Indicator variables, in SQL, 301–302
Infrared beaming, 269
Initializing launch, 83–85
Inner joins, of tables, 233
Input focus, of fields, 142
Insertion sort algorithm, 192–193
INSERT statement, 233–234
   host variables in, 297
Integer types, 29–30
IntelliSync, 4
Interactive SQL tool, 345–346
Interrupting applications, for debugging, 40–41
IS NULL operator, in SELECT statement, 229
Items, in tables, 151–155

J

JOIN clause, in SELECT statement, 233
Joins, in relational databases, 230–233

K

Kadak Products Ltd., 15
Kernel, of Palm OS, 15–16
Keyboard dialog, 143
Keyboard events, 100–102
keyDownEvent, 101
KEY JOIN clause, in SELECT statement, 232
Key joins, in relational databases, 232
Keys, in tables, 209, 210

L

Labels, 134, 136–137
Launch codes, 80, 88–91
   with PilotMain function, 79
Launch flags, 80, 91
Launching applications, 79, 80–91
   with initializing launch, 83–85
   launch codes for, 88–91
   launch flags for, 91
   with normal launch, 80–81
   with notification launch, 85–86
   recovering global data and, 87–88
   with subcall launch, 81–83
Left origin, of components, 136
Left outer joins, of tables, 233
Libraries, C runtime, 46–47, 48
LIKE operator, in SELECT statement, 229
Lines, in forms, 129
Lists, 134, 144–146
Loading of forms, 124–126
Local IDs, 22–23
Long operations, in event processing, 102–105
Low-level events, 98
LstGetSelection function, 146

LstPopupList function, 146
lstSelectEvent function, 144–145
LstSetDrawFunction function, 145–146
LstSetListChoices function, 145, 146
LstSetSelection function, 146

M

Macintosh files, Windows and, 35
MainForm.cpp file, from AppSkeleton, 106
Main processor, for Palm devices, 13–14
Makefiles, with GNU tools, 43
Make tool, 43
Manage Adaptive Server Anywhere shortcut, in creating databases, 274–277
Managing resources in databases, 186–187
Masks, for record attributes, 188, 189
Materialization, of database objects, 211
.mch files, 50
MDI (multiple document interface), 31
Memory
   allocation of, 53–54
   with Palm platforms, 18–24
   used by applications, 91–92
Memory blocks
   allocation of, 23, 53–54, 91–92
   with applications, 91–92
   as database headers, 172–173
   locking and unlocking, 22
   in Palm databases, 171, 172
Memory cards, 20–21
Memory handles, 22, 172
Memory heaps, 21–22
Memory images, creating databases from, 173–174
Memory Manager, error handling by, 80
Memory Manager APIs, object allocation with, 53–54
Memory managers, 16
   databases and, 23–24
   object allocation with, 53–54
MemPtrFree pointer, 23
MemPtrNew operator, 23
Menubar editor, with Constructor, 132–133
Menubars, 131
menuEvent, 134
MenuHandleEvent function, 99
Menu items, 131
MENU resource, 133
Menus, 131–134
   creating, 132–133
   designing, 131–132
   edit, 143
   handling events from, 134

Metadata
   in Consolidator databases, 328, 331–333
   in databases, 210
MobiLink conduits, in deploying UltraLite applications, 283–288
MobiLink server, 268–271
   in deploying UltraLite applications, 283–288
   error handling by, 321–322
MobiLink synchronization, with UltraLite databases, 262–263, 268–271
MobiLink system tables, 283–284
Modal forms. *See* Dialogs
Modification anomalies, in tables, 219
Modified soft resets, 25
Moving resources among databases, 186–187
Multimedia databases, 212
Multiple selection, from databases, 229–233
Multisegment applications, 70
Multi-Segment Read Me.txt file, 70

N

Names
   of applications, 33–34
   of databases, 171
Natural equi-joins, in relational databases, 231
NATURAL JOIN clause, in SELECT statement, 232
Natural joins, in relational databases, 232
Networks, data synchronization in, 246
New operator, memory object allocation with, 53–54
New Project menu item, 32
nilEvent, 95
Normal forms, of tables, 219–221
Normalization
   of Phone Book application, 239
   of tables, 219–221
Normal launch, 80–81
Notification launch, 85–86
   recovering global data in, 87–88
N-to-*M* (*N:M*) relationship, among databases, 215, 216, 217–218
NULL value, 301–302
Null values
   in SQL, 301–302
   in tables, 209

O

Object-oriented databases, 211
Object-relational mapping, 211
Objects. *See* Components

Occasionally connected computing, data synchronization and, 246
One-to-*N* (1:*N*) relationship, among databases, 215, 216
One-to-one (1:1) relationship, among databases, 215
One-way complete snapshot synchronization, with UltraLite, 316–317
Open Database Connectivity (ODBC) interface, 207–208
  with UltraLite, 261, 278, 279
Opening databases, 175–176
Operating systems, for Palm platform, 2, 15–18
Optimistic concurrency, in tables, 235
Optimization, of tables, 219, 221–223
Options menu, 131–132
Oracle, 1, 4, 6, 325
Oracle8 Navigator tool, 329–330
Oracle Lite, 326
Oracle Lite Consolidator. *See* Consolidator
Oracle Lite databases
  deploying, 328
  developing, 327–328
Order
  of records, 187
  in tables, 209
ORDER BY clause, in SELECT statement, 227–230, 234
Ordinary users, of databases, 218–219
OR operation, in SELECT statement, 228–229
Outer joins, of tables, 233

P

Palm Computing platforms, 13–26, 339–340
  advantages of, 2
  basic information on, 7–8
  C/C++ languages and, 46–71
  Consolidator and, 325–337
  data synchronization and, 247–248
  deploying UltraLite applications to, 268–271
  developing applications for, 1–3, 77–167
  documentation for, 9–10
  hardware for, 13–15
  memory for, 18–20
  operating systems for, 2, 15–18
  resetting, 25–26
  synchronization capabilities of, 3
  UltraLite databases and, 262, 263
Palm Conduit Development Kit (CDK), 74–75
Palm databases, 171–203
  closing, 176–177
  creating, 173–174
  custom information blocks for, 181–184
  deleting, 177
  enumerating, 184–185
  headers for, 172–173, 177–181
  opening, 175–176
  organization of, 171
  and Phone Book application, 201
  records in, 172, 187–200
  resources in, 172, 185–187
PalmDBPhoneData class, 201
Palm III, 1
  operating system for, 16
Palm IIIx, operating system for, 16
Palm OS, 15–18
  checking version number of, 93–94
  console for, 74
  header files for, 28–30
  reference guide to, 27–28
  upgrading, 16–17
  versions of, 16–18
Palm OS 1.0
  CategoryEdit routines and, 19
  compatibility with later versions, 17–18
  floating-point computations in, 70
Palm OS 2.0
  CategoryEdit routines and, 19
  compatibility with other versions, 17–18
  floating-point computations in, 70–71
Palm OS 3.0
  CategoryEdit routines and, 19
  compatibility with earlier versions, 17–18
  floating-point computations in, 70–71
Palm OS Emulator (POSE), 71–74
  debugging programs running in, 39, 45–46
  error messages with, 47–50
  history of, 71–72
Palm OS Software Development Kit. *See* SDK
Palm OS String Manager, C library functions in, 47
PalmPilot Personal, operating system for, 16
PalmPilot Professional, 1
  operating system for, 16
Palm V, operating system for, 16
Palm VII, operating system for, 16
Partitioned snapshot synchronization, with UltraLite, 318–319
Passwords, for databases, 218–219
PDB files, 173
penDownEvent, 100–101
Pen events, 100–102
penMoveEvent, 100–101
penUpEvent, 100–101
Permissions, for databases, 218–219, 226
Persistence, of database objects, 211
Phone Book application, 5–7
  abstract model of, 237–238
  consolidated database for, 274–278
  Consolidator and, 337
  database for, 240–241
  data in, 237
  MobiLink conduit for, 285–288
  Palm databases and, 201
  physical model of, 238–239
  queries in, 241–242
  as relational database, 236–242
  UltraLite and, 323
  user interface for, 164–167
PhoneData class, 167
PhoneEntry class, 167, 201
Physical models
  of databases, 212–213, 215–218
  of Phone Book application, 238–239
Pila cross-assembler, 14
<Pilot.h> header file, 28, 50
PilotMain.cpp file, from AppSkeleton, 106–110
PilotMain function
  for applications, 79
  in AppSkeleton, 105
  recursive calls to, 81–83
PilRC resource compiler, 42–44
  alerts in, 115
  bitmaps and icons in, 157
  creating components with, 135
  creating menus with, 133
  forms with, 123–124
  string lists with, 117
  string resources in, 116
  and user interface elements, 113–114
Placement variant, of new operator, 53–54
Platforms, 3. *See also* Palm Computing platforms
popSelectEvent function, 139–140
Popup triggers, as controls, 137, 139–140
Pragmas, 70
.prc target, 32, 34, 44–45
Prc-tools release, 42
Precompiled headers, in CodeWarrior, 50
PrefGetAppPreferences function, 163–164
Prefix strings, 118
PrefSetAppPreferences function, 163
Preparing SQL commands, 225

Primary entity identifiers, in databases, 214, 216
Primary key pooling
  Consolidator and, 337
  in data synchronization, 259, 321
Primary keys
  in databases, 216
  in tables, 209
Private header files, 29
Private records, 200
Project files, 35–36
Projects
  building, 38, 43–45
  debugging, 38–41
  launching new, 32–34, 43–45
Project stationery templates, 32
  with UltraLite, 273
Project window, with CodeWarrior, 32–33
Proxies, cover classes as, 62–65
PString class, 167
Publications, with Consolidator, 331–333
Push buttons, as controls, 137, 138–139

Q
QUALCOMM pdQ Smartphone, 1
Querying databases, 226–236. *See also* Structured query language (SQL); Subqueries
  for Phone Book application, 241–242
Quicksort algorithm, 193–193

R
RAM. *See* Read-write memory (RAM)
RAM sizes, for Palm devices, 20
RctGetIntersection function, 129
RctPtInRectangle function, 129
Reading resources in databases, 185–186
Read-only memory (ROM), for Palm devices, 20
Read-write memory (RAM), for Palm devices, 20
Real-time clock, sleep mode and, 15
Record databases, 24, 172, 187–200
Record menu, 131–132
Record-oriented databases, 204–205
Records, 24, 172
  accessing in databases, 190
  archiving, 191
  attributes of, 188
  categories of, 197–200
  creating in databases, 189–190
  in databases, 159, 204–205
  deallocating from databases, 191
  deleting from databases, 191
  described, 187–189
  detaching from databases, 191–192
  finding in databases, 192
  modifying in databases, 190
  private, 200
  removing from databases, 190–192
  secret, 200
  sorting in databases, 192–197
Rectangles, in forms, 129
Recursive calls, to PilotMain function, 81–83
Reference database, with UltraLite applications, 266–268
Reference guide, in Software Development Kit, 27–28
Referential integrity, of relational databases, 210
Refreshing data, in data synchronization, 255–256
Registering Creator ID, 78
Relational algebra, 209
Relational databases, 203–242. *See also* UltraLite databases
  abstract models of, 212–215
  databases other than, 211–212
  described, 209–211
  joins in, 230–233
  management system interfaces for, 207–208
  management systems for, 206–207
  multiple selection from, 229–233
  normalization of, 219–221
  optimization of, 219, 221–223
  ownership of data in, 218–219
  Palm databases and, 204
  Phone Book application as, 236–242
  physical models of, 212–213, 215–218
  record-oriented, 204–205
  from Sybase ASA system, 203
Relationships, in databases, 213–215
Relaunching applications, 65–70
RelaunchWithGlobals function, 87–88
Removing records, 190–192
Removing resources, 187
Repeating buttons, as controls, 137, 138
Replication of data, in data synchronization, 246
Resetting, 25–26
Resizing resources, 187
Resource databases, 24, 172, 185–187
  applications as, 77–78
Resource editor window, for Constructor, 35–36
Resource files, 35–36
Resources, 24, 172
  in AppSkeleton, 105–106
  creating in databases, 186
  deleting, 187
  enumerating, 187
  managing in databases, 186–187
  moving among databases, 186–187
  reading in databases, 185–186
  resizing, 187
  for user interfaces, 112–114
Responsiveness, in event processing, 102–103
Restoring states, in applications, 163–164
REVOKE TABLE statement, 226
Right outer joins, of tables, 233
Rollback, of transactions, 207
ROLLBACK statement, 235–236, 304
ROM. *See* Read-only memory (ROM)
Row partitioning, in data synchronization, 255–256, 257
Rows
  adding to tables, 233–234
  changing in tables, 234–235
  deleting from tables, 235
  fetching multiple, 302–304
  fetching single, 302
  retrieving from tables, 226–229
.rsrc files, 35–36
Running modes, 14–15

S
Saving states, in applications, 163–164
sclEnterEvent function, 148
sclExitEvent function, 148–149
SclGetScrollBar function, 148
sclRepeatEvent function, 148–149
SclSetScrollBar function, 148
Screen, for Palm devices, 14
screenX member, 100–101
screenY member, 100–101
Script parameters, in UltraLite synchronization, 311–312
Scripts, in UltraLite synchronization, 270–271, 310–311, 311–312
Scroll bars, 134, 147–149
  with fields, 143–144
Scroll cars, 148
Scrolling
  of cursors, 304
  of tables, 156
Scroll thumbs, 148
SDK (Software Development Kit), 27–30, 248
Second normal form (2NF), of tables, 220
Secret bits, in records, 188
Secret records, 200
SelectCategory function, 199
Selector triggers, as controls, 137, 139
SELECT statement, 226–233
  host variables in, 297
  subsetting data with, 255, 257
  with UltraLite, 302–304

Index

Self-describing databases, 210
Serial channels, 304
Serial synchronization, with MobiLink and UltraLite, 308–309
Server windows, for ASA, 344
SetCategory function, 188–189
Settings window, for CodeWarrior, 34
shiftKeyMask, 102
Shortcut sequences, 40
Single-threaded applications, 16
Sleep mode, 15
Snapshot synchronization, 255–256, 316–319
Soft resets, 25
sortInfo block, 184
Sorting information block, 184
Sorting records, 192–197
  optimization for, 221–223
  in SELECT statement, 227–228
SortRecordInfoType structures, 193–195
.sqc files, 280
SQLCODE macro, 293
SQL communications area (SQLCA), with UltraLite, 291–292
sqlerr.h file, 292
SQLERROR, 292
SQL preprocessor, with UltraLite, 290–291
SQL preprocessor (SQLPP), 267, 282
SQL statements, with UltraLite, 295–297
SQLWARNING, 292
StartApplication function, 92–93
Static data, memory management for, 91–92
Static SQL statements, 296
Static user interface elements, 35
StopApplication function, 92–93
Storage heaps, 21–22
  applications and, 92
  databases and, 23–24, 171
  enumerating databases in, 184–185
  hard reset and, 26
Stored procedures, for databases, 218
strAsTyped member, in Find request, 159
String editor, with Constructor, 116, 117
String lists, 117–122
StringListType class, 119–121, 145
String resources, with user interfaces, 116–117
strToFind member, in Find request, 159
Structured query language (SQL), 224–236. *See also* Embedded SQL
  data description language of, 225–226

data manipulation language of, 226–236
  preparing commands for, 225
Sybase tools with, 345–347
UltraLite and, 264, 267, 280–283
Styles, of items, 152–156
Subcall launch, 81–83
Subqueries, with SELECT statements, 229–230
Subscriptions, with Consolidator, 331–333
Subsetting data, in data synchronization, 254–257
Sybase, 1, 4, 6. *See also* UltraLite databases
Sybase Central tool, 345–347
  in creating databases, 274–277, 279
  in UltraLite database deployment, 284–285
Synchronization channels, with UltraLite, 269, 304–310
Synchronization of data, 165, 245–259. *See also* Data synchronization
  dirty bit and, 188, 190
  with Palm platform, 3, 4
  removing records and, 190–191
sysAppLaunchCmdAlarmTriggered launch code, 90
sysAppLaunchCmdDisplayAlarm launch code, 90
sysAppLaunchCmdFind launch code, 89, 157, 158, 159
sysAppLaunchCmdGoTo launch code, 81–82, 84, 89, 157, 158–159
sysAppLaunchCmdInitDatabase launch code, 90–91
sysAppLaunchCmdNormalLaunch launch code, 80–81, 89
sysAppLaunchCmdSaveData launch code, 90, 157, 158
sysAppLaunchCmdSyncNotify launch code, 89, 303
sysAppLaunchCmdSystemReset launch code, 90
sysAppLaunchCmdTimeChange launch code, 90
sysAppLaunchFlagNewGlobals launch code, 83–85
  in notification launches, 85–86
sysAppLaunchFlagNewStack launch flag, 91
sysAppLaunchFlagNewThread launch flag, 91
sysAppLaunchFlagSubCall launch code, 83–84
SysAppLaunchFlagSubCall launch code
  in notification launches, 85–86

sysAppLaunchFlagUIApp launch flag, 91
SysAppLaunch function, 65–70
SysFormPointerArrayToStrings function, 121
SysHandleEvent function, 98–99
SysStringByIndex, 117
System crashes, resetting after, 25–26
<System/ErrorMgr.h> file, 47
  exception handling and, 50–51
<System/Globals.h> header file, 28
System managers, 16
<System/SysAll.h> header file, 28
  error classes in, 80
  launch codes in, 86, 88–91
System traps, 19
SysTicksPerSecond function, 5

T

Table events, in UltraLite synchronization, 311–312
Table items. *See* Items
Tables, 134, 150–156
  adding rows to, 233–234
  changing rows in, 234–235
  creating, 225–226
  creating with Consolidator, 328, 329–330
  in database design, 212–223
  deleting, 226
  deleting rows from, 235
  events and, 155–156
  foreign, 210
  initializing, 155
  items in, 151–155
  joining, 230–233
  normalization of, 219–221
  in object-relational mapping, 211
  optimization of, 219, 221–223
  in relational databases, 209–210
  rows and columns in, 150–151, 209
  scrolling, 156
Table scan, 223
Target objects
  cover classes for, 63–65
  in relaunching applications, 65–70
Target Settings button, 33
Taskbar icon, for ASA, 345
TblFindRowID function, 151
TblInsertRow function, 156
TblMarkTableInvalid function, 156
TblRedrawTable function, 156
TblRemoveRow function, 156
TblSetItemStyle function, 152
TblSetRowStaticHeight function, 151
TCP/IP channels, 304
TCP/IP synchronization, with MobiLink and UltraLite, 307–308
Text databases, 212

Index

Text editing, in fields, 142–143
Third normal form (3NF), of tables, 221
Threads, 16
Ticks, 95
Time Book application, 248–251
  synchronization challenges with, 251–252
Time Book sample program, 7
Timestamps, in UltraLite synchronization, 319–320
Timestamp synchronization, 319–320
Top origin, of components, 136
Touch-sensitive screen, for Palm devices, 14
Transactions
  database management with, 207
  in SQL, 235–236
  with UltraLite, 304
Transformation of data, in data synchronization, 245
Transitive dependency, of tables, 221
Triggers
  for databases, 218
  synchronization events as, 311–312
Two-way complete snapshot synchronization, with UltraLite, 317–318
Types
  appl, 78
  of database columns (list), 222–223
  resource, 112
  in SQL, 298–298

U

UI (user interface) managers, 16
UI Test application, 111
<UI/UIAll.h> header file, 28
<UI/UIGlobals.h> header file, 28
ulglobal.h header file, 291
ULPalmExit routine, 293, 307–308
  selecting synchronization channel with, 304
ULPalmLaunch routine, 282, 293, 307–308
  selecting synchronization channel with, 304
ULSynchronize function, 282, 307–309
  selecting synchronization channel with, 304
UltraLite analyzer, 267–268
UltraLite databases, 261–323
  applications with, 272–290
  capabilities of, 262
  debugging applications with, 322–323
  described, 261–265
  embedded SQL for, 290–304
  fetching data from, 302–304
  licensing of, 265
  limitations and restrictions with, 263–265
  MobiLink synchronization with, 262–263
  operation of, 265–271
  Phone Book application and, 323
  platforms supporting, 263
  without synchronization, 288–290
  synchronization channels for, 304–310
  synchronization with, 310–322
UltraLite generator (ULGEN), 282, 283
UltraLite stationery, 273
UnderlineModeType enumeration, 130
Underlining, in forms, 130
Unique identifiers (unique IDs), of records, 187
Unix Amiga Emulator (UAE), 71
Unloading of forms, 124–126
UPDATE statement, 234–235
  host variables in, 297
Upload stream, in UltraLite synchronization, 270–271, 314
User interfaces, 110–157. *See also* Graphical user interfaces (GUIs)
  alerts in, 114–116
  bitmaps in, 156–157
  components in, 134–156
  controls in, 134, 137–140
  designing, 111
  dialogs with, 122, 130–131
  fields in, 134, 140–144
  form bitmaps in, 135, 146
  forms with, 122–130
  gadgets in, 135, 147
  graffiti shift indicators in, 135, 146
  icons in, 156–157
  lists in, 134, 144–146
  menus in, 131–134
  for Phone Book application, 164–167
  resources for, 112–114
  scroll bars in, 134, 147–149
  string lists with, 117–122
  strings with, 116–117
  tables in, 134, 150–156
User name, in UltraLite database synchronization, 305–306

V

Virtual functions, 54–70
  for Phone Book application, 167
  simulating, 55–63, 63–65
Virtual keys, 101–102
Virtual memory, 18–20
Vtables, 19
  simulating virtual functions with, 55–63

W

WHENEVER statement, in SQL, 293–295
WHERE clause
  in DELETE statement, 235
  in SELECT statement, 228, 231, 232, 257
  in UPDATE statement, 234
Width
  of columns, 151
  of components, 136
Win32 programming, Palm platform and, 2
Windows
  CodeWarrior for, 30–31
  Macintosh files and, 35
WorkPad, 1

Develop Applications for
Palm Computing Platform Handhelds

CodeWarrior® for the Palm Computing® platform is the official tool for building applications based on the Palm OS™ software. With the award-winning CodeWarrior Integrated Development Environment (IDE) you can create software programs that will run directly on a Palm Computing platform device. CodeWarrior can be hosted on Windows® 95/98/NT® or Mac® OS computers.

The CodeWarrior IDE gives you everything you need to develop Palm OS™ applications: a GUI layout tool (Constructor for Palm Computing platform), editor, project manager, C/C++ compiler, source- and assembly-level debuggers, direct-to-device debugger, stand-alone assembler, and linker.

The CodeWarrior IDE offers unsurpassed ease-of-use to develop applications for the 3Com PalmPilot, Palm III, Palm IIIX, Palm V, Palm VII (supported in Release 6), the IBM Workpad, the QUALCOMM pdQ Smartphone and the Symbol Technologies SPT family.

Palm Computing
CodeWarrior®
for Palm Computing platform

The complete programming tool for
Palm Computing® platform handhelds

PALM COMPUTING PLATFORM

3Com, the 3Com logo, Palm Computing, Graffiti, HotSync and Palm Modem are registered trademarks, and Palm III, Palm IIIx, Palm V, Palm OS, Palm, the Palm Computing platform logo, Palm III logo, Palm IIIx logo, Palm V logo and HotSync logos are trademarks of Palm Computing, Inc., 3Com Corporation or its subsidiaries.

3Com®

Order on-line:
http://www.palm.com/catalog/codewar.html

By phone: 1-800-881-7256 (US) 1-800-891-6342 (Canada)
1-801-431-1536 (International)

Fax (512) 873-4901

Email your information to: cwregister@palm.com

Mail: Palm Computing, Inc., Dept 334, PO Box 9700, Austin, TX 78766-9700

CUSTOMER NOTE: IF THIS BOOK IS ACCOMPANIED BY SOFTWARE, PLEASE READ THE FOLLOWING BEFORE OPENING THE PACKAGE.

This software contains files to help you utilize the models described in the accompanying book. By opening the package, you are agreeing to be bound by the following agreement:

This software product is protected by copyright and all rights are reserved by the author, John Wiley & Sons, Inc., or their licensors. You are licensed to use this software as described in the software and the accompanying book. Copying the software for any other purpose may be a violation of the U.S. Copyright Law.

This software product is sold as is without warranty of any kind, either express or implied, including but not limited to the implied warranty of merchantability and fitness for a particular purpose. Neither Wiley nor its dealers or distributors assumes any liability for any alleged or actual damages arising from the use of or the inability to use this software. (Some states do not allow the exclusion of implied warranties, so the exclusion may not apply to you.)

To use this CD-ROM, your system must meet the following requirements:

Platform/Processor/Operating System. Windows 95, Windows 98 or Windows NT 4.0.

RAM. 16MB RAM minimum, 32MB RAM recommended.

Hard Drive Space. 200MB disk space required to install tools.

Peripherals. None.